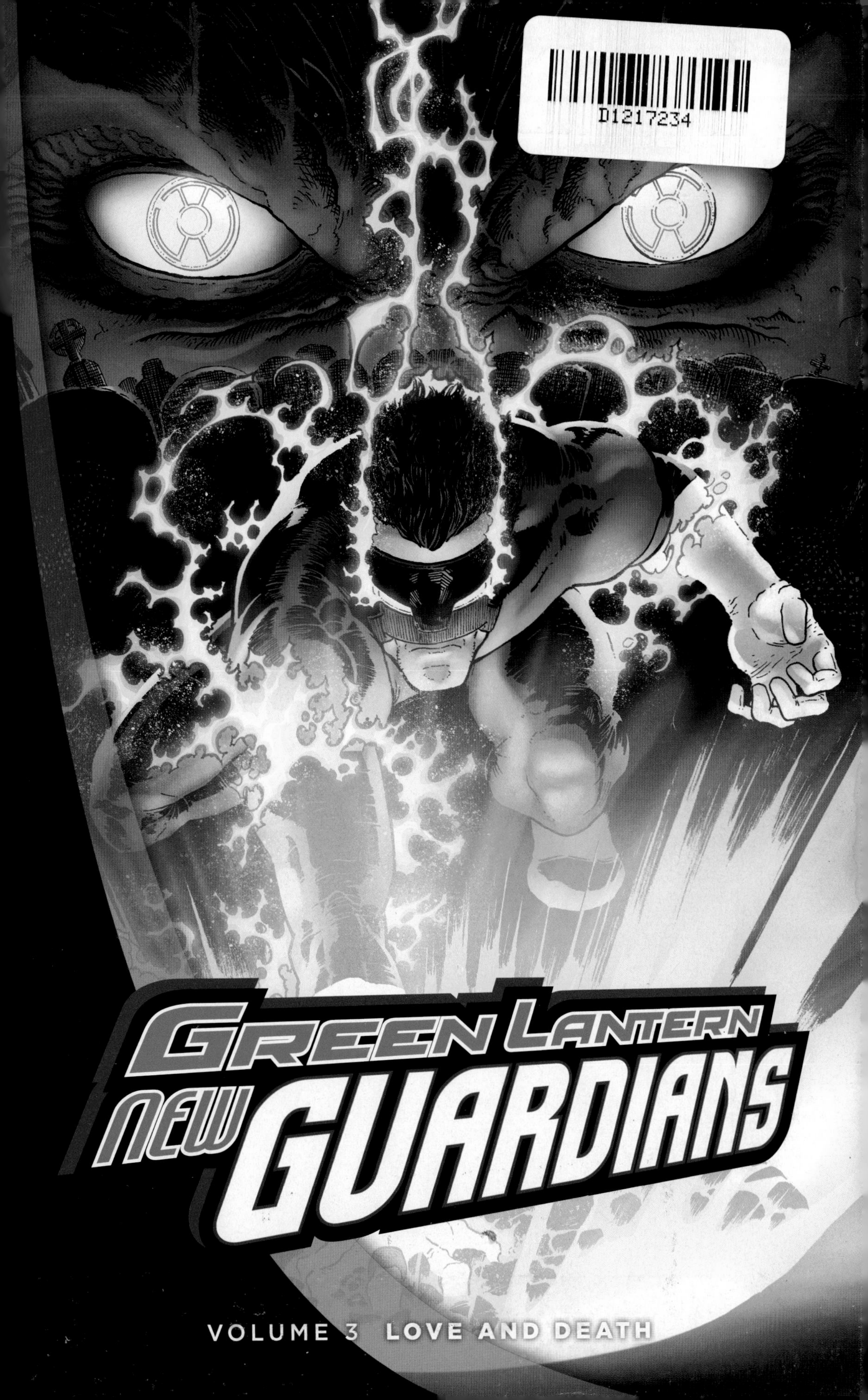
GREEN LANTERN
NEW GUARDIANS
VOLUME 3 LOVE AND DEATH

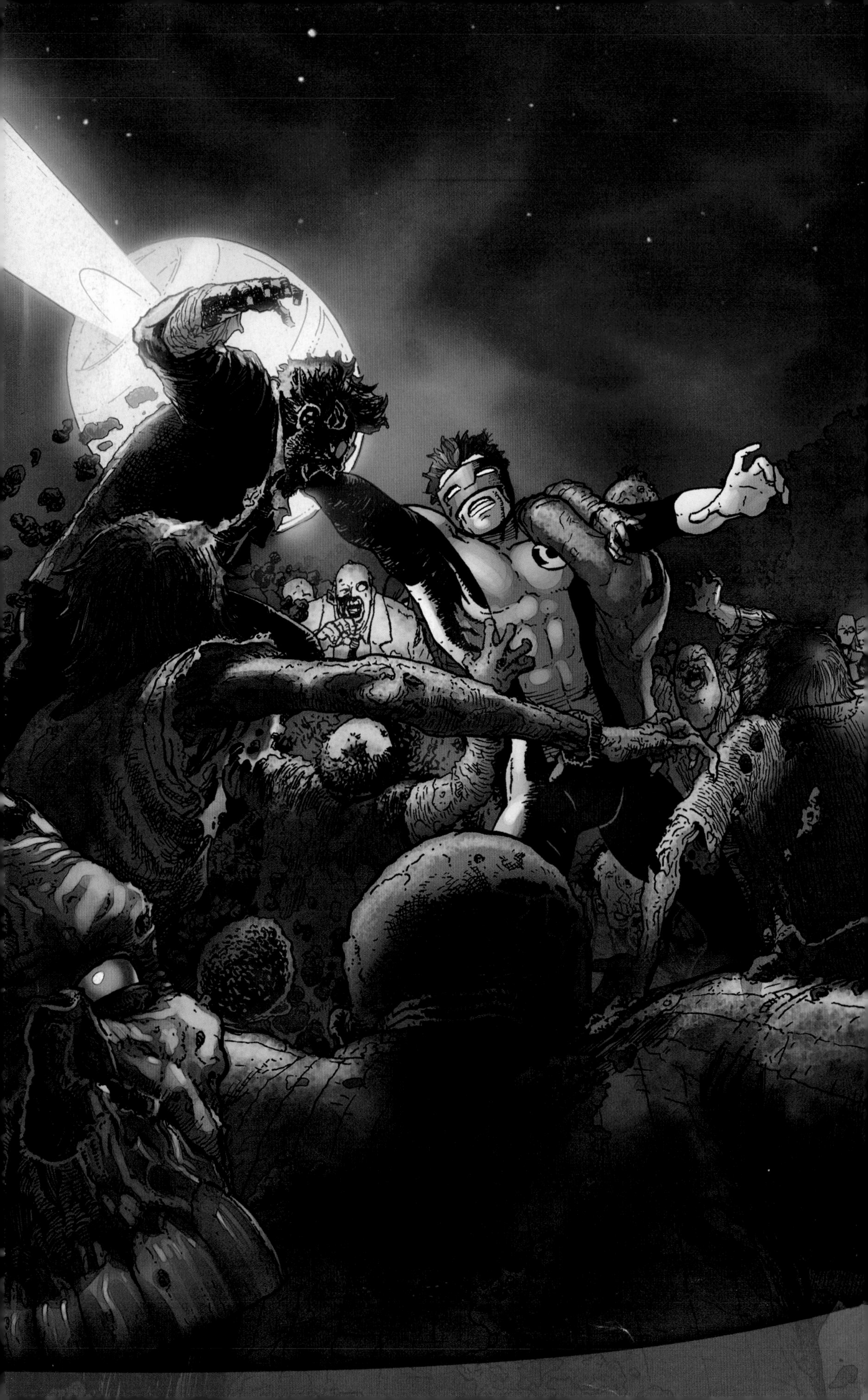

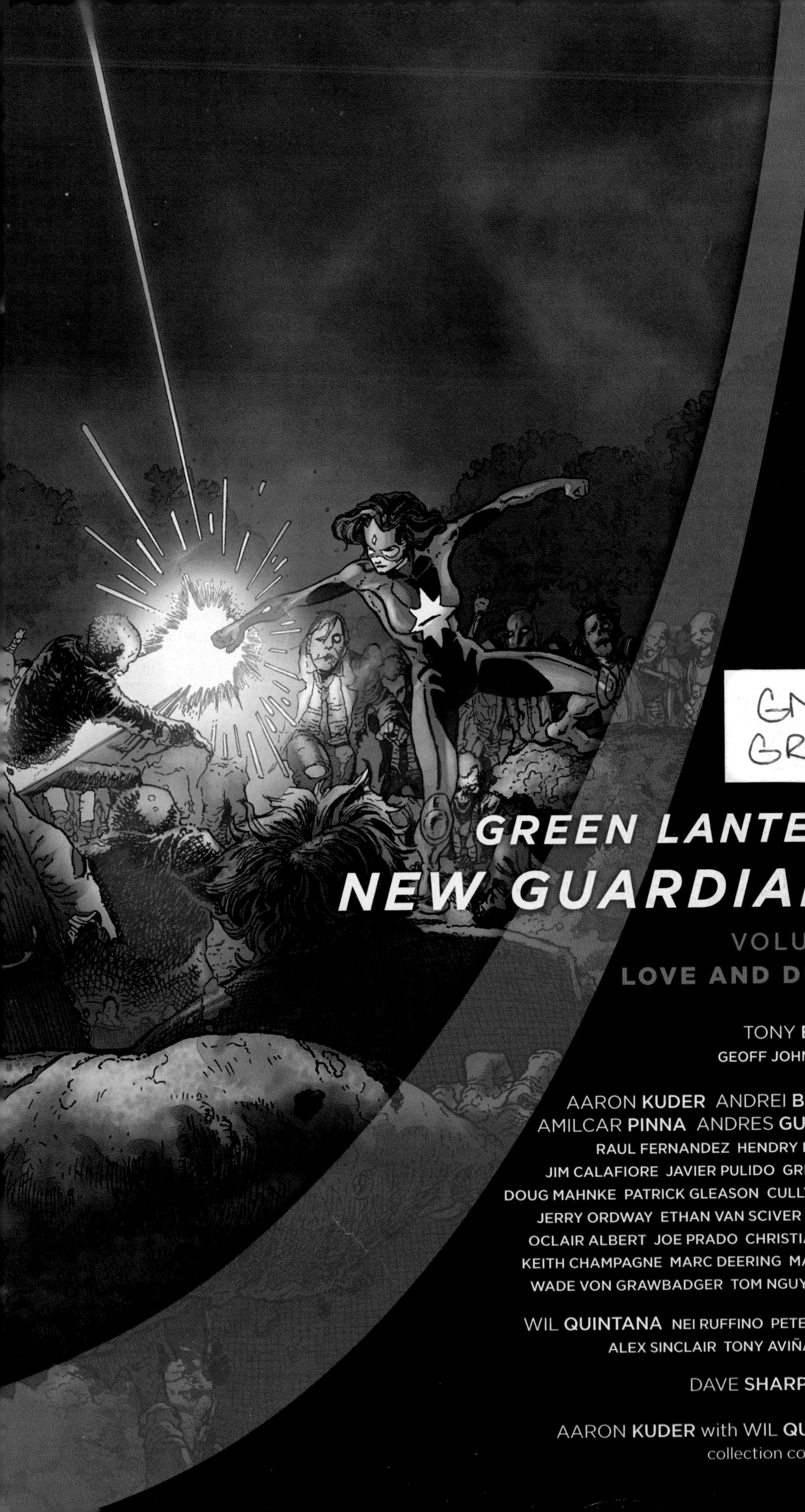

GREEN LANTERN
NEW GUARDIANS

VOLUME 3
LOVE AND DEATH

TONY **BEDARD**
GEOFF JOHNS writers

AARON **KUDER** ANDREI **BRESSAN**
AMILCAR **PINNA** ANDRES **GUINALDO**
RAUL FERNANDEZ HENDRY PRASETYO
JIM CALAFIORE JAVIER PULIDO GREG ADAMS
DOUG MAHNKE PATRICK GLEASON CULLY HAMNER
JERRY ORDWAY ETHAN VAN SCIVER IVAN REIS
OCLAIR ALBERT JOE PRADO CHRISTIAN ALAMY
KEITH CHAMPAGNE MARC DEERING MARK IRWIN
WADE VON GRAWBADGER TOM NGUYEN artists

WIL **QUINTANA** **NEI RUFFINO PETE PANTAZIS**
ALEX SINCLAIR TONY AVIÑA colorists

DAVE **SHARPE** letterer

AARON **KUDER** with WIL **QUINTANA**
collection cover artists

MATT IDELSON PAT MCCALLUM WIL MOSS Editors – Original Series CHRIS CONROY Associate Editor – Original Series
SEAN MACKIEWICZ KATE STEWART Assistant Editors – Original Series
PETER HAMBOUSSI Editor RACHEL PINNELAS Assistant Editor
ROBBIN BROSTERMAN Design Director – Books ROBBIE BIEDERMAN Publication Design

BOB HARRAS Senior VP – Editor-in-Chief, DC Comics

DIANE NELSON President DAN DIDIO and JIM LEE Co-Publishers GEOFF JOHNS Chief Creative Officer
AMIT DESAI Senior VP – Marketing and Franchise Management
AMY GENKINS Senior VP – Business and Legal Affairs NAIRI GARDINER Senior VP – Finance
JEFF BOISON VP – Publishing Planning MARK CHIARELLO VP – Art Direction and Design
JOHN CUNNINGHAM VP – Marketing TERRI CUNNINGHAM VP – Editorial Administration
LARRY GANEM VP – Talent Relations and Services ALISON GILL Senior VP – Manufacturing and Operations
HANK KANALZ Senior VP – Vertigo and Integrated Publishing JAY KOGAN VP – Business and Legal Affairs, Publishing
JACK MAHAN VP – Business Affairs, Talent NICK NAPOLITANO VP – Manufacturing Administration SUE POHJA VP – Book Sales
FRED RUIZ VP – Manufacturing Operations COURTNEY SIMMONS Senior VP – Publicity BOB WAYNE Senior VP – Sales

GREEN LANTERN - NEW GUARDIANS VOLUME 3: LOVE AND DEATH

DC Comics, 1700 Broadway, New York, NY 10019
A Warner Bros. Entertainment Company.
Printed by RR Donnelley, Salem, VA, USA. 5/30/14. First Printing.

ISBN: 978-1-4012-4710-2

SUSTAINABLE
FORESTRY
INITIATIVE

Certified Chain of Custody
20% Certified Forest Content,
80% Certified Sourcing
www.sfiprogram.org
SFI-01042
APPLIES TO TEXT STOCK ONLY

Library of Congress Cataloging-in-Publication Data

Bedard, Tony, author.
Green Lantern, New Guardians. Volume 3, Love & Death / Tony Bedard ; [illustrated by] Aaron Kuder.
pages cm
ISBN 978-1-4012-4710-2
1. Graphic novels. I. Kuder, Aaron, illustrator. II. Title. III. Title: Love & Death.
PN6728.G74B35 2014
741.5'973—dc23
2013039607

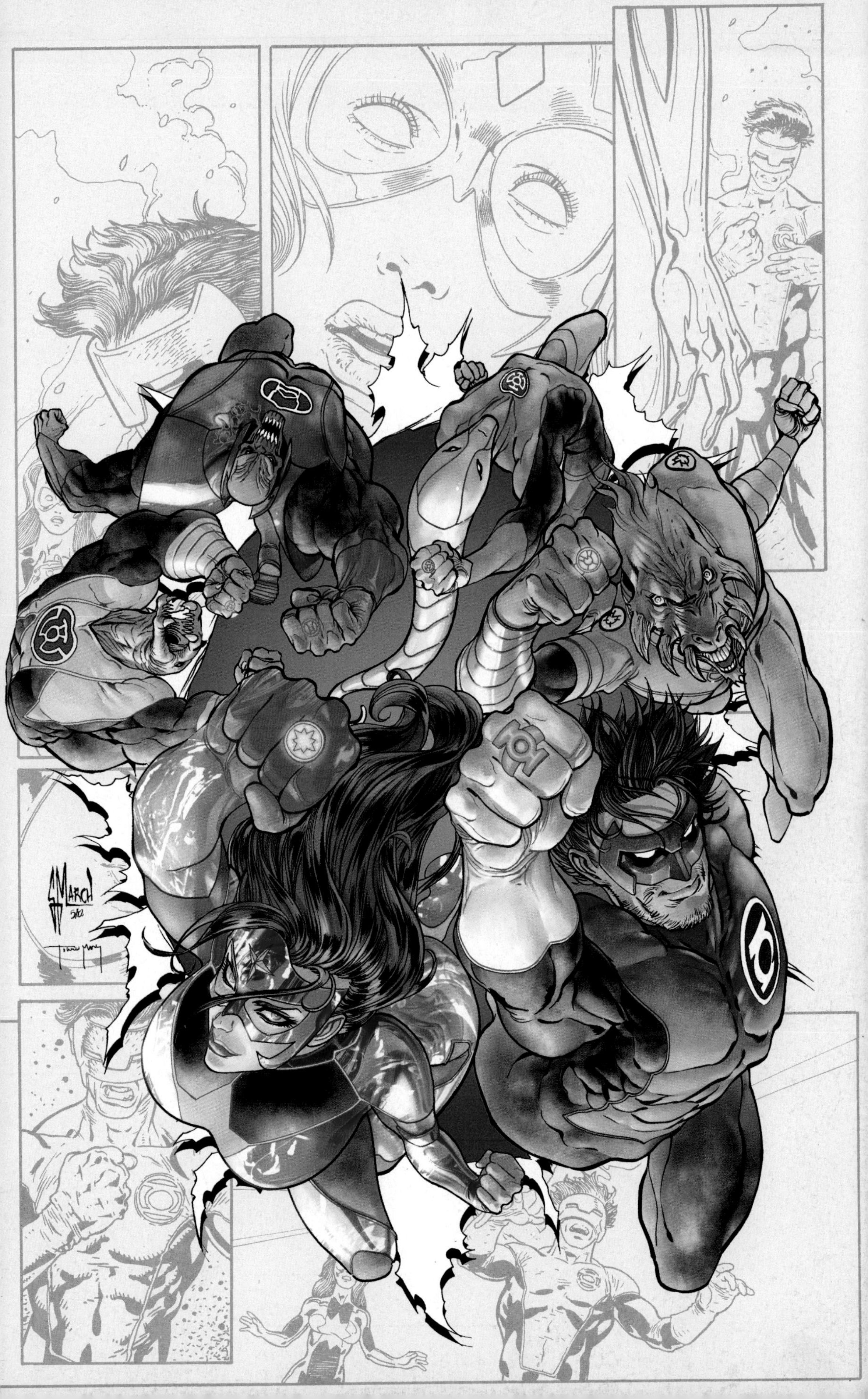

LOVE AND DEATH

TONY BEDARD writer **AARON KUDER & ANDREI BRESSAN** artists **GREG ADAMS** inker
GUILLEM MARCH cover

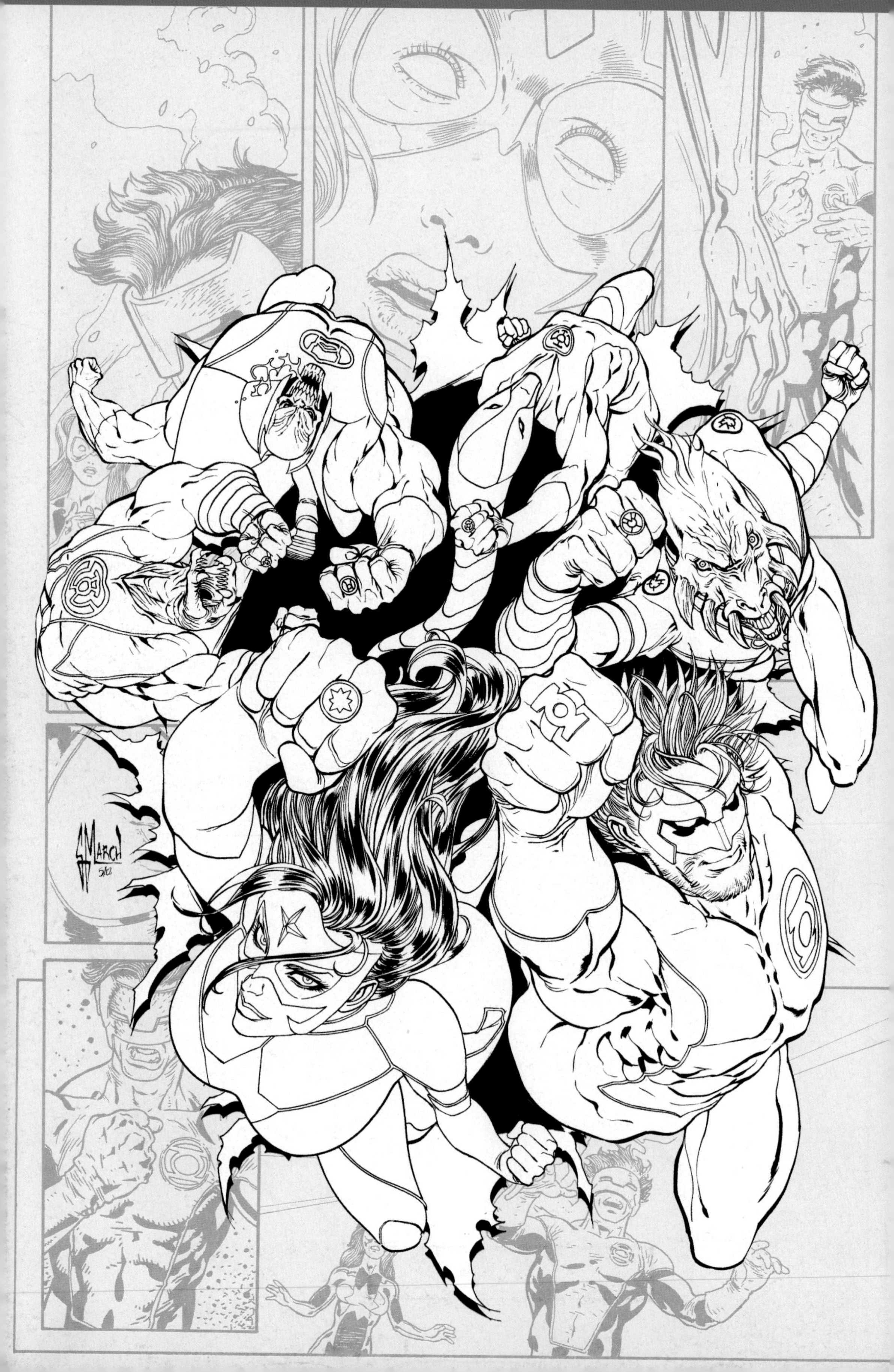
G. MARCH
5/12

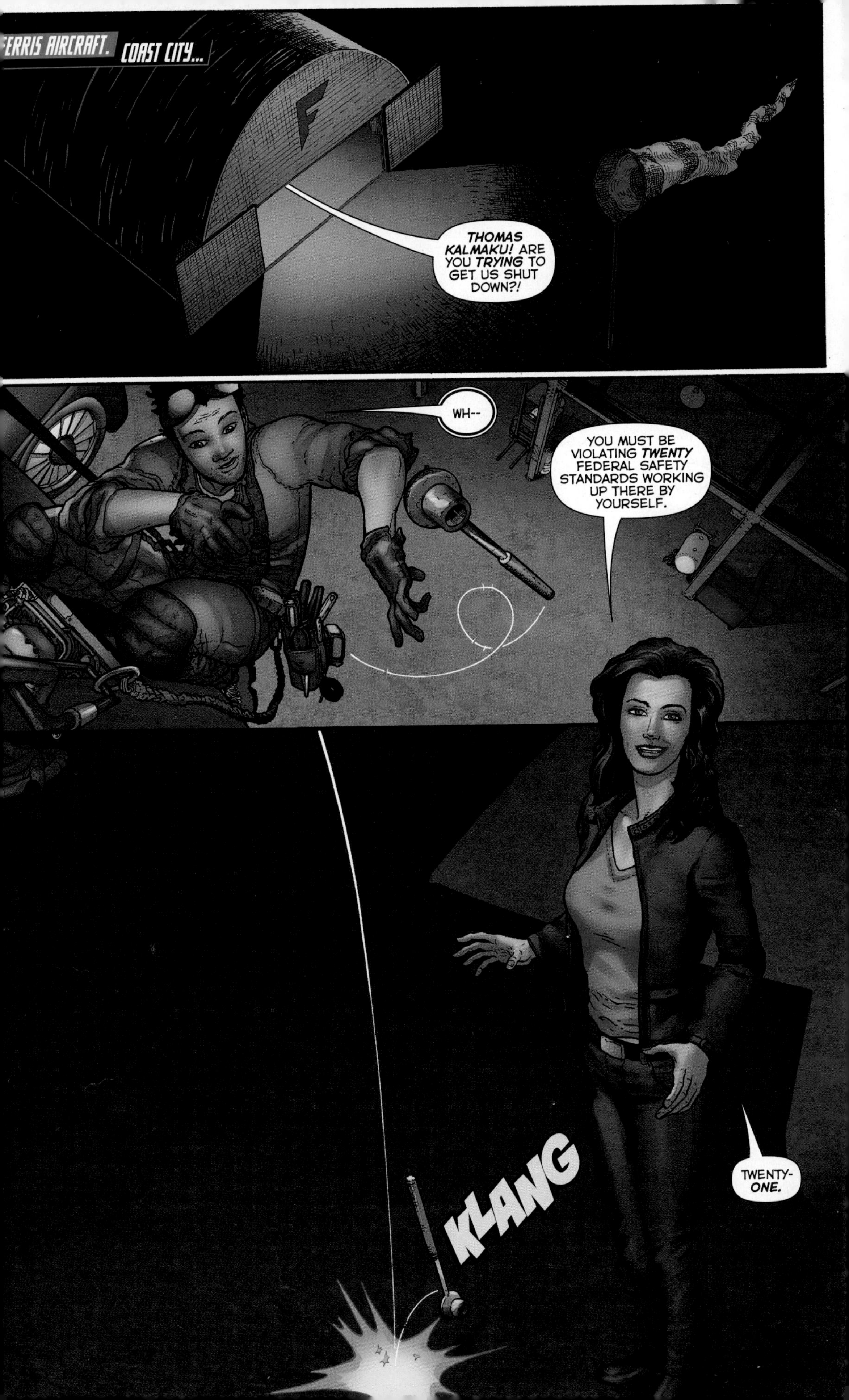
FERRIS AIRCRAFT. COAST CITY...
THOMAS KALMAKU! ARE YOU TRYING TO GET US SHUT DOWN?!
WH--
YOU MUST BE VIOLATING TWENTY FEDERAL SAFETY STANDARDS WORKING UP THERE BY YOURSELF.
KLANG
TWENTY-ONE.

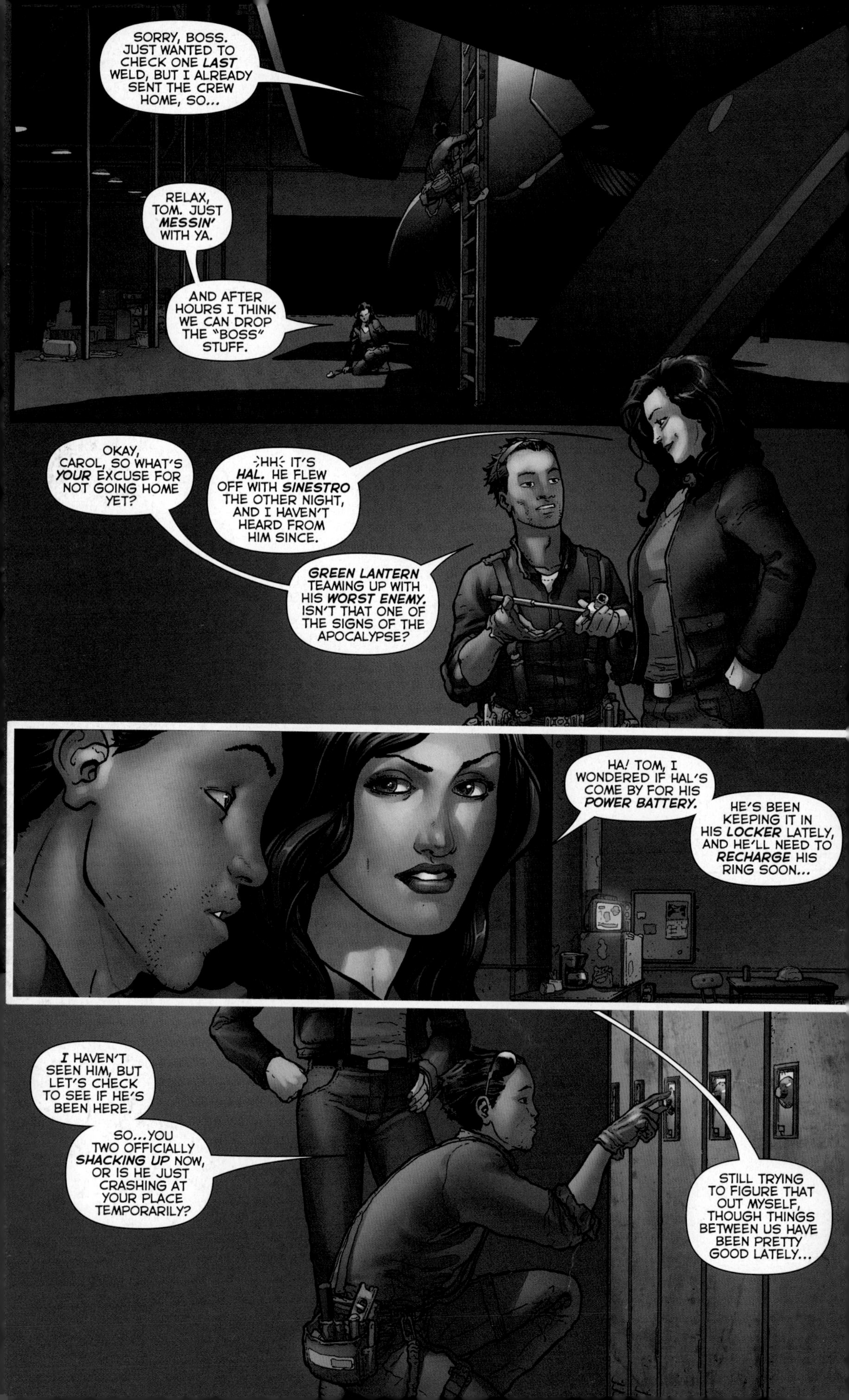
SORRY, BOSS. JUST WANTED TO CHECK ONE LAST WELD, BUT I ALREADY SENT THE CREW HOME, SO...
RELAX, TOM. JUST MESSIN' WITH YA.
AND AFTER HOURS I THINK WE CAN DROP THE "BOSS" STUFF.
OKAY, CAROL, SO WHAT'S YOUR EXCUSE FOR NOT GOING HOME YET?
HH IT'S HAL. HE FLEW OFF WITH SINESTRO THE OTHER NIGHT, AND I HAVEN'T HEARD FROM HIM SINCE.
GREEN LANTERN TEAMING UP WITH HIS WORST ENEMY. ISN'T THAT ONE OF THE SIGNS OF THE APOCALYPSE?
HA! TOM, I WONDERED IF HAL'S COME BY FOR HIS POWER BATTERY.
HE'S BEEN KEEPING IT IN HIS LOCKER LATELY, AND HE'LL NEED TO RECHARGE HIS RING SOON...
I HAVEN'T SEEN HIM, BUT LET'S CHECK TO SEE IF HE'S BEEN HERE.
SO...YOU TWO OFFICIALLY SHACKING UP NOW, OR IS HE JUST CRASHING AT YOUR PLACE TEMPORARILY?
STILL TRYING TO FIGURE THAT OUT MYSELF, THOUGH THINGS BETWEEN US HAVE BEEN PRETTY GOOD LATELY...

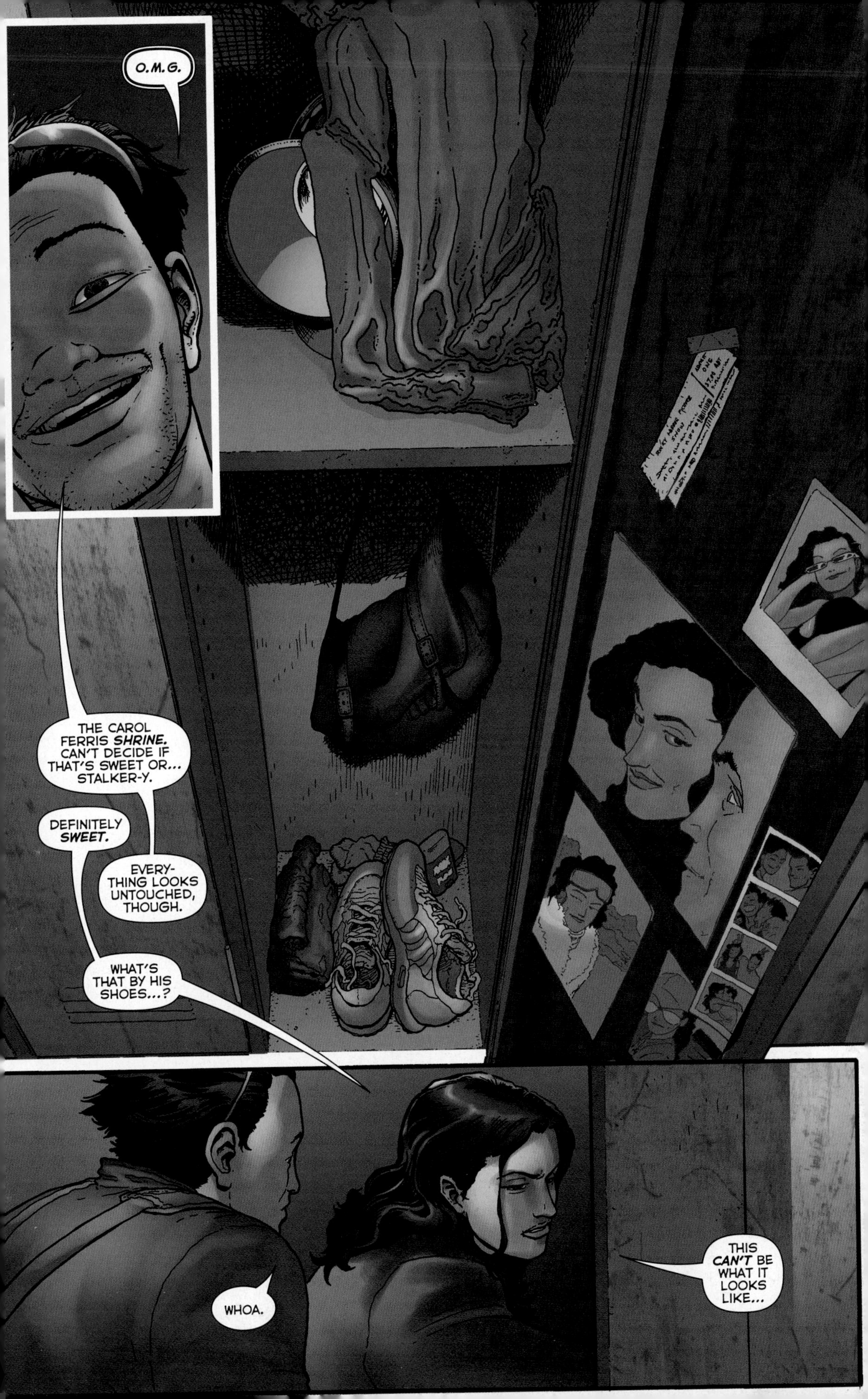

O.M.G.
THE CAROL FERRIS SHRINE. CAN'T DECIDE IF THAT'S SWEET OR... STALKER-Y.
DEFINITELY SWEET.
EVERY-THING LOOKS UNTOUCHED, THOUGH.
WHAT'S THAT BY HIS SHOES...?
WHOA.
THIS CAN'T BE WHAT IT LOOKS LIKE...

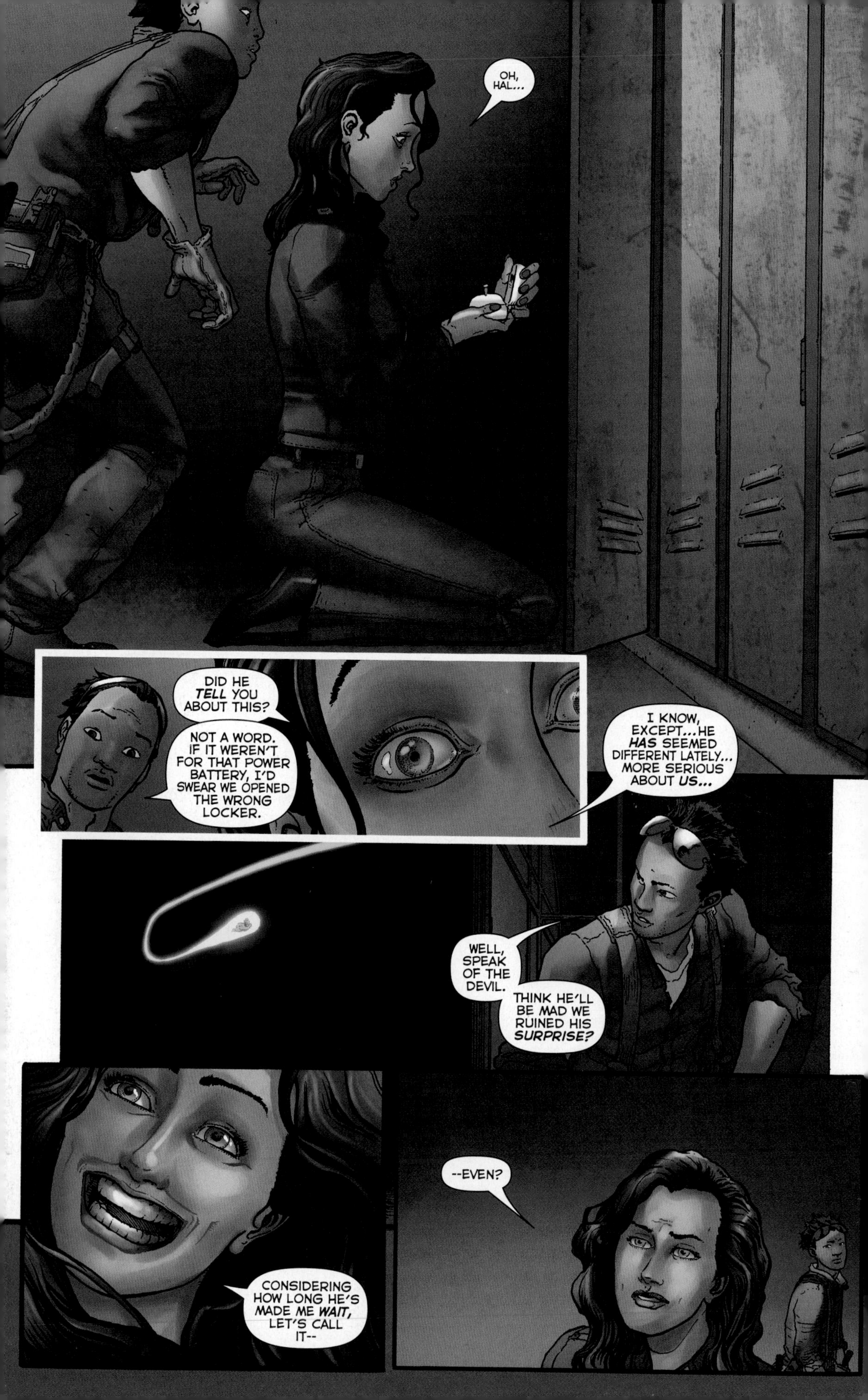
OH, HAL...
DID HE TELL YOU ABOUT THIS?
NOT A WORD. IF IT WEREN'T FOR THAT POWER BATTERY, I'D SWEAR WE OPENED THE WRONG LOCKER.
I KNOW, EXCEPT...HE HAS SEEMED DIFFERENT LATELY... MORE SERIOUS ABOUT US...
WELL, SPEAK OF THE DEVIL.
THINK HE'LL BE MAD WE RUINED HIS SURPRISE?
CONSIDERING HOW LONG HE'S MADE ME WAIT, LET'S CALL IT--
--EVEN?

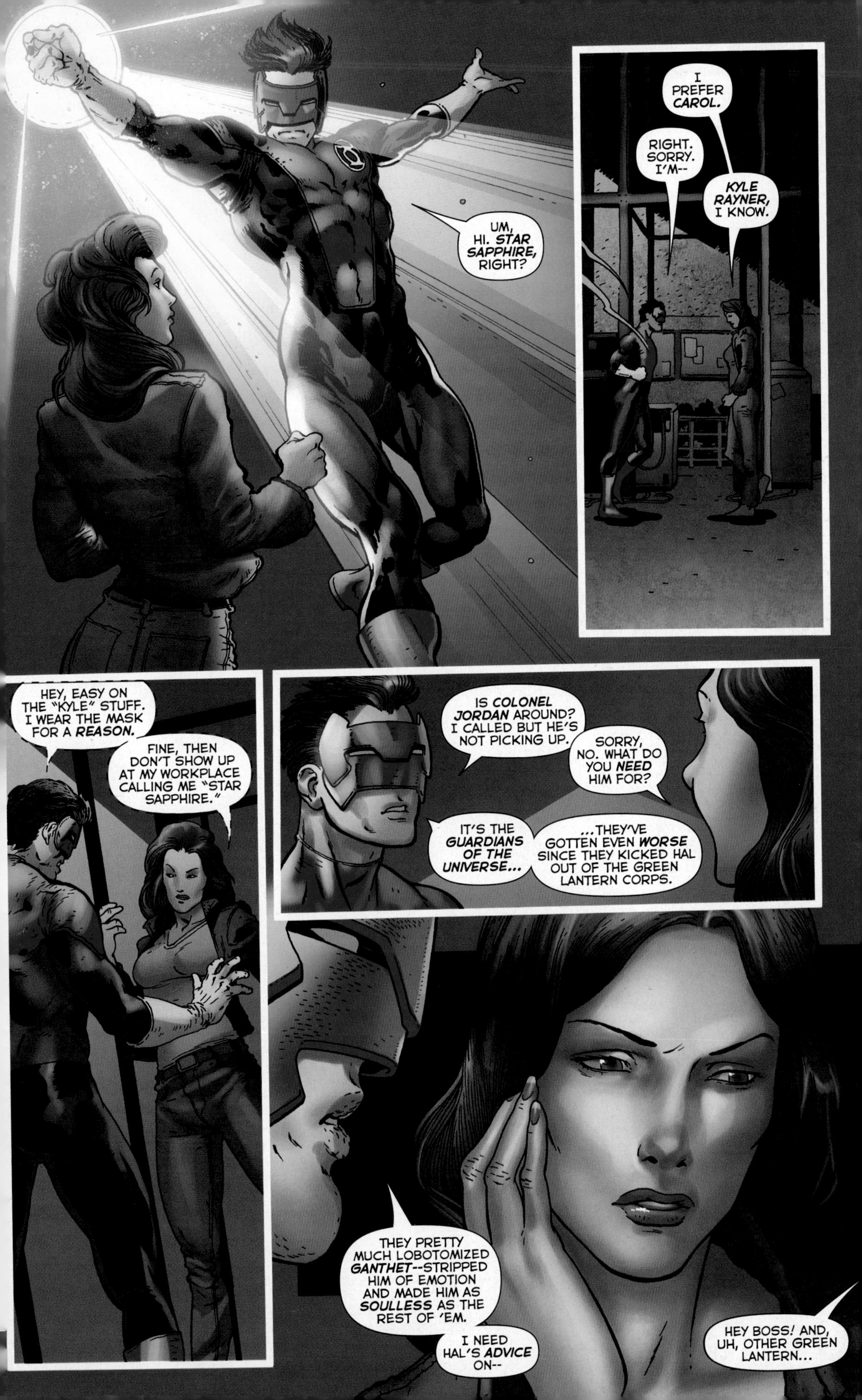
UM, HI. STAR SAPPHIRE, RIGHT?
I PREFER CAROL.
RIGHT. SORRY. I'M--
KYLE RAYNER, I KNOW.
HEY, EASY ON THE "KYLE" STUFF. I WEAR THE MASK FOR A REASON.
FINE, THEN DON'T SHOW UP AT MY WORKPLACE CALLING ME "STAR SAPPHIRE."
IS COLONEL JORDAN AROUND? I CALLED BUT HE'S NOT PICKING UP.
SORRY, NO. WHAT DO YOU NEED HIM FOR?
IT'S THE GUARDIANS OF THE UNIVERSE...
...THEY'VE GOTTEN EVEN WORSE SINCE THEY KICKED HAL OUT OF THE GREEN LANTERN CORPS.
THEY PRETTY MUCH LOBOTOMIZED GANTHET--STRIPPED HIM OF EMOTION AND MADE HIM AS SOULLESS AS THE REST OF 'EM.
I NEED HAL'S ADVICE ON--
HEY BOSS! AND, UH, OTHER GREEN LANTERN...

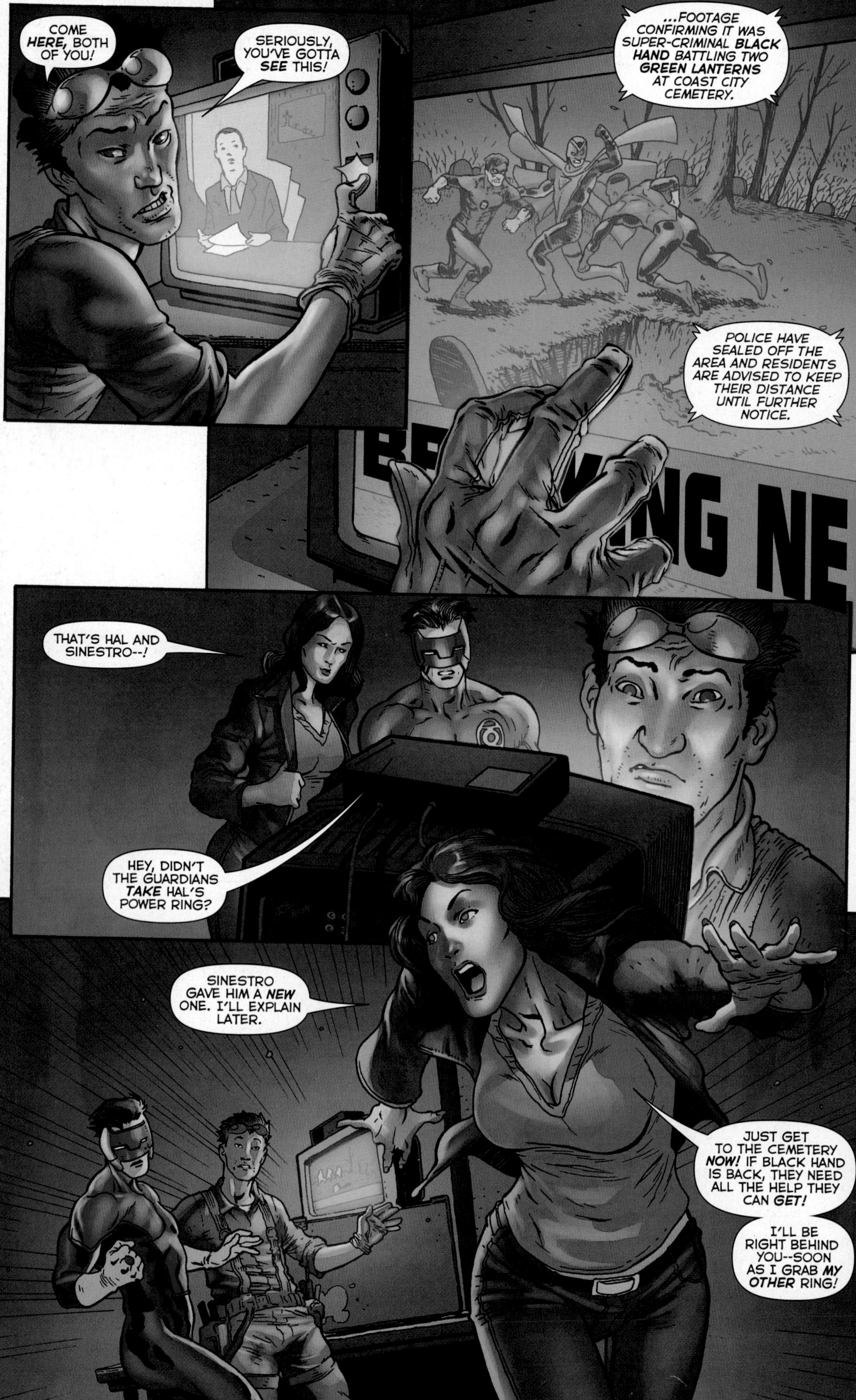
COME *HERE,* BOTH OF YOU!
SERIOUSLY, YOU'VE GOTTA *SEE* THIS!
...FOOTAGE CONFIRMING IT WAS SUPER-CRIMINAL **BLACK HAND** BATTLING TWO **GREEN LANTERNS** AT COAST CITY CEMETERY.
POLICE HAVE SEALED OFF THE AREA AND RESIDENTS ARE ADVISED TO KEEP THEIR DISTANCE UNTIL FURTHER NOTICE.
THAT'S HAL AND SINESTRO--!
HEY, DIDN'T THE GUARDIANS *TAKE* HAL'S POWER RING?
SINESTRO GAVE HIM A *NEW* ONE. I'LL EXPLAIN LATER.
JUST GET TO THE CEMETERY *NOW!* IF BLACK HAND IS BACK, THEY NEED ALL THE HELP THEY CAN *GET!*
I'LL BE RIGHT BEHIND YOU--SOON AS I GRAB *MY OTHER* RING!

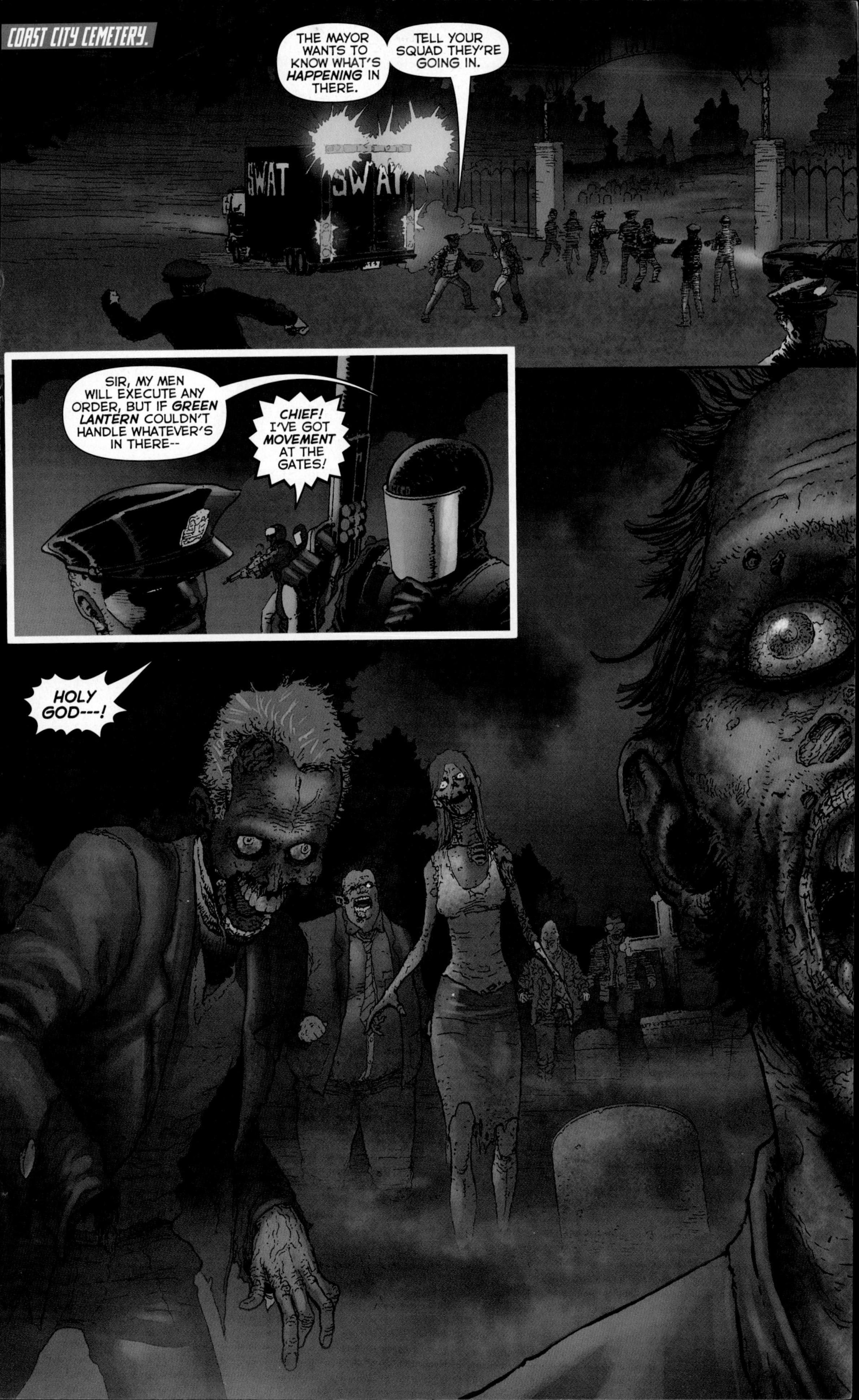
COAST CITY CEMETERY.
THE MAYOR WANTS TO KNOW WHAT'S HAPPENING IN THERE.
TELL YOUR SQUAD THEY'RE GOING IN.
SWAT
SWAT
SIR, MY MEN WILL EXECUTE ANY ORDER, BUT IF GREEN LANTERN COULDN'T HANDLE WHATEVER'S IN THERE--
CHIEF! I'VE GOT MOVEMENT AT THE GATES!
HOLY GOD---!

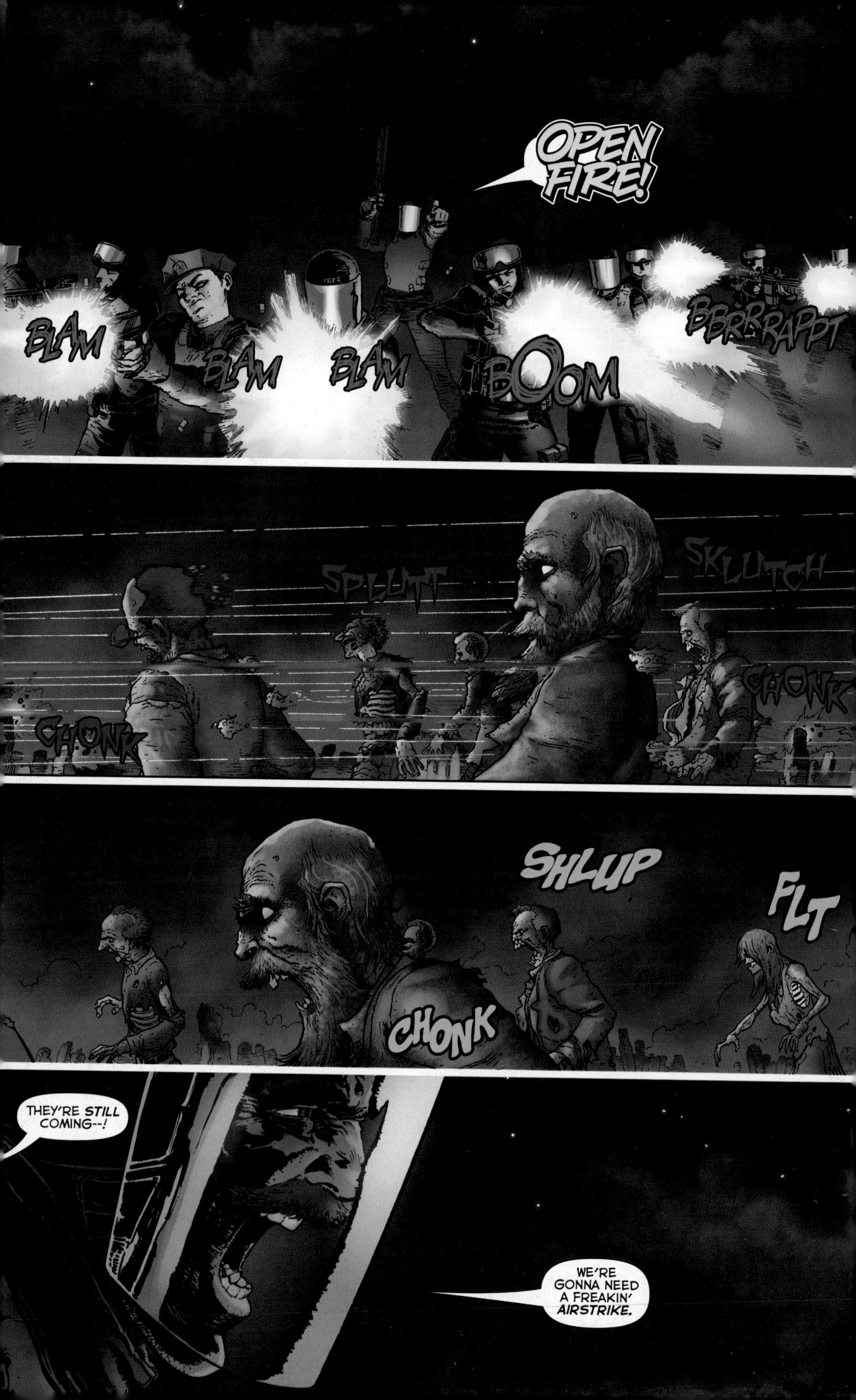

OPEN FIRE!
BLAM
BLAM
BLAM
BOOM
BBRRRAPPT
SPLUTT
SKLUTCH
CHONK
CHONK
SHLUP
FLT
CHONK
THEY'RE STILL COMING--!
WE'RE GONNA NEED A FREAKIN' AIRSTRIKE.

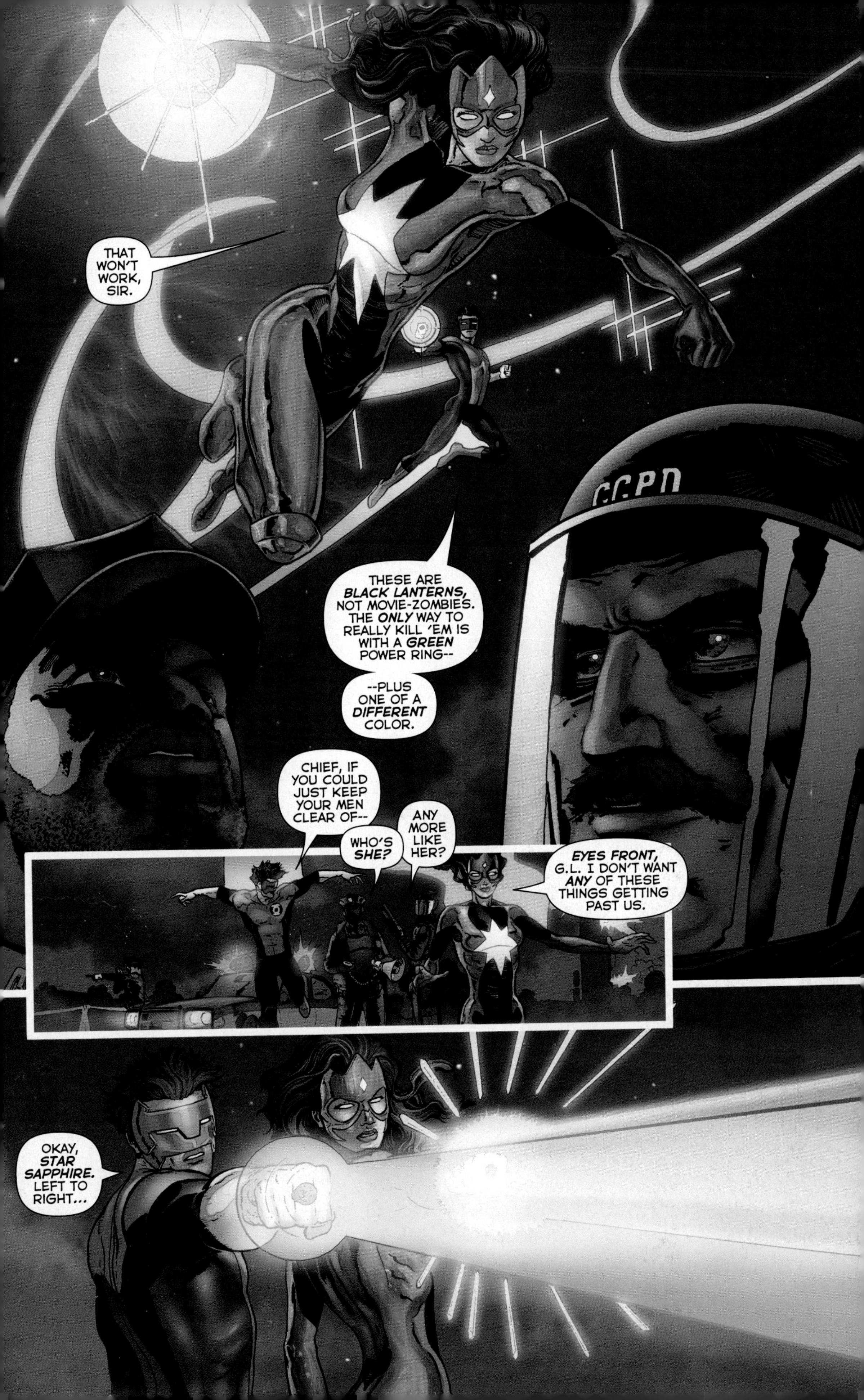
THAT WON'T WORK, SIR.
C.C.P.D
THESE ARE BLACK LANTERNS, NOT MOVIE-ZOMBIES. THE ONLY WAY TO REALLY KILL 'EM IS WITH A GREEN POWER RING--
--PLUS ONE OF A DIFFERENT COLOR.
CHIEF, IF YOU COULD JUST KEEP YOUR MEN CLEAR OF--
WHO'S SHE?
ANY MORE LIKE HER?
EYES FRONT, G.L. I DON'T WANT ANY OF THESE THINGS GETTING PAST US.
OKAY, STAR SAPPHIRE. LEFT TO RIGHT...

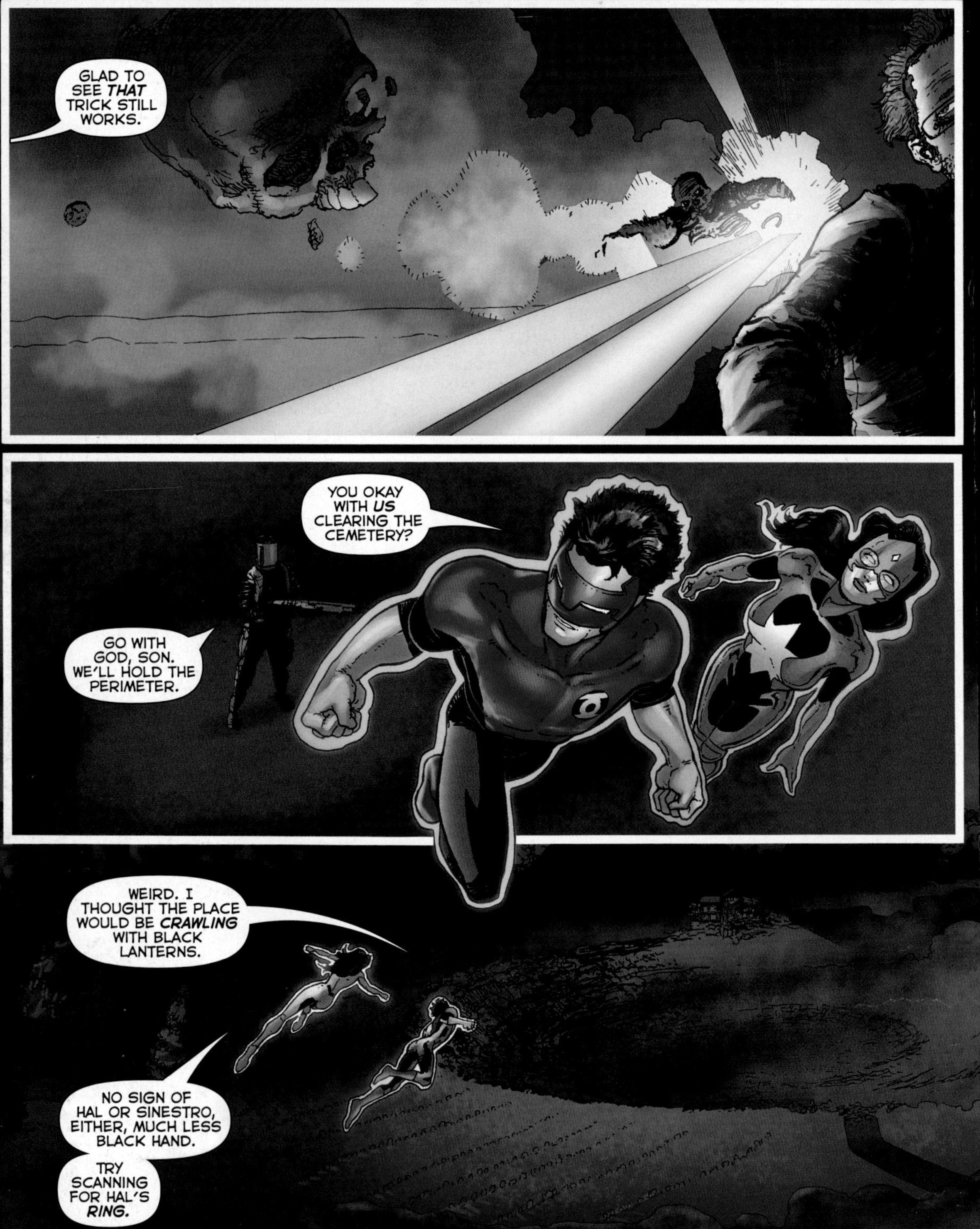
GLAD TO SEE *THAT* TRICK STILL WORKS.
YOU OKAY WITH *US* CLEARING THE CEMETERY?
GO WITH GOD, SON. WE'LL HOLD THE PERIMETER.
WEIRD. I THOUGHT THE PLACE WOULD BE *CRAWLING* WITH BLACK LANTERNS.
NO SIGN OF HAL OR SINESTRO, EITHER, MUCH LESS BLACK HAND.
TRY SCANNING FOR HAL'S *RING*.

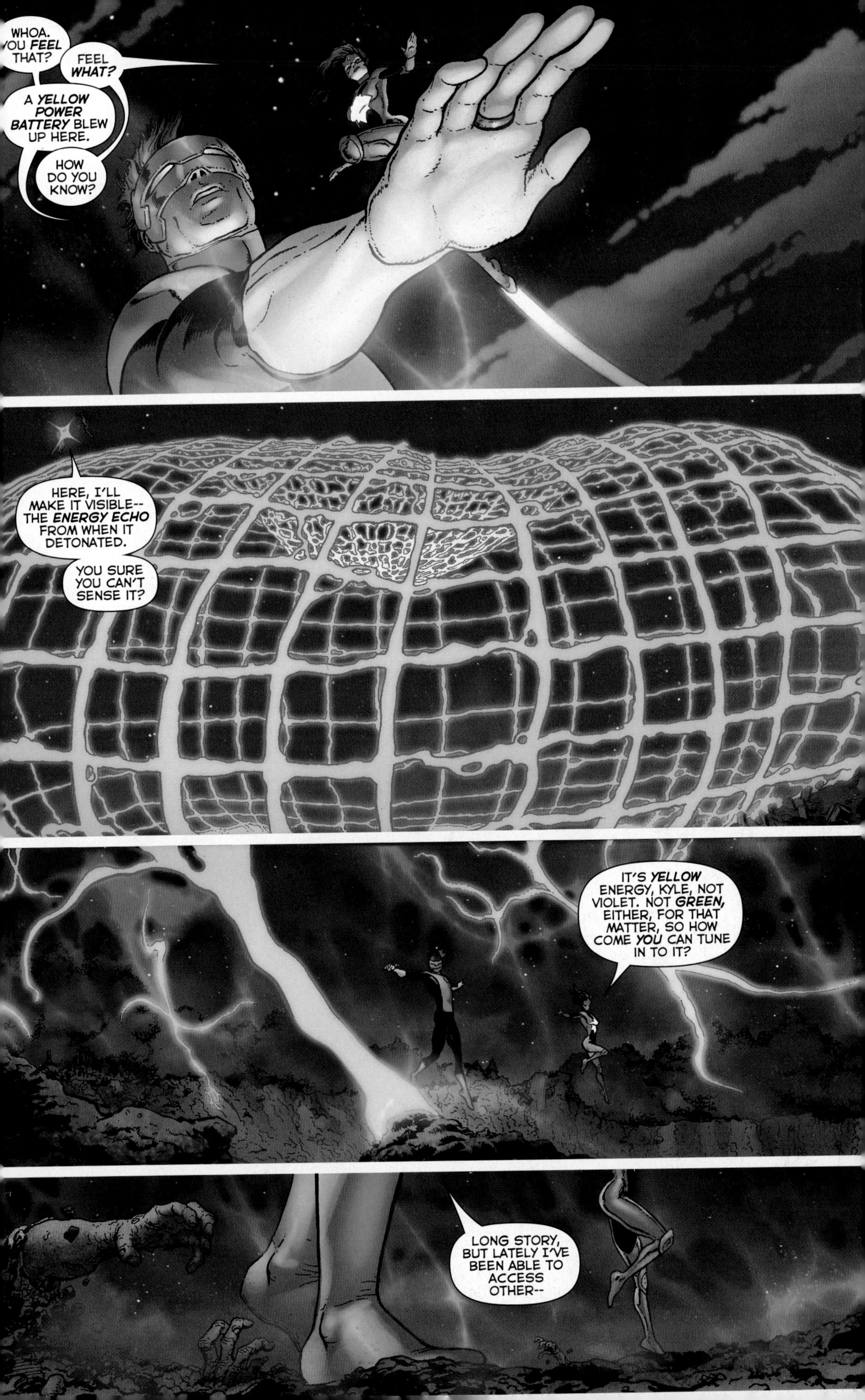
WHOA. YOU FEEL THAT?
FEEL WHAT?
A YELLOW POWER BATTERY BLEW UP HERE.
HOW DO YOU KNOW?
HERE, I'LL MAKE IT VISIBLE-- THE ENERGY ECHO FROM WHEN IT DETONATED.
YOU SURE YOU CAN'T SENSE IT?
IT'S YELLOW ENERGY, KYLE, NOT VIOLET. NOT GREEN, EITHER, FOR THAT MATTER, SO HOW COME YOU CAN TUNE IN TO IT?
LONG STORY, BUT LATELY I'VE BEEN ABLE TO ACCESS OTHER--

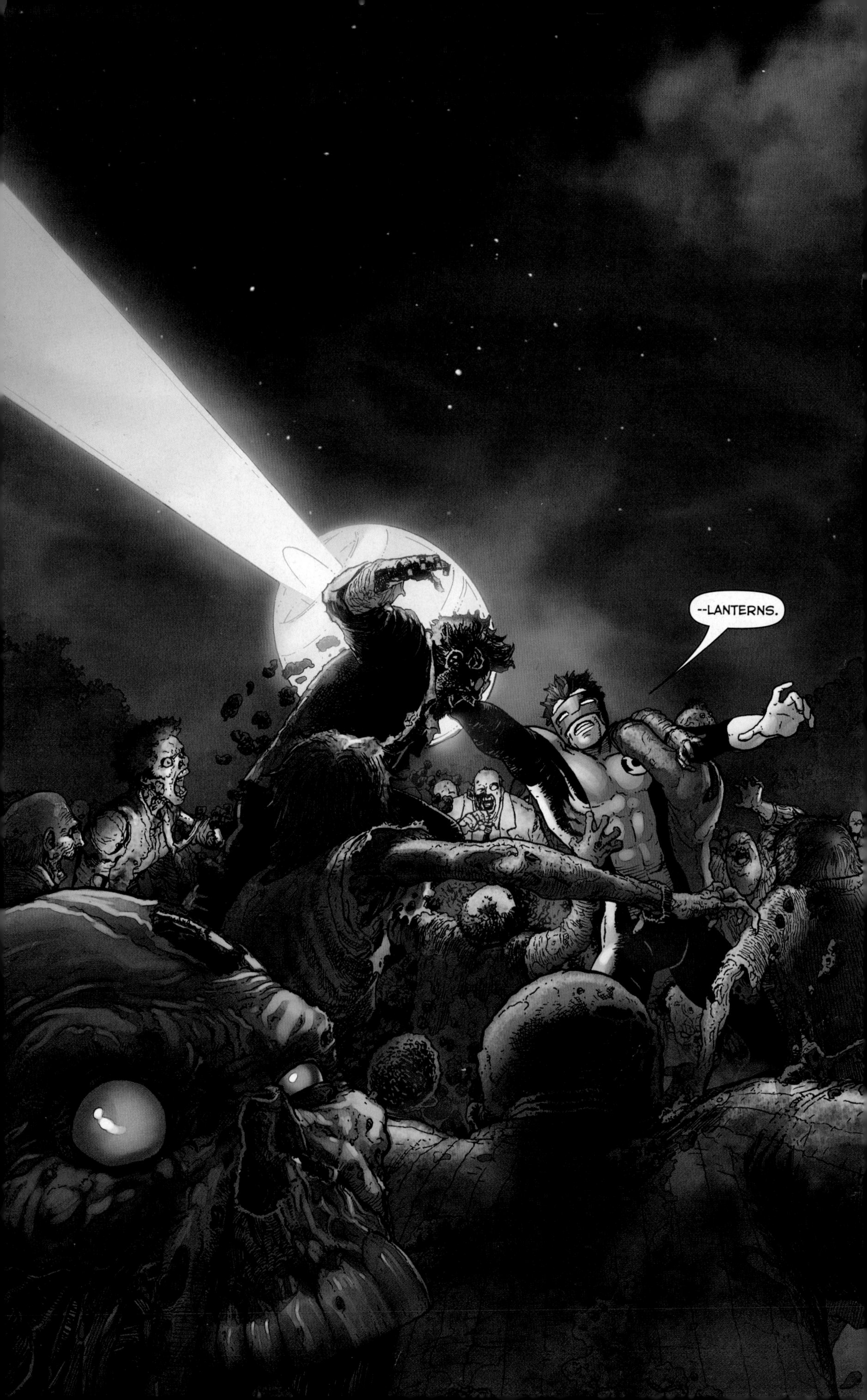
--LANTERNS.

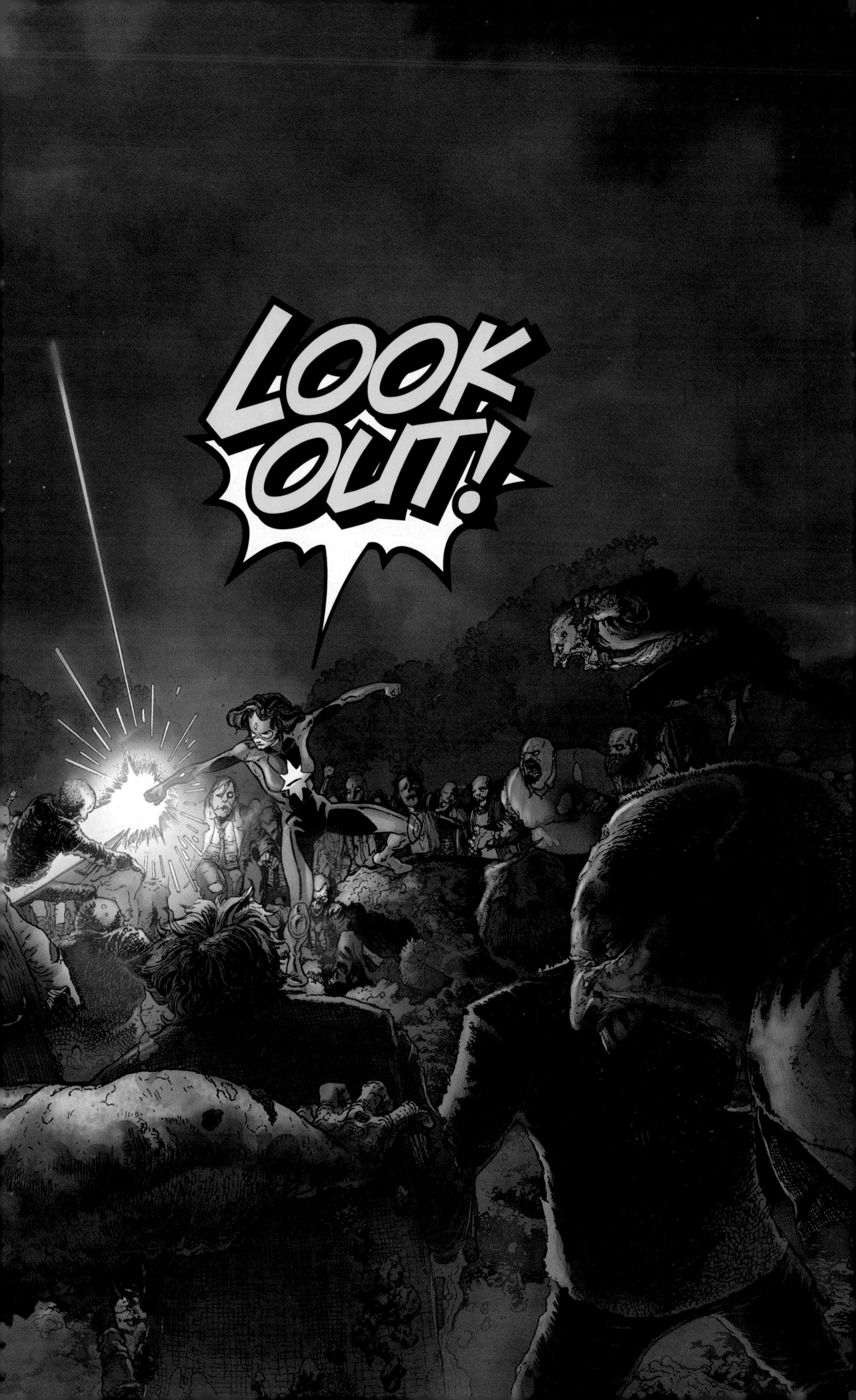
LOOK OUT!

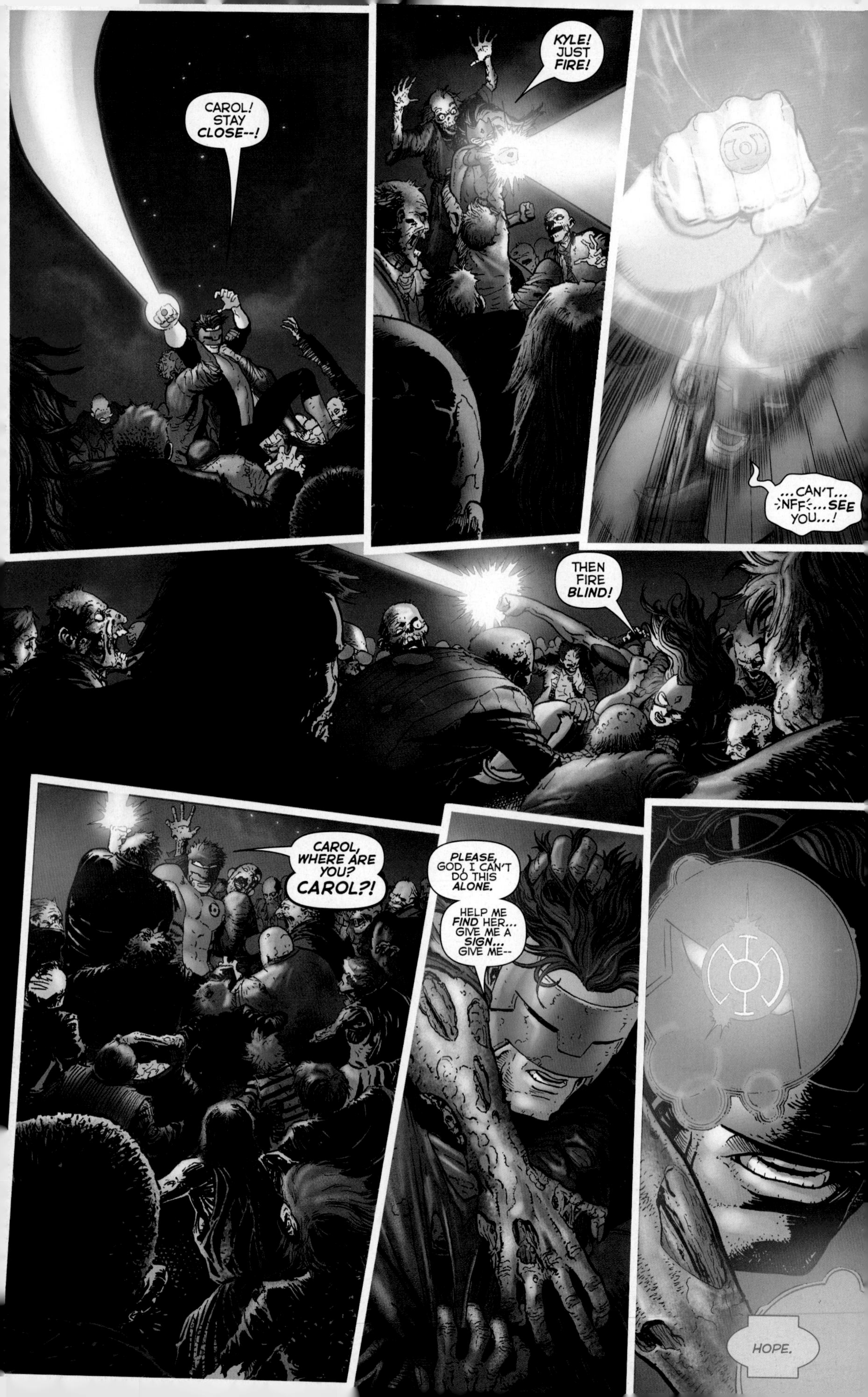
CAROL! STAY CLOSE--!
KYLE! JUST FIRE!
...CAN'T... NFF... SEE YOU...!
THEN FIRE BLIND!
CAROL, WHERE ARE YOU? CAROL?!
PLEASE, GOD, I CAN'T DO THIS ALONE.
HELP ME FIND HER... GIVE ME A SIGN... GIVE ME--
HOPE.

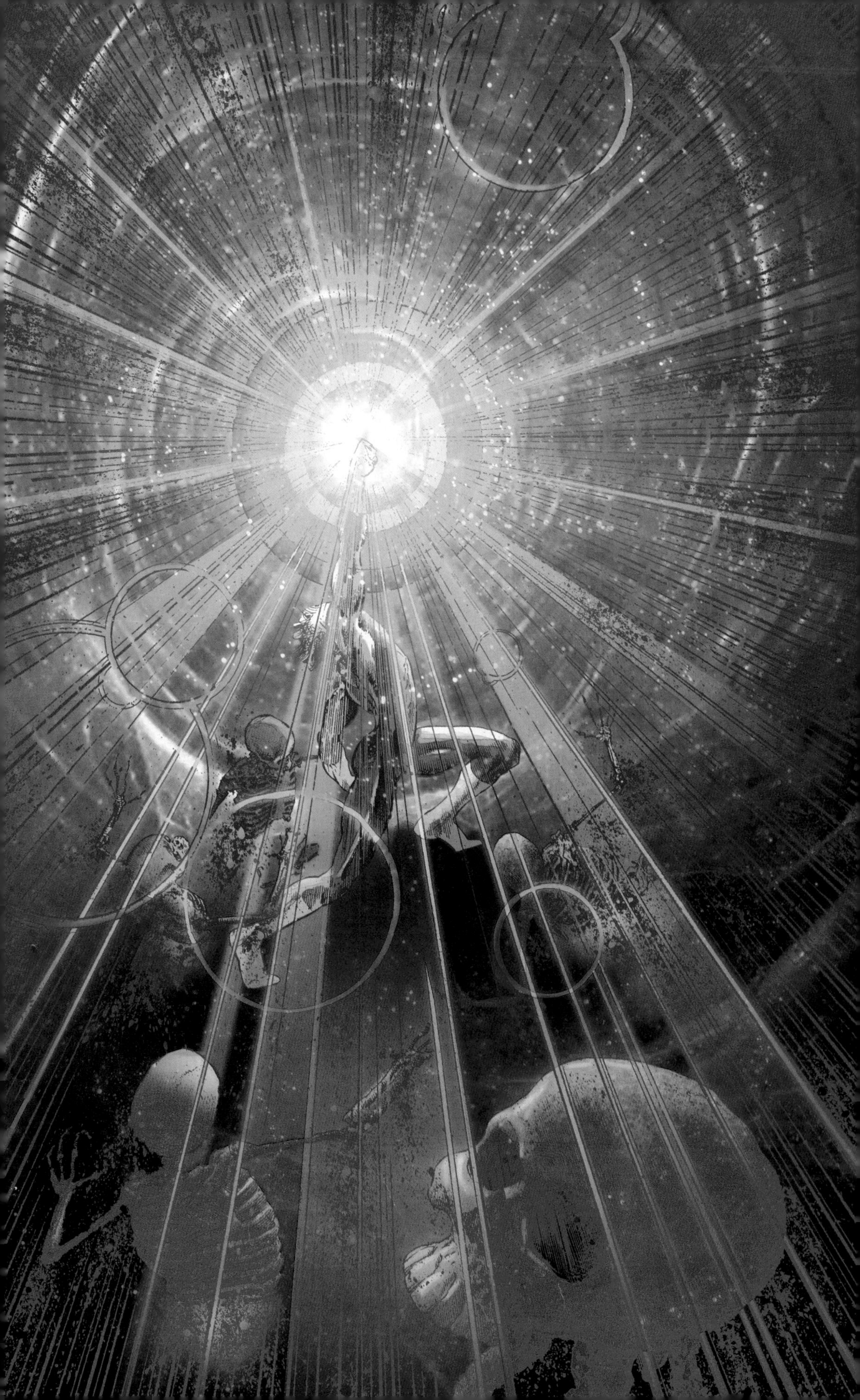

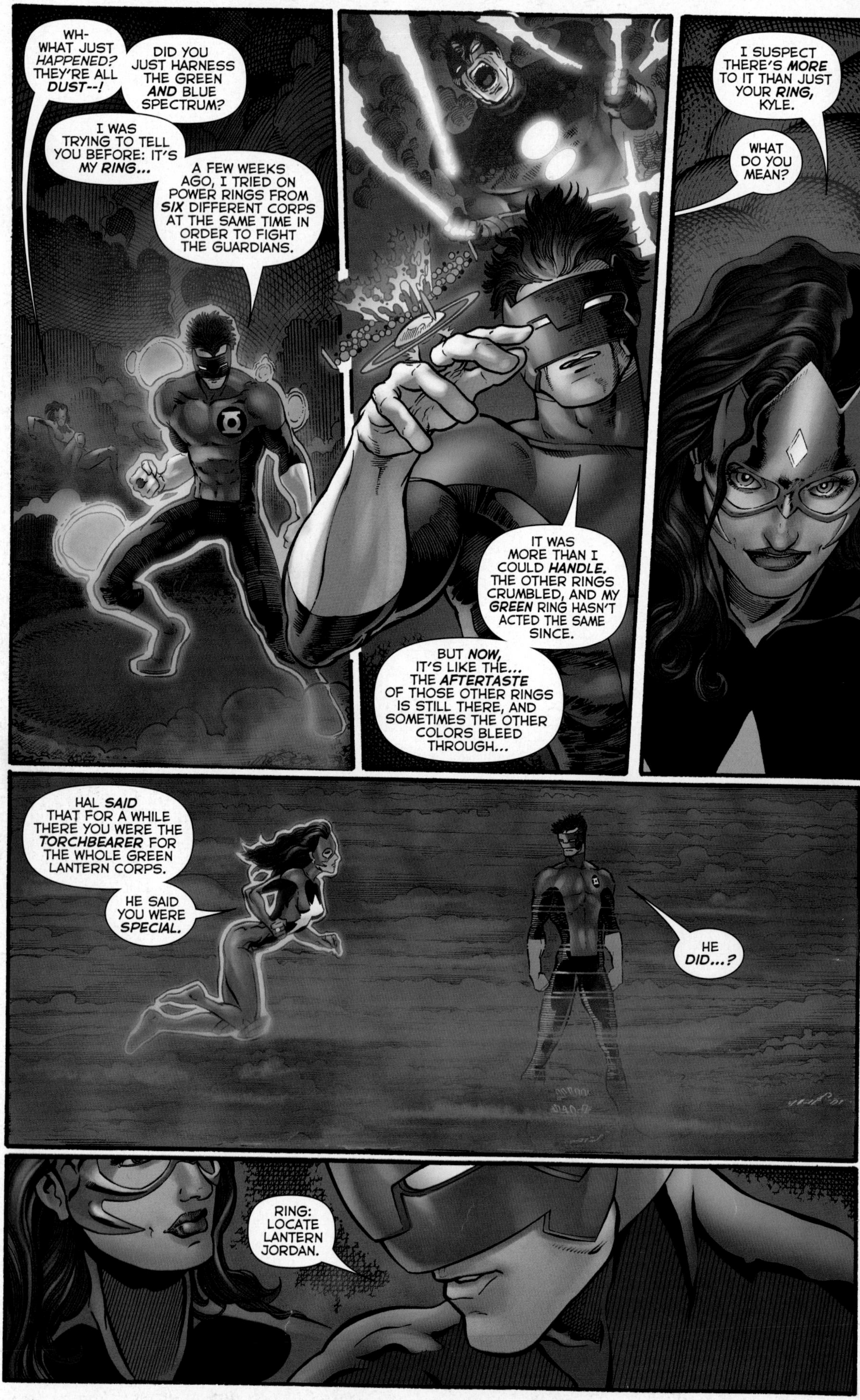
WH- WHAT JUST HAPPENED? THEY'RE ALL DUST--!
DID YOU JUST HARNESS THE GREEN AND BLUE SPECTRUM?
I WAS TRYING TO TELL YOU BEFORE: IT'S MY RING...
A FEW WEEKS AGO, I TRIED ON POWER RINGS FROM SIX DIFFERENT CORPS AT THE SAME TIME IN ORDER TO FIGHT THE GUARDIANS.
IT WAS MORE THAN I COULD HANDLE. THE OTHER RINGS CRUMBLED, AND MY GREEN RING HASN'T ACTED THE SAME SINCE.
BUT NOW, IT'S LIKE THE... THE AFTERTASTE OF THOSE OTHER RINGS IS STILL THERE, AND SOMETIMES THE OTHER COLORS BLEED THROUGH...
I SUSPECT THERE'S MORE TO IT THAN JUST YOUR RING, KYLE.
WHAT DO YOU MEAN?
HAL SAID THAT FOR A WHILE THERE YOU WERE THE TORCHBEARER FOR THE WHOLE GREEN LANTERN CORPS.
HE SAID YOU WERE SPECIAL.
HE DID...?
RING: LOCATE LANTERN JORDAN.

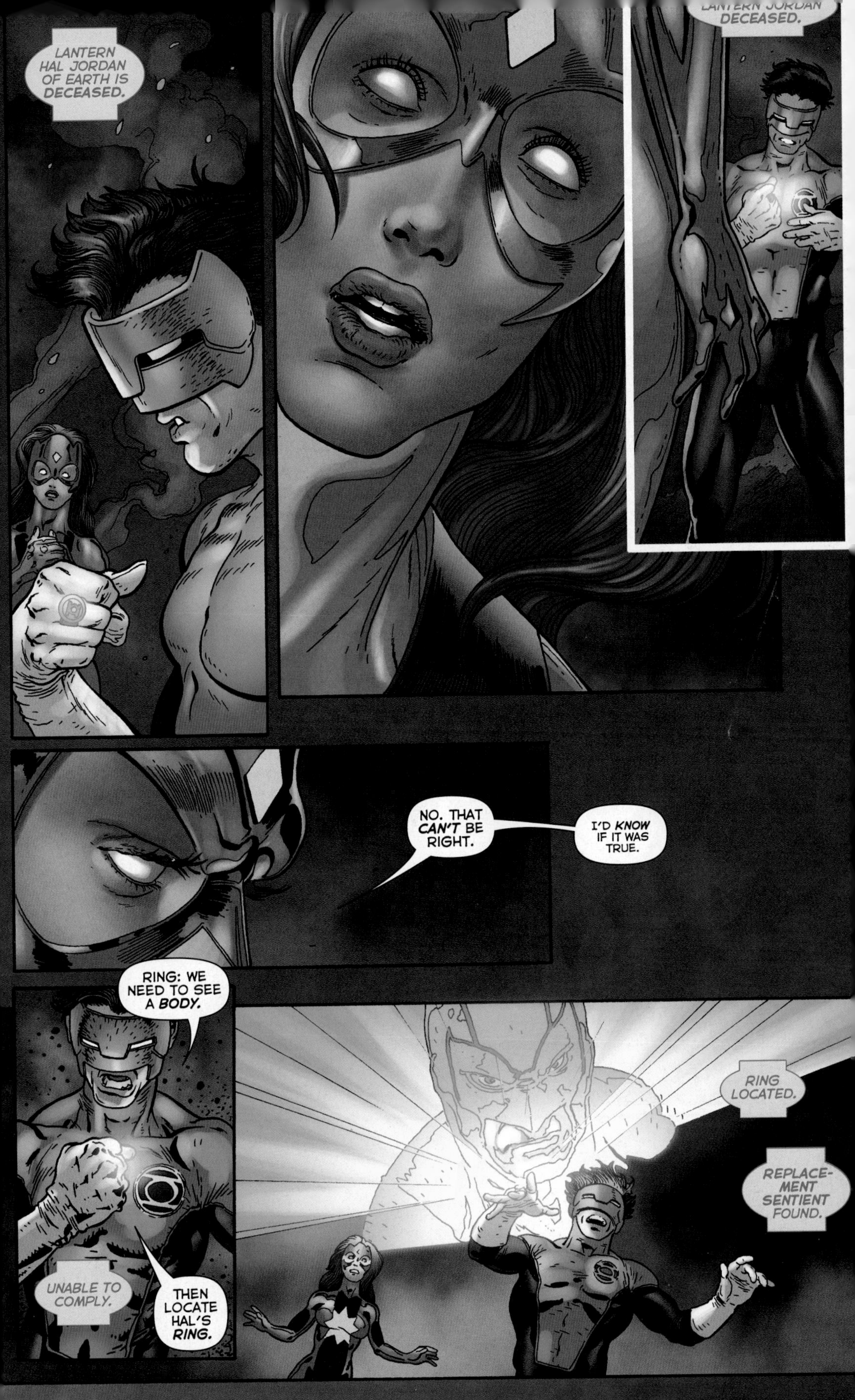
LANTERN HAL JORDAN OF EARTH IS DECEASED.
LANTERN JORDAN DECEASED.
NO. THAT CAN'T BE RIGHT.
I'D KNOW IF IT WAS TRUE.
RING: WE NEED TO SEE A BODY.
UNABLE TO COMPLY.
THEN LOCATE HAL'S RING.
RING LOCATED.
REPLACEMENT SENTIENT FOUND.

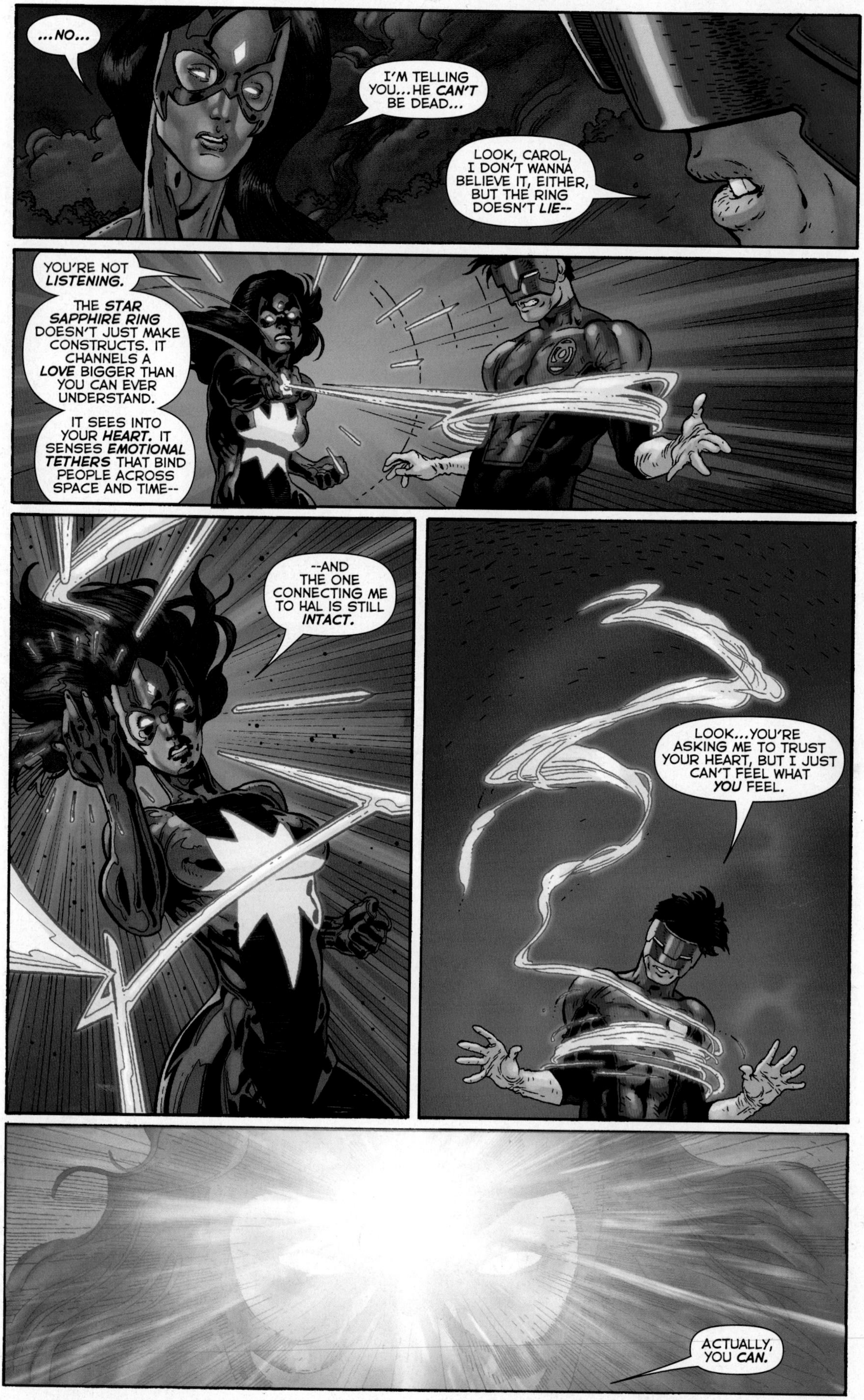
...NO...
I'M TELLING YOU...HE CAN'T BE DEAD...
LOOK, CAROL, I DON'T WANNA BELIEVE IT, EITHER, BUT THE RING DOESN'T LIE--
YOU'RE NOT LISTENING.
THE STAR SAPPHIRE RING DOESN'T JUST MAKE CONSTRUCTS. IT CHANNELS A LOVE BIGGER THAN YOU CAN EVER UNDERSTAND.
IT SEES INTO YOUR HEART. IT SENSES EMOTIONAL TETHERS THAT BIND PEOPLE ACROSS SPACE AND TIME--
--AND THE ONE CONNECTING ME TO HAL IS STILL INTACT.
LOOK...YOU'RE ASKING ME TO TRUST YOUR HEART, BUT I JUST CAN'T FEEL WHAT YOU FEEL.
ACTUALLY, YOU CAN.

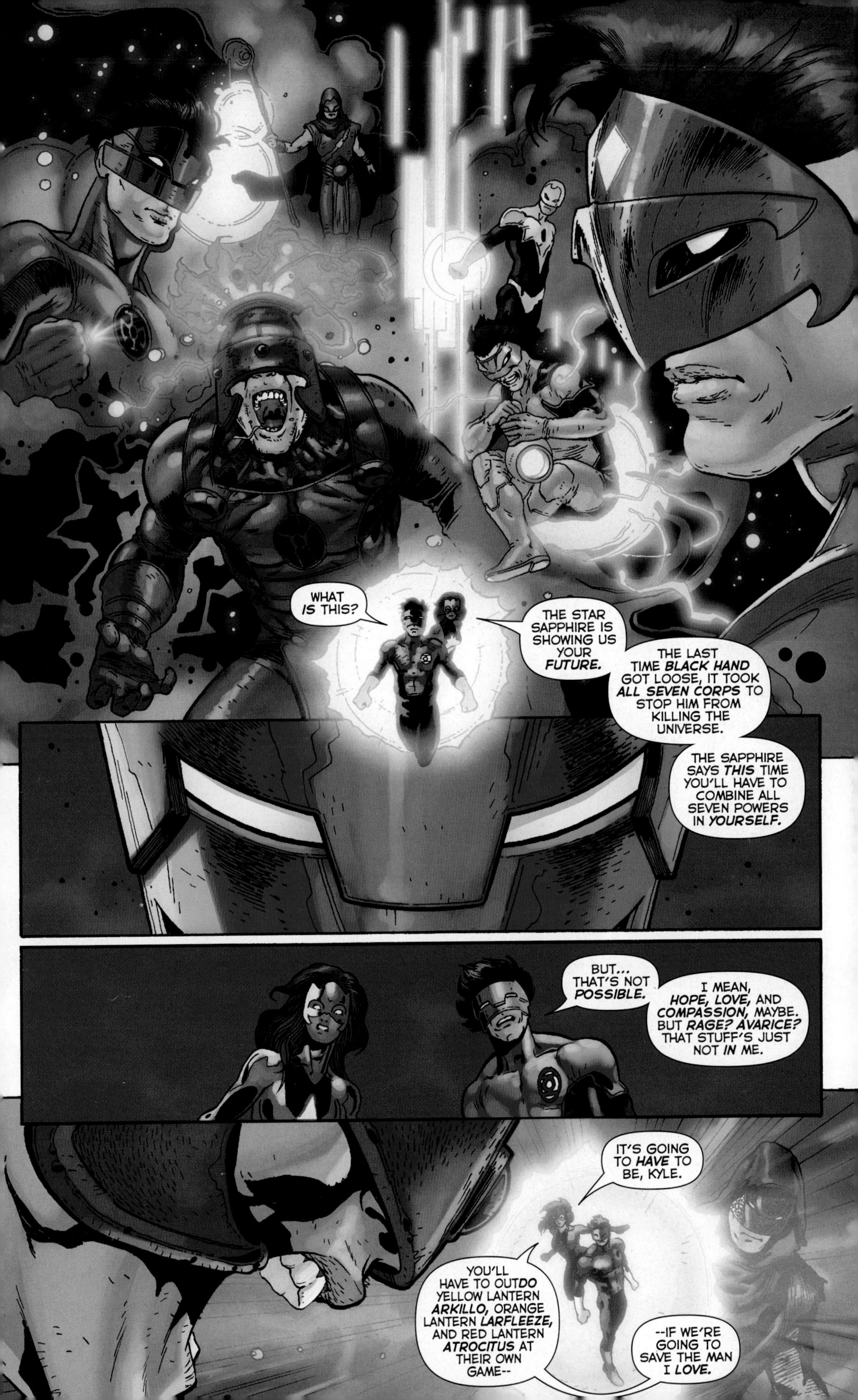
WHAT IS THIS?
THE STAR SAPPHIRE IS SHOWING US YOUR FUTURE.
THE LAST TIME BLACK HAND GOT LOOSE, IT TOOK ALL SEVEN CORPS TO STOP HIM FROM KILLING THE UNIVERSE.
THE SAPPHIRE SAYS THIS TIME YOU'LL HAVE TO COMBINE ALL SEVEN POWERS IN YOURSELF.
BUT... THAT'S NOT POSSIBLE.
I MEAN, HOPE, LOVE, AND COMPASSION, MAYBE. BUT RAGE? AVARICE? THAT STUFF'S JUST NOT IN ME.
IT'S GOING TO HAVE TO BE, KYLE.
YOU'LL HAVE TO OUTDO YELLOW LANTERN ARKILLO, ORANGE LANTERN LARFLEEZE, AND RED LANTERN ATROCITUS AT THEIR OWN GAME--
--IF WE'RE GOING TO SAVE THE MAN I LOVE.

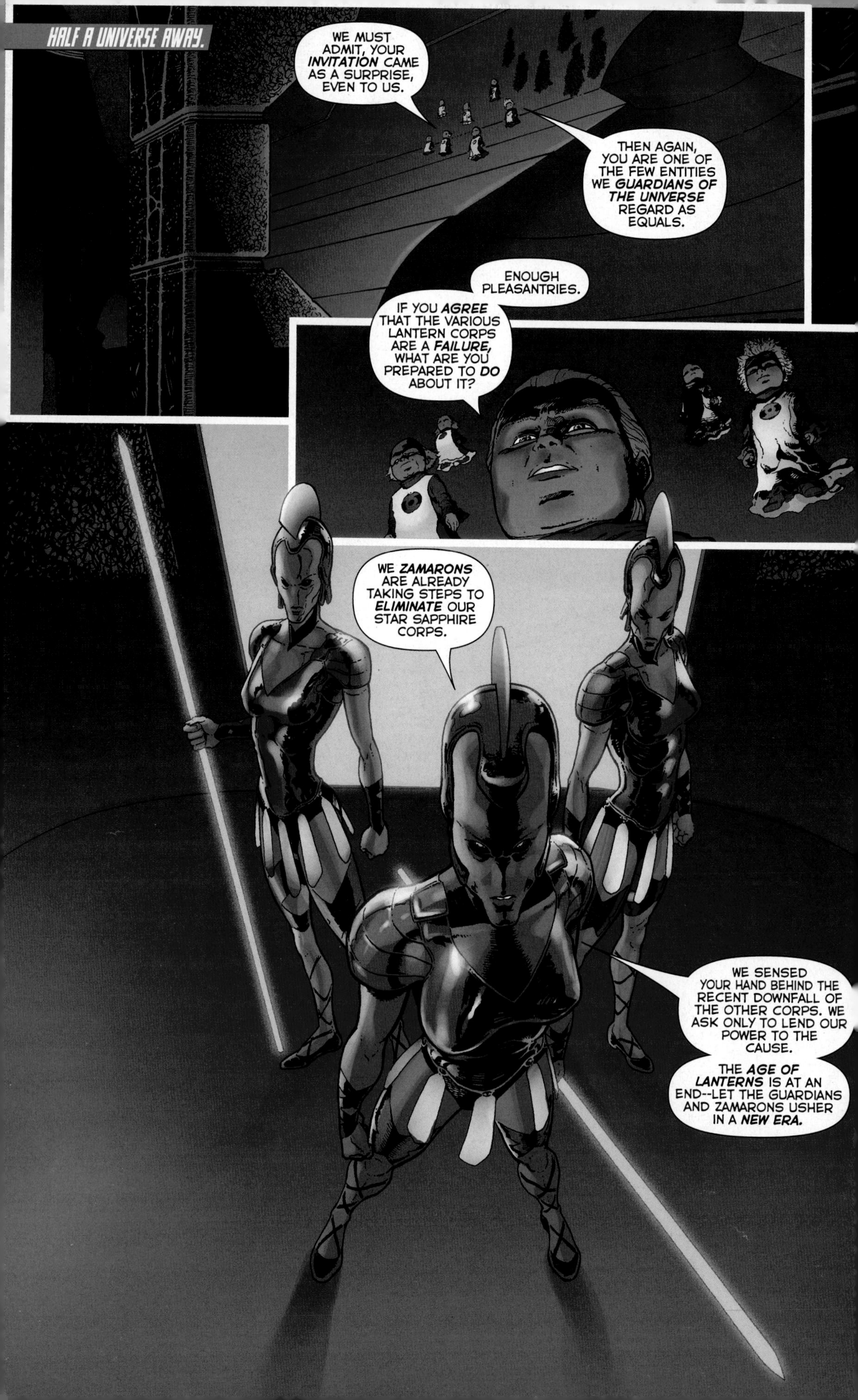
HALF A UNIVERSE AWAY.
WE MUST ADMIT, YOUR INVITATION CAME AS A SURPRISE, EVEN TO US.
THEN AGAIN, YOU ARE ONE OF THE FEW ENTITIES WE GUARDIANS OF THE UNIVERSE REGARD AS EQUALS.
ENOUGH PLEASANTRIES.
IF YOU AGREE THAT THE VARIOUS LANTERN CORPS ARE A FAILURE, WHAT ARE YOU PREPARED TO DO ABOUT IT?
WE ZAMARONS ARE ALREADY TAKING STEPS TO ELIMINATE OUR STAR SAPPHIRE CORPS.
WE SENSED YOUR HAND BEHIND THE RECENT DOWNFALL OF THE OTHER CORPS. WE ASK ONLY TO LEND OUR POWER TO THE CAUSE.
THE AGE OF LANTERNS IS AT AN END--LET THE GUARDIANS AND ZAMARONS USHER IN A NEW ERA.

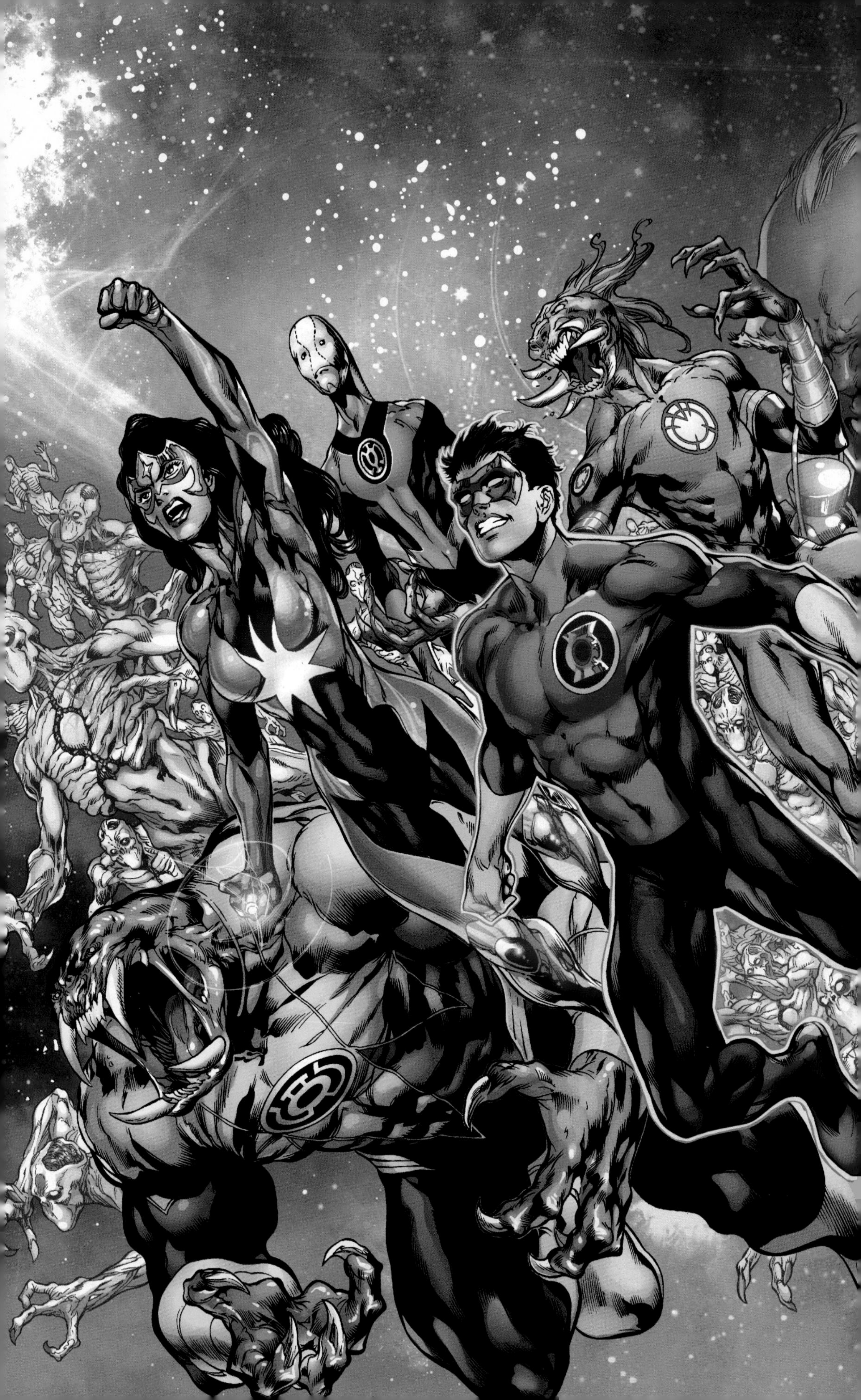

ALL THE RAGE

TONY BEDARD writer ANDREI BRESSAN & AMILCAR PINNA artists
IVAN REIS, OCLAIR ALBERT & ROD REIS cover

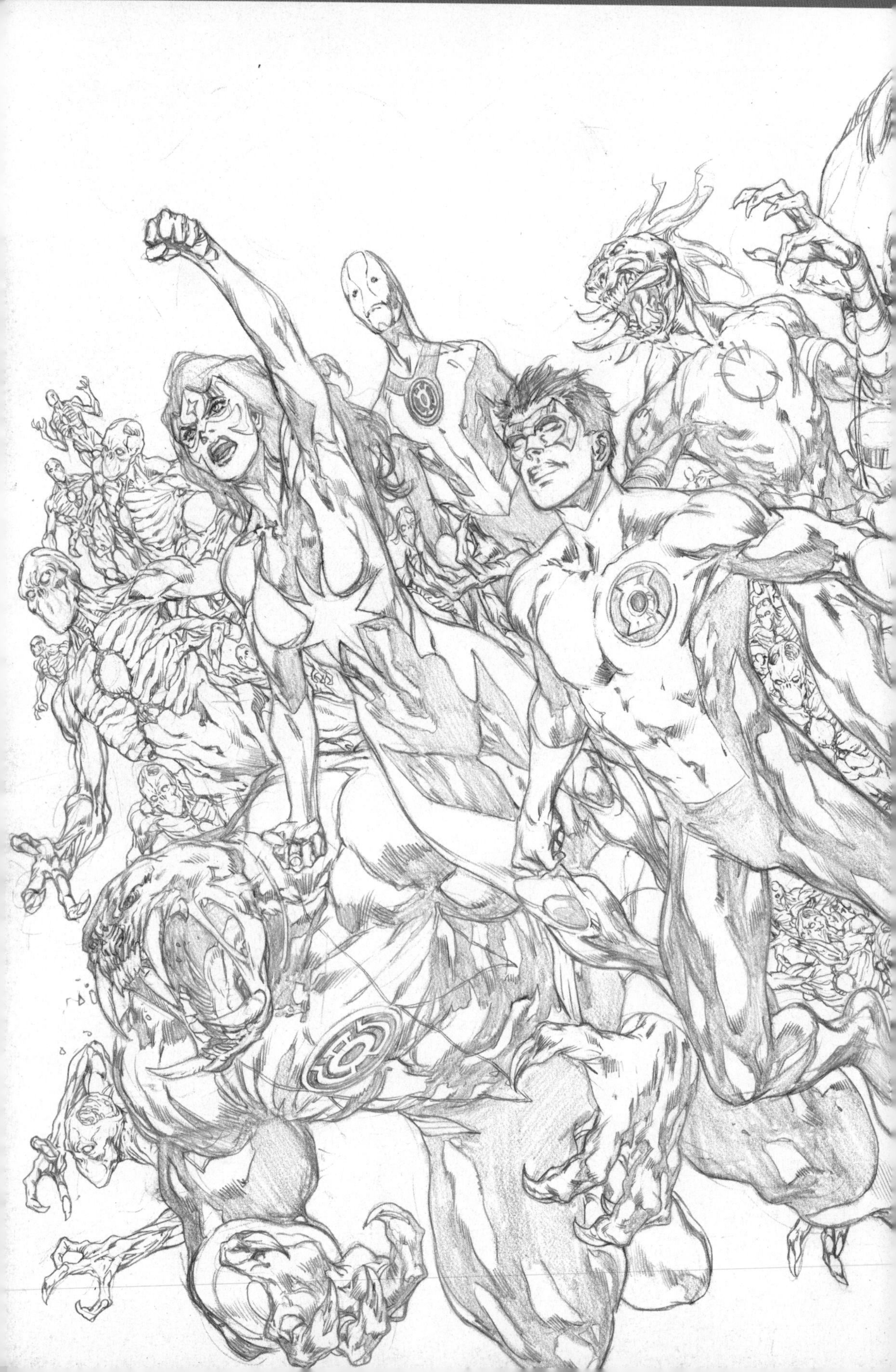

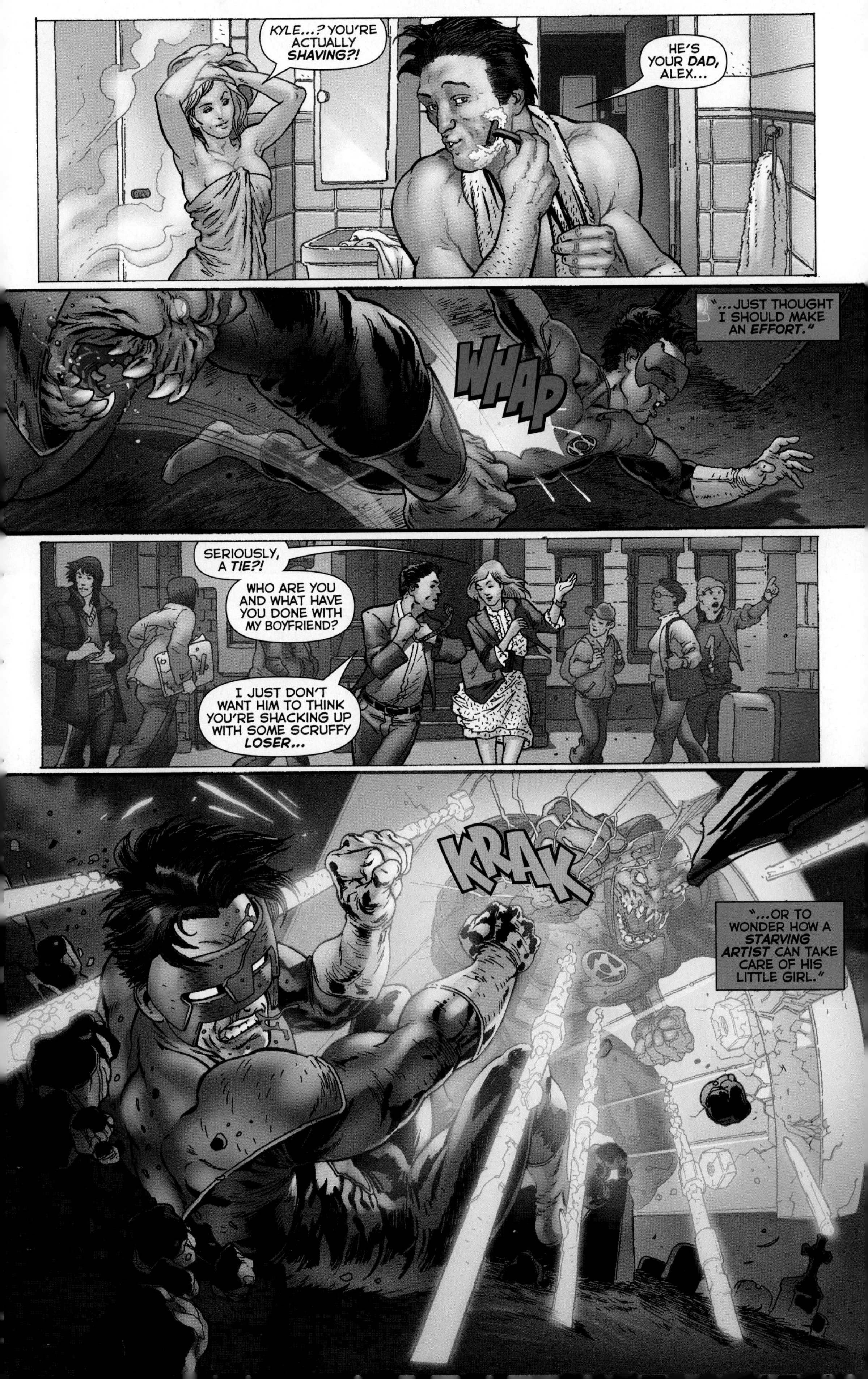
KYLE...? YOU'RE ACTUALLY SHAVING?!
HE'S YOUR DAD, ALEX...
"...JUST THOUGHT I SHOULD MAKE AN EFFORT."
WHAP
SERIOUSLY, A TIE?!
WHO ARE YOU AND WHAT HAVE YOU DONE WITH MY BOYFRIEND?
I JUST DON'T WANT HIM TO THINK YOU'RE SHACKING UP WITH SOME SCRUFFY LOSER...
KRAK
"...OR TO WONDER HOW A STARVING ARTIST CAN TAKE CARE OF HIS LITTLE GIRL."

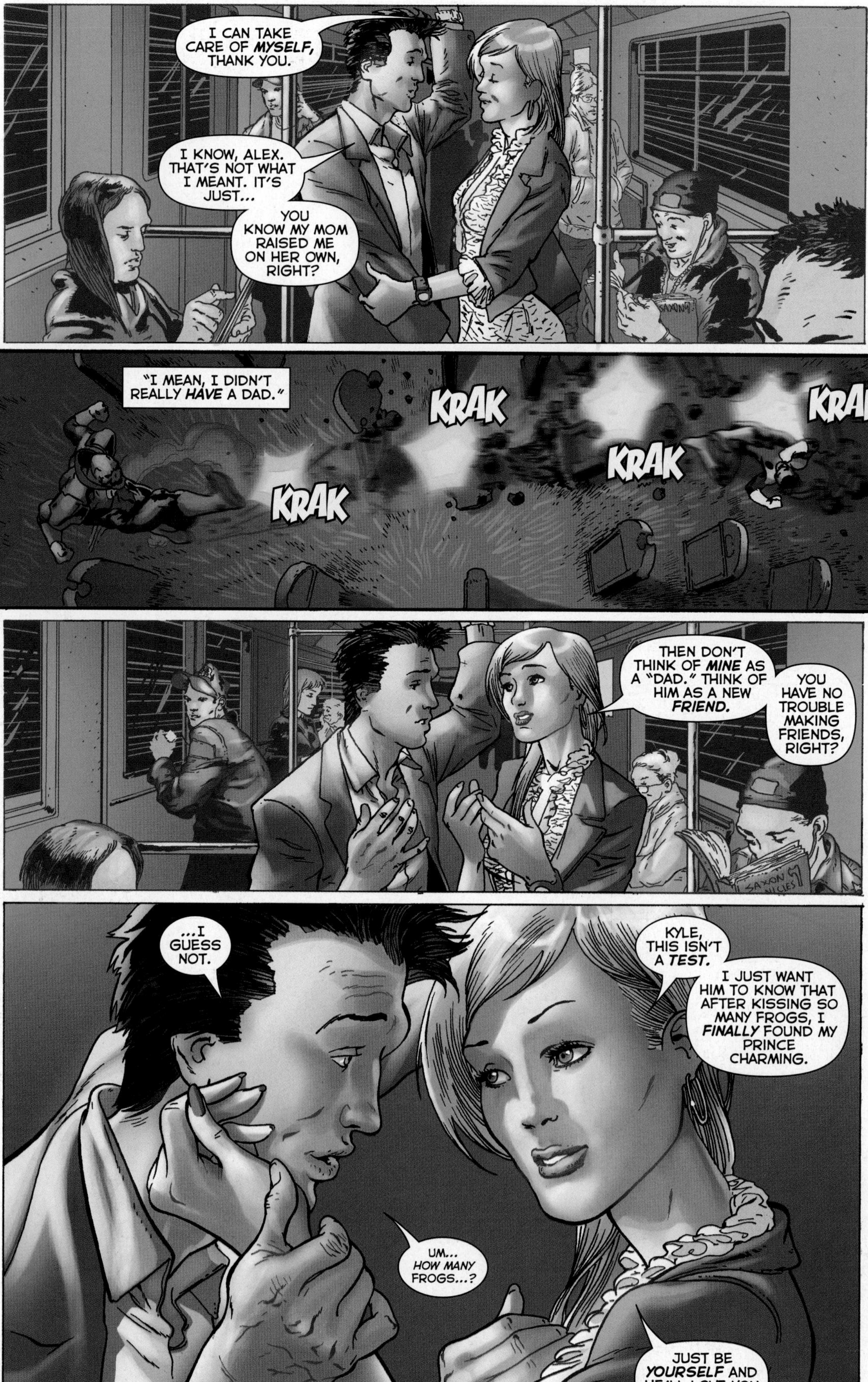
I CAN TAKE CARE OF *MYSELF,* THANK YOU.
I KNOW, ALEX. THAT'S NOT WHAT I MEANT. IT'S JUST...
YOU KNOW MY MOM RAISED ME ON HER OWN, RIGHT?
"I MEAN, I DIDN'T REALLY *HAVE* A DAD."
KRAK
KRAK
KRAK
KRAK
THEN DON'T THINK OF *MINE* AS A "DAD." THINK OF HIM AS A NEW *FRIEND.*
YOU HAVE NO TROUBLE MAKING FRIENDS, RIGHT?
...I GUESS NOT.
KYLE, THIS ISN'T A *TEST.*
I JUST WANT HIM TO KNOW THAT AFTER KISSING SO MANY FROGS, I *FINALLY* FOUND MY PRINCE CHARMING.
UM... *HOW MANY* FROGS...?
JUST BE *YOURSELF* AND HE'LL LOVE YOU LIKE I DO.

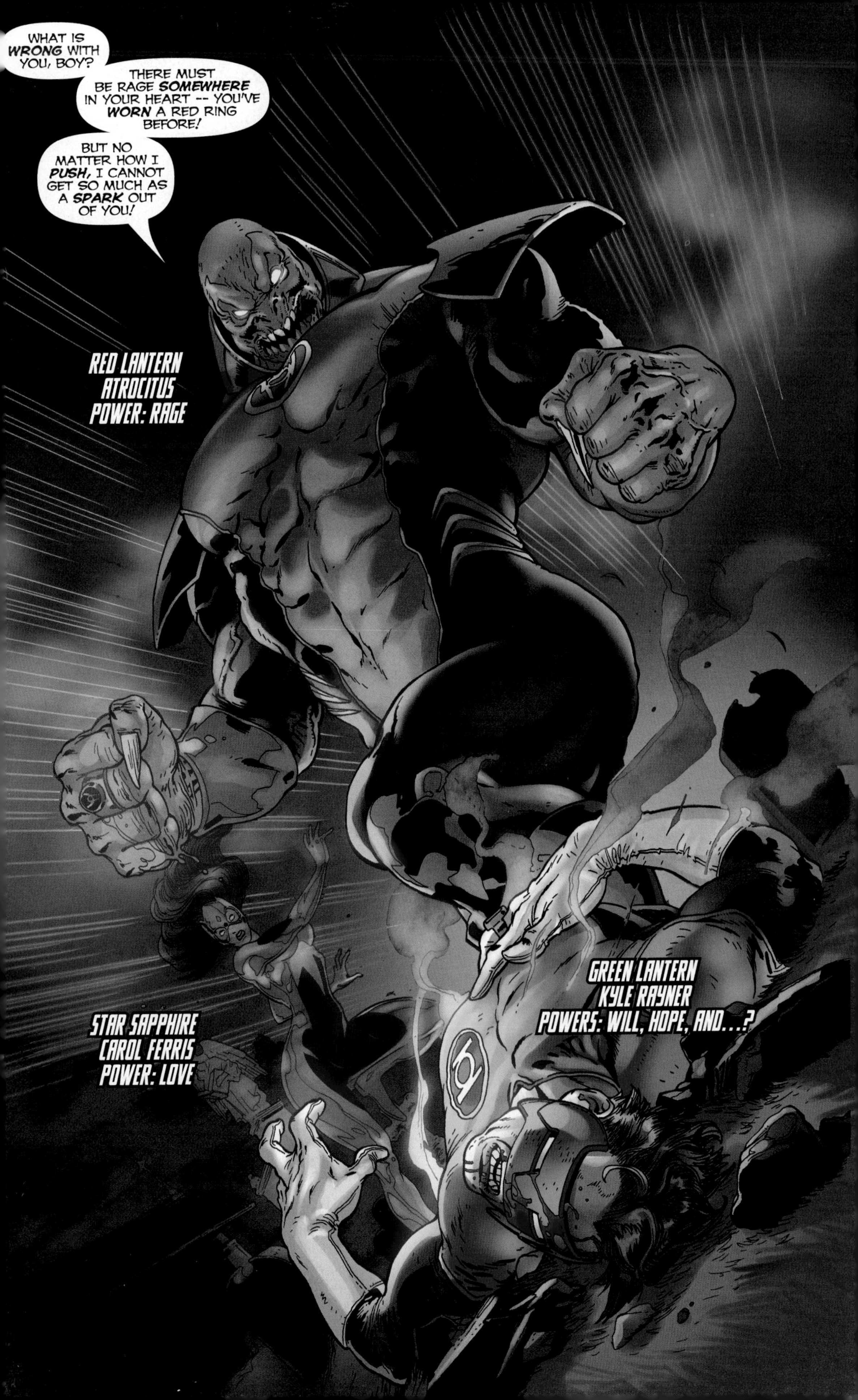
WHAT IS WRONG WITH YOU, BOY?
THERE MUST BE RAGE SOMEWHERE IN YOUR HEART -- YOU'VE WORN A RED RING BEFORE!
BUT NO MATTER HOW I PUSH, I CANNOT GET SO MUCH AS A SPARK OUT OF YOU!
RED LANTERN ATROCITUS POWER: RAGE
GREEN LANTERN KYLE RAYNER POWERS: WILL, HOPE, AND...?
STAR SAPPHIRE CAROL FERRIS POWER: LOVE

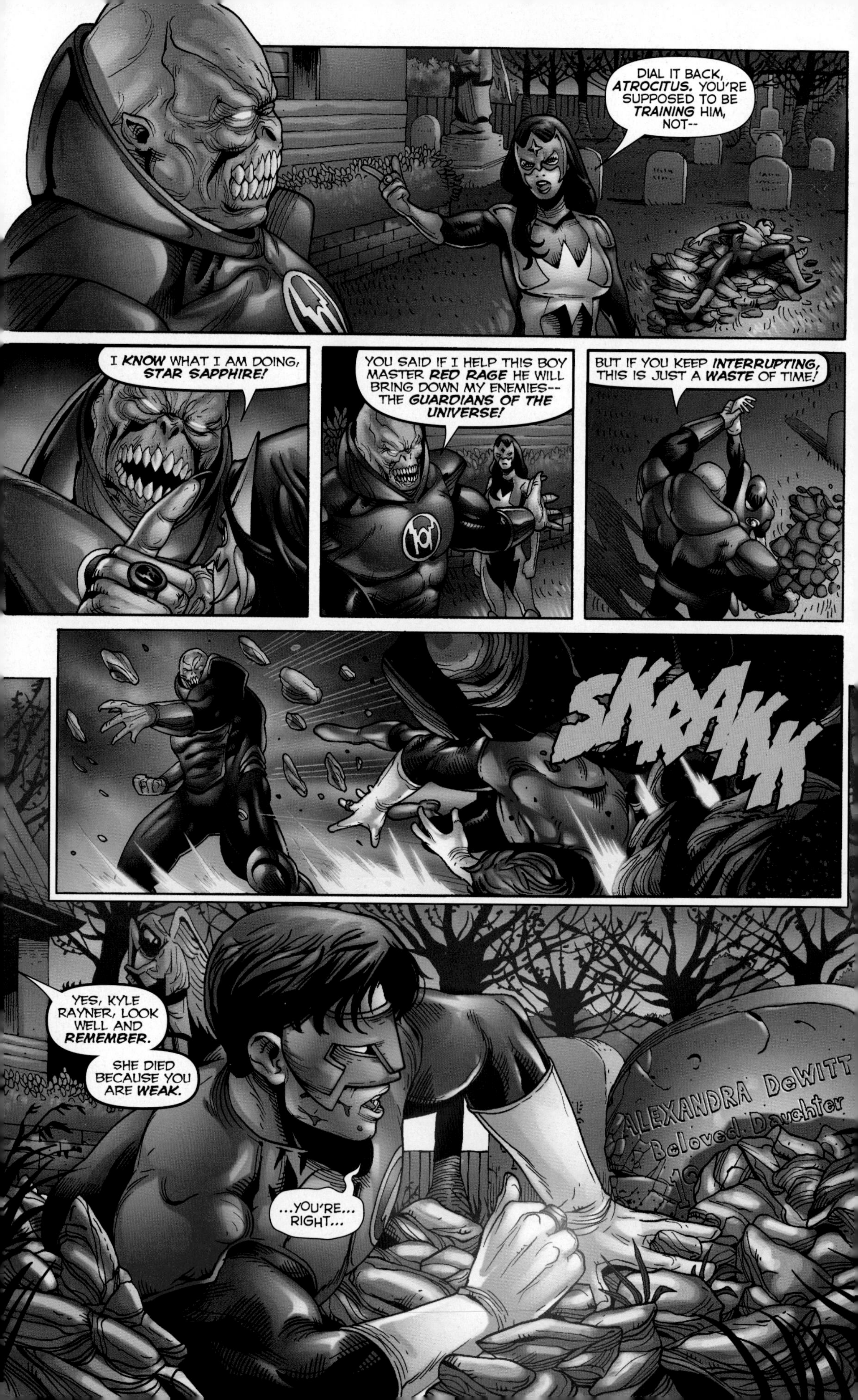
DIAL IT BACK, ATROCITUS. YOU'RE SUPPOSED TO BE TRAINING HIM, NOT--
I KNOW WHAT I AM DOING, STAR SAPPHIRE!
YOU SAID IF I HELP THIS BOY MASTER RED RAGE HE WILL BRING DOWN MY ENEMIES-- THE GUARDIANS OF THE UNIVERSE!
BUT IF YOU KEEP INTERRUPTING, THIS IS JUST A WASTE OF TIME!
SKRAKK
YES, KYLE RAYNER, LOOK WELL AND REMEMBER.
SHE DIED BECAUSE YOU ARE WEAK.
ALEXANDRA DeWITT
Beloved Daughter
...YOU'RE... RIGHT...

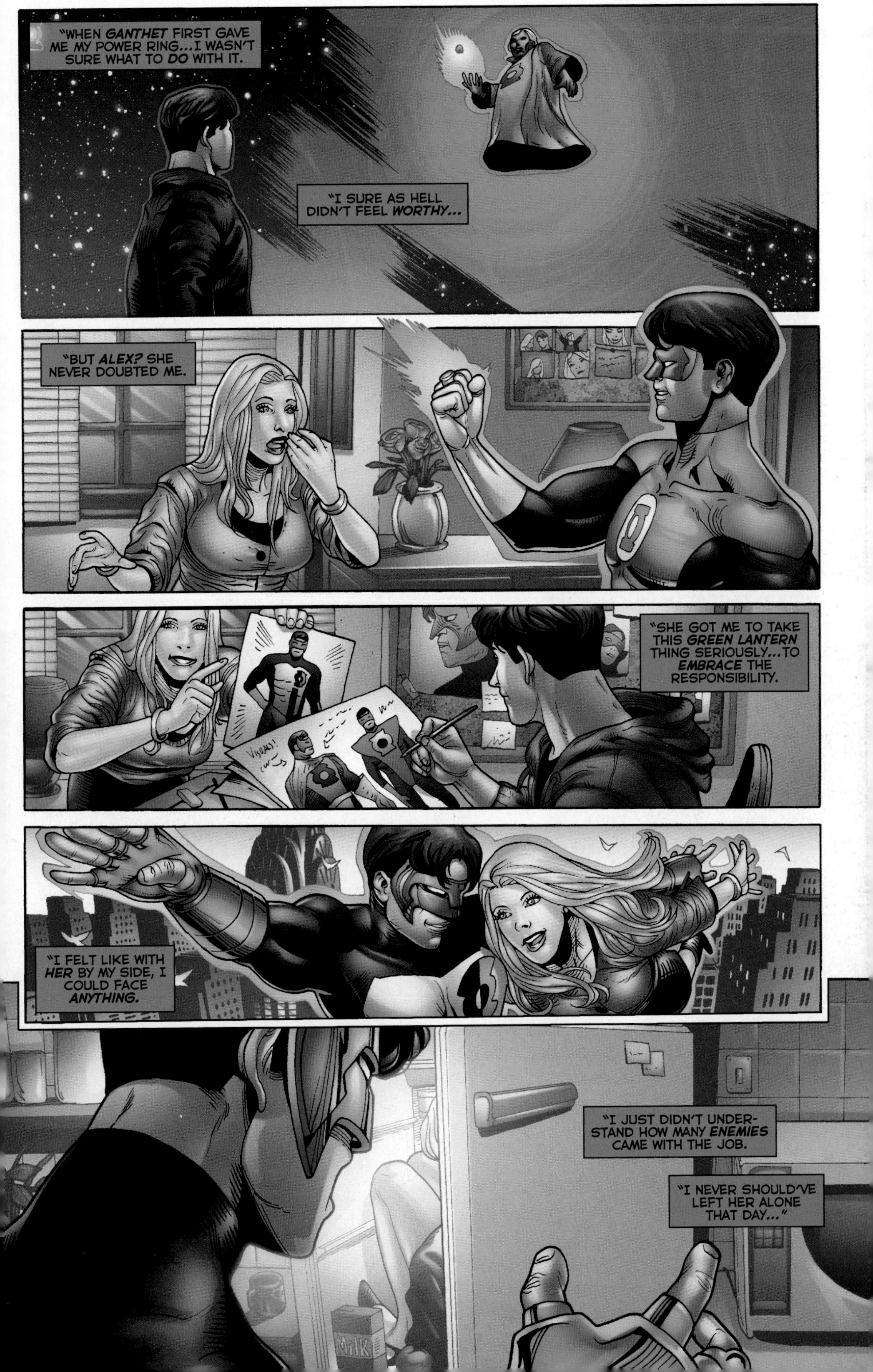
"WHEN GANTHET FIRST GAVE ME MY POWER RING...I WASN'T SURE WHAT TO DO WITH IT.
"I SURE AS HELL DIDN'T FEEL WORTHY...
"BUT ALEX? SHE NEVER DOUBTED ME.
"SHE GOT ME TO TAKE THIS GREEN LANTERN THING SERIOUSLY...TO EMBRACE THE RESPONSIBILITY.
"I FELT LIKE WITH HER BY MY SIDE, I COULD FACE ANYTHING.
"I JUST DIDN'T UNDERSTAND HOW MANY ENEMIES CAME WITH THE JOB.
"I NEVER SHOULD'VE LEFT HER ALONE THAT DAY..."
MILK

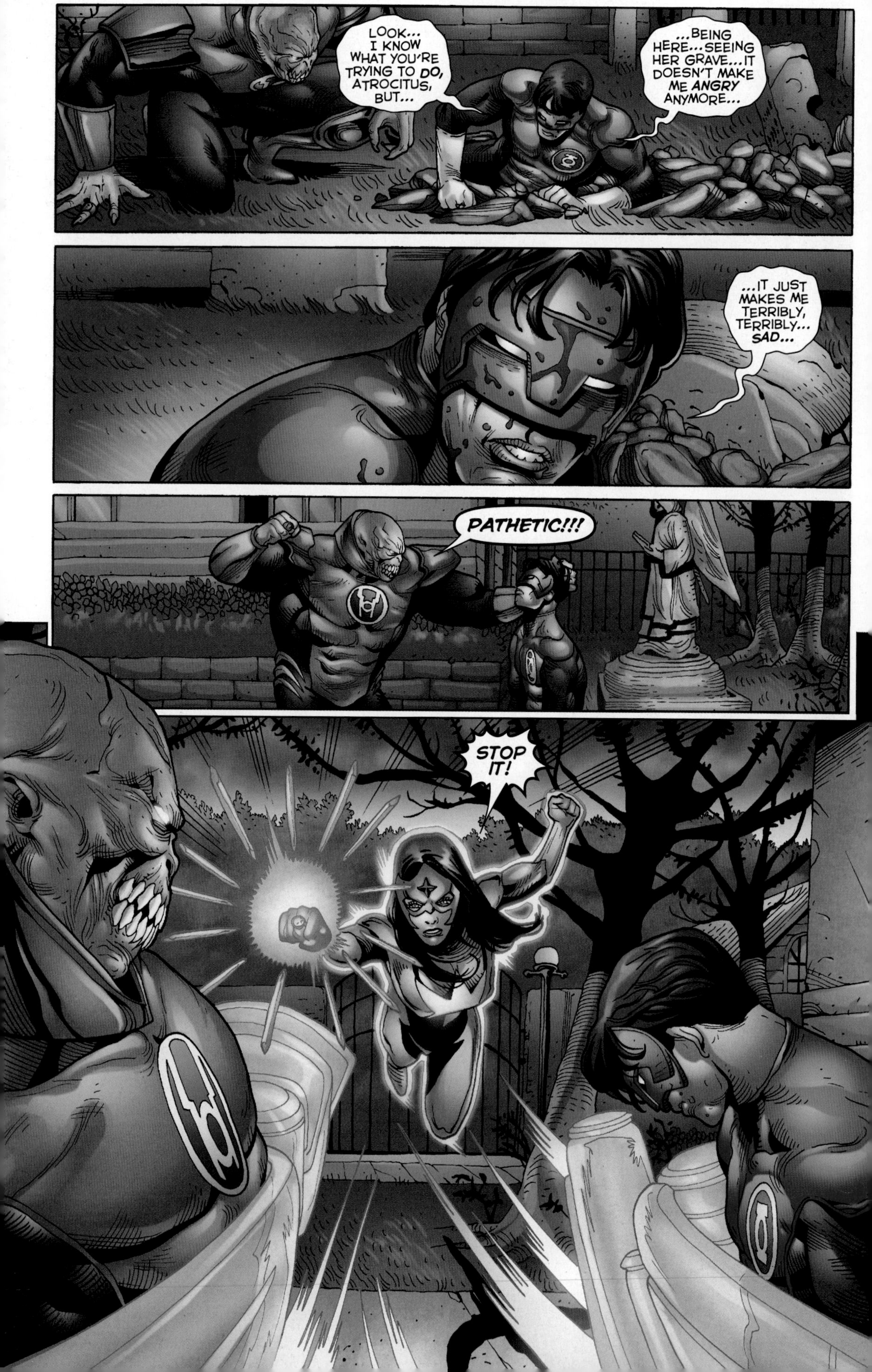
LOOK... I KNOW WHAT YOU'RE TRYING TO DO, ATROCITUS, BUT...
...BEING HERE...SEEING HER GRAVE...IT DOESN'T MAKE ME ANGRY ANYMORE...
...IT JUST MAKES ME TERRIBLY, TERRIBLY... SAD...
PATHETIC!!!
STOP IT!

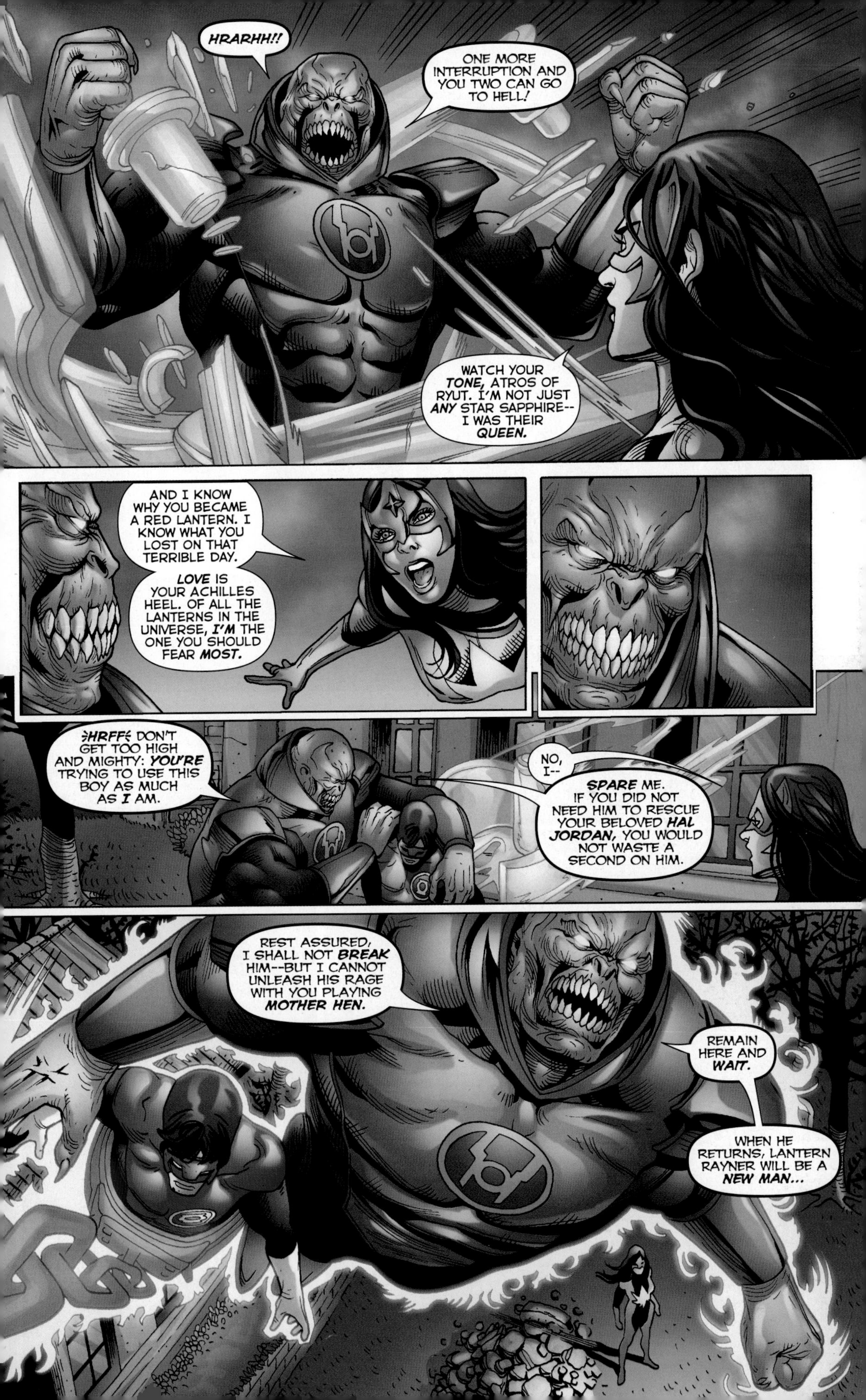
HRARHH!!
ONE MORE INTERRUPTION AND YOU TWO CAN GO TO HELL!
WATCH YOUR TONE, ATROS OF RYUT. I'M NOT JUST ANY STAR SAPPHIRE-- I WAS THEIR QUEEN.
AND I KNOW WHY YOU BECAME A RED LANTERN. I KNOW WHAT YOU LOST ON THAT TERRIBLE DAY.
LOVE IS YOUR ACHILLES HEEL. OF ALL THE LANTERNS IN THE UNIVERSE, I'M THE ONE YOU SHOULD FEAR MOST.
HRFF DON'T GET TOO HIGH AND MIGHTY: YOU'RE TRYING TO USE THIS BOY AS MUCH AS I AM.
NO, I--
SPARE ME. IF YOU DID NOT NEED HIM TO RESCUE YOUR BELOVED HAL JORDAN, YOU WOULD NOT WASTE A SECOND ON HIM.
REST ASSURED, I SHALL NOT BREAK HIM--BUT I CANNOT UNLEASH HIS RAGE WITH YOU PLAYING MOTHER HEN.
REMAIN HERE AND WAIT.
WHEN HE RETURNS, LANTERN RAYNER WILL BE A NEW MAN...

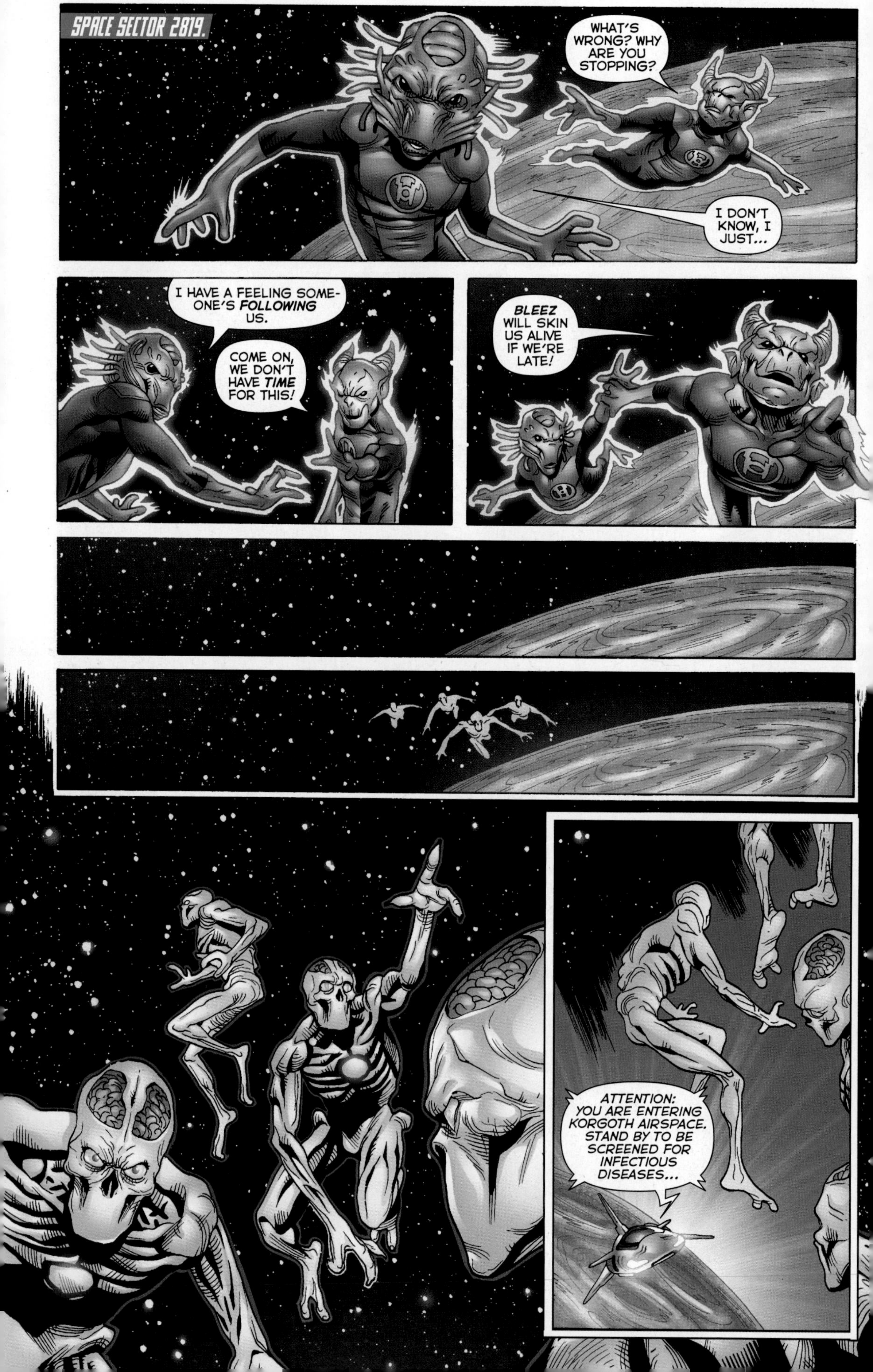
SPACE SECTOR 2819.
WHAT'S WRONG? WHY ARE YOU STOPPING?
I DON'T KNOW, I JUST...
I HAVE A FEELING SOME-ONE'S FOLLOWING US.
COME ON, WE DON'T HAVE TIME FOR THIS!
BLEEZ WILL SKIN US ALIVE IF WE'RE LATE!
ATTENTION: YOU ARE ENTERING KORGOTH AIRSPACE. STAND BY TO BE SCREENED FOR INFECTIOUS DISEASES...

PLANET EARTH.

<YUSUF, BE *BRAVE!* GOD WILL NOT LET THIS *HAPPEN* TO US!>*

*TRANSLATED FROM ARABIC.

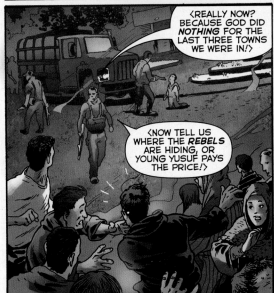

<REALLY NOW? BECAUSE GOD DID *NOTHING* FOR THE LAST THREE TOWNS WE WERE IN!>

<NOW TELL US WHERE THE *REBELS* ARE HIDING, OR YOUNG YUSUF PAYS THE PRICE!>

WHAT *IS* THIS, ATROCITUS? WHY BRING ME *HERE?*

TO REMIND YOU THERE'S NO SHORTAGE OF *EVIL* IN THE UNIVERSE-- EVEN ON THIS MUDBALL YOU CALL HOME.

<WAIT! HE IS MY ONLY SON!>

<LET *ME* TAKE HIS PLACE!>

OKAY, *LET GO* NOW. THIS HAS GONE *FAR* ENOUGH.

OH, THIS IS ONLY *BEGINNING.* SOON YOU SHALL *BURN* WITH HELPLESSNESS AND *OUTRAGE* -- JUST AS *I* DID ON THE DAY I WAS *REBORN...*

"THE *MANHUNTERS* HAD GONE BERSERK, ANNIHILATING EVERY LIVING THING IN SECTOR 666.

"I KNEW NOT *WHY* OUR PROTECTORS HAD TURNED AGAINST US. I ONLY KNEW I HAD TO REACH MY *FAMILY.*

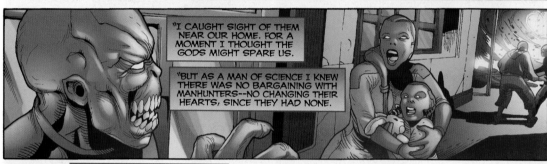

"I CAUGHT SIGHT OF THEM NEAR OUR HOME. FOR A MOMENT I THOUGHT THE GODS MIGHT SPARE US.

"BUT AS A MAN OF SCIENCE I KNEW THERE WAS NO BARGAINING WITH MANHUNTERS--NO CHANGING THEIR HEARTS, SINCE THEY HAD NONE.

"ONCE COMMITTED TO ACTION, THEY WOULD CARRY OUT THEIR PROGRAMMING...

"...WITHOUT HESITATION, WITHOUT REMORSE.

"AN ENTIRE *SECTOR* WAS LOST THAT DAY. COUNTLESS *TRILLIONS* OF LIVES.

"NO HEART COULD POSSIBLY CONTAIN *HATRED* AND *OUTRAGE* TO EQUAL SUCH AN ACT--AND YET MINE FOUND A WAY."

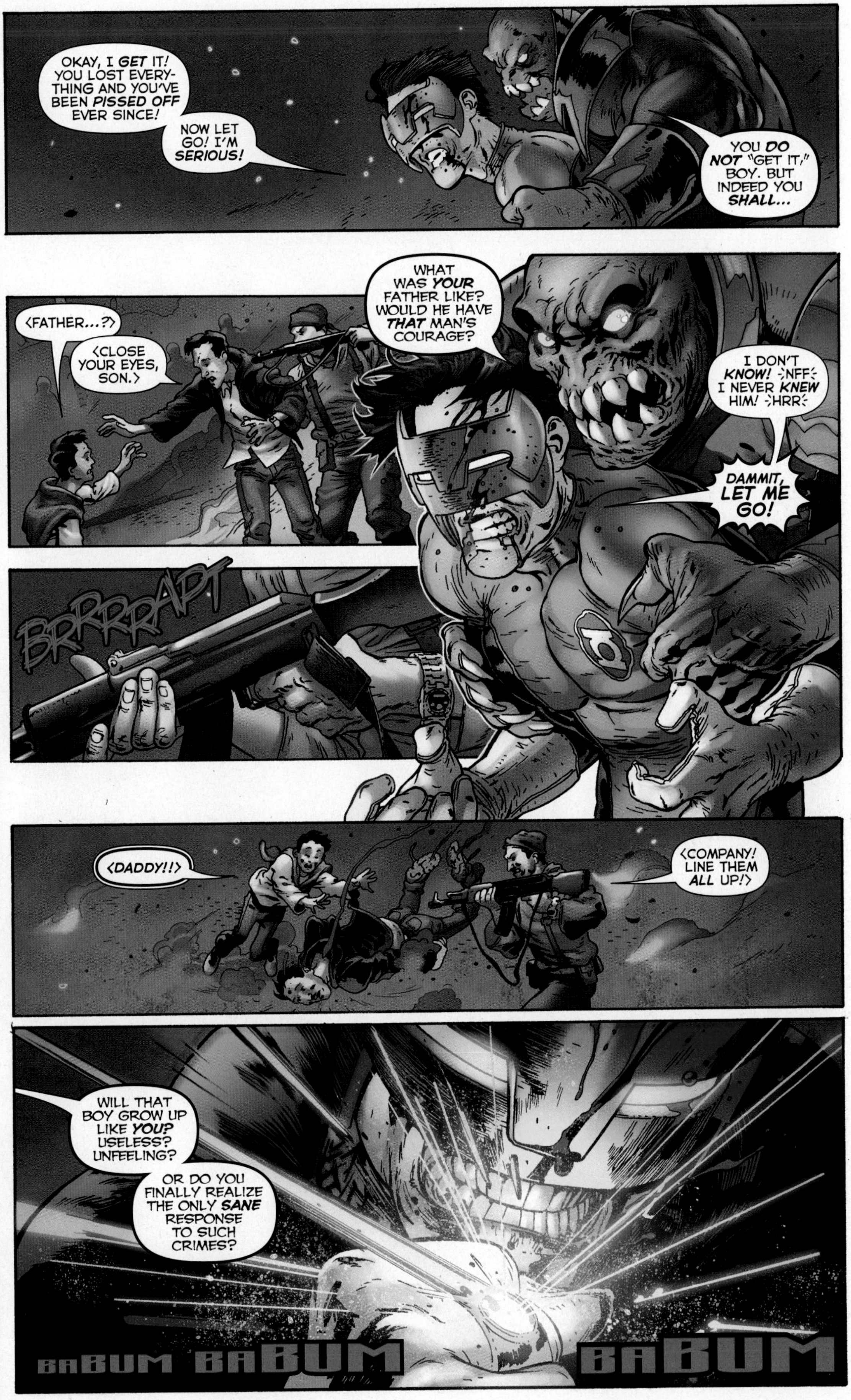
OKAY, I GET IT! YOU LOST EVERYTHING AND YOU'VE BEEN PISSED OFF EVER SINCE!
NOW LET GO! I'M SERIOUS!
YOU DO NOT "GET IT," BOY. BUT INDEED YOU SHALL...
<FATHER...?>
<CLOSE YOUR EYES, SON.>
WHAT WAS YOUR FATHER LIKE? WOULD HE HAVE THAT MAN'S COURAGE?
I DON'T KNOW! NFF I NEVER KNEW HIM! HRR
DAMMIT, LET ME GO!
BRRRRAPT
<DADDY!!>
<COMPANY! LINE THEM ALL UP!>
WILL THAT BOY GROW UP LIKE YOU? USELESS? UNFEELING?
OR DO YOU FINALLY REALIZE THE ONLY SANE RESPONSE TO SUCH CRIMES?
BABUM BABUM BABUM

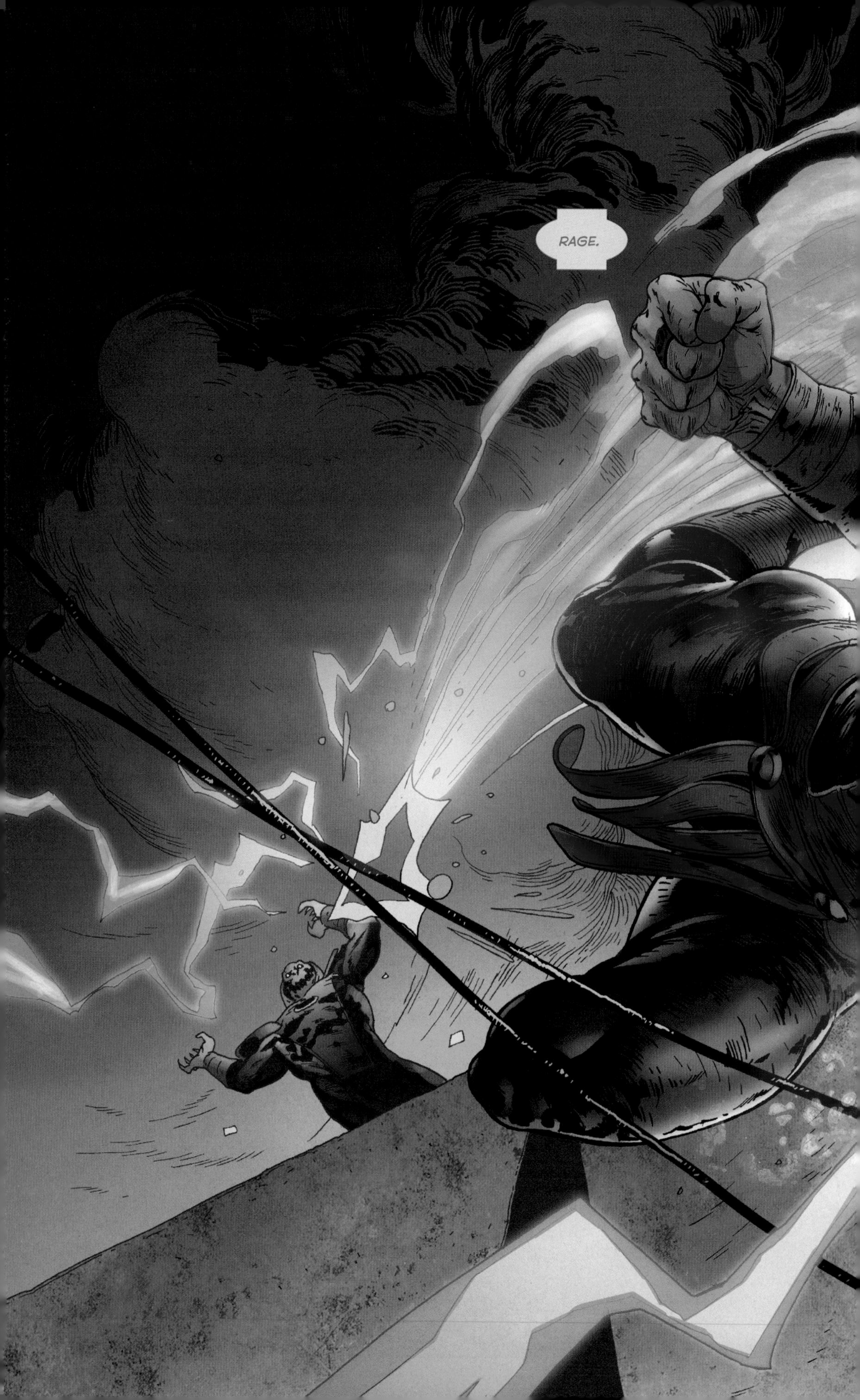
RAGE.

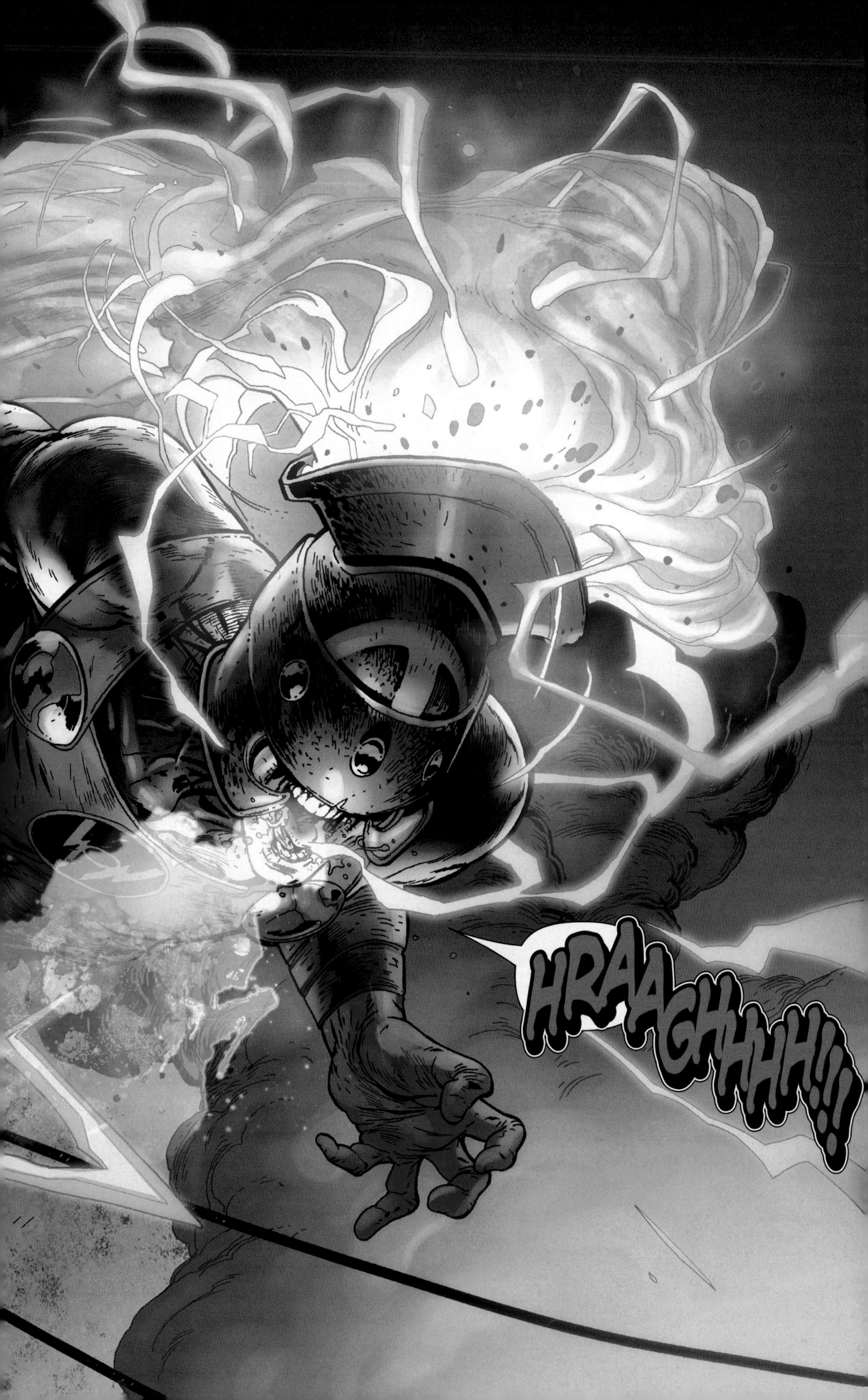
HRAAGHHHH!!!

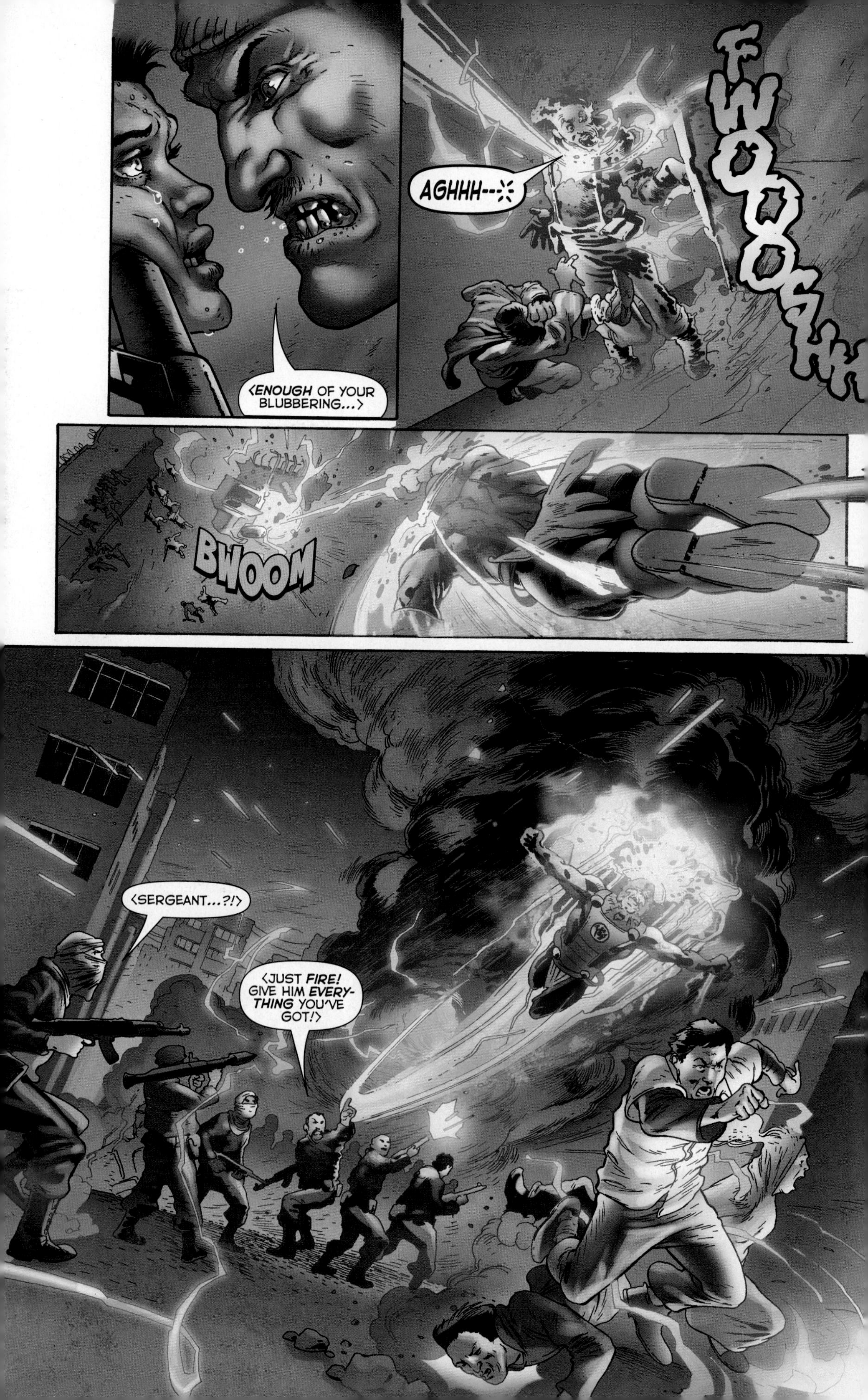

<ENOUGH OF YOUR BLUBBERING...>
AGHHH--
FWOOOSHH
BWOOM
<SERGEANT...?!>
<JUST FIRE! GIVE HIM EVERY-THING YOU'VE GOT!>

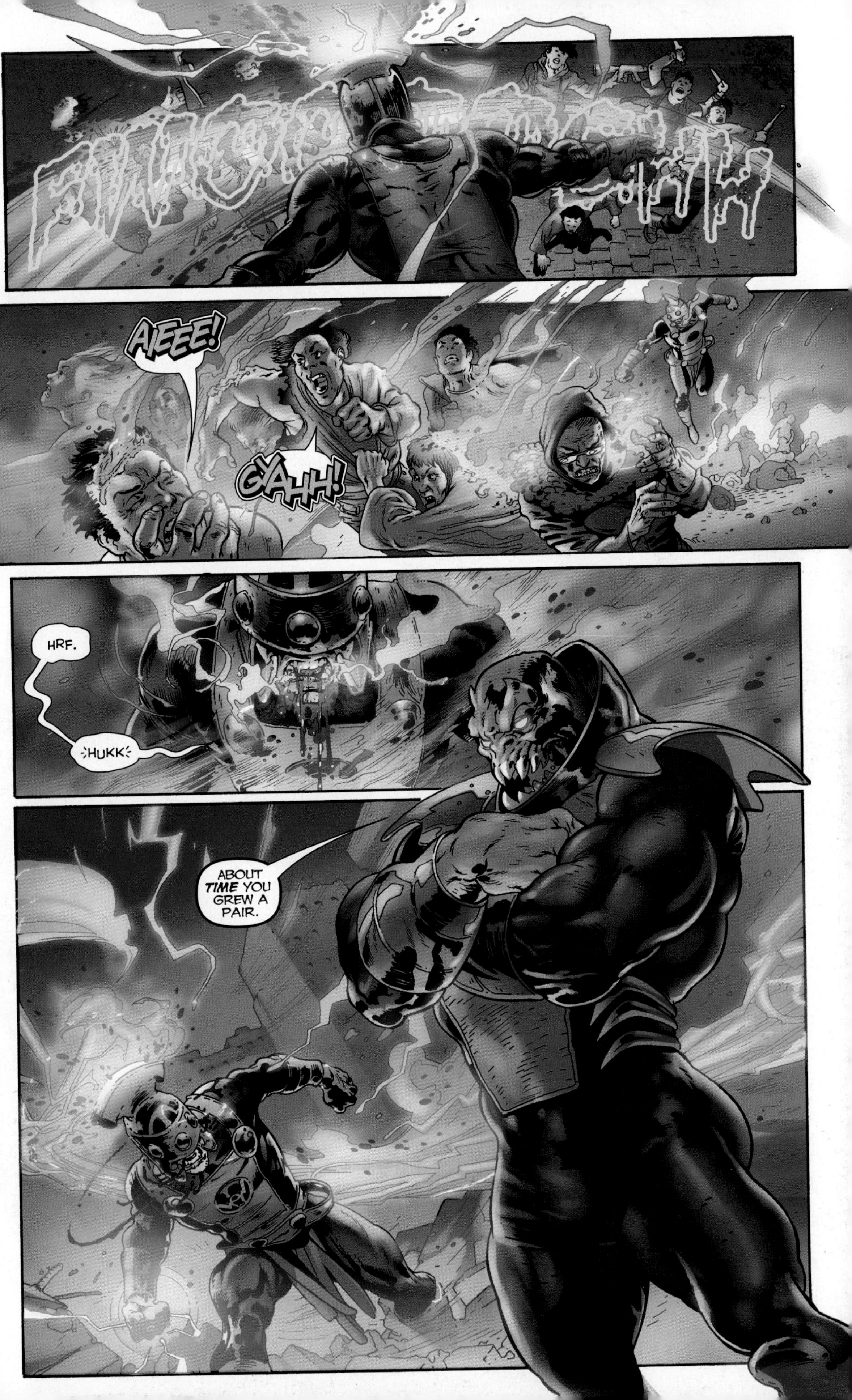
AIEEE!
GYAHH!
HRF.
HUKK
ABOUT TIME YOU GREW A PAIR.

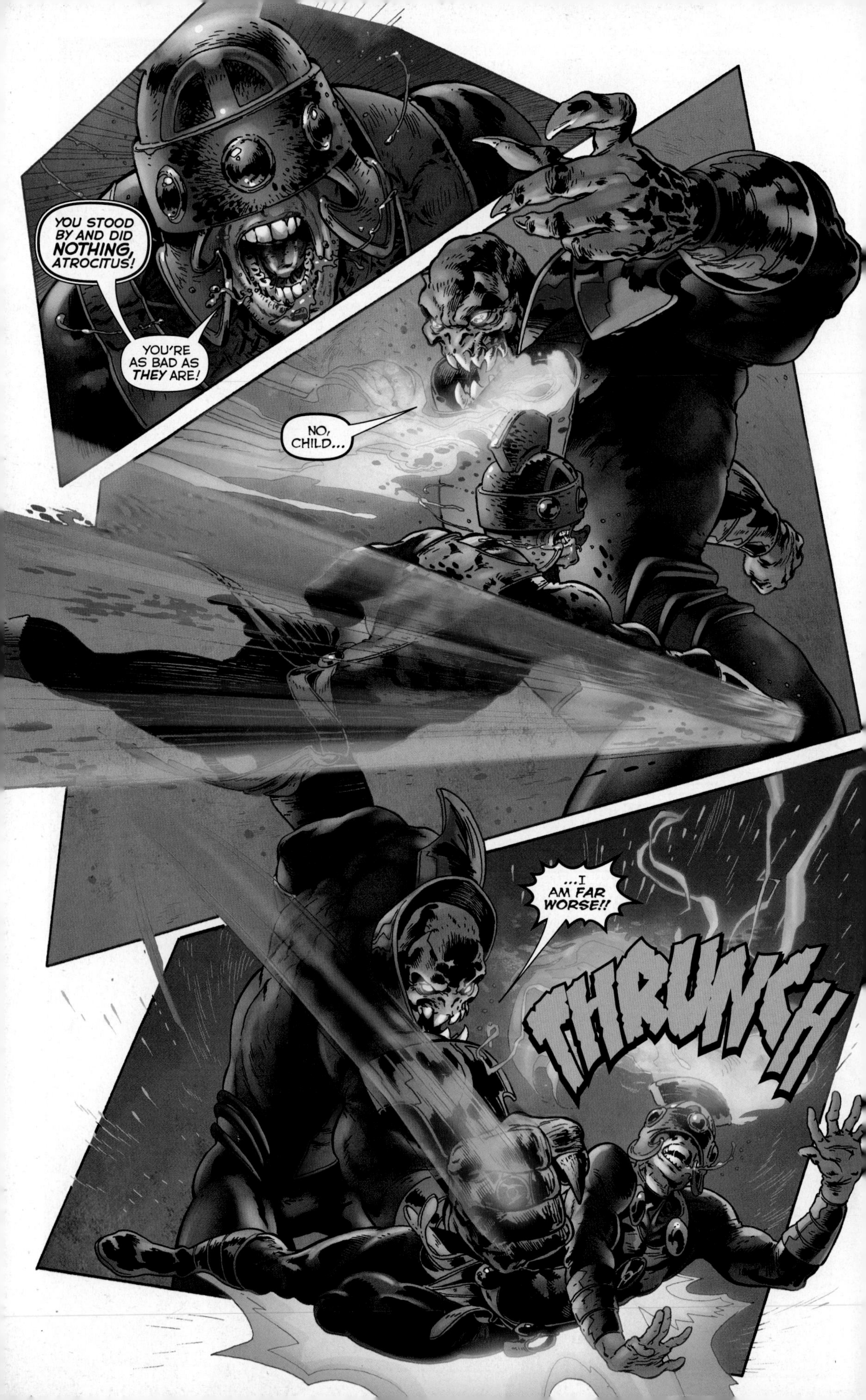
YOU STOOD BY AND DID NOTHING, ATROCITUS!
YOU'RE AS BAD AS THEY ARE!
NO, CHILD...
...I AM FAR WORSE!!
THRUNCH

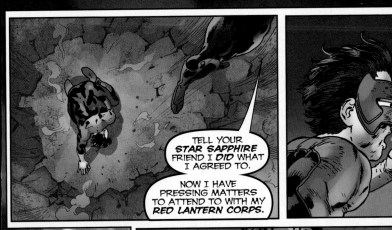

TELL YOUR *STAR SAPPHIRE* FRIEND I *DID* WHAT I AGREED TO.

NOW I HAVE PRESSING MATTERS TO ATTEND TO WITH MY *RED LANTERN CORPS.*

WHEN THE TIME COMES TO FINALLY DESTROY THE *GUARDIANS*, YOU HAD *BETTER* LEAVE ONE OR TWO FOR *ME!*

‹S-SIR, PLEASE...WE HAVE SUFFERED ENOUGH...!›

RING: *HEAL* THEIR WOUNDS.

BE *QUICK* ABOUT IT.

HOPE.

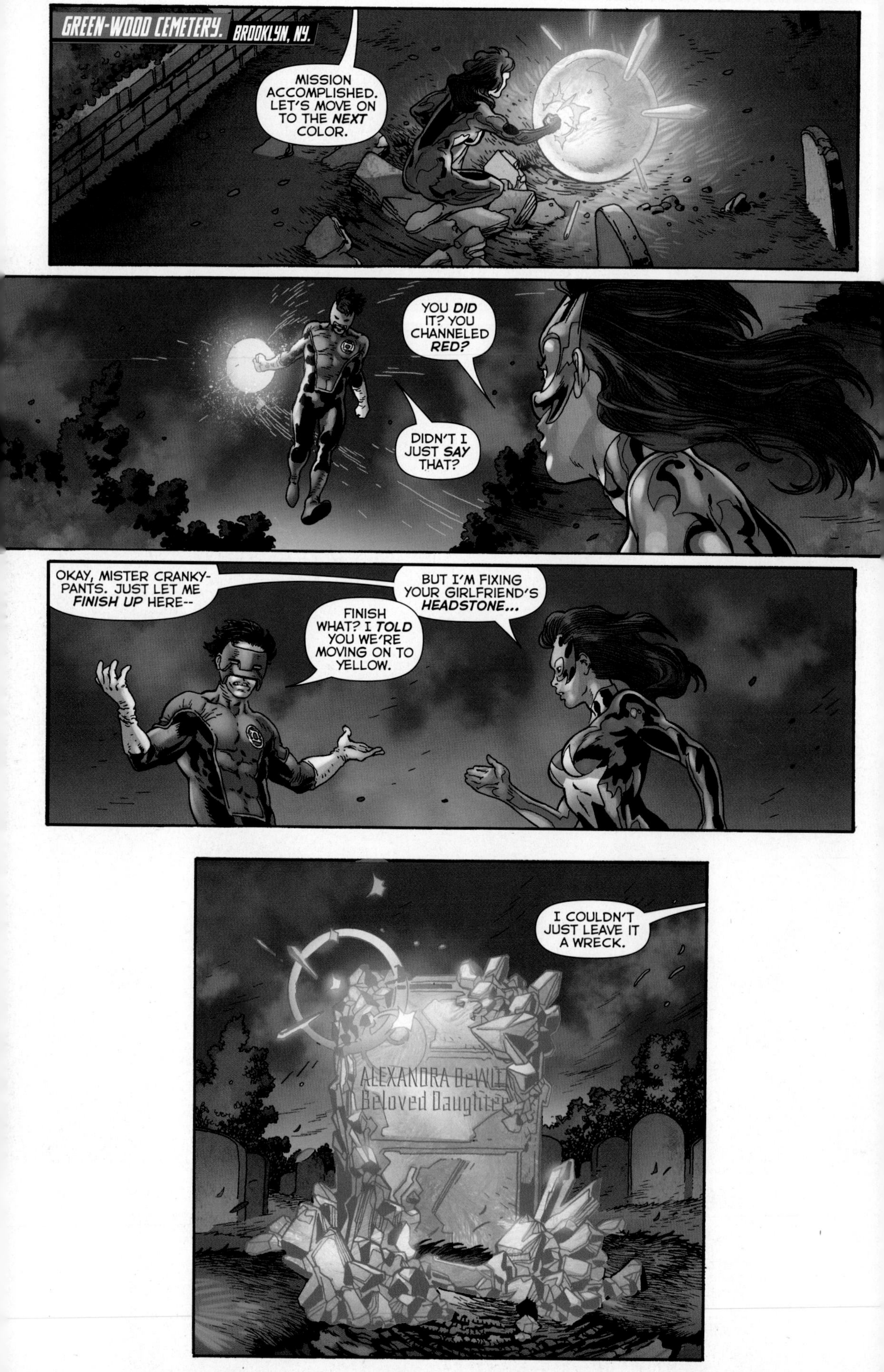
GREEN-WOOD CEMETERY. BROOKLYN, NY.
MISSION ACCOMPLISHED. LET'S MOVE ON TO THE NEXT COLOR.
YOU DID IT? YOU CHANNELED RED?
DIDN'T I JUST SAY THAT?
OKAY, MISTER CRANKY-PANTS. JUST LET ME FINISH UP HERE--
FINISH WHAT? I TOLD YOU WE'RE MOVING ON TO YELLOW.
BUT I'M FIXING YOUR GIRLFRIEND'S HEADSTONE...
I COULDN'T JUST LEAVE IT A WRECK.
ALEXANDRA DeWIT
Beloved Daughter

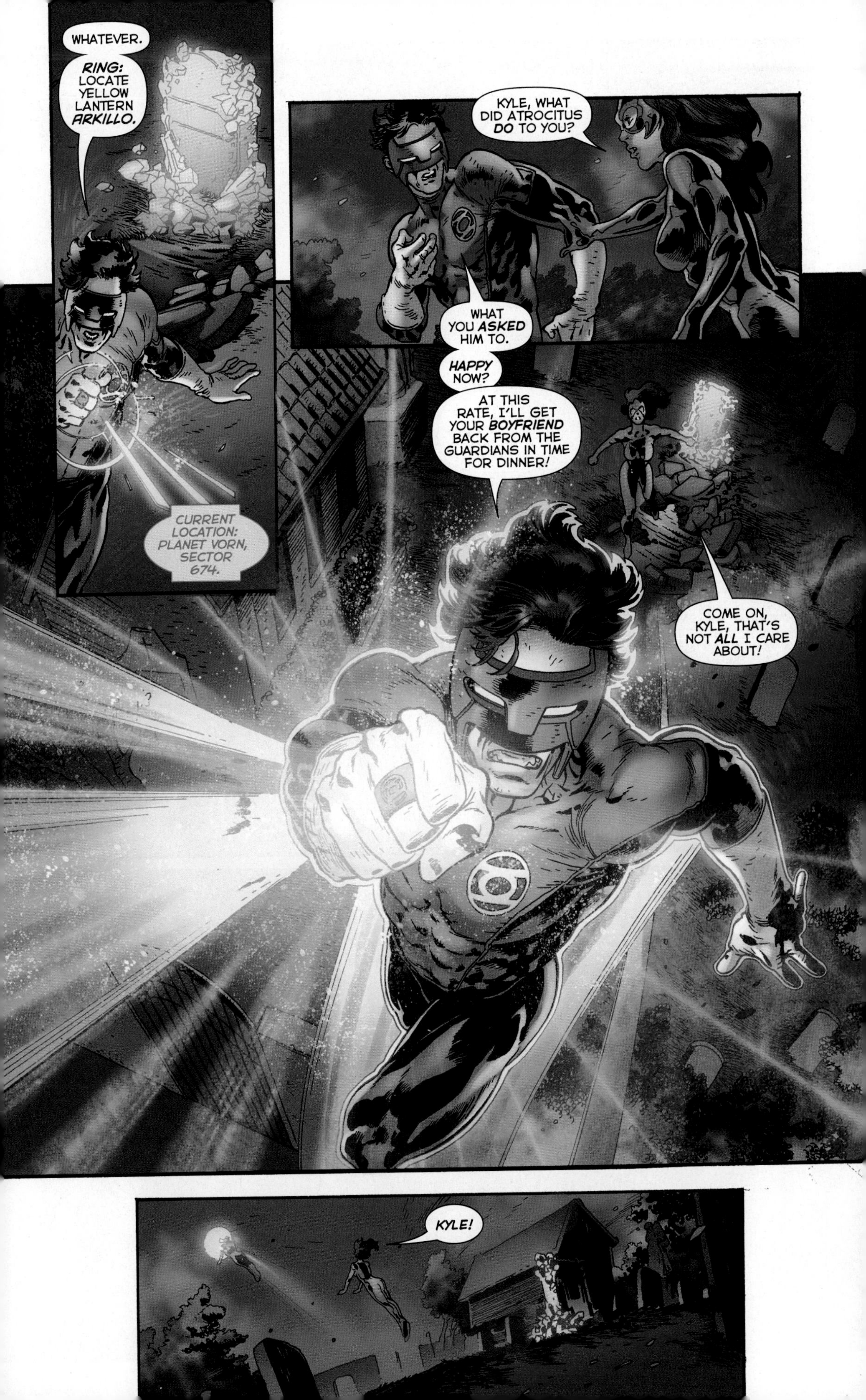
WHATEVER.
RING: LOCATE YELLOW LANTERN ARKILLO.
CURRENT LOCATION: PLANET VORN, SECTOR 674.
KYLE, WHAT DID ATROCITUS DO TO YOU?
WHAT YOU ASKED HIM TO.
HAPPY NOW?
AT THIS RATE, I'LL GET YOUR BOYFRIEND BACK FROM THE GUARDIANS IN TIME FOR DINNER!
COME ON, KYLE, THAT'S NOT ALL I CARE ABOUT!
KYLE!

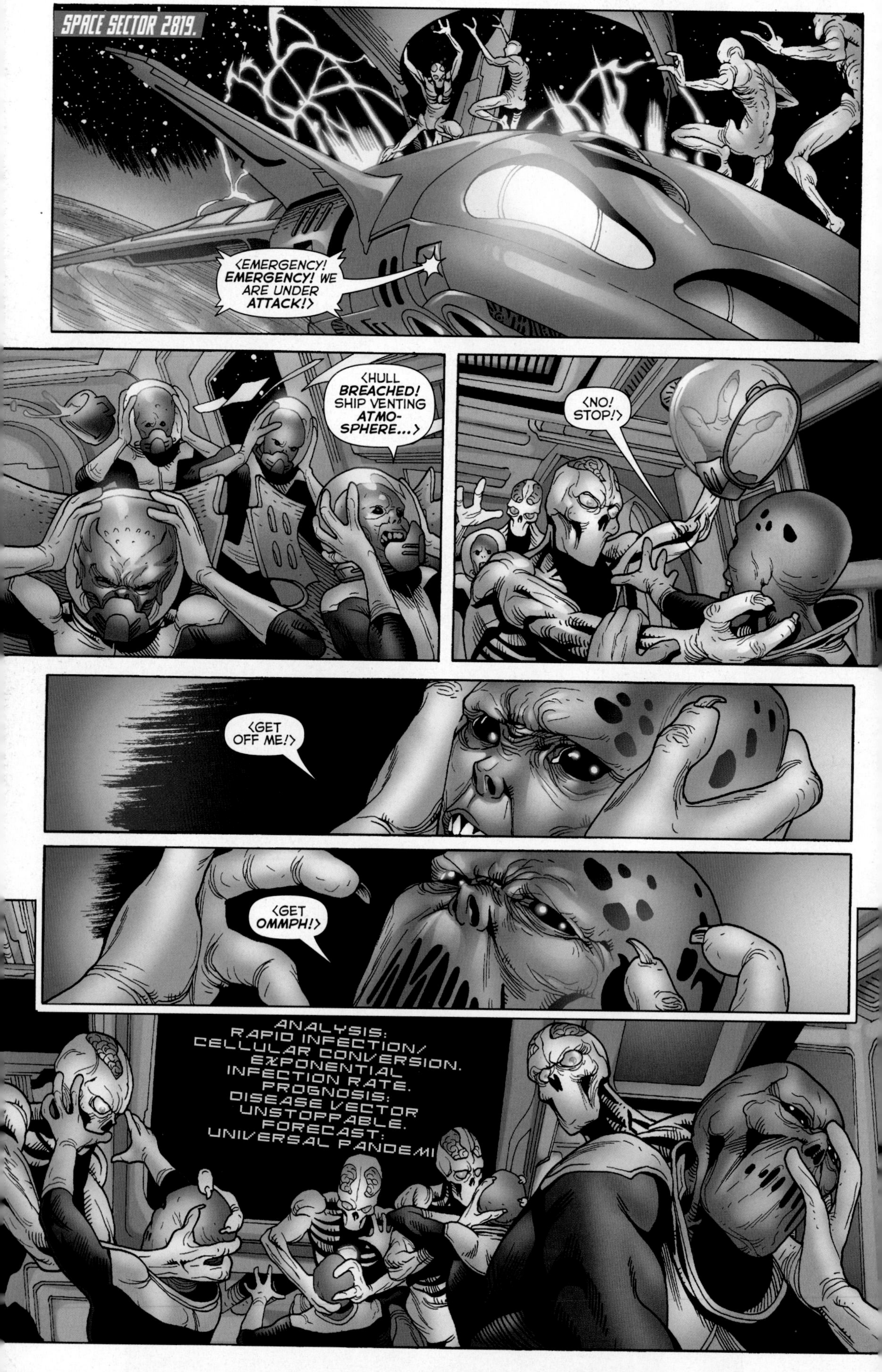
SPACE SECTOR 2819.
<EMERGENCY! EMERGENCY! WE ARE UNDER ATTACK!>
<HULL BREACHED! SHIP VENTING ATMO-SPHERE...>
<NO! STOP!>
<GET OFF ME!>
<GET OMMPH!>
ANALYSIS: RAPID INFECTION/ CELLULAR CONVERSION. EXPONENTIAL INFECTION RATE. PROGNOSIS: DISEASE VECTOR UNSTOPPABLE. FORECAST: UNIVERSAL PANDEMI

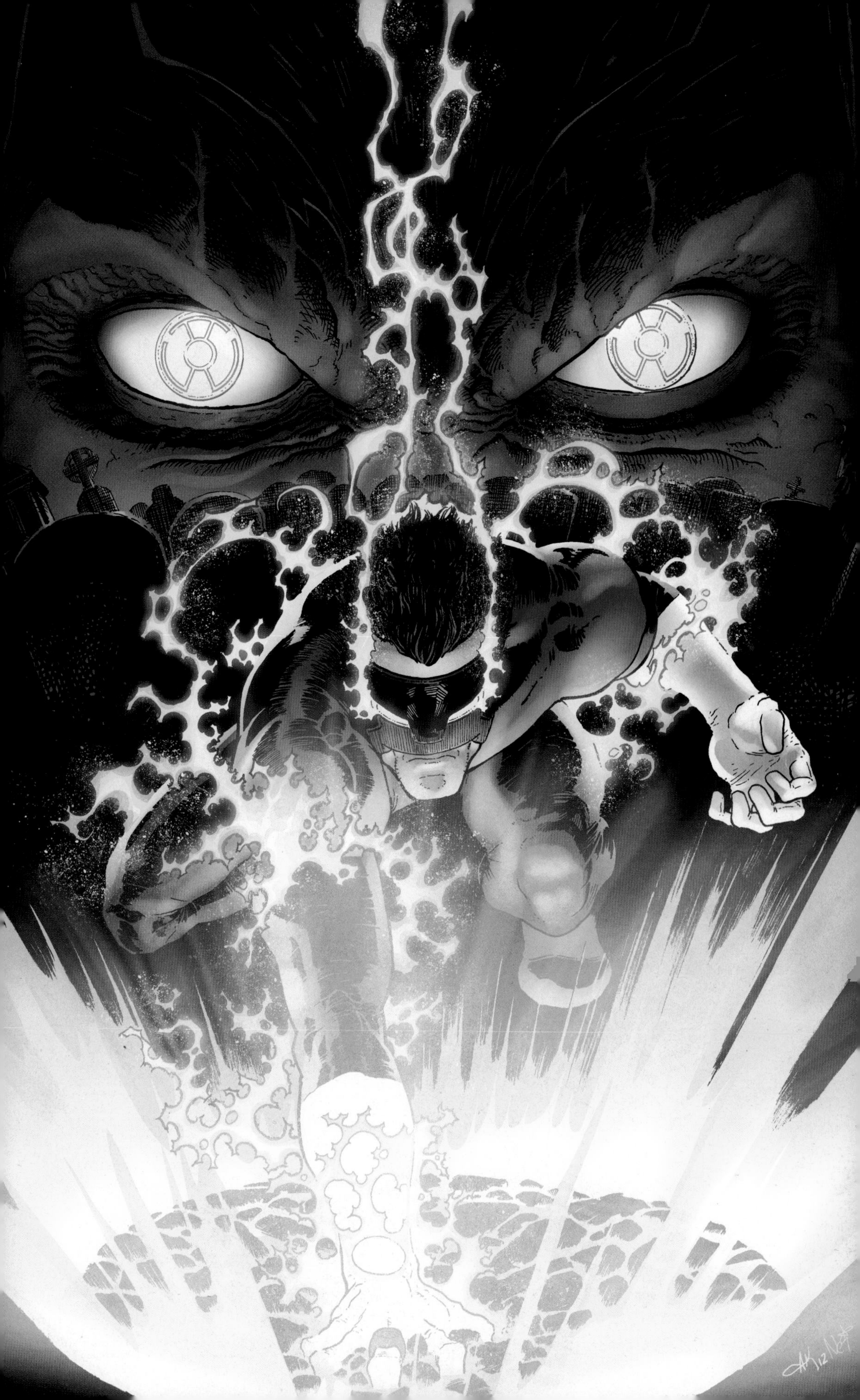

FEAR FACTOR

TONY BEDARD writer ANDREI BRESSAN & AMILCAR PINNA artists
AARON KUDER & NEI RUFFINO cover

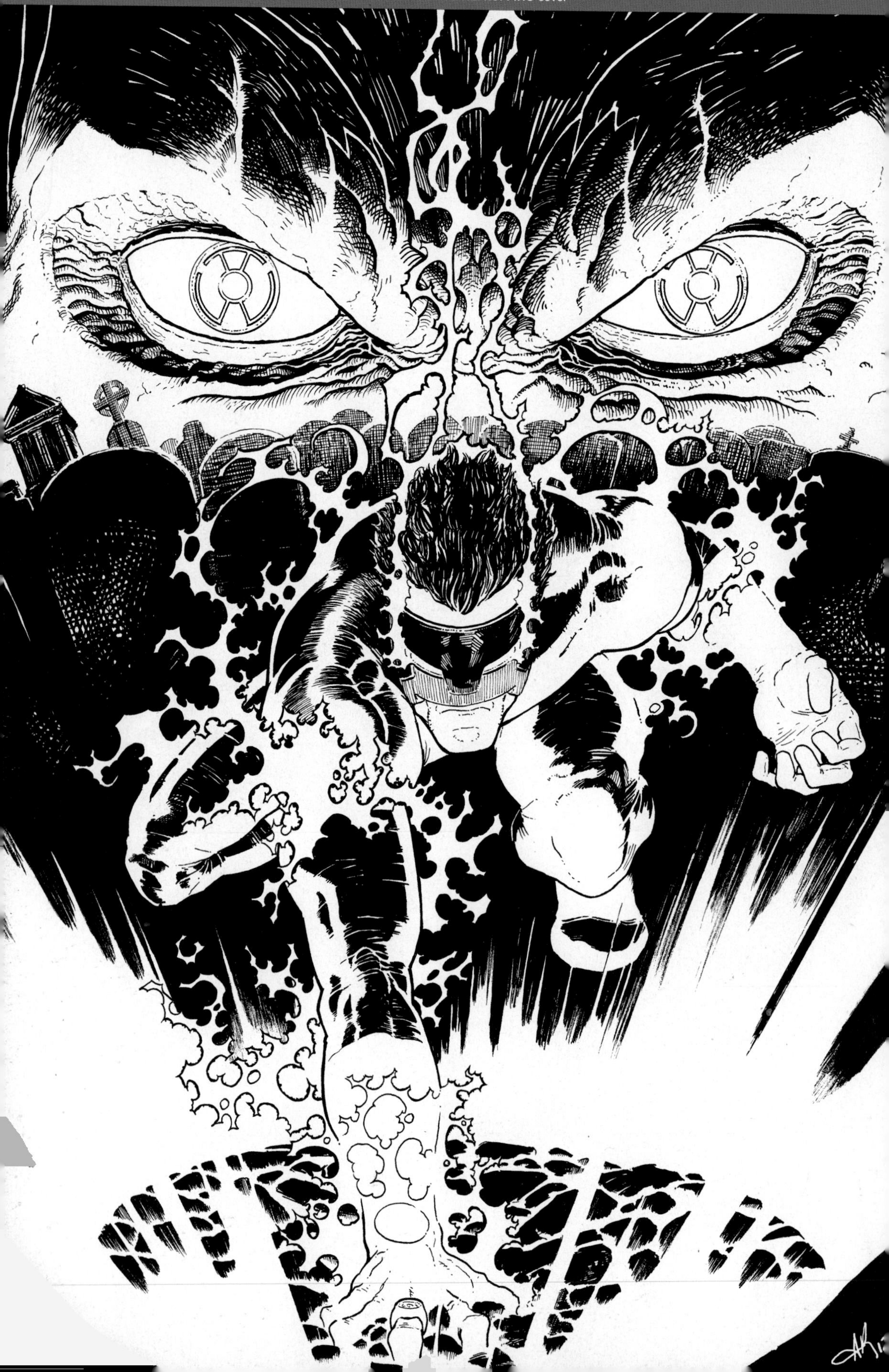

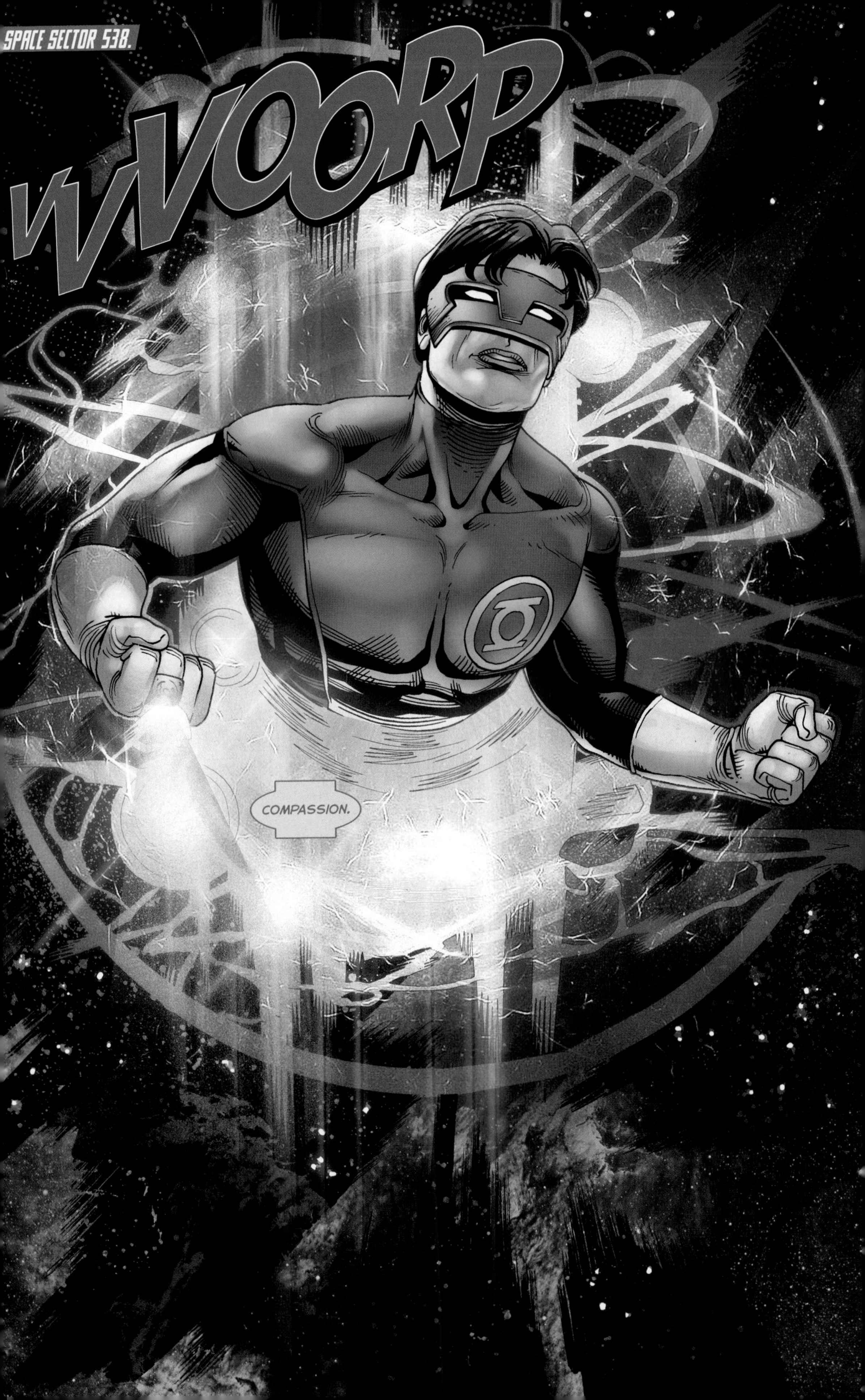
SPACE SECTOR 538.
VVVOORP
COMPASSION.

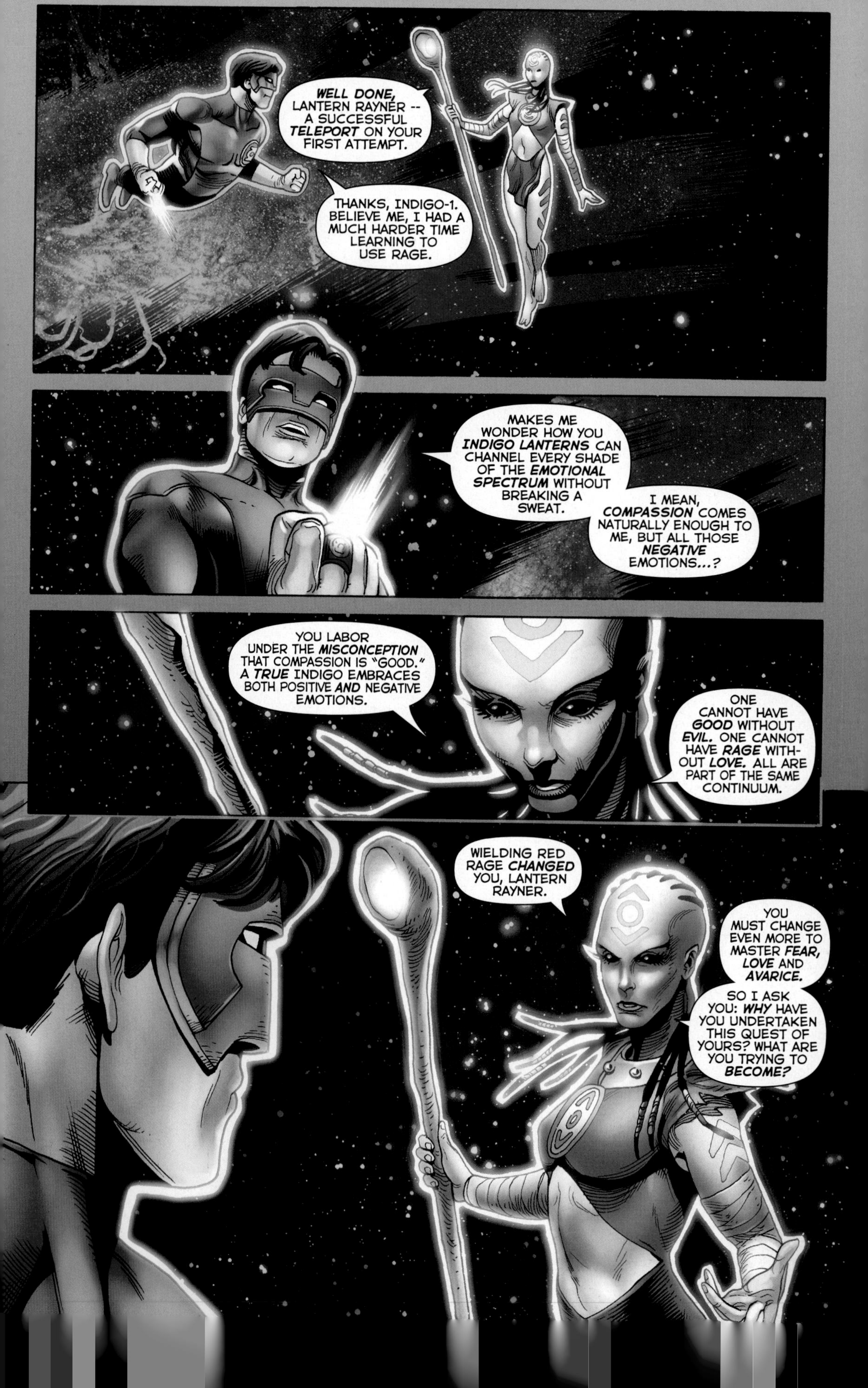

WELL DONE, LANTERN RAYNER -- A SUCCESSFUL TELEPORT ON YOUR FIRST ATTEMPT.
THANKS, INDIGO-1. BELIEVE ME, I HAD A MUCH HARDER TIME LEARNING TO USE RAGE.
MAKES ME WONDER HOW YOU INDIGO LANTERNS CAN CHANNEL EVERY SHADE OF THE EMOTIONAL SPECTRUM WITHOUT BREAKING A SWEAT.
I MEAN, COMPASSION COMES NATURALLY ENOUGH TO ME, BUT ALL THOSE NEGATIVE EMOTIONS...?
YOU LABOR UNDER THE MISCONCEPTION THAT COMPASSION IS "GOOD." A TRUE INDIGO EMBRACES BOTH POSITIVE AND NEGATIVE EMOTIONS.
ONE CANNOT HAVE GOOD WITHOUT EVIL. ONE CANNOT HAVE RAGE WITH-OUT LOVE. ALL ARE PART OF THE SAME CONTINUUM.
WIELDING RED RAGE CHANGED YOU, LANTERN RAYNER.
YOU MUST CHANGE EVEN MORE TO MASTER FEAR, LOVE AND AVARICE.
SO I ASK YOU: WHY HAVE YOU UNDERTAKEN THIS QUEST OF YOURS? WHAT ARE YOU TRYING TO BECOME?

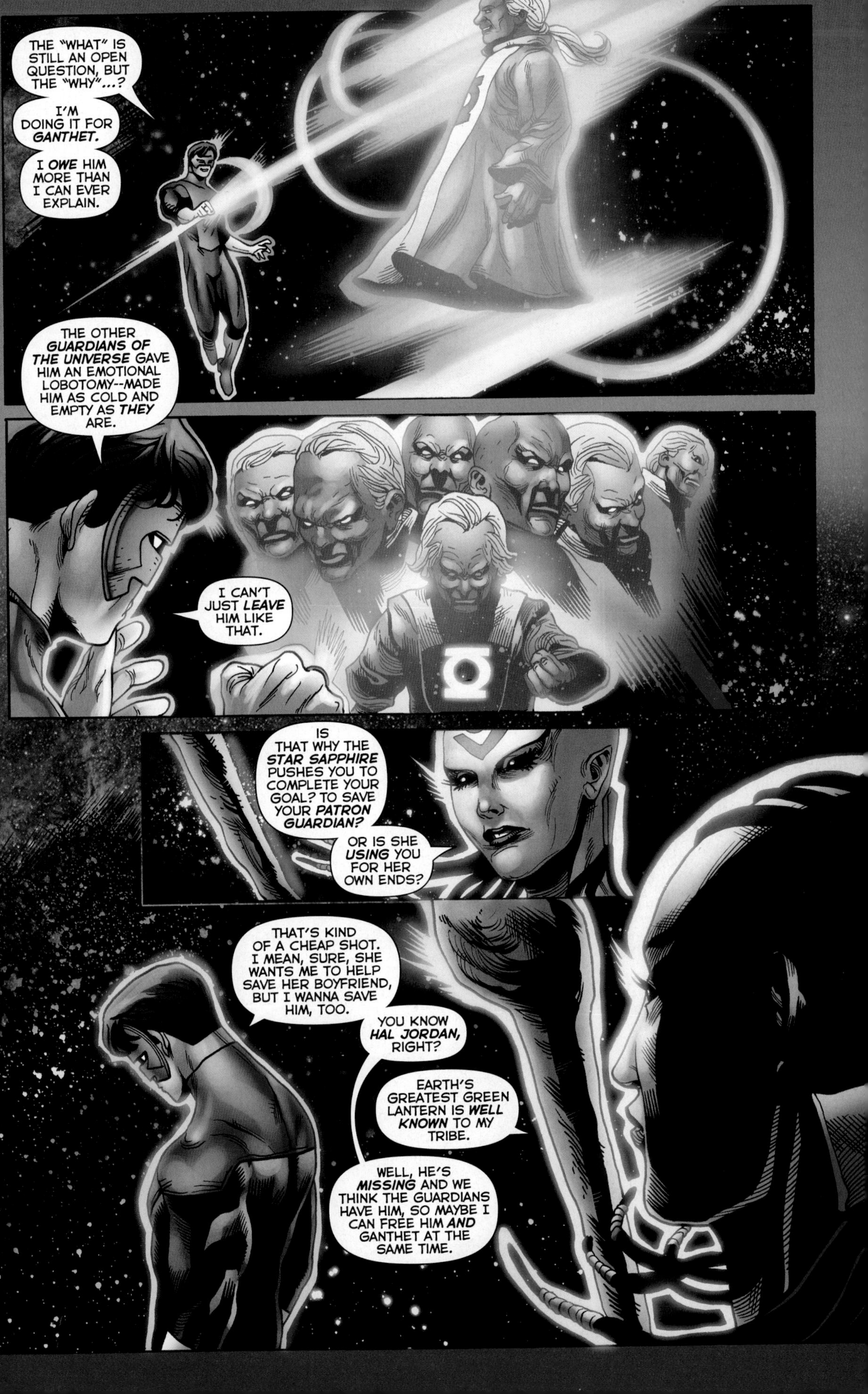
THE "WHAT" IS STILL AN OPEN QUESTION, BUT THE "WHY"...?
I'M DOING IT FOR GANTHET.
I OWE HIM MORE THAN I CAN EVER EXPLAIN.
THE OTHER GUARDIANS OF THE UNIVERSE GAVE HIM AN EMOTIONAL LOBOTOMY--MADE HIM AS COLD AND EMPTY AS THEY ARE.
I CAN'T JUST LEAVE HIM LIKE THAT.
IS THAT WHY THE STAR SAPPHIRE PUSHES YOU TO COMPLETE YOUR GOAL? TO SAVE YOUR PATRON GUARDIAN?
OR IS SHE USING YOU FOR HER OWN ENDS?
THAT'S KIND OF A CHEAP SHOT. I MEAN, SURE, SHE WANTS ME TO HELP SAVE HER BOYFRIEND, BUT I WANNA SAVE HIM, TOO.
YOU KNOW HAL JORDAN, RIGHT?
EARTH'S GREATEST GREEN LANTERN IS WELL KNOWN TO MY TRIBE.
WELL, HE'S MISSING AND WE THINK THE GUARDIANS HAVE HIM, SO MAYBE I CAN FREE HIM AND GANTHET AT THE SAME TIME.

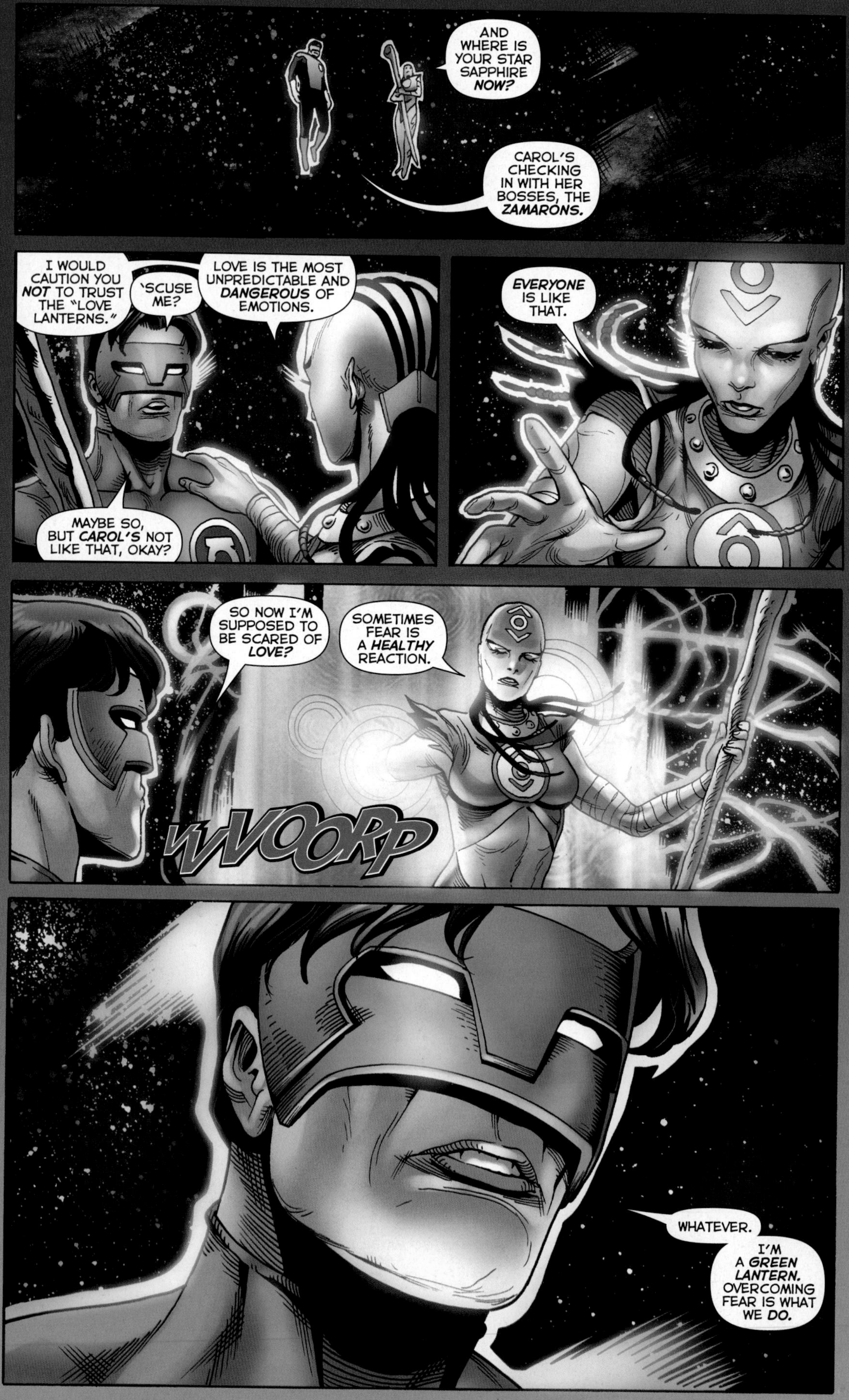
AND WHERE IS YOUR STAR SAPPHIRE NOW?
CAROL'S CHECKING IN WITH HER BOSSES, THE ZAMARONS.
I WOULD CAUTION YOU NOT TO TRUST THE "LOVE LANTERNS."
'SCUSE ME?
LOVE IS THE MOST UNPREDICTABLE AND DANGEROUS OF EMOTIONS.
MAYBE SO, BUT CAROL'S NOT LIKE THAT, OKAY?
EVERYONE IS LIKE THAT.
SO NOW I'M SUPPOSED TO BE SCARED OF LOVE?
SOMETIMES FEAR IS A HEALTHY REACTION.
VVVOORP
WHATEVER.
I'M A GREEN LANTERN. OVERCOMING FEAR IS WHAT WE DO.

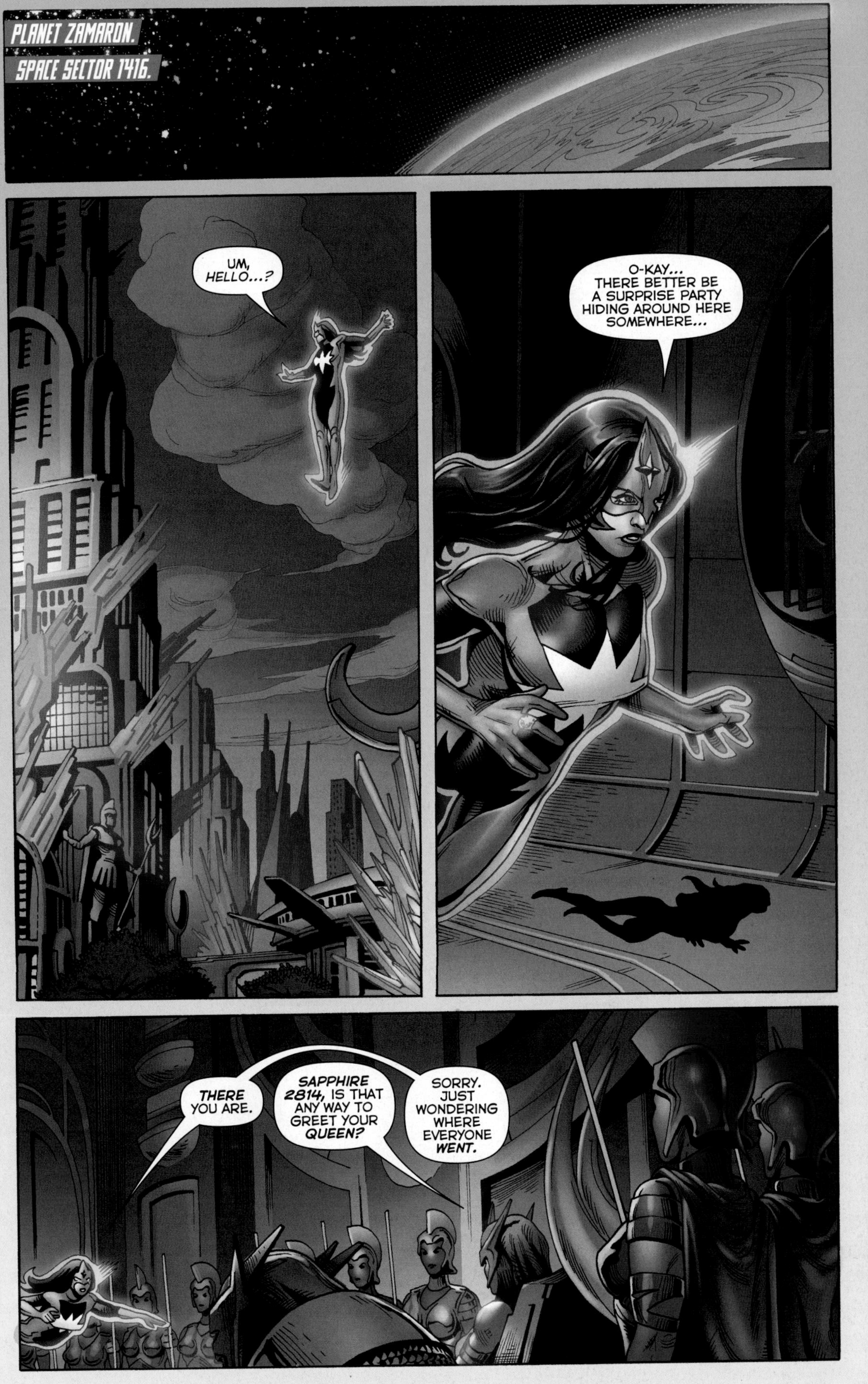
PLANET ZAMARON.
SPACE SECTOR 1416.
UM, HELLO...?
O-KAY... THERE BETTER BE A SURPRISE PARTY HIDING AROUND HERE SOMEWHERE...
THERE YOU ARE.
SAPPHIRE 2814, IS THAT ANY WAY TO GREET YOUR QUEEN?
SORRY. JUST WONDERING WHERE EVERYONE WENT.

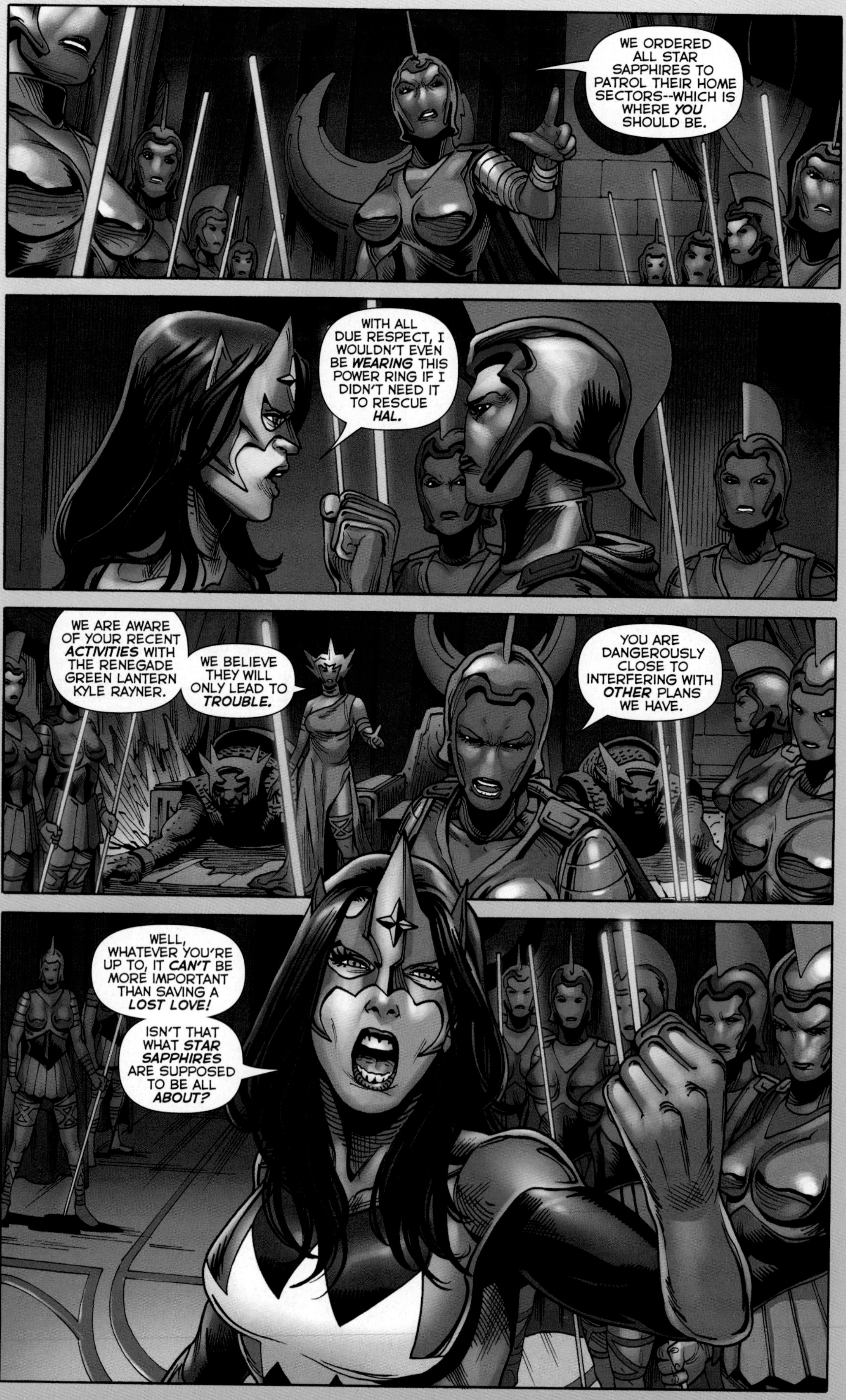

WE ORDERED ALL STAR SAPPHIRES TO PATROL THEIR HOME SECTORS--WHICH IS WHERE *YOU* SHOULD BE.
WITH ALL DUE RESPECT, I WOULDN'T EVEN BE *WEARING* THIS POWER RING IF I DIDN'T NEED IT TO RESCUE *HAL.*
WE ARE AWARE OF YOUR RECENT *ACTIVITIES* WITH THE RENEGADE GREEN LANTERN KYLE RAYNER.
WE BELIEVE THEY WILL ONLY LEAD TO *TROUBLE.*
YOU ARE DANGEROUSLY CLOSE TO INTERFERING WITH *OTHER* PLANS WE HAVE.
WELL, WHATEVER YOU'RE UP TO, IT *CAN'T* BE MORE IMPORTANT THAN SAVING A *LOST LOVE!*
ISN'T THAT WHAT *STAR SAPPHIRES* ARE SUPPOSED TO BE ALL *ABOUT?*

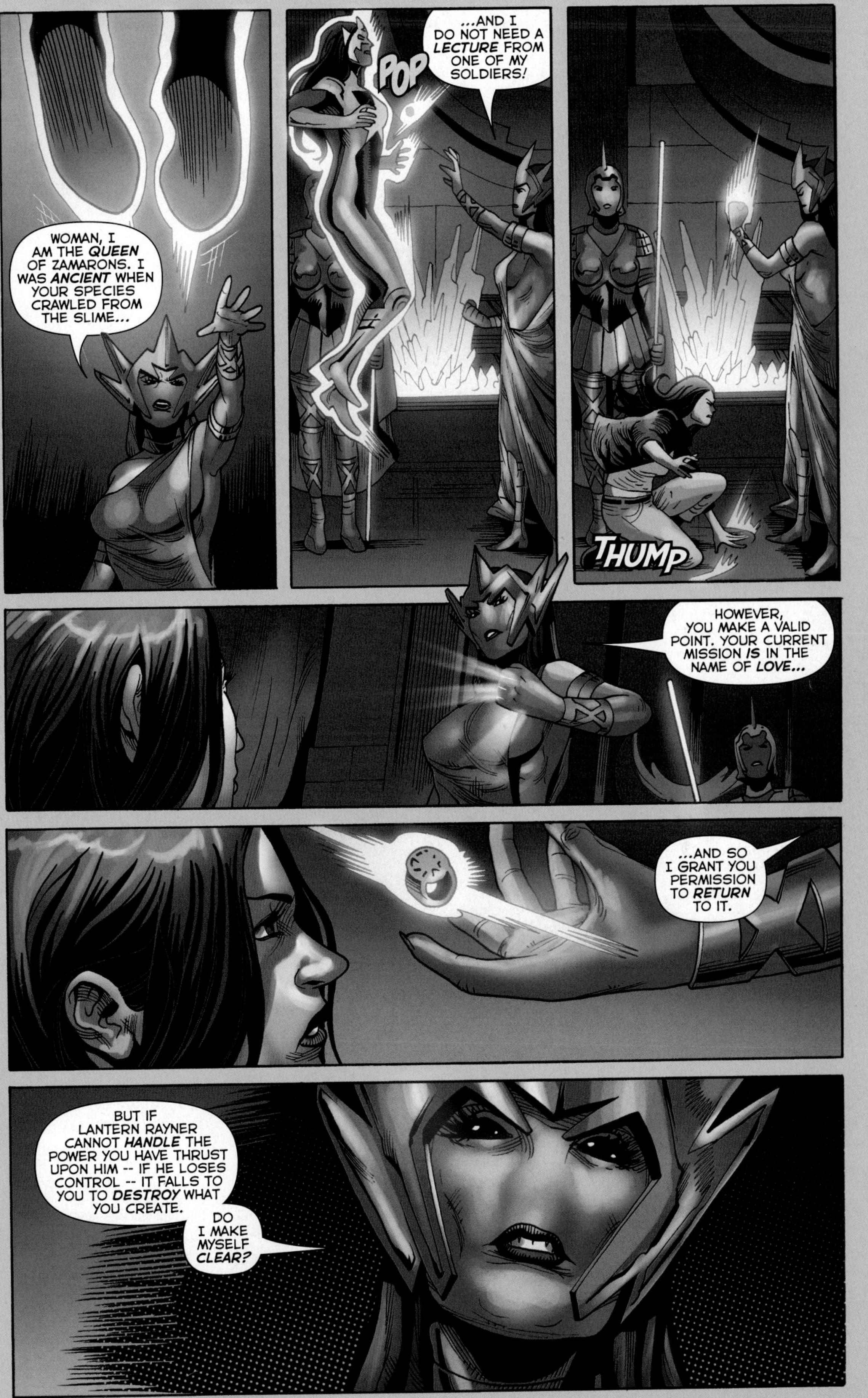
WOMAN, I AM THE QUEEN OF ZAMARONS. I WAS ANCIENT WHEN YOUR SPECIES CRAWLED FROM THE SLIME...
POP
...AND I DO NOT NEED A LECTURE FROM ONE OF MY SOLDIERS!
THUMP
HOWEVER, YOU MAKE A VALID POINT. YOUR CURRENT MISSION IS IN THE NAME OF LOVE...
...AND SO I GRANT YOU PERMISSION TO RETURN TO IT.
BUT IF LANTERN RAYNER CANNOT HANDLE THE POWER YOU HAVE THRUST UPON HIM -- IF HE LOSES CONTROL -- IT FALLS TO YOU TO DESTROY WHAT YOU CREATE.
DO I MAKE MYSELF CLEAR?

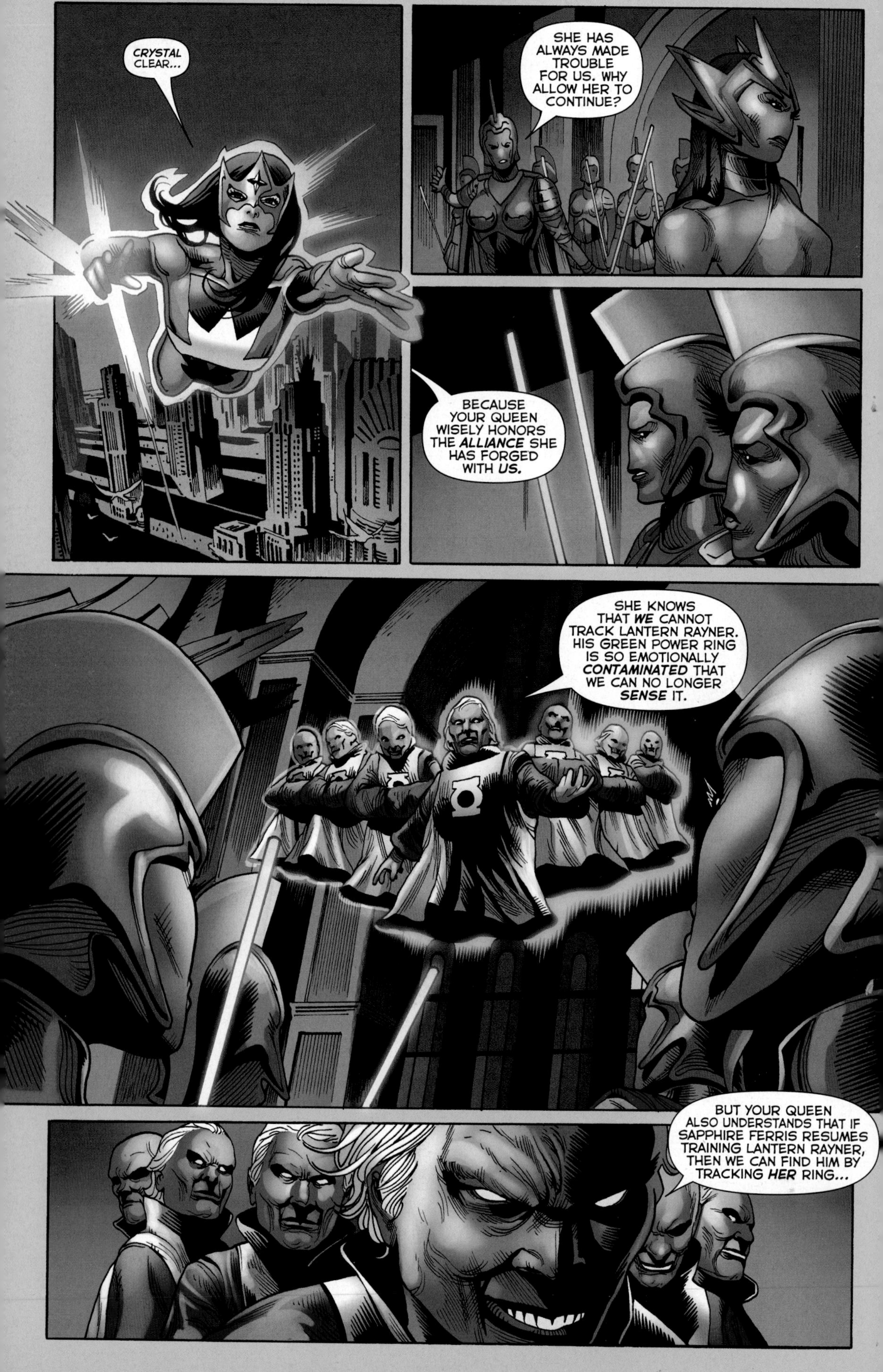
CRYSTAL CLEAR...
SHE HAS ALWAYS MADE TROUBLE FOR US. WHY ALLOW HER TO CONTINUE?
BECAUSE YOUR QUEEN WISELY HONORS THE ALLIANCE SHE HAS FORGED WITH US.
SHE KNOWS THAT WE CANNOT TRACK LANTERN RAYNER. HIS GREEN POWER RING IS SO EMOTIONALLY CONTAMINATED THAT WE CAN NO LONGER SENSE IT.
BUT YOUR QUEEN ALSO UNDERSTANDS THAT IF SAPPHIRE FERRIS RESUMES TRAINING LANTERN RAYNER, THEN WE CAN FIND HIM BY TRACKING HER RING...

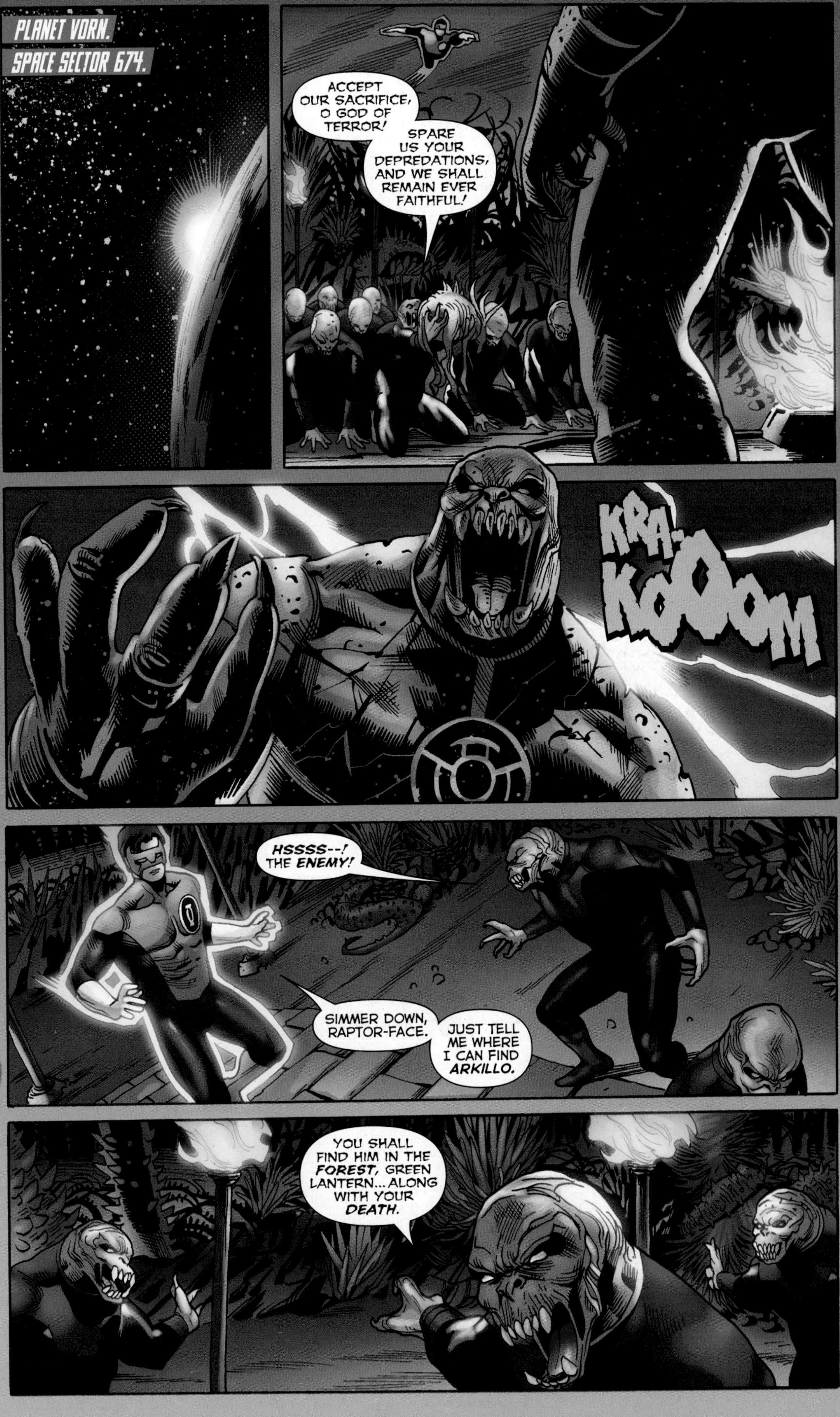
PLANET VORN.
SPACE SECTOR 674.
ACCEPT OUR SACRIFICE, O GOD OF TERROR!
SPARE US YOUR DEPREDATIONS, AND WE SHALL REMAIN EVER FAITHFUL!
KRA-KOOOM
HSSSS--! THE ENEMY!
SIMMER DOWN, RAPTOR-FACE.
JUST TELL ME WHERE I CAN FIND ARKILLO.
YOU SHALL FIND HIM IN THE FOREST, GREEN LANTERN... ALONG WITH YOUR DEATH.

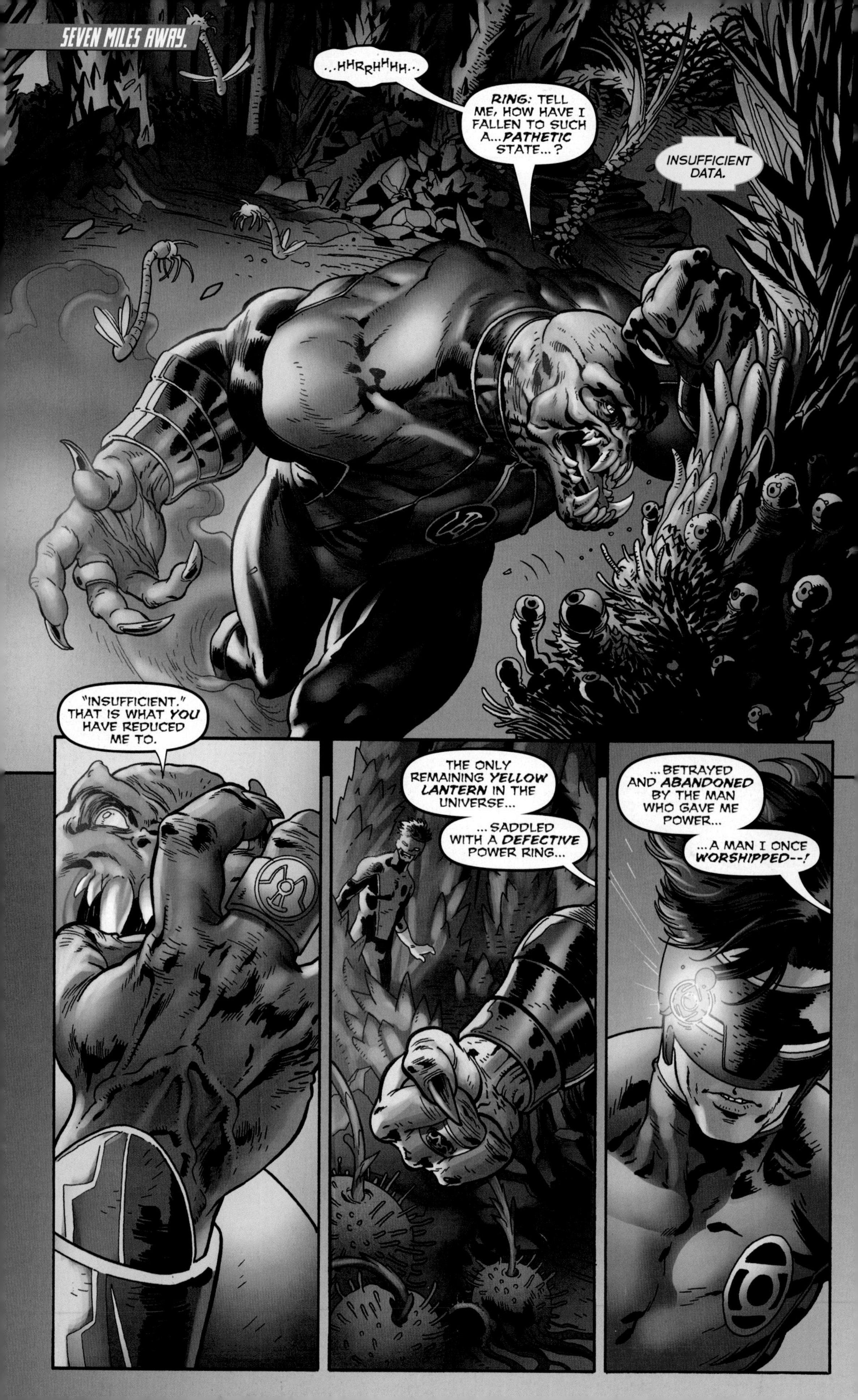
SEVEN MILES AWAY.
...HHRRHHHH...
RING: TELL ME, HOW HAVE I FALLEN TO SUCH A...PATHETIC STATE...?
INSUFFICIENT DATA.
"INSUFFICIENT." THAT IS WHAT YOU HAVE REDUCED ME TO.
THE ONLY REMAINING YELLOW LANTERN IN THE UNIVERSE...
...SADDLED WITH A DEFECTIVE POWER RING...
...BETRAYED AND ABANDONED BY THE MAN WHO GAVE ME POWER...
...A MAN I ONCE WORSHIPPED--!

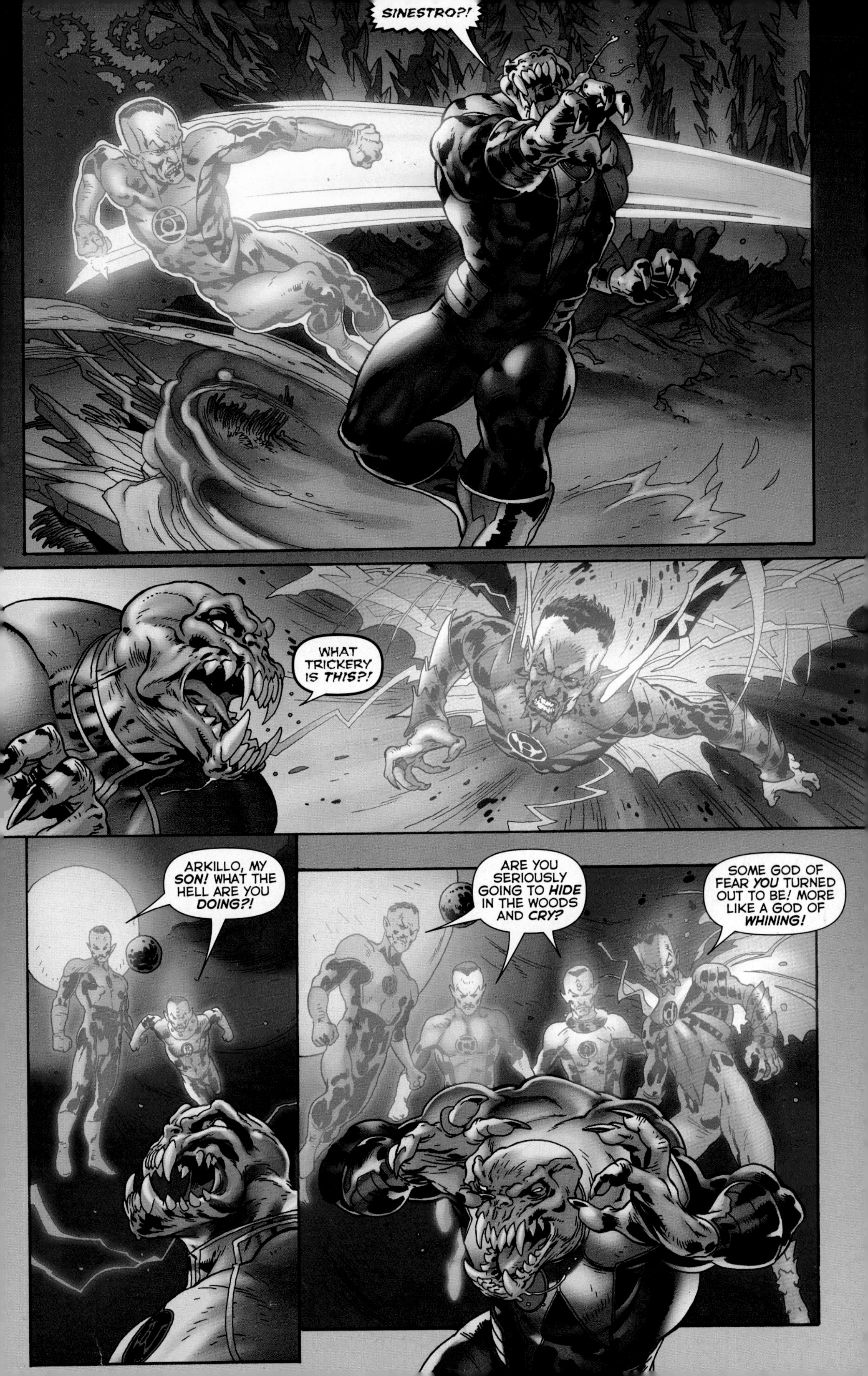
SINESTRO?!
WHAT TRICKERY IS THIS?!
ARKILLO, MY SON! WHAT THE HELL ARE YOU DOING?!
ARE YOU SERIOUSLY GOING TO HIDE IN THE WOODS AND CRY?
SOME GOD OF FEAR YOU TURNED OUT TO BE! MORE LIKE A GOD OF WHINING!

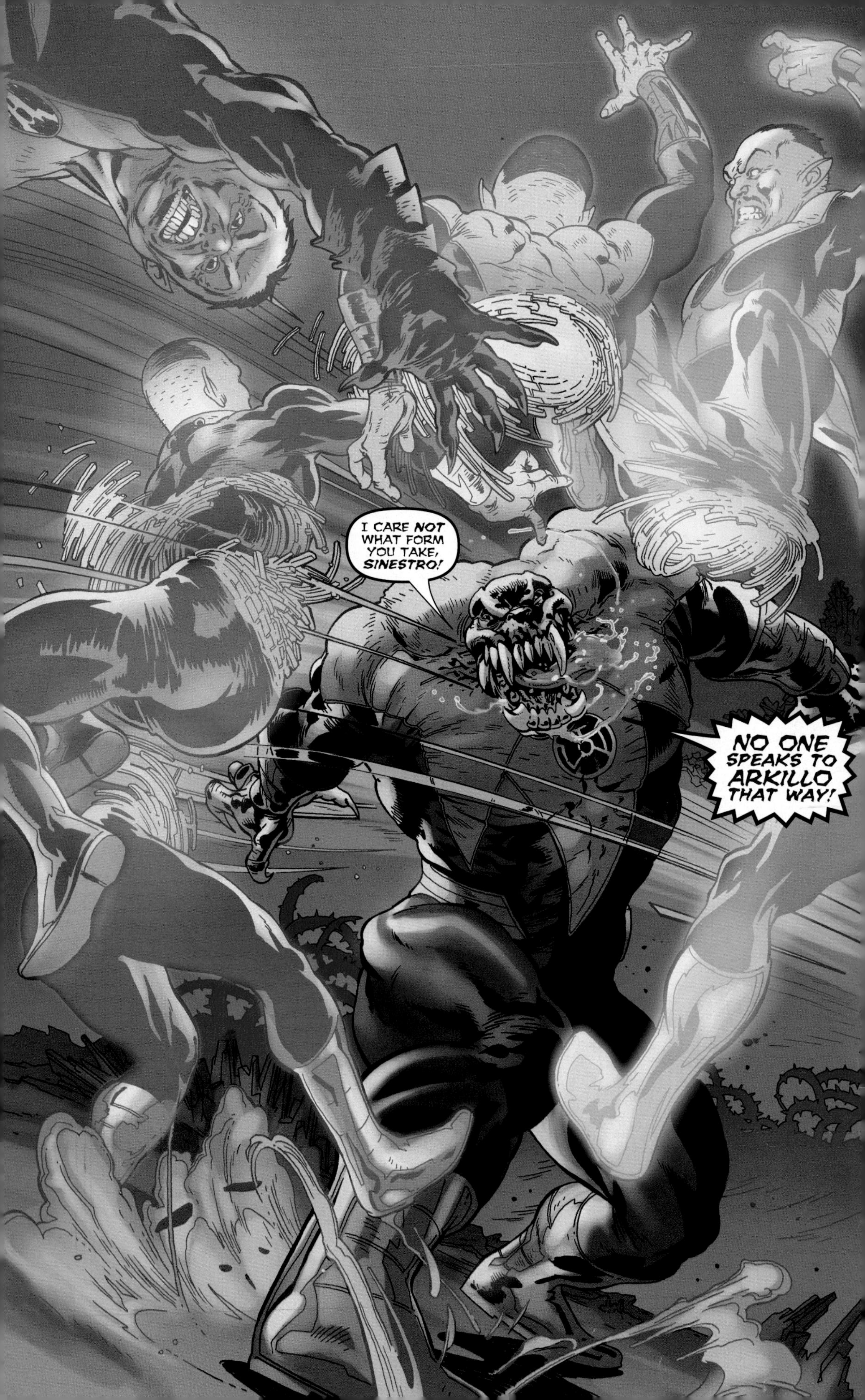
I CARE NOT WHAT FORM YOU TAKE, SINESTRO!
NO ONE SPEAKS TO ARKILLO THAT WAY!

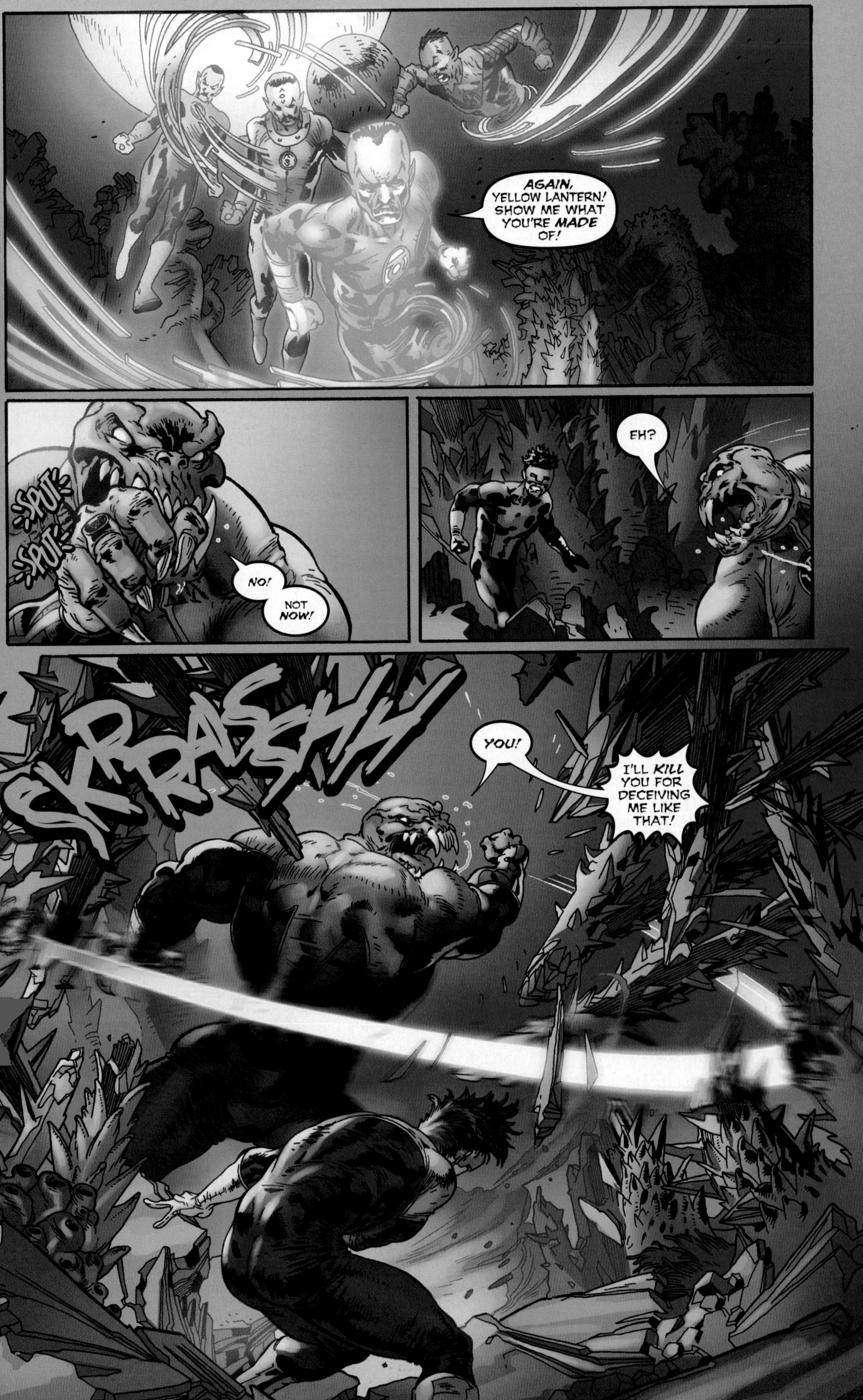
AGAIN, YELLOW LANTERN! SHOW ME WHAT YOU'RE MADE OF!
SPUT
SPUT
NO!
NOT NOW!
EH?
SKRASHH
YOU!
I'LL KILL YOU FOR DECEIVING ME LIKE THAT!

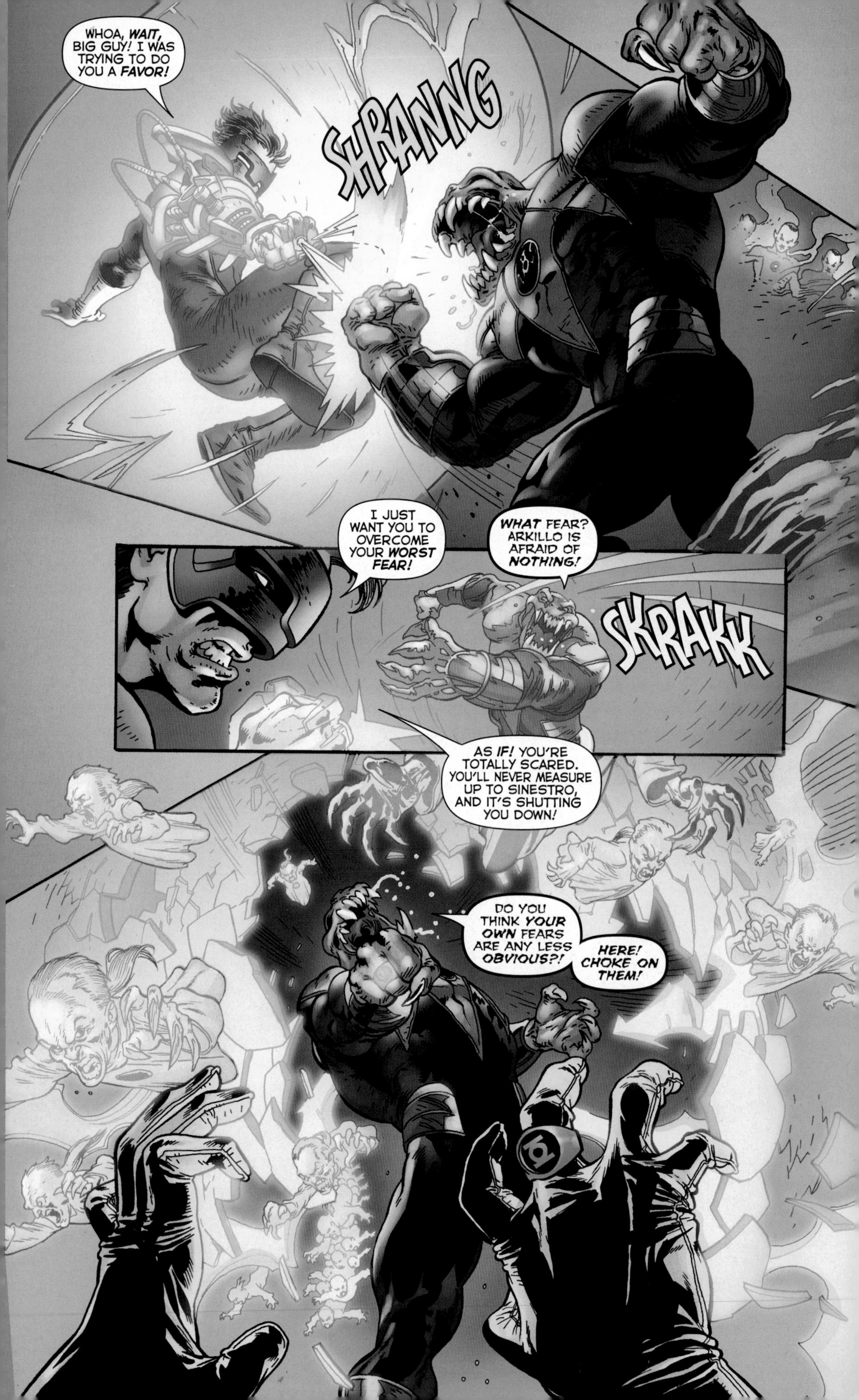
WHOA, *WAIT*, BIG GUY! I WAS TRYING TO DO YOU A *FAVOR*!
SHRANNG
I JUST WANT YOU TO OVERCOME YOUR *WORST* FEAR!
WHAT FEAR? ARKILLO IS AFRAID OF *NOTHING*!
SKRAKK
AS *IF*! YOU'RE TOTALLY SCARED. YOU'LL NEVER MEASURE UP TO SINESTRO, AND IT'S SHUTTING YOU DOWN!
DO YOU THINK *YOUR OWN* FEARS ARE ANY LESS *OBVIOUS*?!
HERE! CHOKE ON THEM!

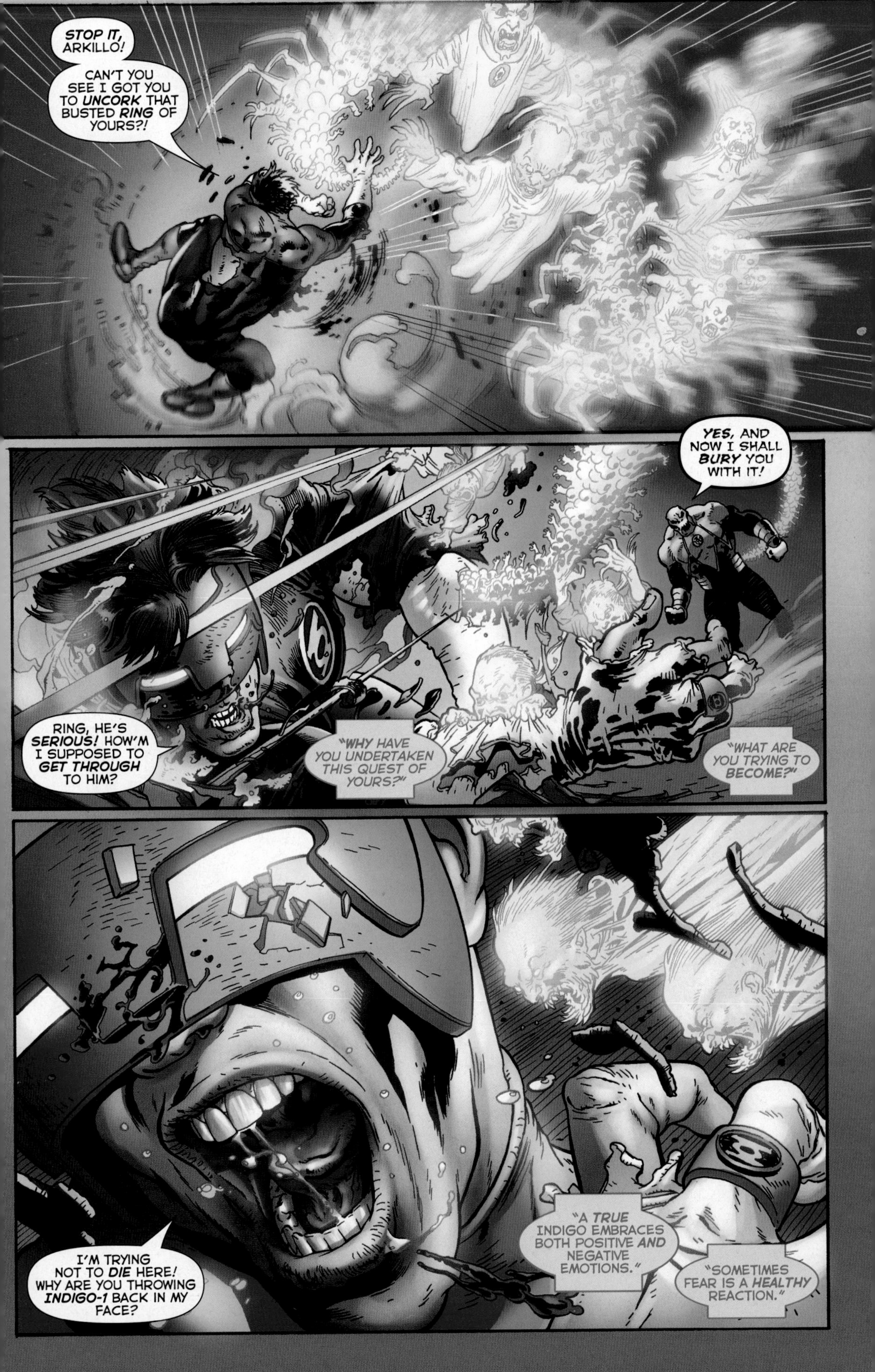
STOP IT, ARKILLO!
CAN'T YOU SEE I GOT YOU TO UNCORK THAT BUSTED RING OF YOURS?!
YES, AND NOW I SHALL BURY YOU WITH IT!
RING, HE'S SERIOUS! HOW'M I SUPPOSED TO GET THROUGH TO HIM?
"WHY HAVE YOU UNDERTAKEN THIS QUEST OF YOURS?"
"WHAT ARE YOU TRYING TO BECOME?"
I'M TRYING NOT TO DIE HERE! WHY ARE YOU THROWING INDIGO-1 BACK IN MY FACE?
"A TRUE INDIGO EMBRACES BOTH POSITIVE AND NEGATIVE EMOTIONS."
"SOMETIMES FEAR IS A HEALTHY REACTION."

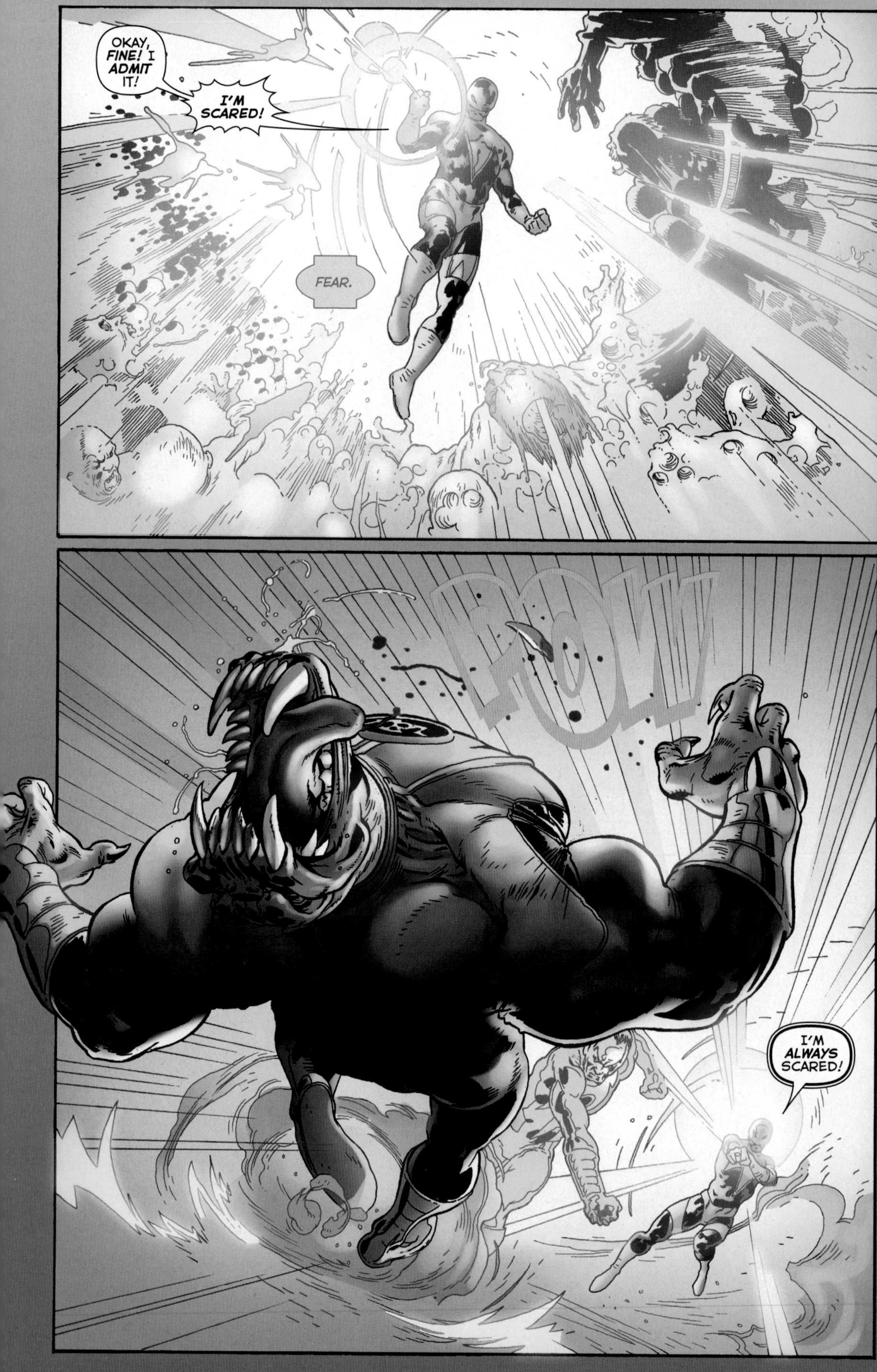
OKAY, FINE! I ADMIT IT!
I'M SCARED!
FEAR.
POW
I'M ALWAYS SCARED!

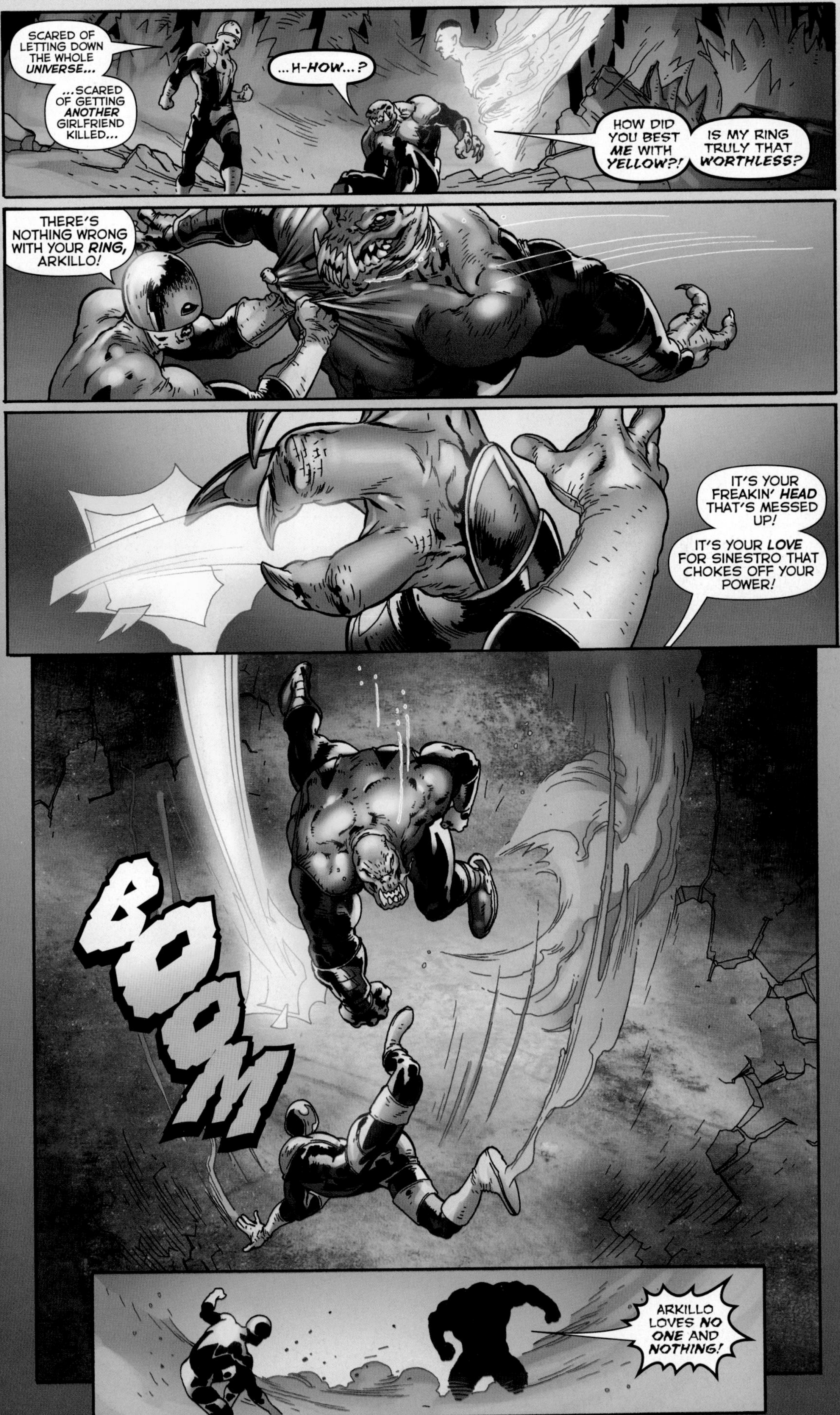
SCARED OF LETTING DOWN THE WHOLE UNIVERSE...
...SCARED OF GETTING ANOTHER GIRLFRIEND KILLED...
...H-HOW...?
HOW DID YOU BEST ME WITH YELLOW?!
IS MY RING TRULY THAT WORTHLESS?
THERE'S NOTHING WRONG WITH YOUR RING, ARKILLO!
IT'S YOUR FREAKIN' HEAD THAT'S MESSED UP!
IT'S YOUR LOVE FOR SINESTRO THAT CHOKES OFF YOUR POWER!
BOOM
ARKILLO LOVES NO ONE AND NOTHING!

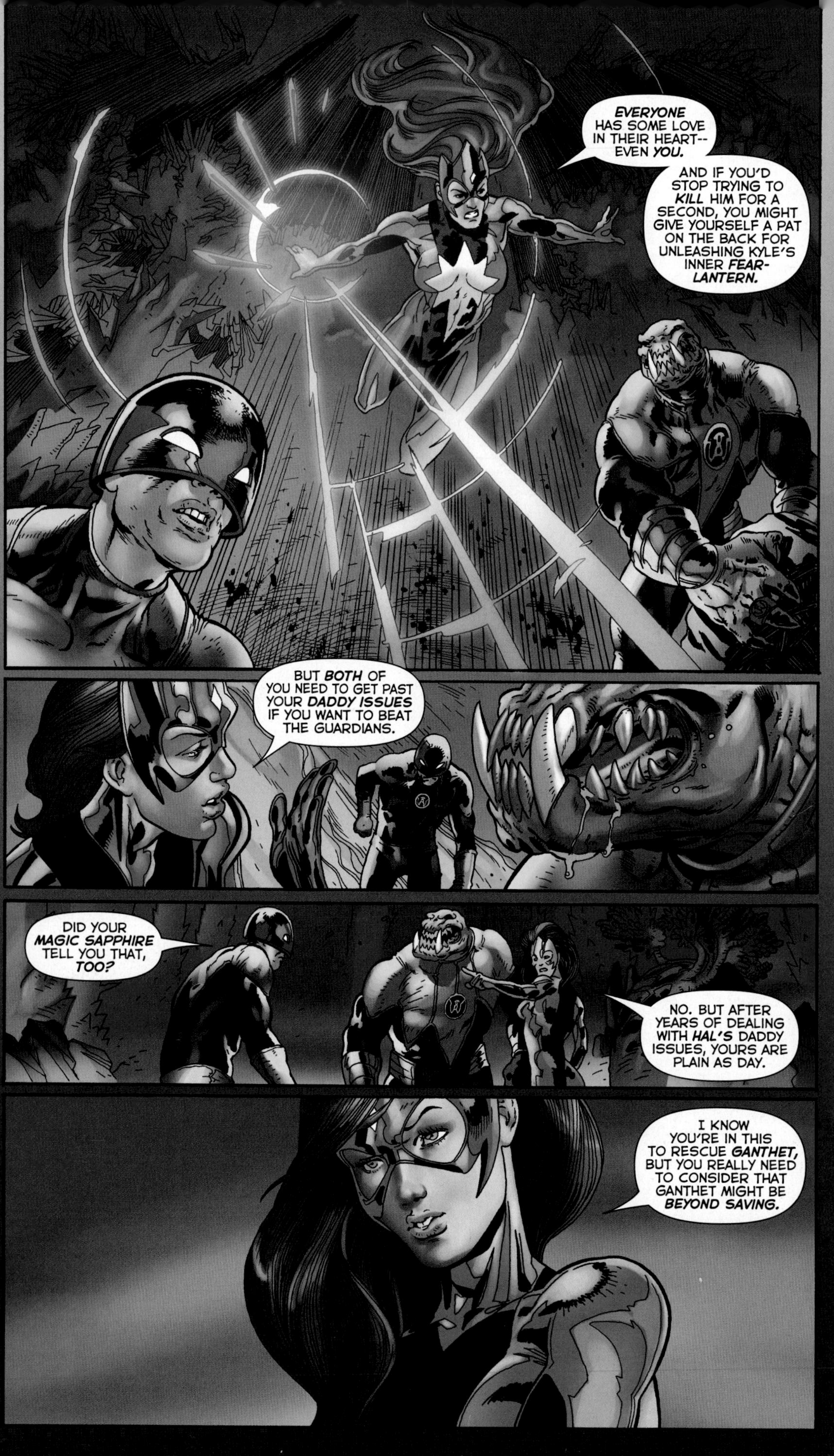
EVERYONE HAS SOME LOVE IN THEIR HEART-- EVEN YOU.
AND IF YOU'D STOP TRYING TO KILL HIM FOR A SECOND, YOU MIGHT GIVE YOURSELF A PAT ON THE BACK FOR UNLEASHING KYLE'S INNER FEAR-LANTERN.
BUT BOTH OF YOU NEED TO GET PAST YOUR DADDY ISSUES IF YOU WANT TO BEAT THE GUARDIANS.
DID YOUR MAGIC SAPPHIRE TELL YOU THAT, TOO?
NO. BUT AFTER YEARS OF DEALING WITH HAL'S DADDY ISSUES, YOURS ARE PLAIN AS DAY.
I KNOW YOU'RE IN THIS TO RESCUE GANTHET, BUT YOU REALLY NEED TO CONSIDER THAT GANTHET MIGHT BE BEYOND SAVING.

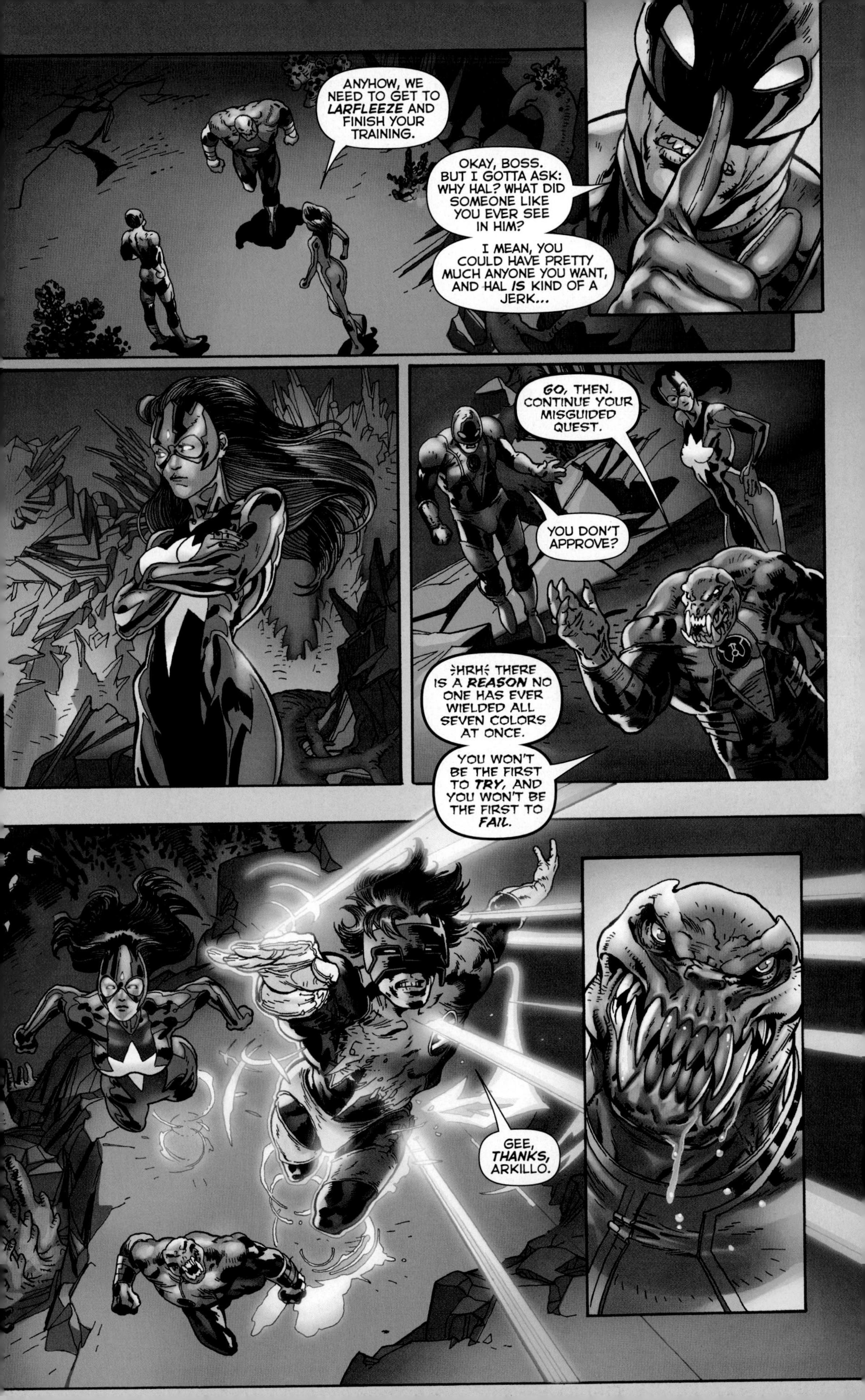
ANYHOW, WE NEED TO GET TO LARFLEEZE AND FINISH YOUR TRAINING.
OKAY, BOSS. BUT I GOTTA ASK: WHY HAL? WHAT DID SOMEONE LIKE YOU EVER SEE IN HIM?
I MEAN, YOU COULD HAVE PRETTY MUCH ANYONE YOU WANT, AND HAL IS KIND OF A JERK...
GO, THEN. CONTINUE YOUR MISGUIDED QUEST.
YOU DON'T APPROVE?
HRH THERE IS A REASON NO ONE HAS EVER WIELDED ALL SEVEN COLORS AT ONCE.
YOU WON'T BE THE FIRST TO TRY, AND YOU WON'T BE THE FIRST TO FAIL.
GEE, THANKS, ARKILLO.

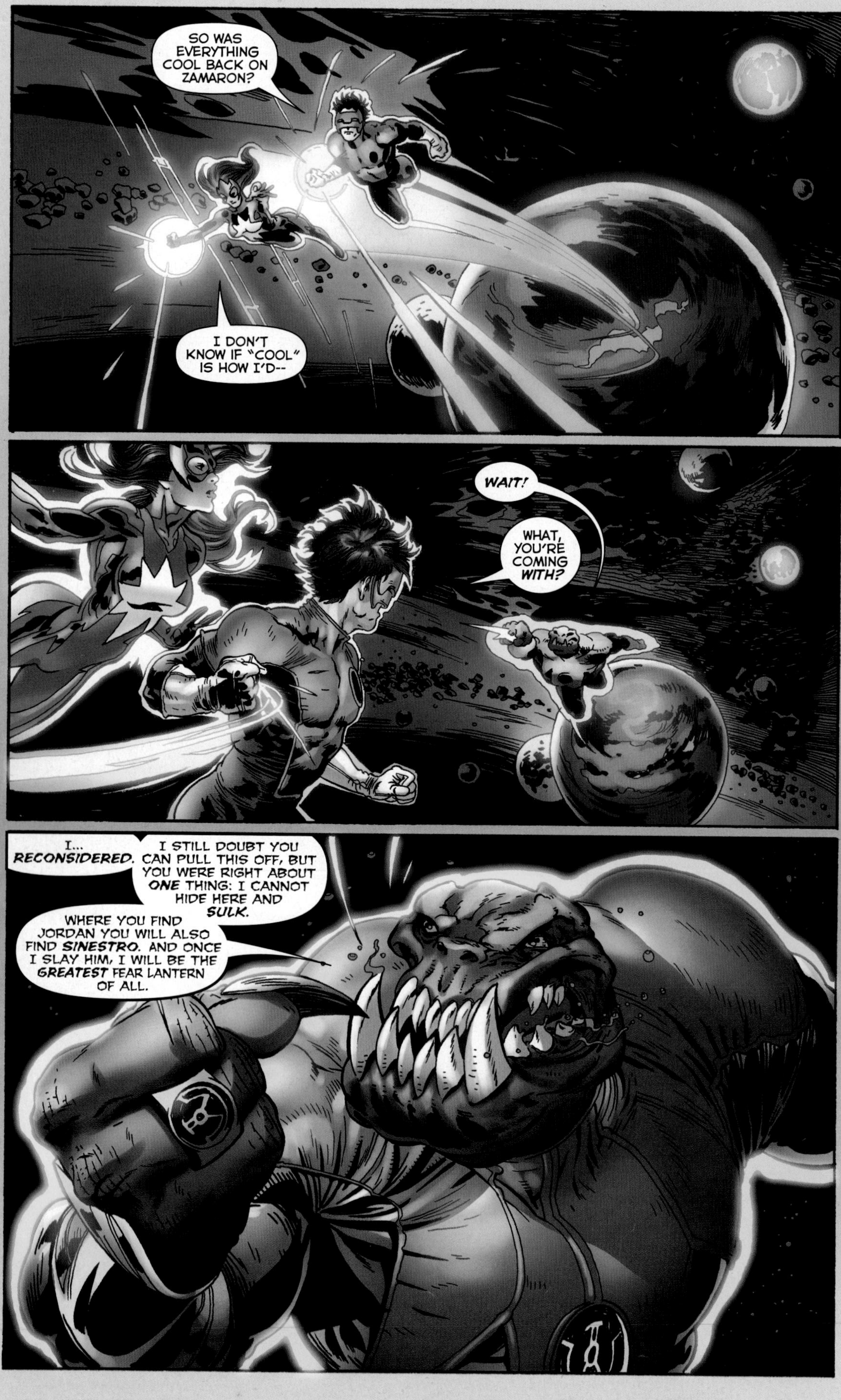
SO WAS EVERYTHING COOL BACK ON ZAMARON?
I DON'T KNOW IF "COOL" IS HOW I'D--
WAIT!
WHAT, YOU'RE COMING WITH?
I... RECONSIDERED.
I STILL DOUBT YOU CAN PULL THIS OFF, BUT YOU WERE RIGHT ABOUT ONE THING: I CANNOT HIDE HERE AND SULK.
WHERE YOU FIND JORDAN YOU WILL ALSO FIND SINESTRO. AND ONCE I SLAY HIM, I WILL BE THE GREATEST FEAR LANTERN OF ALL.

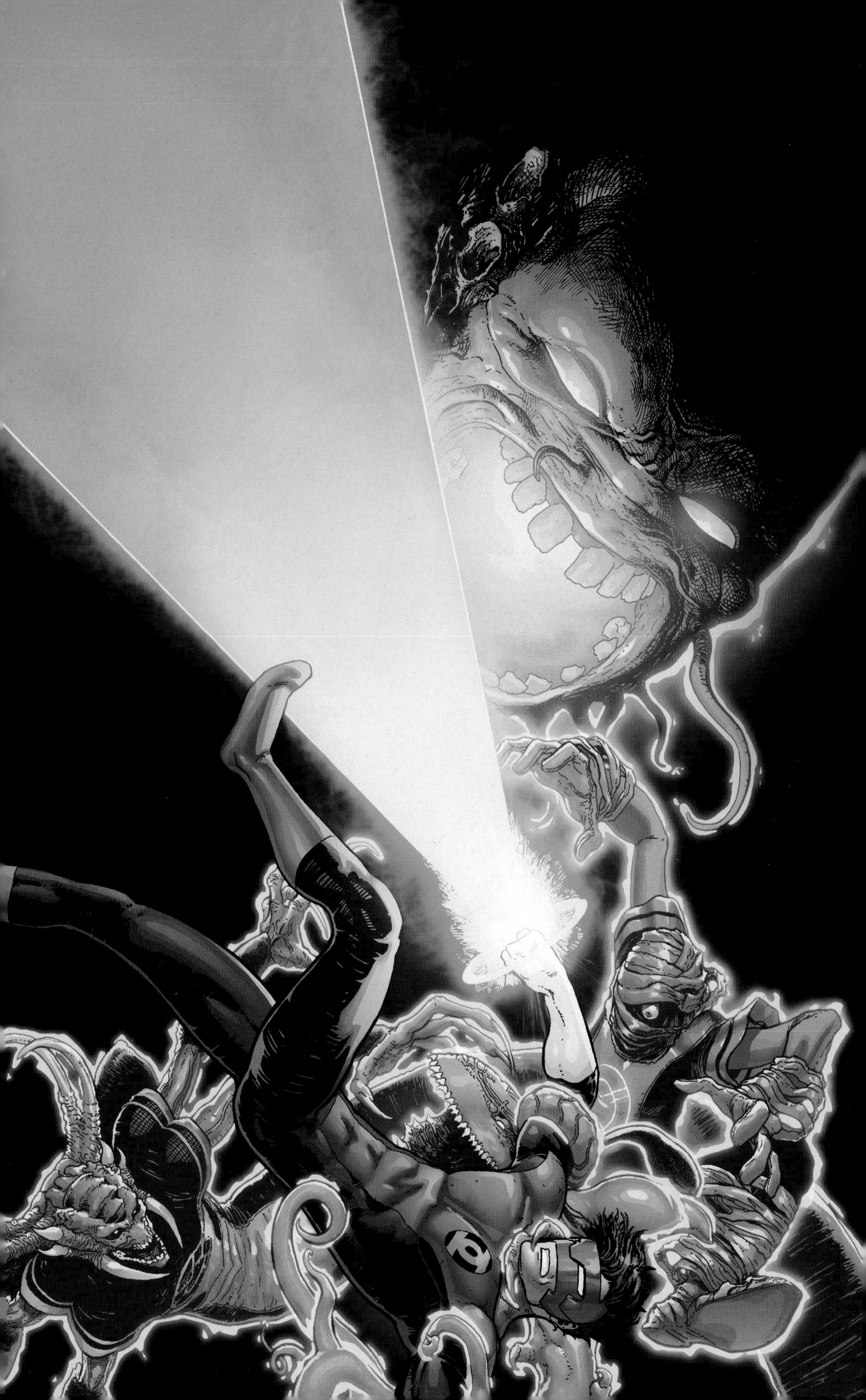

THE NEED FOR GREED

TONY BEDARD writer AARON KUDER artist
AARON KUDER & HI-FI cover

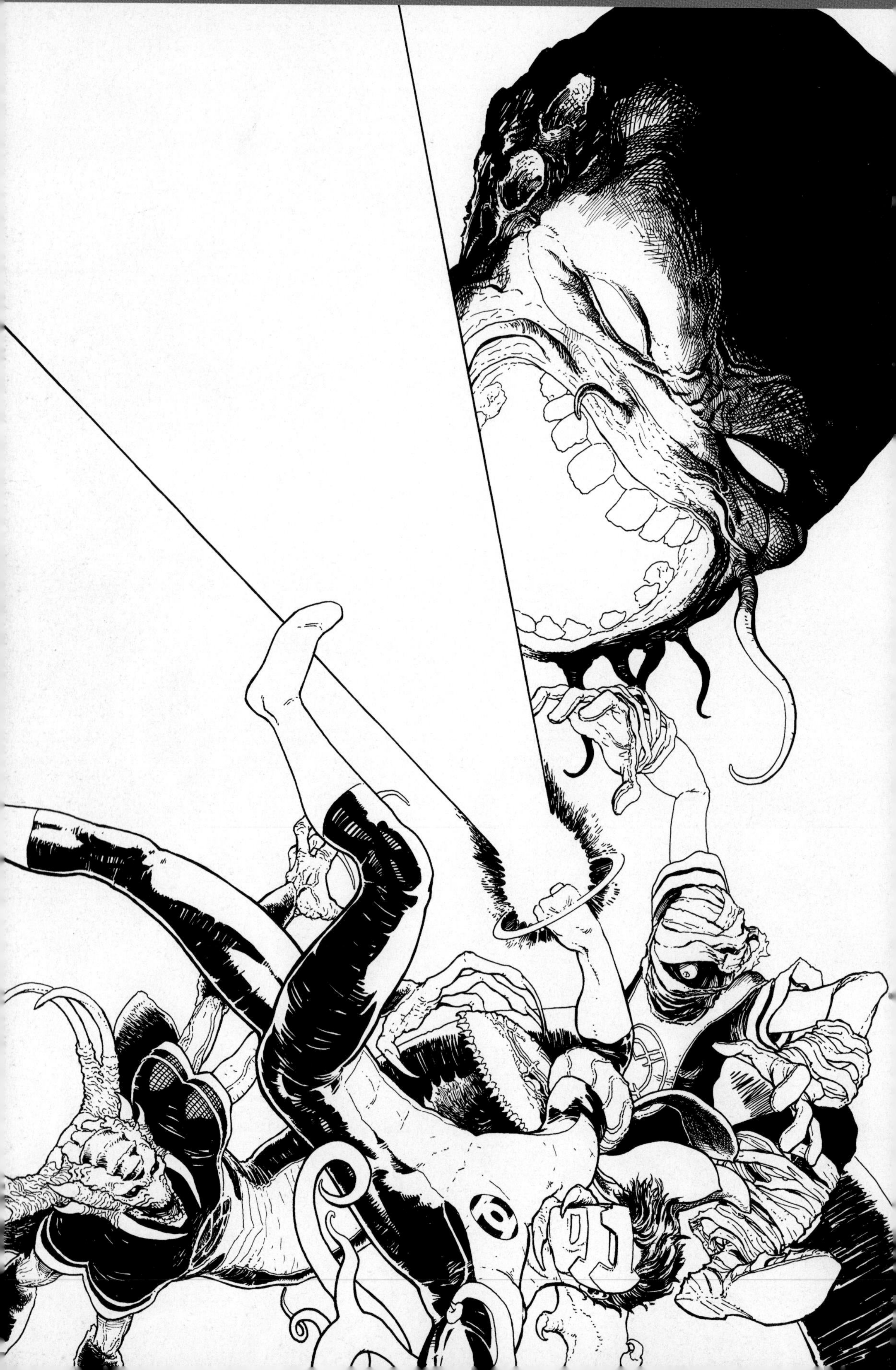

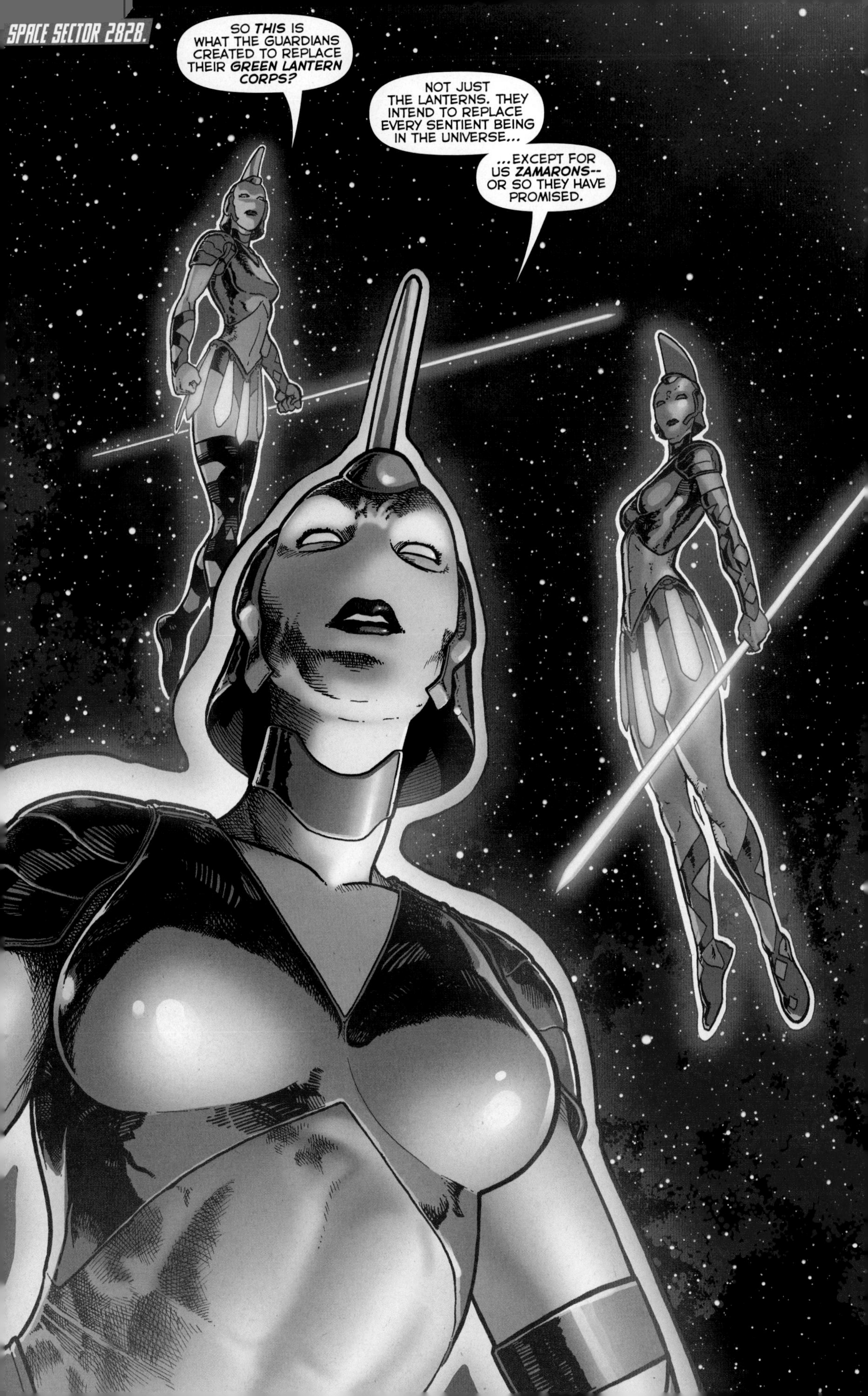
SPACE SECTOR 2828.
SO THIS IS WHAT THE GUARDIANS CREATED TO REPLACE THEIR GREEN LANTERN CORPS?
NOT JUST THE LANTERNS. THEY INTEND TO REPLACE EVERY SENTIENT BEING IN THE UNIVERSE...
...EXCEPT FOR US ZAMARONS-- OR SO THEY HAVE PROMISED.

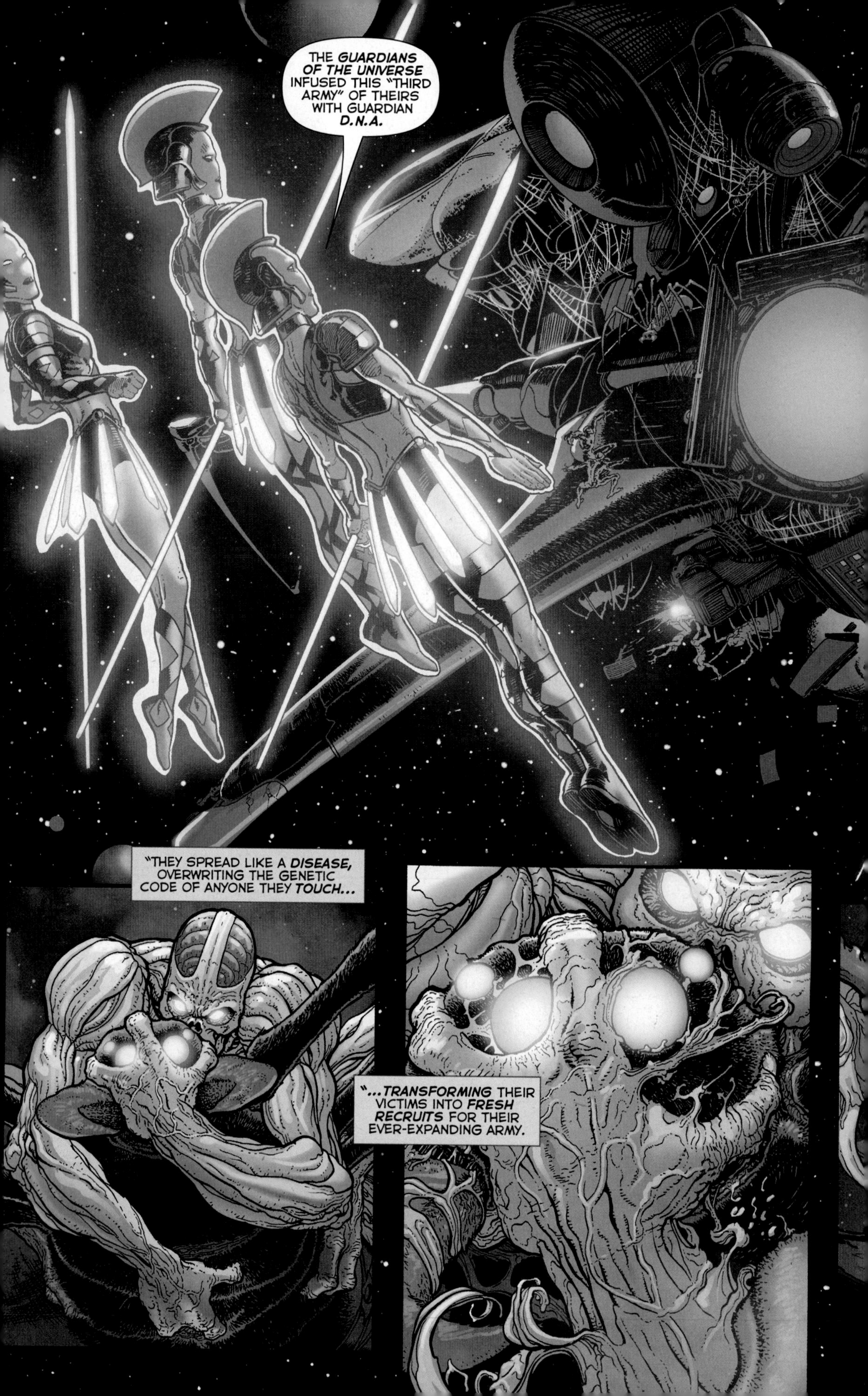
THE GUARDIANS OF THE UNIVERSE INFUSED THIS "THIRD ARMY" OF THEIRS WITH GUARDIAN D.N.A.
"THEY SPREAD LIKE A DISEASE, OVERWRITING THE GENETIC CODE OF ANYONE THEY TOUCH...
"...TRANSFORMING THEIR VICTIMS INTO FRESH RECRUITS FOR THEIR EVER-EXPANDING ARMY.

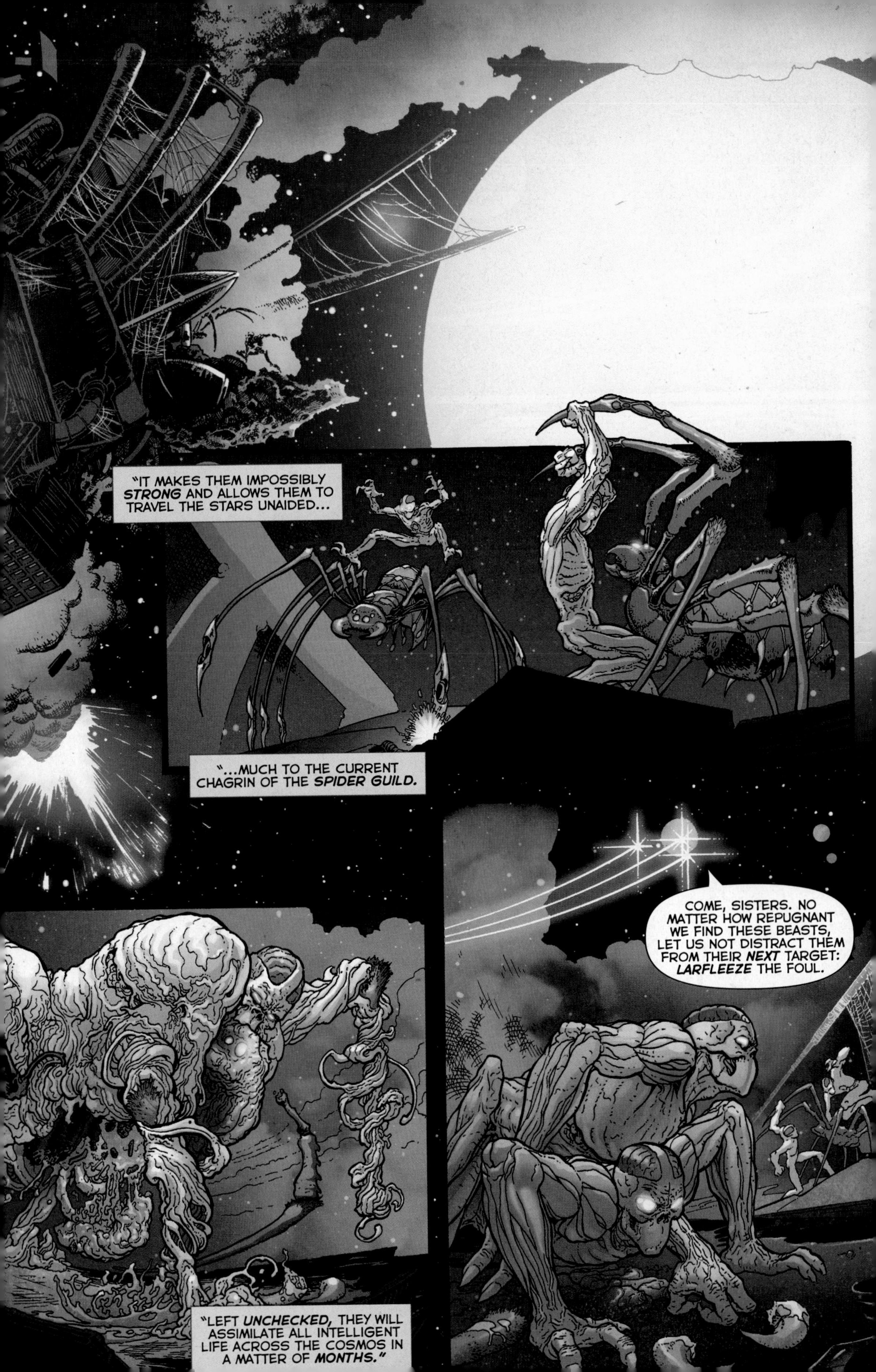
"IT MAKES THEM IMPOSSIBLY STRONG AND ALLOWS THEM TO TRAVEL THE STARS UNAIDED...
"...MUCH TO THE CURRENT CHAGRIN OF THE SPIDER GUILD.
COME, SISTERS. NO MATTER HOW REPUGNANT WE FIND THESE BEASTS, LET US NOT DISTRACT THEM FROM THEIR NEXT TARGET: LARFLEEZE THE FOUL.
"LEFT UNCHECKED, THEY WILL ASSIMILATE ALL INTELLIGENT LIFE ACROSS THE COSMOS IN A MATTER OF MONTHS."

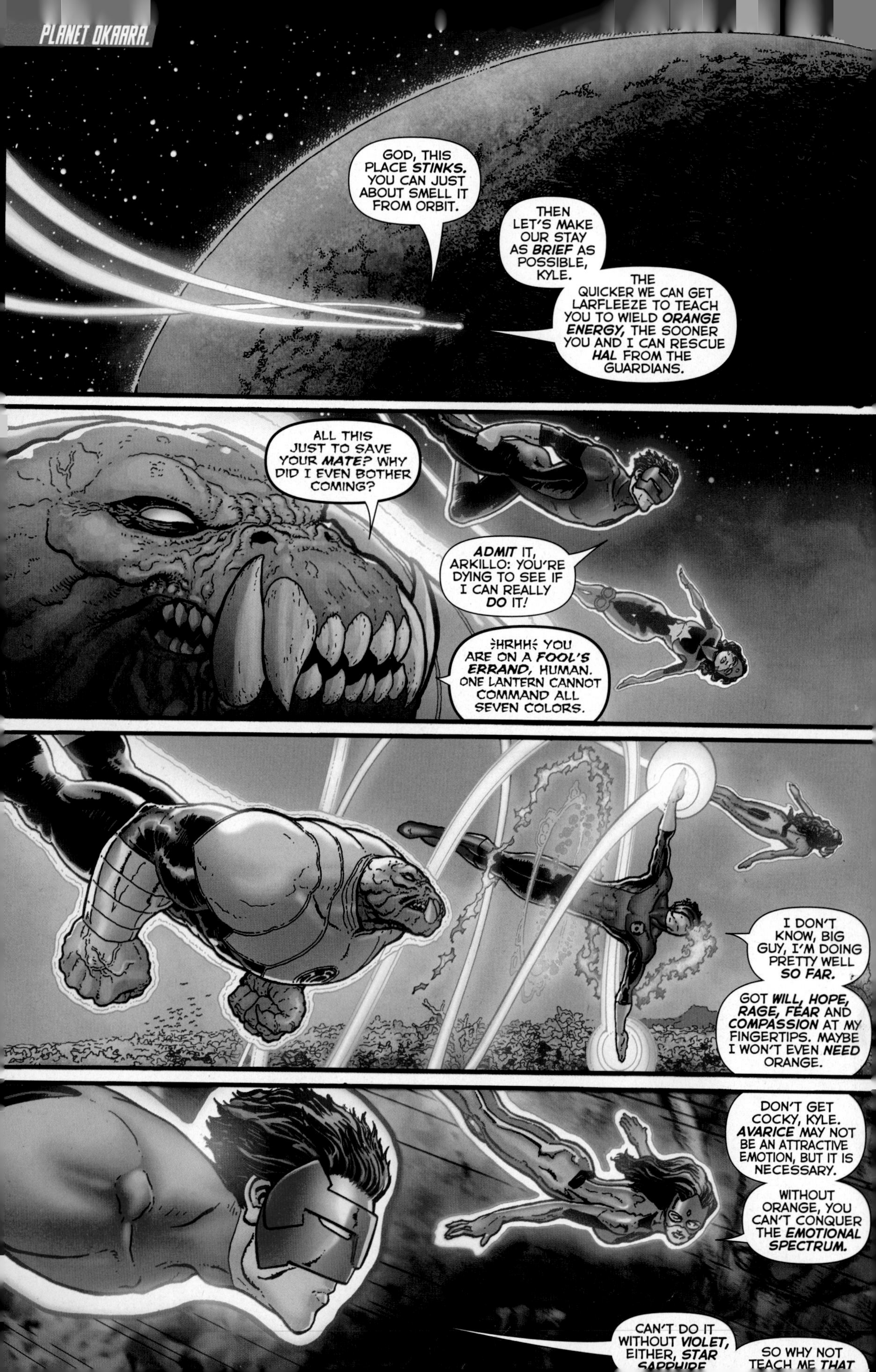
PLANET OKAARA.
GOD, THIS PLACE STINKS. YOU CAN JUST ABOUT SMELL IT FROM ORBIT.
THEN LET'S MAKE OUR STAY AS BRIEF AS POSSIBLE, KYLE.
THE QUICKER WE CAN GET LARFLEEZE TO TEACH YOU TO WIELD ORANGE ENERGY, THE SOONER YOU AND I CAN RESCUE HAL FROM THE GUARDIANS.
ALL THIS JUST TO SAVE YOUR MATE? WHY DID I EVEN BOTHER COMING?
ADMIT IT, ARKILLO: YOU'RE DYING TO SEE IF I CAN REALLY DO IT!
HRHH YOU ARE ON A FOOL'S ERRAND, HUMAN. ONE LANTERN CANNOT COMMAND ALL SEVEN COLORS.
I DON'T KNOW, BIG GUY, I'M DOING PRETTY WELL SO FAR.
GOT WILL, HOPE, RAGE, FEAR AND COMPASSION AT MY FINGERTIPS. MAYBE I WON'T EVEN NEED ORANGE.
DON'T GET COCKY, KYLE. AVARICE MAY NOT BE AN ATTRACTIVE EMOTION, BUT IT IS NECESSARY.
WITHOUT ORANGE, YOU CAN'T CONQUER THE EMOTIONAL SPECTRUM.
CAN'T DO IT WITHOUT VIOLET, EITHER, STAR
SO WHY NOT TEACH ME THAT

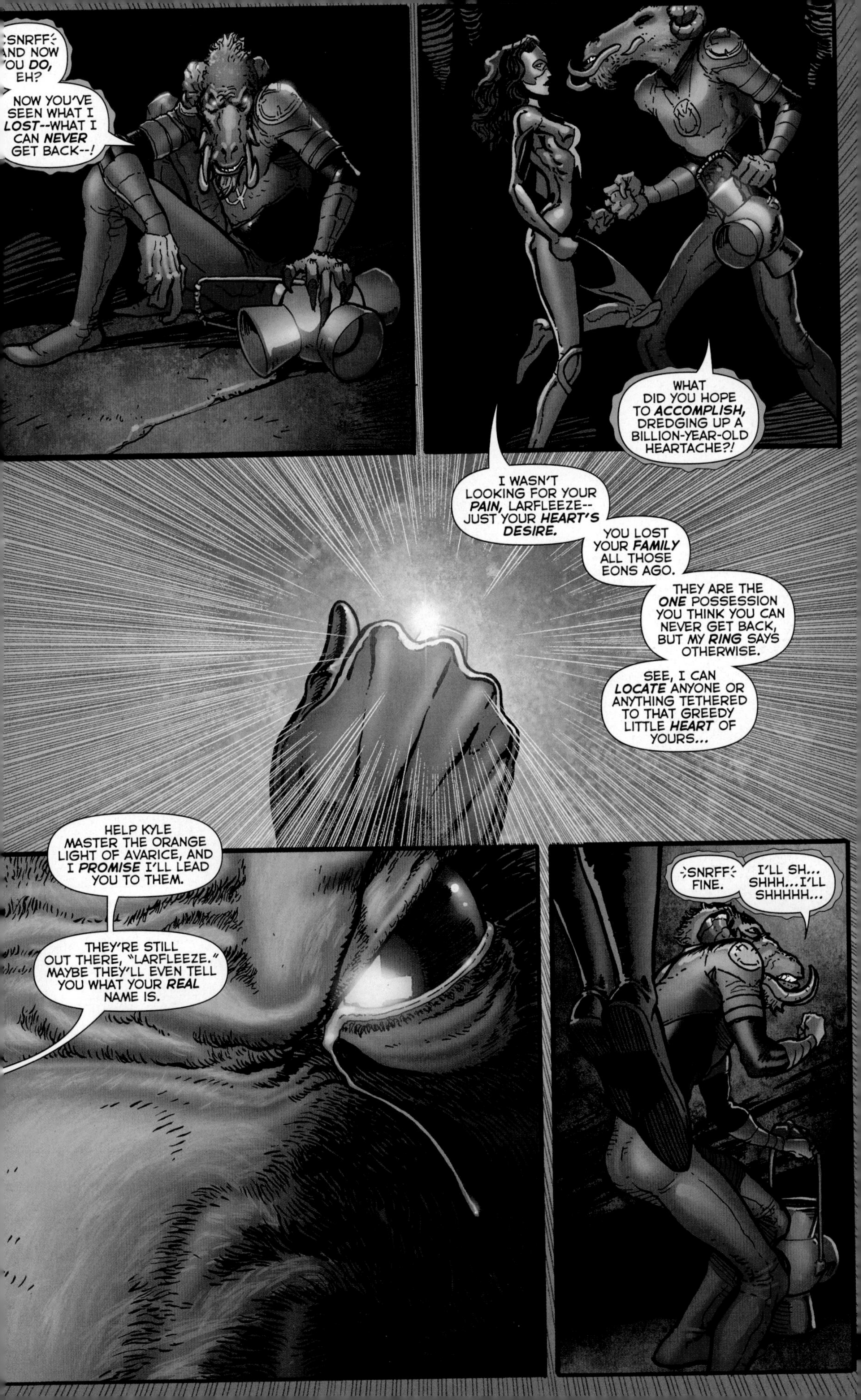

SNRFF AND NOW YOU DO, EH?
NOW YOU'VE SEEN WHAT I LOST--WHAT I CAN NEVER GET BACK--!
WHAT DID YOU HOPE TO ACCOMPLISH, DREDGING UP A BILLION-YEAR-OLD HEARTACHE?!
I WASN'T LOOKING FOR YOUR PAIN, LARFLEEZE--JUST YOUR HEART'S DESIRE.
YOU LOST YOUR FAMILY ALL THOSE EONS AGO.
THEY ARE THE ONE POSSESSION YOU THINK YOU CAN NEVER GET BACK, BUT MY RING SAYS OTHERWISE.
SEE, I CAN LOCATE ANYONE OR ANYTHING TETHERED TO THAT GREEDY LITTLE HEART OF YOURS...
HELP KYLE MASTER THE ORANGE LIGHT OF AVARICE, AND I PROMISE I'LL LEAD YOU TO THEM.
THEY'RE STILL OUT THERE, "LARFLEEZE." MAYBE THEY'LL EVEN TELL YOU WHAT YOUR REAL NAME IS.
SNRFF FINE.
I'LL SH... SHHH...I'LL SHHHHH...

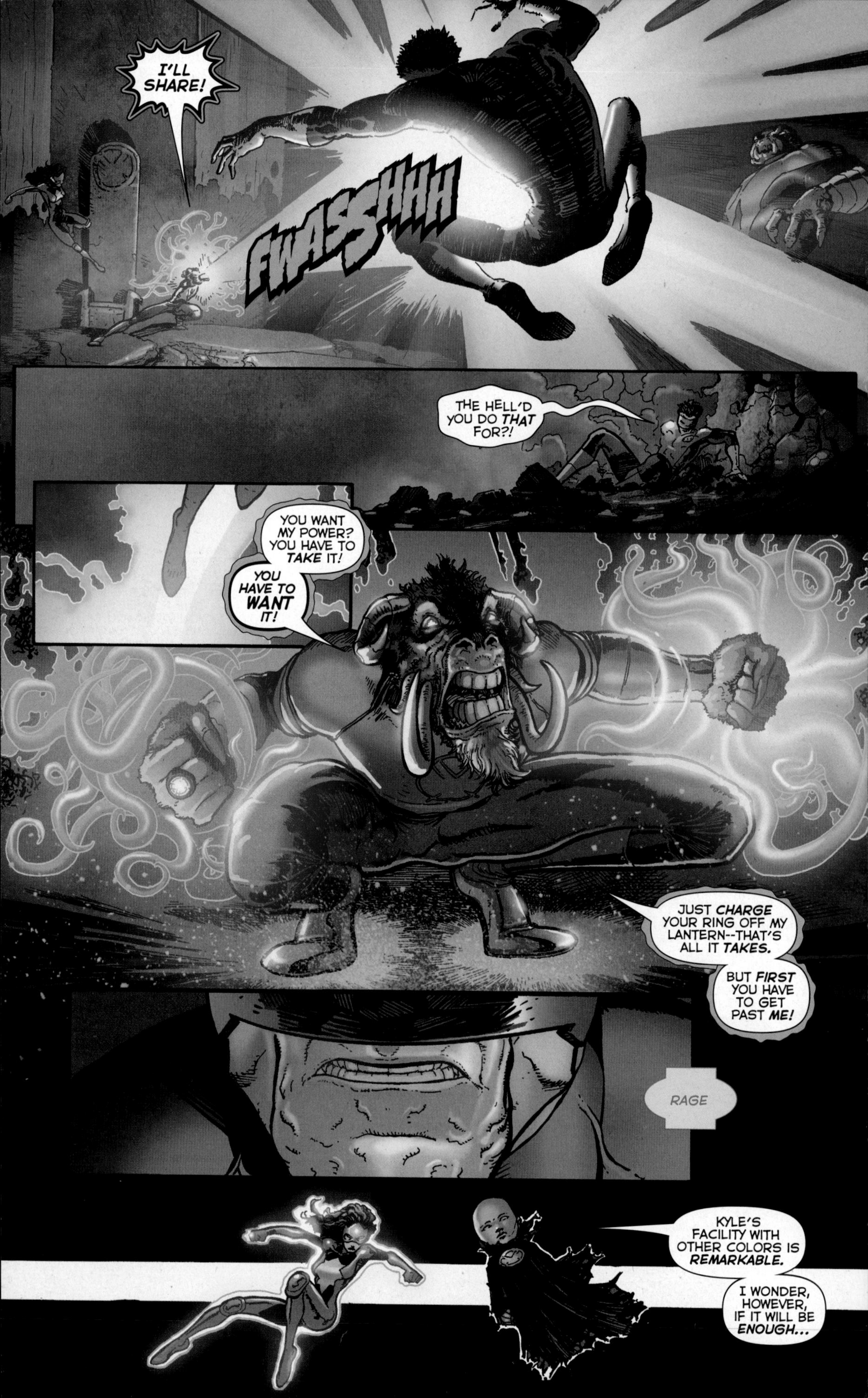
I'LL SHARE!
FWASSHHH
THE HELL'D YOU DO THAT FOR?!
YOU WANT MY POWER? YOU HAVE TO TAKE IT!
YOU HAVE TO WANT IT!
JUST CHARGE YOUR RING OFF MY LANTERN--THAT'S ALL IT TAKES.
BUT FIRST YOU HAVE TO GET PAST ME!
RAGE
KYLE'S FACILITY WITH OTHER COLORS IS REMARKABLE.
I WONDER, HOWEVER, IF IT WILL BE ENOUGH...

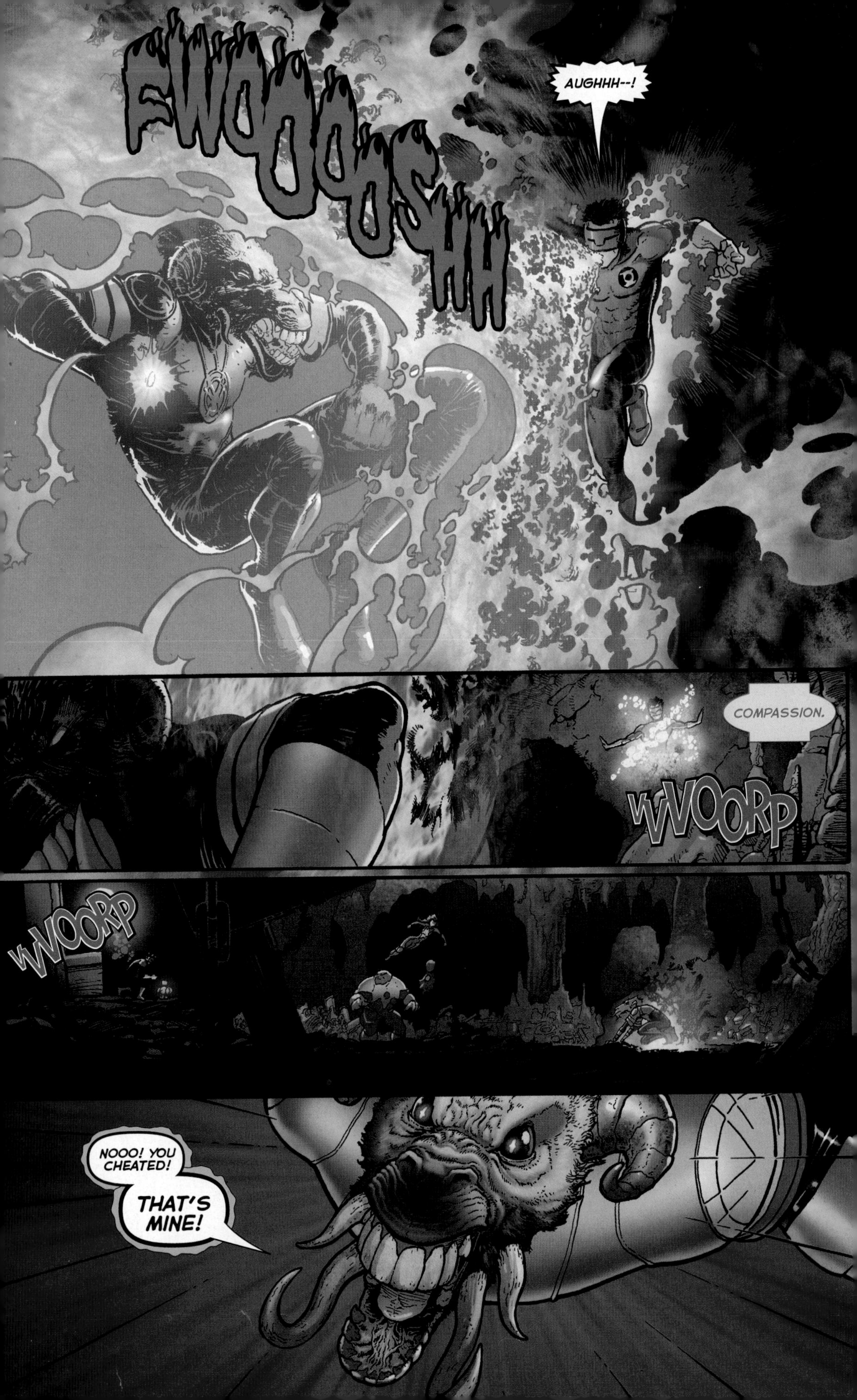
FWOOOOSHH
AUGHHH--!
COMPASSION.
VVVOORP
VVVOORP
NOOO! YOU CHEATED!
THAT'S MINE!

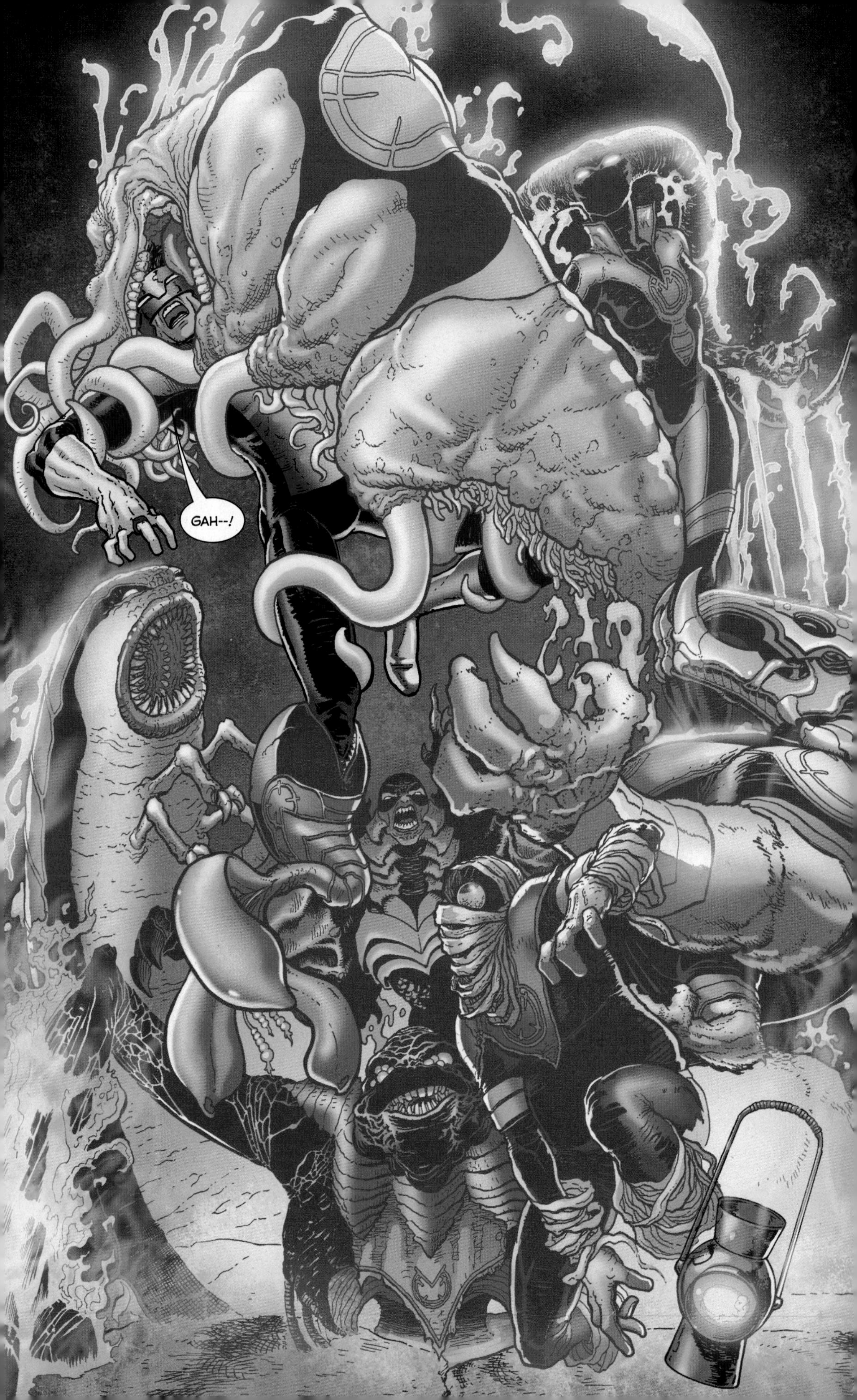
GAH--!

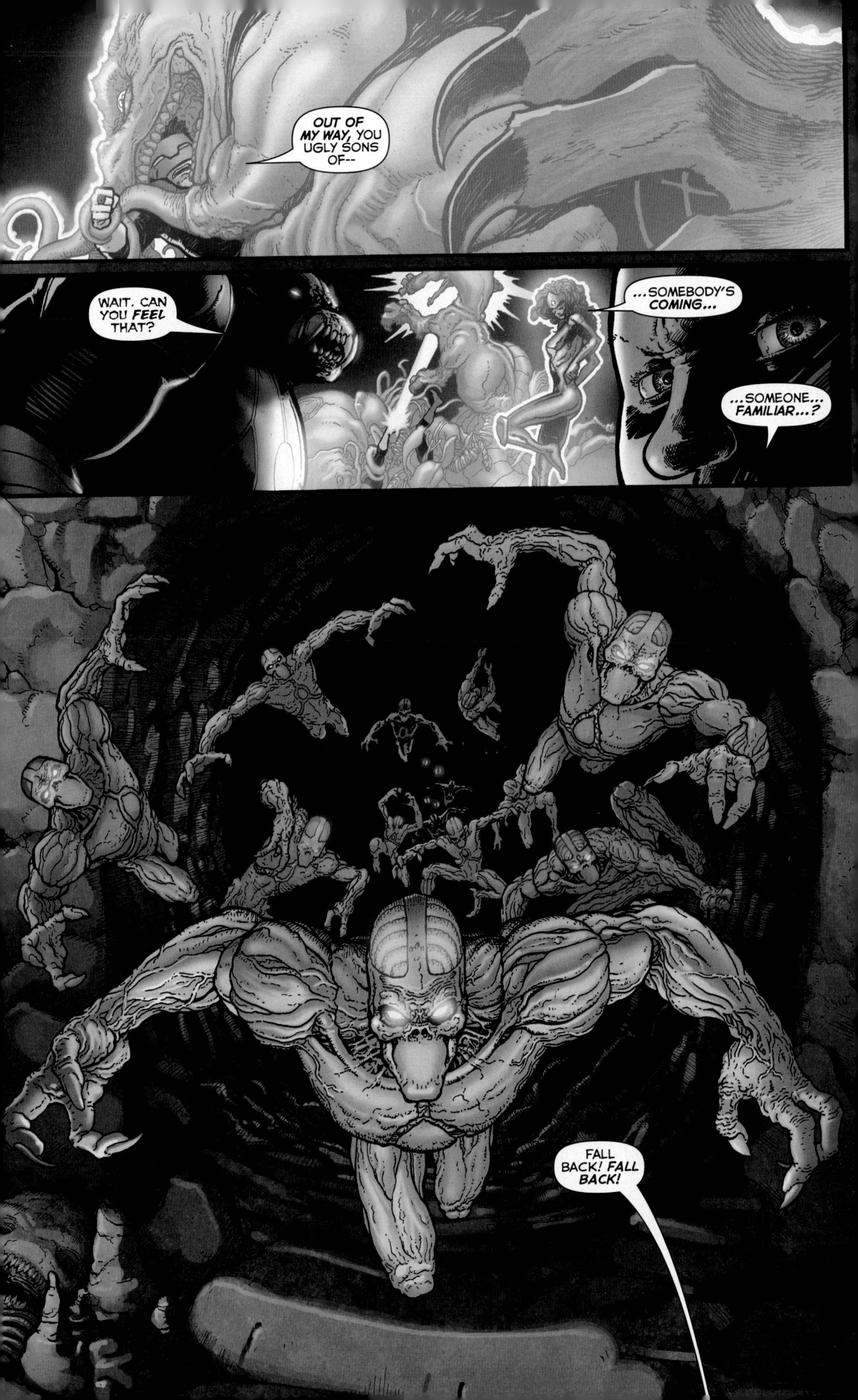
OUT OF MY WAY, YOU UGLY SONS OF--
WAIT. CAN YOU FEEL THAT?
...SOMEBODY'S COMING...
...SOMEONE... FAMILIAR...?
FALL BACK! FALL BACK!

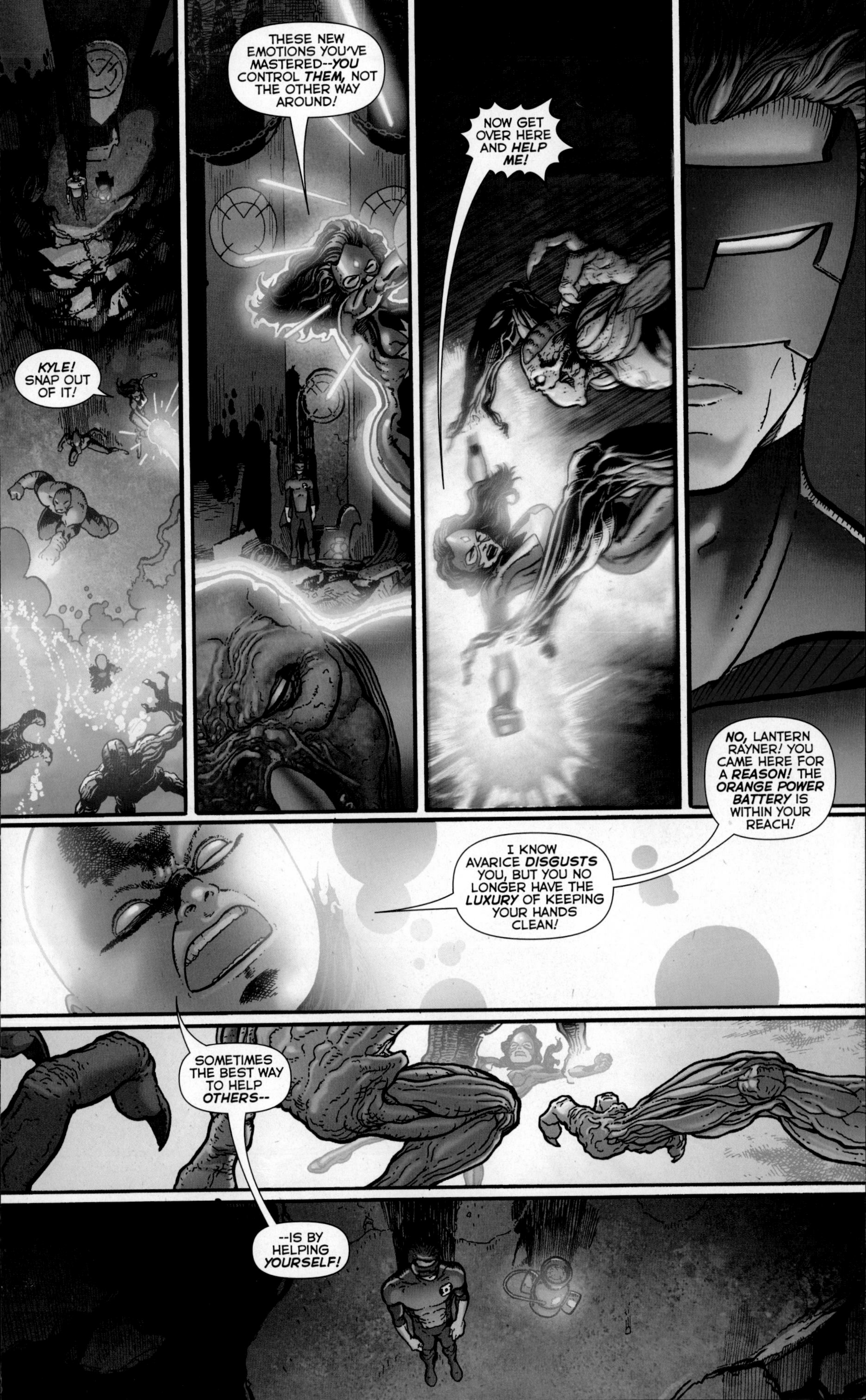
KYLE! SNAP OUT OF IT!
THESE NEW EMOTIONS YOU'VE MASTERED--YOU CONTROL THEM, NOT THE OTHER WAY AROUND!
NOW GET OVER HERE AND HELP ME!
NO, LANTERN RAYNER! YOU CAME HERE FOR A REASON! THE ORANGE POWER BATTERY IS WITHIN YOUR REACH!
I KNOW AVARICE DISGUSTS YOU, BUT YOU NO LONGER HAVE THE LUXURY OF KEEPING YOUR HANDS CLEAN!
SOMETIMES THE BEST WAY TO HELP OTHERS--
--IS BY HELPING YOURSELF!

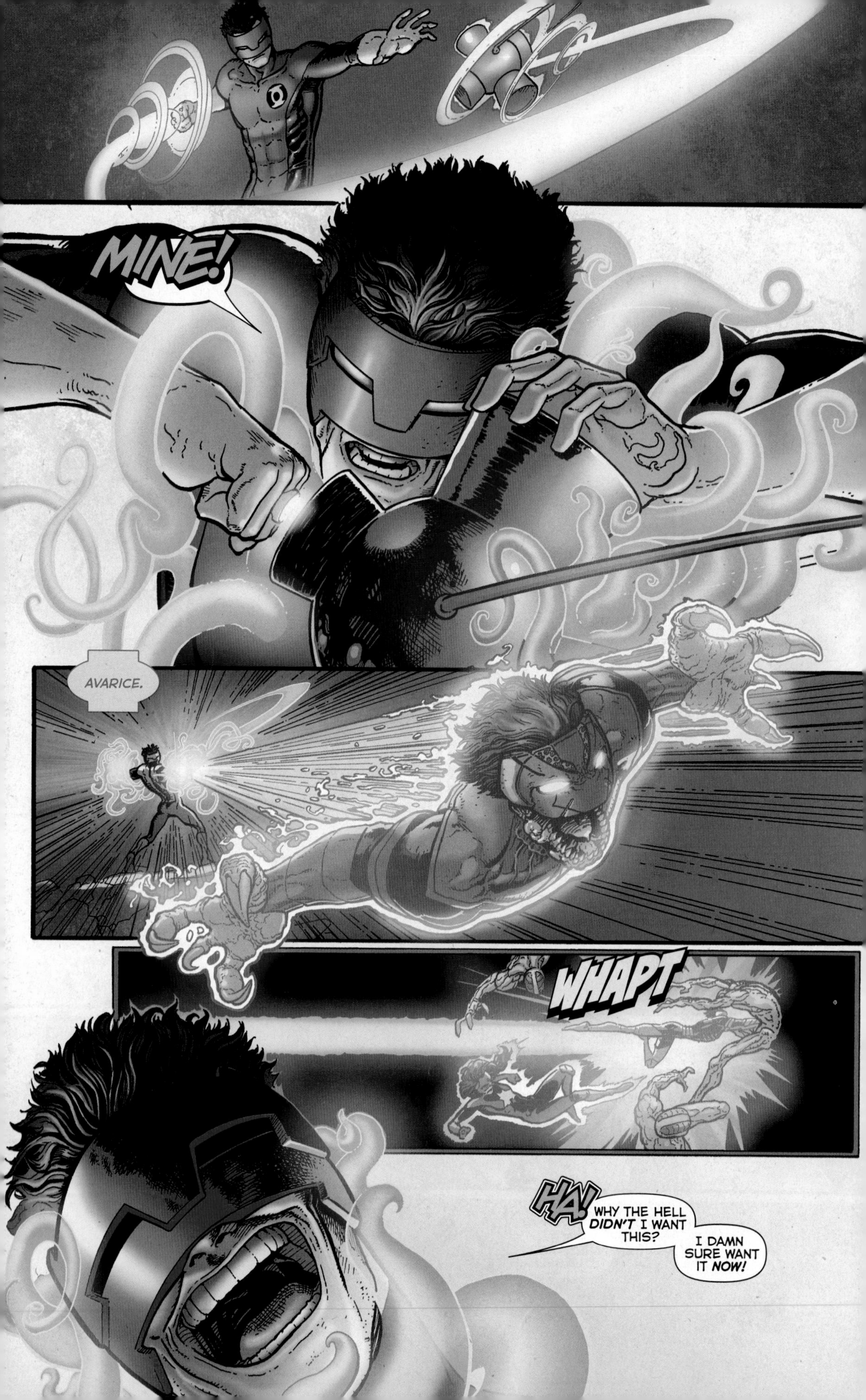
MINE!
AVARICE.
WHAPT
HA!
WHY THE HELL DIDN'T I WANT THIS?
I DAMN SURE WANT IT NOW!

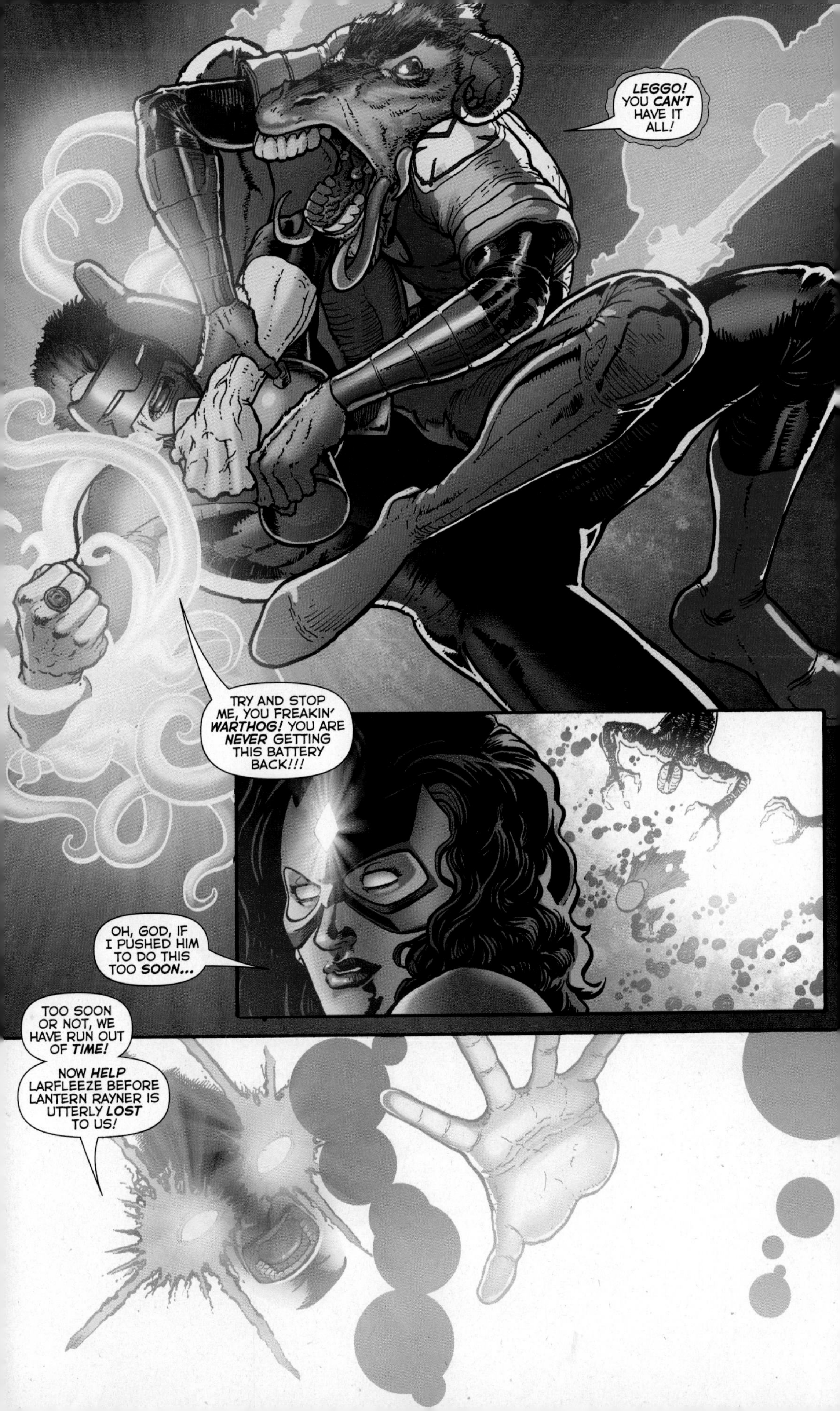
LEGGO! YOU CAN'T HAVE IT ALL!
TRY AND STOP ME, YOU FREAKIN' WARTHOG! YOU ARE NEVER GETTING THIS BATTERY BACK!!!
OH, GOD, IF I PUSHED HIM TO DO THIS TOO SOON...
TOO SOON OR NOT, WE HAVE RUN OUT OF TIME!
NOW HELP LARFLEEZE BEFORE LANTERN RAYNER IS UTTERLY LOST TO US!

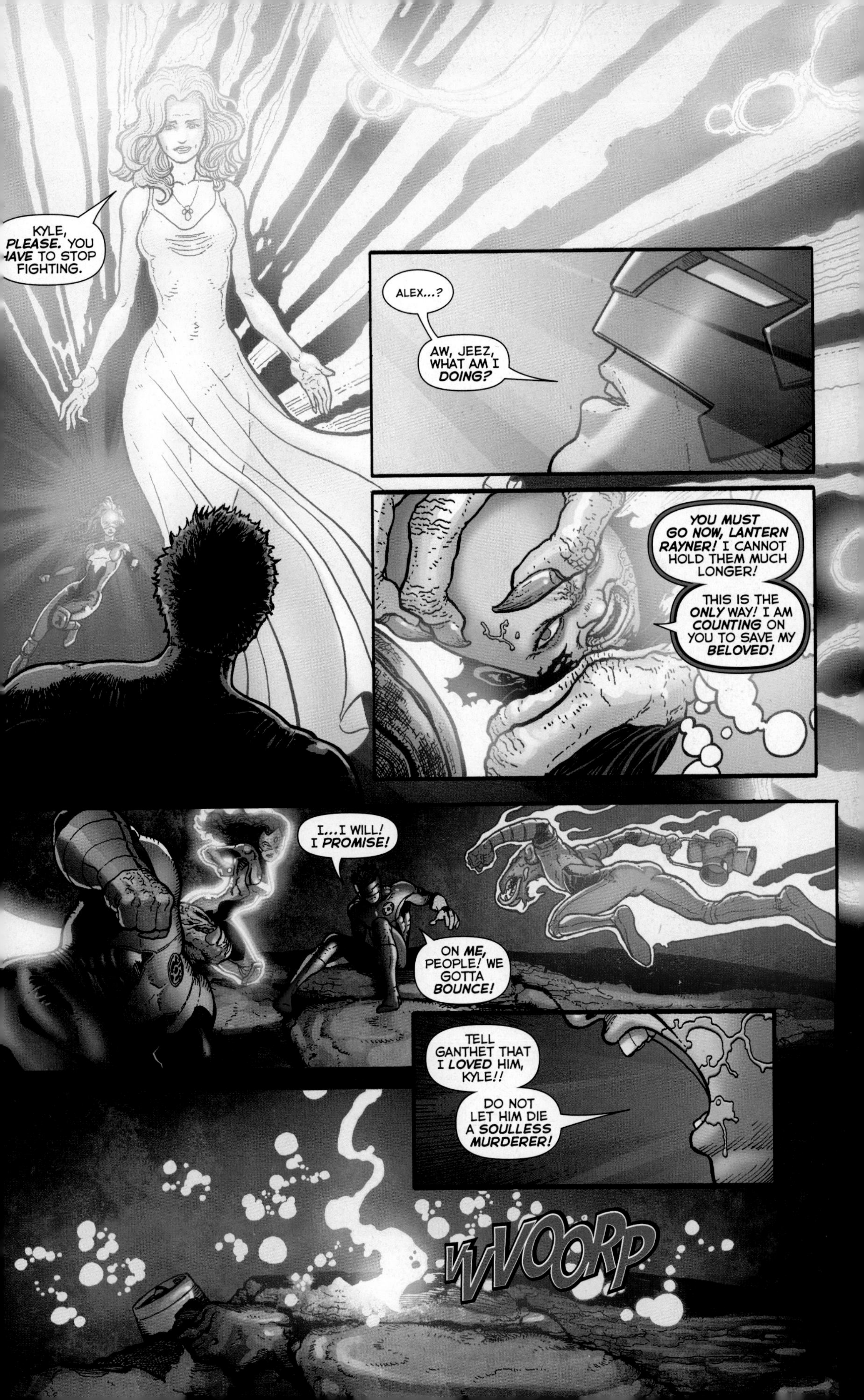
KYLE, PLEASE. YOU HAVE TO STOP FIGHTING.
ALEX...?
AW, JEEZ, WHAT AM I DOING?
YOU MUST GO NOW, LANTERN RAYNER! I CANNOT HOLD THEM MUCH LONGER!
THIS IS THE ONLY WAY! I AM COUNTING ON YOU TO SAVE MY BELOVED!
I...I WILL! I PROMISE!
ON ME, PEOPLE! WE GOTTA BOUNCE!
TELL GANTHET THAT I LOVED HIM, KYLE!!
DO NOT LET HIM DIE A SOULLESS MURDERER!
VVVOORP

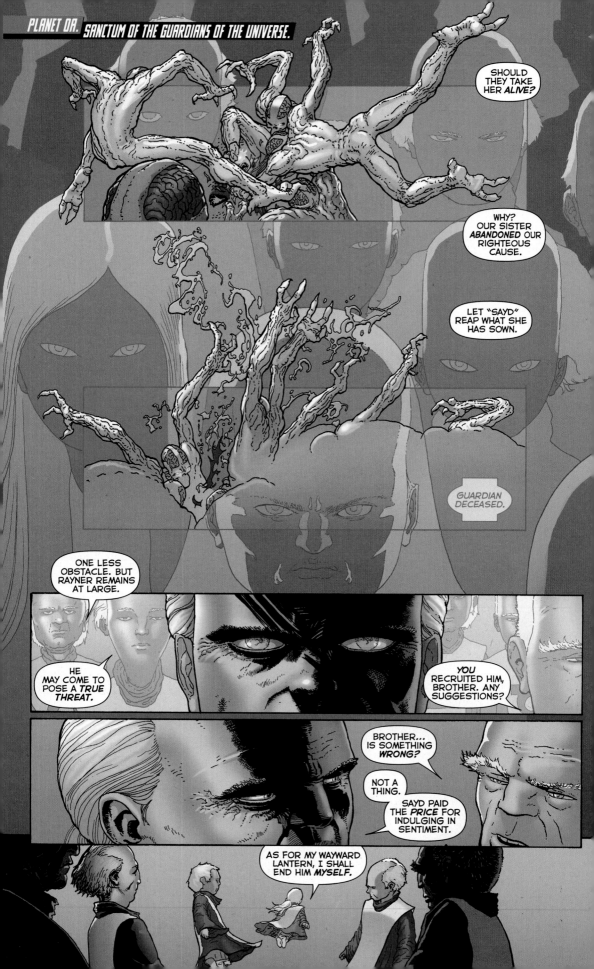

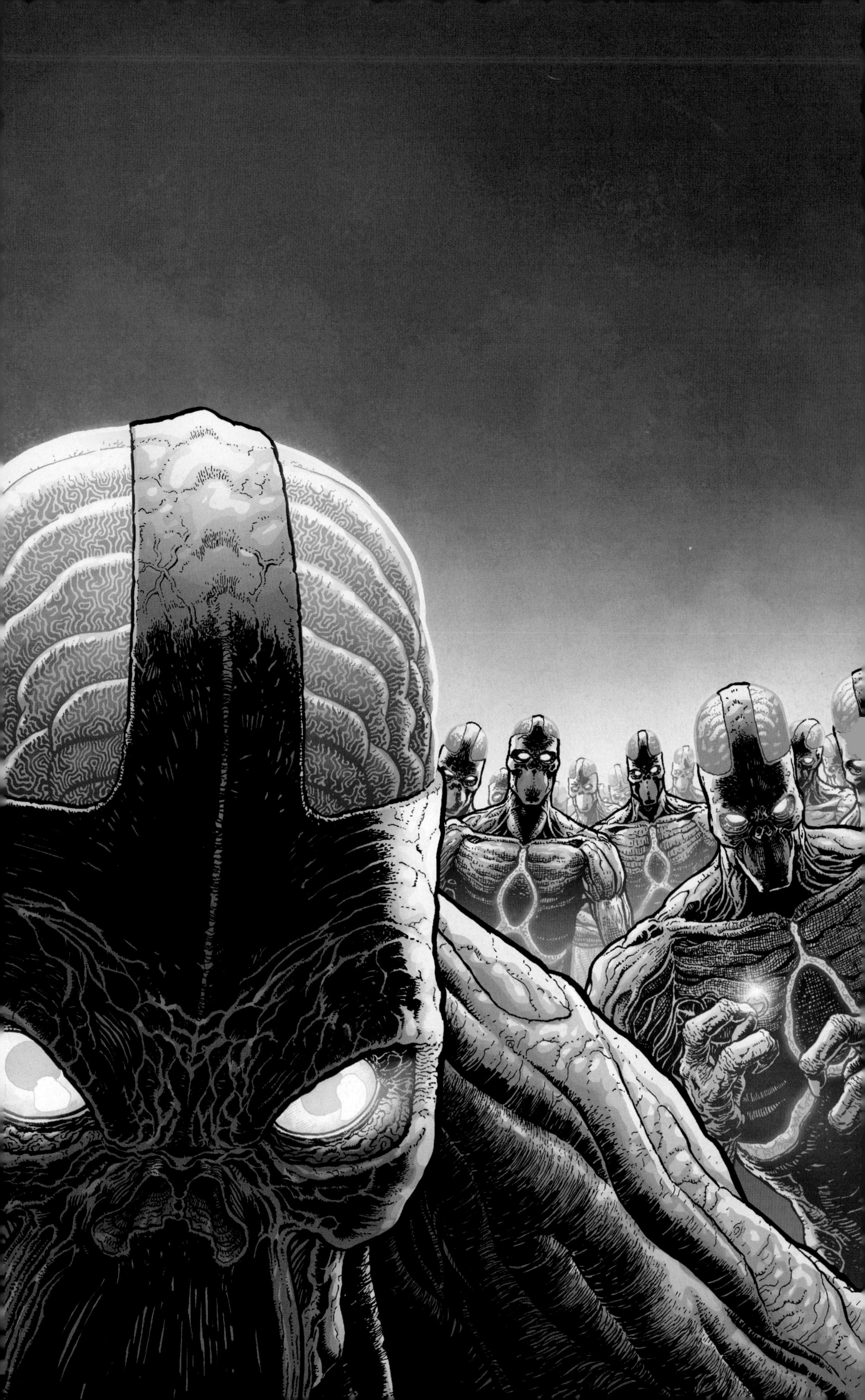

LET LOVE RULE

TONY BEDARD writer AARON KUDER artist

AARON KUDER & HI-FI cover

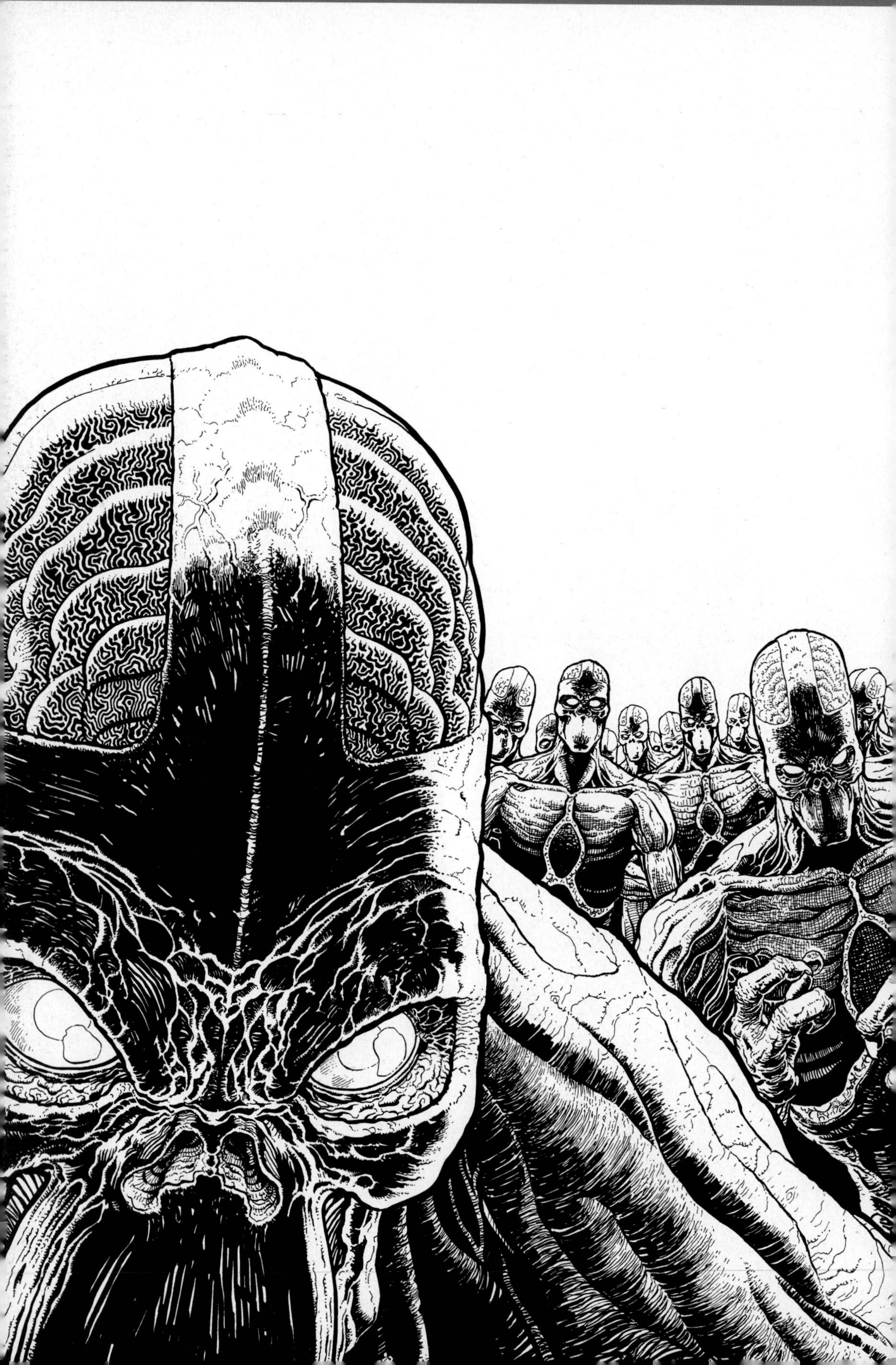

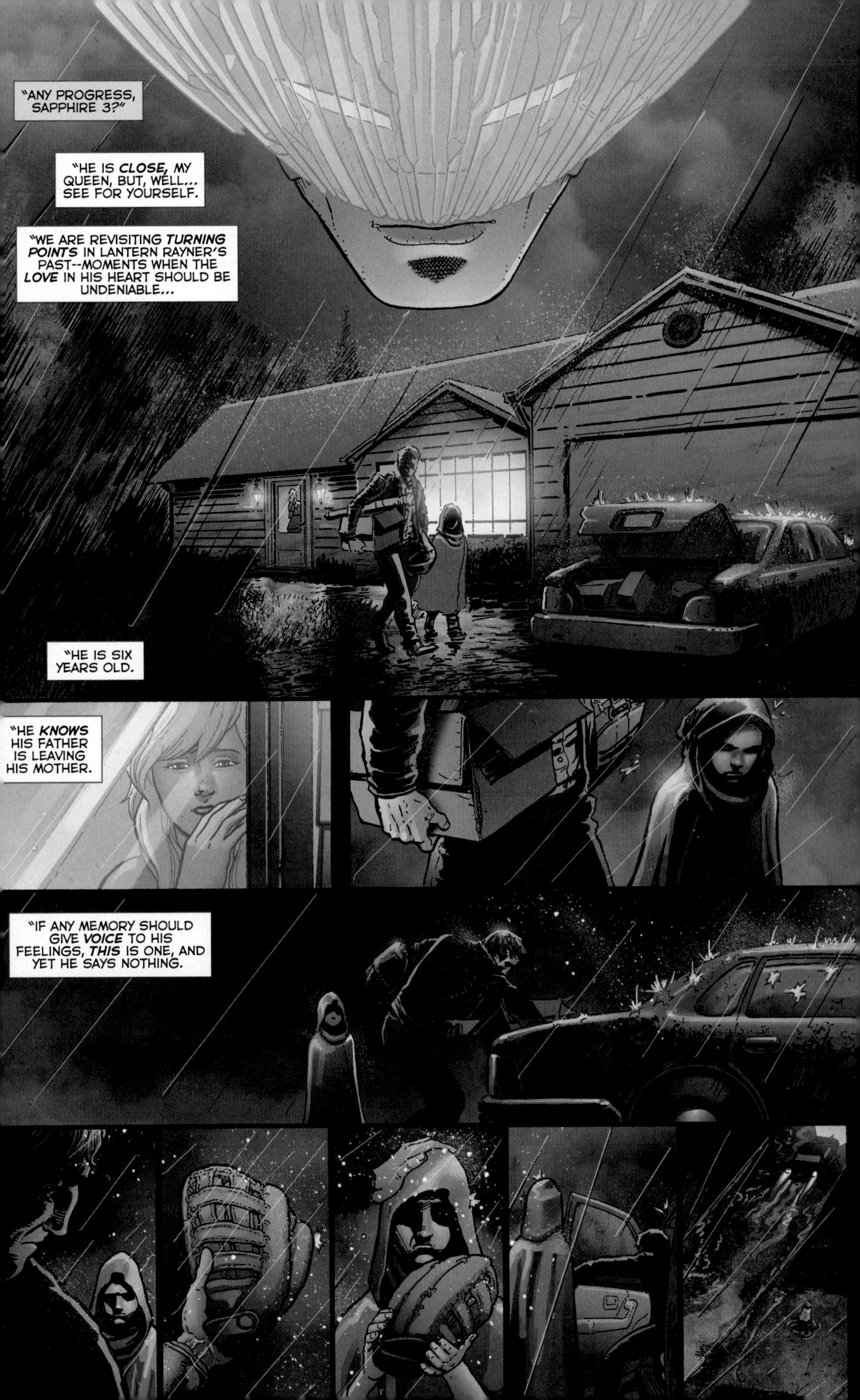
"ANY PROGRESS, SAPPHIRE 3?"
"HE IS CLOSE, MY QUEEN, BUT, WELL... SEE FOR YOURSELF.
"WE ARE REVISITING TURNING POINTS IN LANTERN RAYNER'S PAST--MOMENTS WHEN THE LOVE IN HIS HEART SHOULD BE UNDENIABLE...
"HE IS SIX YEARS OLD.
"HE KNOWS HIS FATHER IS LEAVING HIS MOTHER.
"IF ANY MEMORY SHOULD GIVE VOICE TO HIS FEELINGS, THIS IS ONE, AND YET HE SAYS NOTHING.

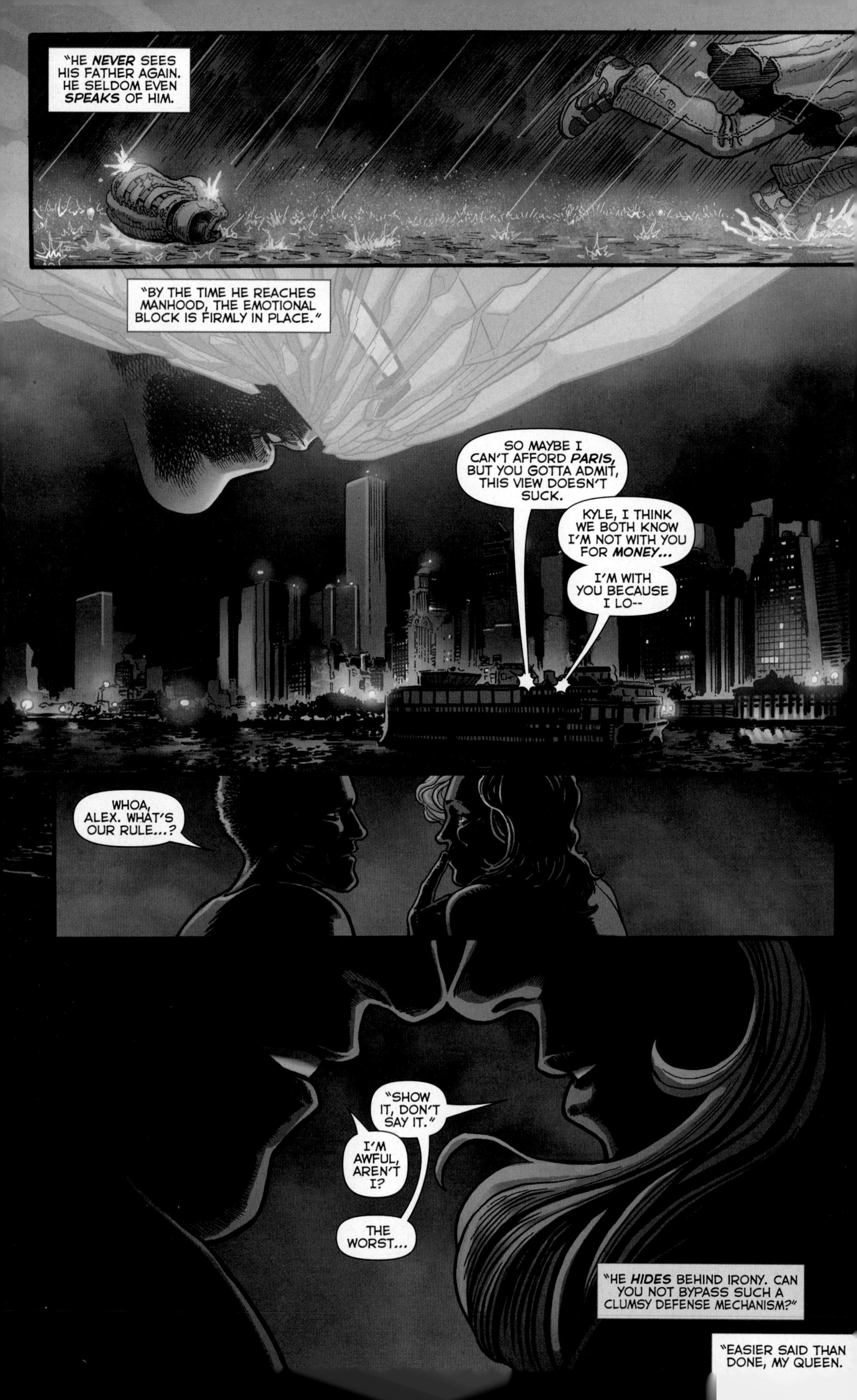
"HE NEVER SEES HIS FATHER AGAIN. HE SELDOM EVEN SPEAKS OF HIM.
"BY THE TIME HE REACHES MANHOOD, THE EMOTIONAL BLOCK IS FIRMLY IN PLACE."
SO MAYBE I CAN'T AFFORD PARIS, BUT YOU GOTTA ADMIT, THIS VIEW DOESN'T SUCK.
KYLE, I THINK WE BOTH KNOW I'M NOT WITH YOU FOR MONEY...
I'M WITH YOU BECAUSE I LO--
WHOA, ALEX. WHAT'S OUR RULE...?
"SHOW IT, DON'T SAY IT."
I'M AWFUL, AREN'T I?
THE WORST...
"HE HIDES BEHIND IRONY. CAN YOU NOT BYPASS SUCH A CLUMSY DEFENSE MECHANISM?"
"EASIER SAID THAN DONE, MY QUEEN.

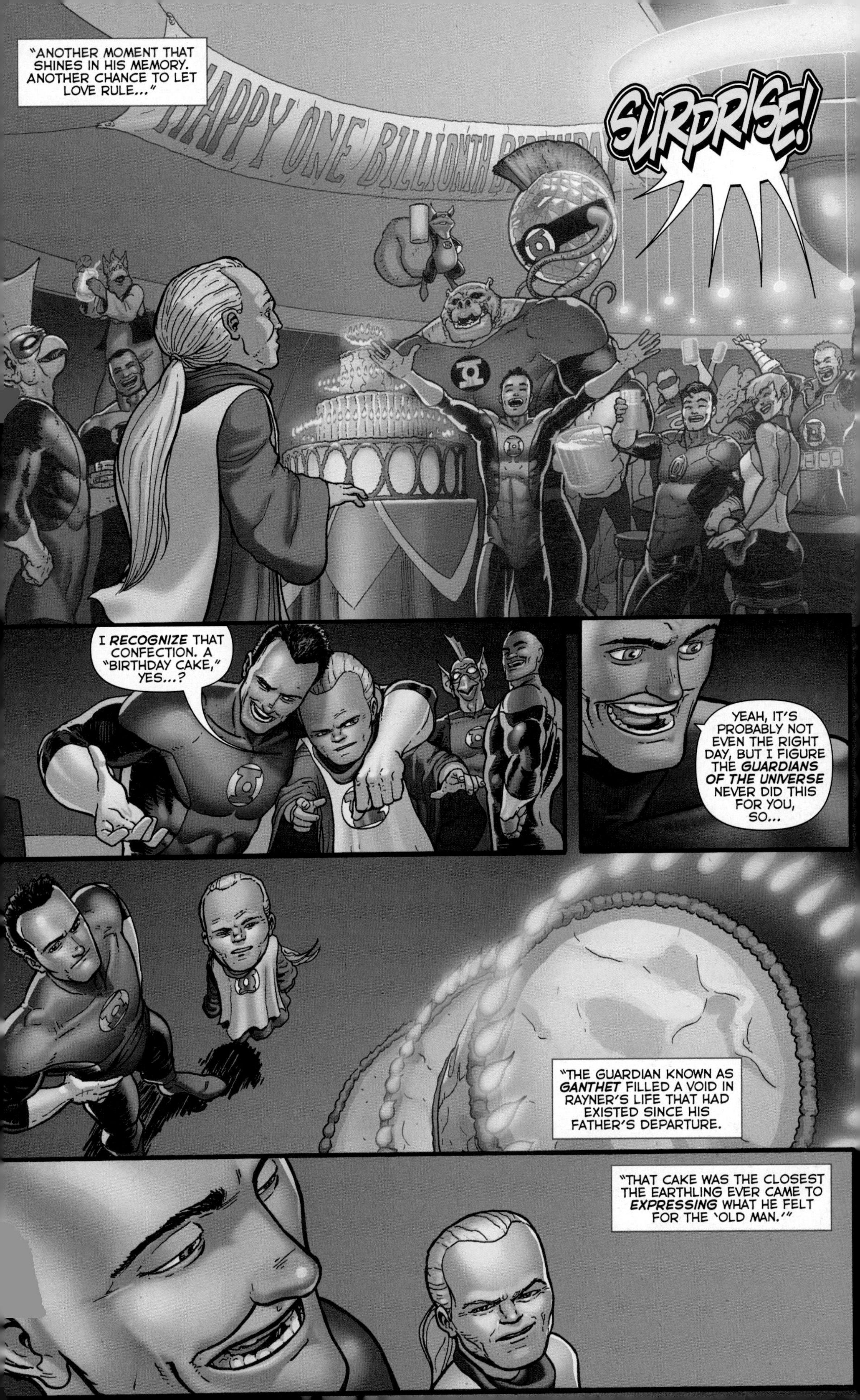
"ANOTHER MOMENT THAT SHINES IN HIS MEMORY. ANOTHER CHANCE TO LET LOVE RULE..."
HAPPY ONE BILLIONTH B
SURPRISE!
I RECOGNIZE THAT CONFECTION. A "BIRTHDAY CAKE," YES...?
YEAH, IT'S PROBABLY NOT EVEN THE RIGHT DAY, BUT I FIGURE THE GUARDIANS OF THE UNIVERSE NEVER DID THIS FOR YOU, SO...
"THE GUARDIAN KNOWN AS GANTHET FILLED A VOID IN RAYNER'S LIFE THAT HAD EXISTED SINCE HIS FATHER'S DEPARTURE.
"THAT CAKE WAS THE CLOSEST THE EARTHLING EVER CAME TO EXPRESSING WHAT HE FELT FOR THE 'OLD MAN.'"

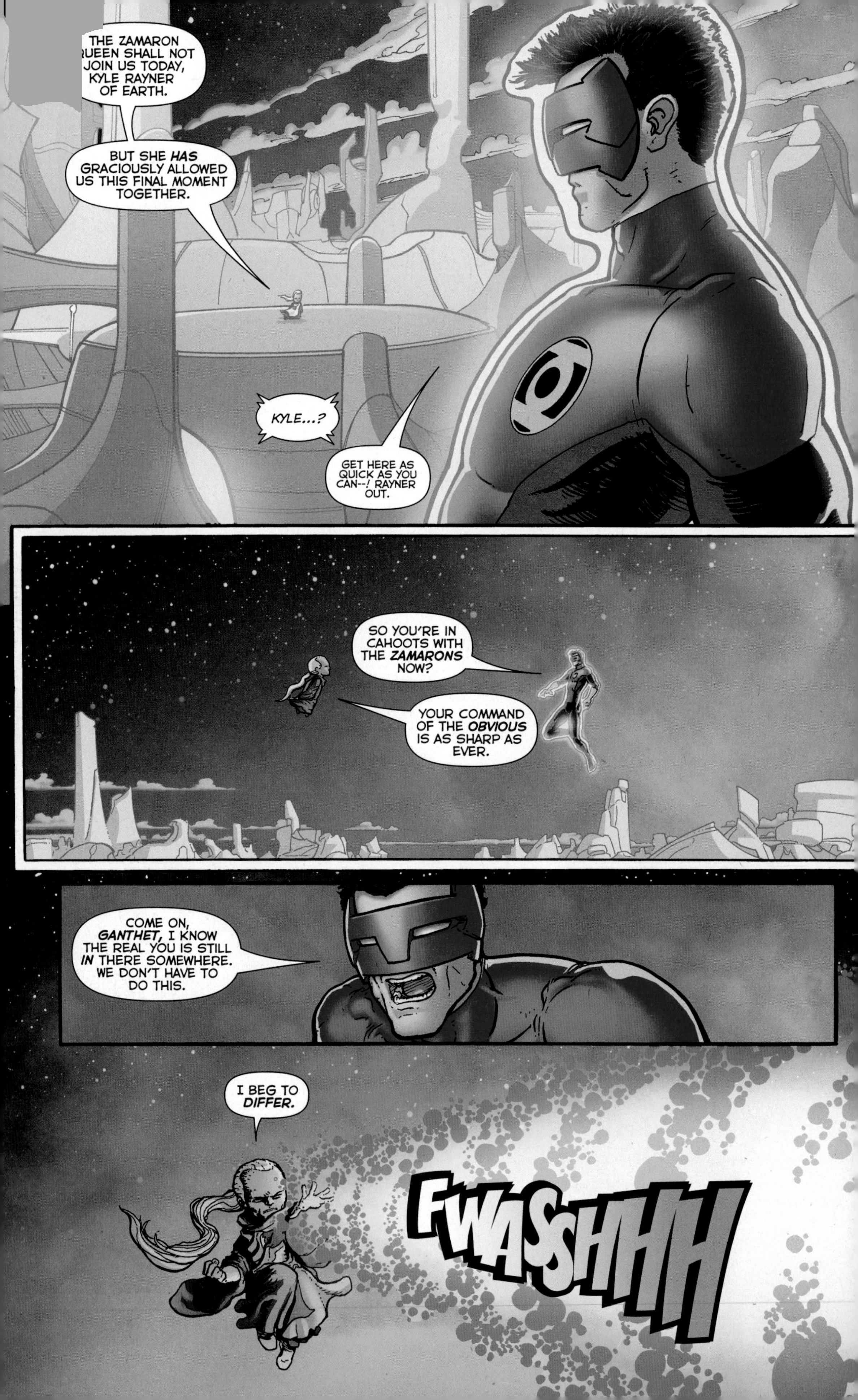
THE ZAMARON QUEEN SHALL NOT JOIN US TODAY, KYLE RAYNER OF EARTH.
BUT SHE *HAS* GRACIOUSLY ALLOWED US THIS FINAL MOMENT TOGETHER.
KYLE...?
GET HERE AS QUICK AS YOU CAN--! RAYNER OUT.
SO YOU'RE IN CAHOOTS WITH THE *ZAMARONS* NOW?
YOUR COMMAND OF THE *OBVIOUS* IS AS SHARP AS EVER.
COME ON, *GANTHET*, I KNOW THE REAL YOU IS STILL *IN* THERE SOMEWHERE. WE DON'T HAVE TO DO THIS.
I BEG TO *DIFFER.*
FWASHHH

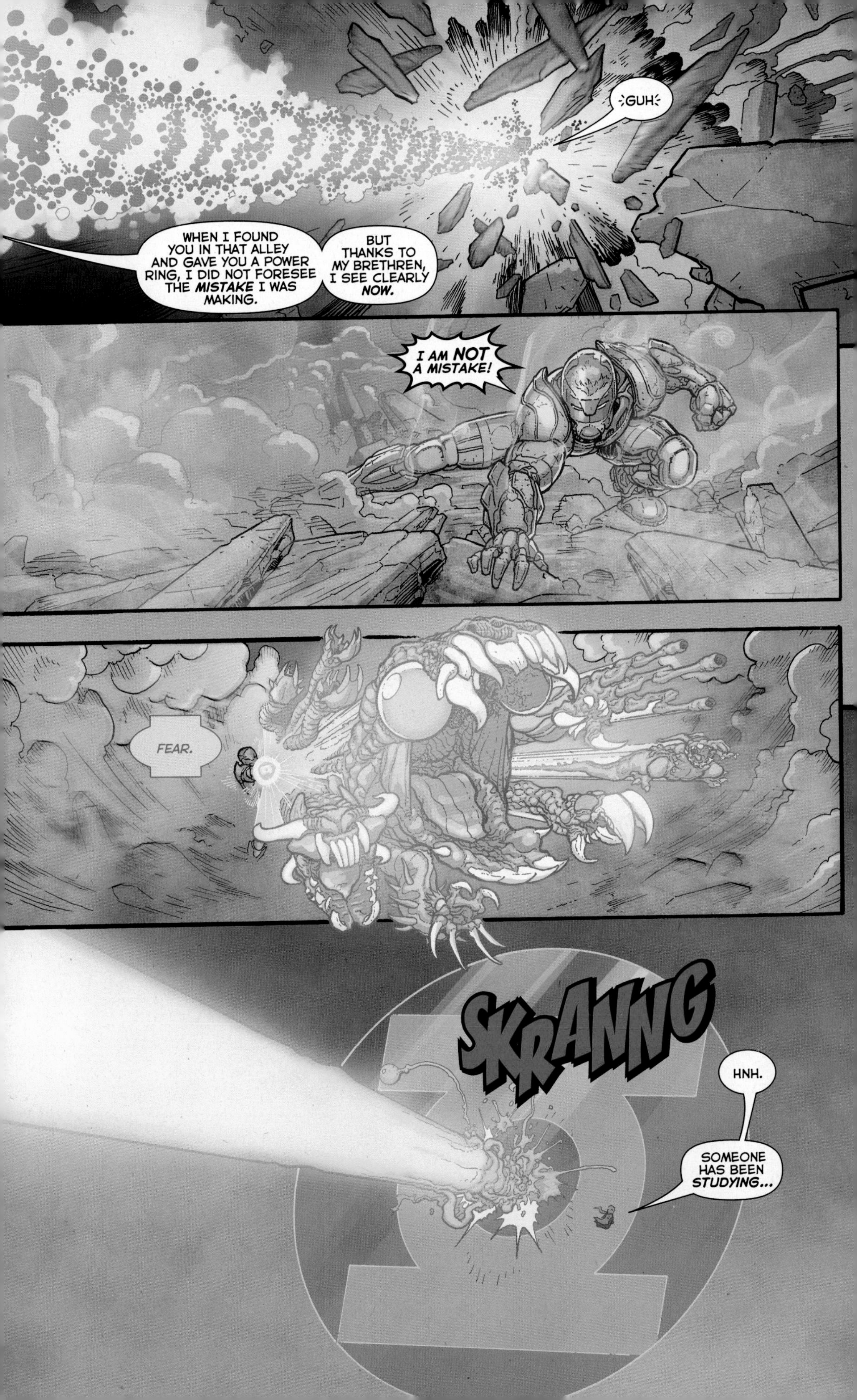
GUH
WHEN I FOUND YOU IN THAT ALLEY AND GAVE YOU A POWER RING, I DID NOT FORESEE THE *MISTAKE* I WAS MAKING.
BUT THANKS TO MY BRETHREN, I SEE CLEARLY *NOW.*
I AM **NOT** A MISTAKE!
FEAR.
SKRANNG
HNH.
SOMEONE HAS BEEN *STUDYING...*

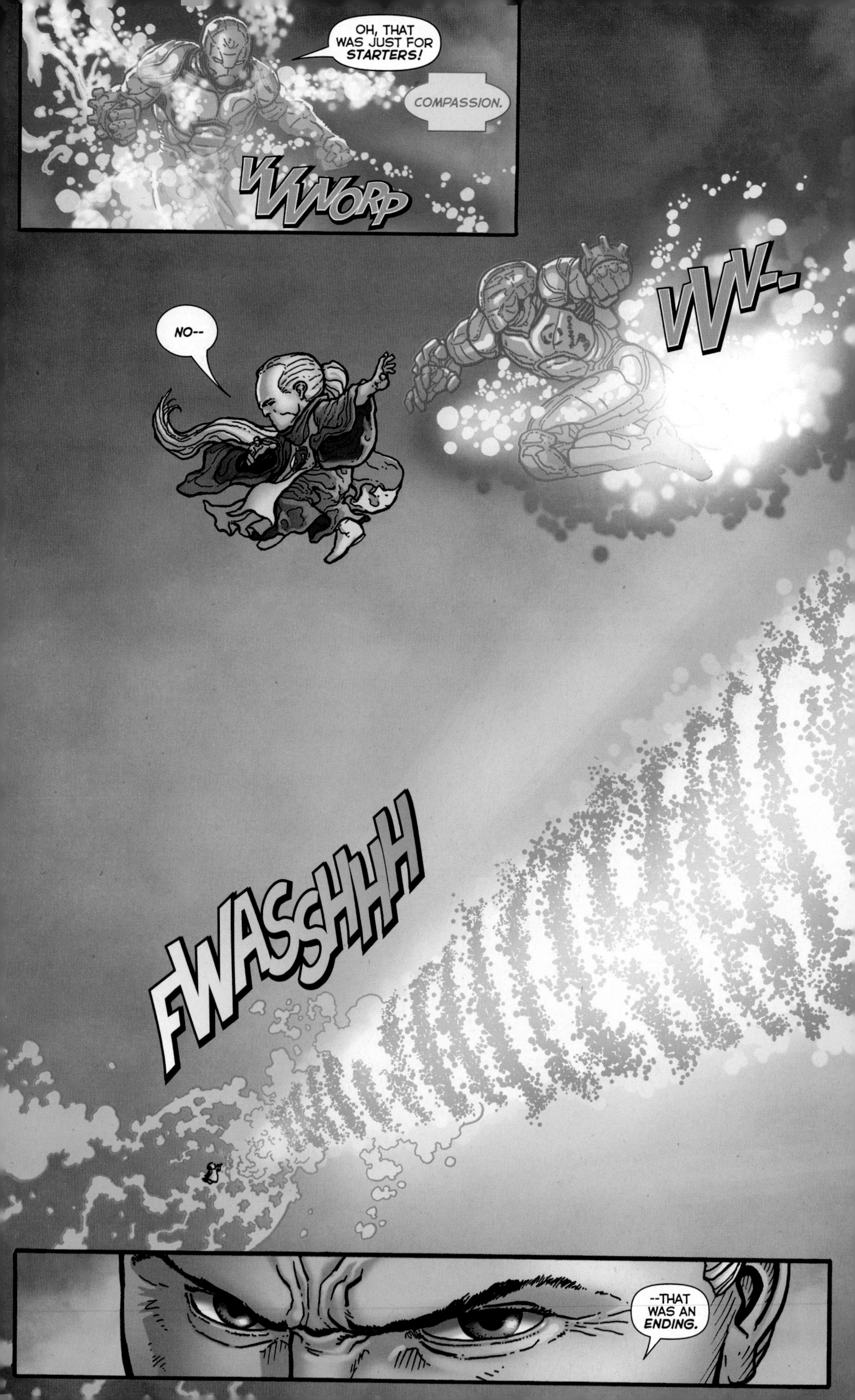
OH, THAT WAS JUST FOR STARTERS!
COMPASSION.
VVVWORP
NO--
VVV--
FWASSHHH
--THAT WAS AN ENDING.

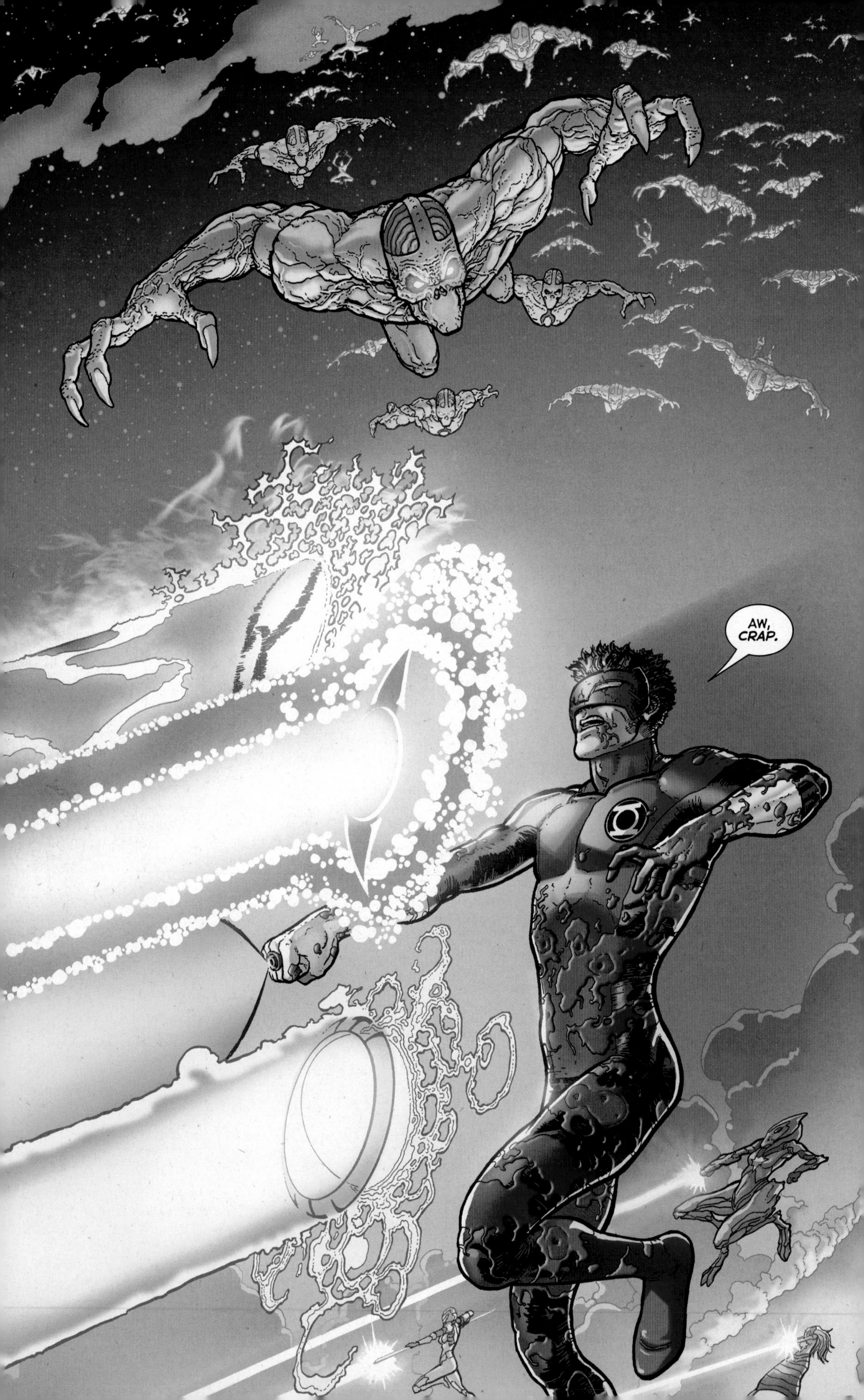
AW, CRAP.

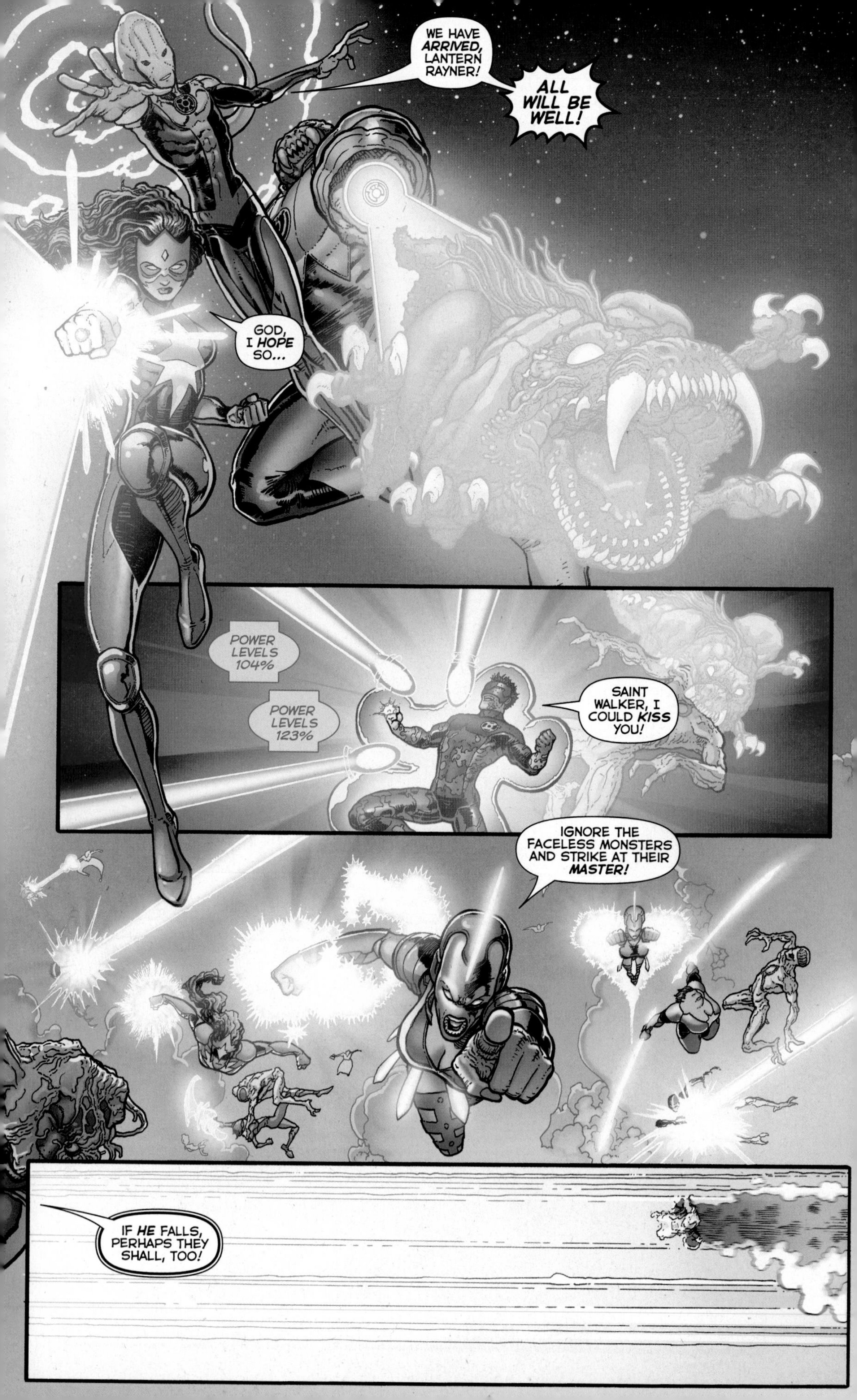
WE HAVE ARRIVED, LANTERN RAYNER!
ALL WILL BE WELL!
GOD, I HOPE SO...
POWER LEVELS 104%
POWER LEVELS 123%
SAINT WALKER, I COULD KISS YOU!
IGNORE THE FACELESS MONSTERS AND STRIKE AT THEIR MASTER!
IF HE FALLS, PERHAPS THEY SHALL, TOO!

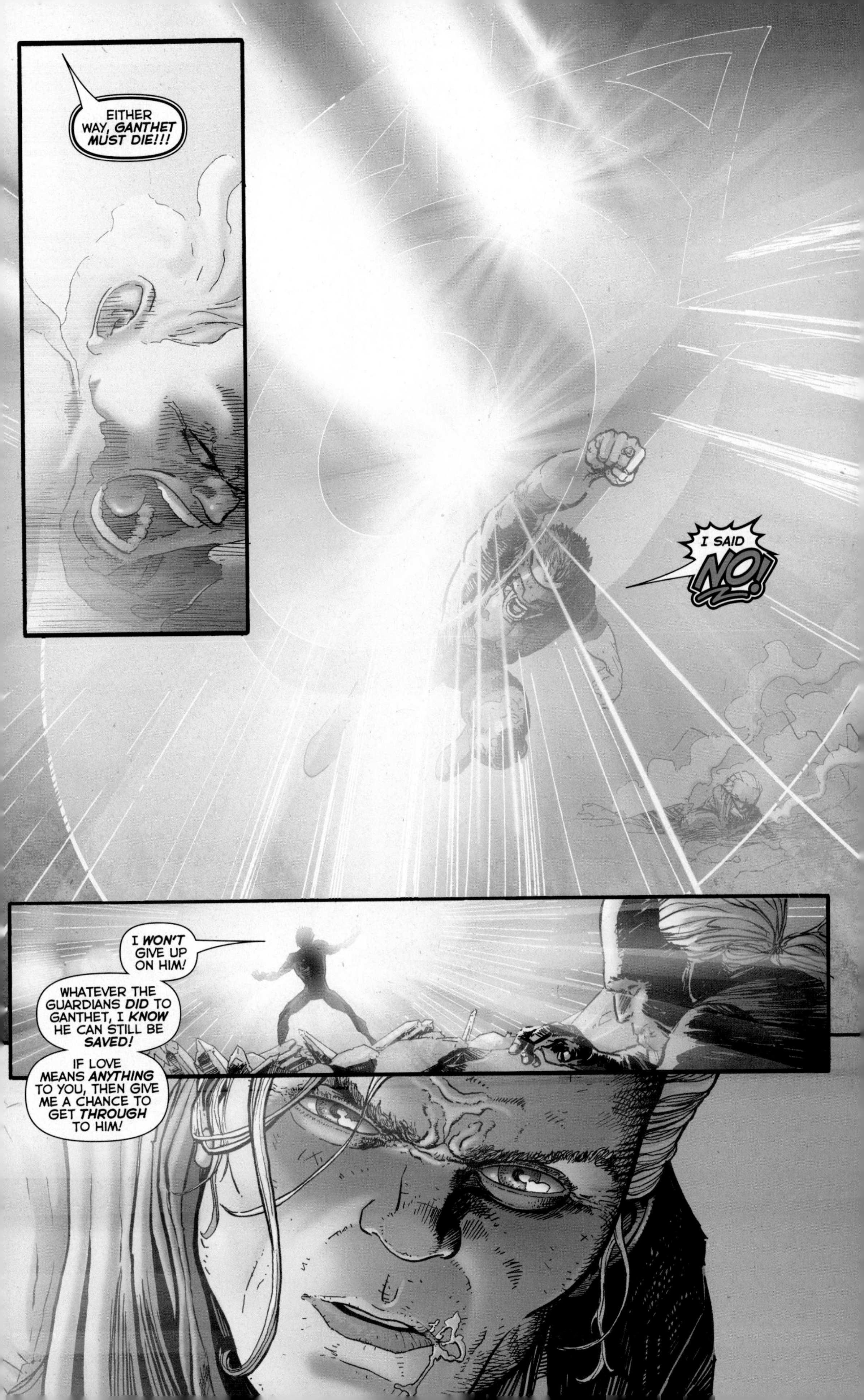
EITHER WAY, GANTHET MUST DIE!!!
I SAID NO!
I WON'T GIVE UP ON HIM!
WHATEVER THE GUARDIANS DID TO GANTHET, I KNOW HE CAN STILL BE SAVED!
IF LOVE MEANS ANYTHING TO YOU, THEN GIVE ME A CHANCE TO GET THROUGH TO HIM!

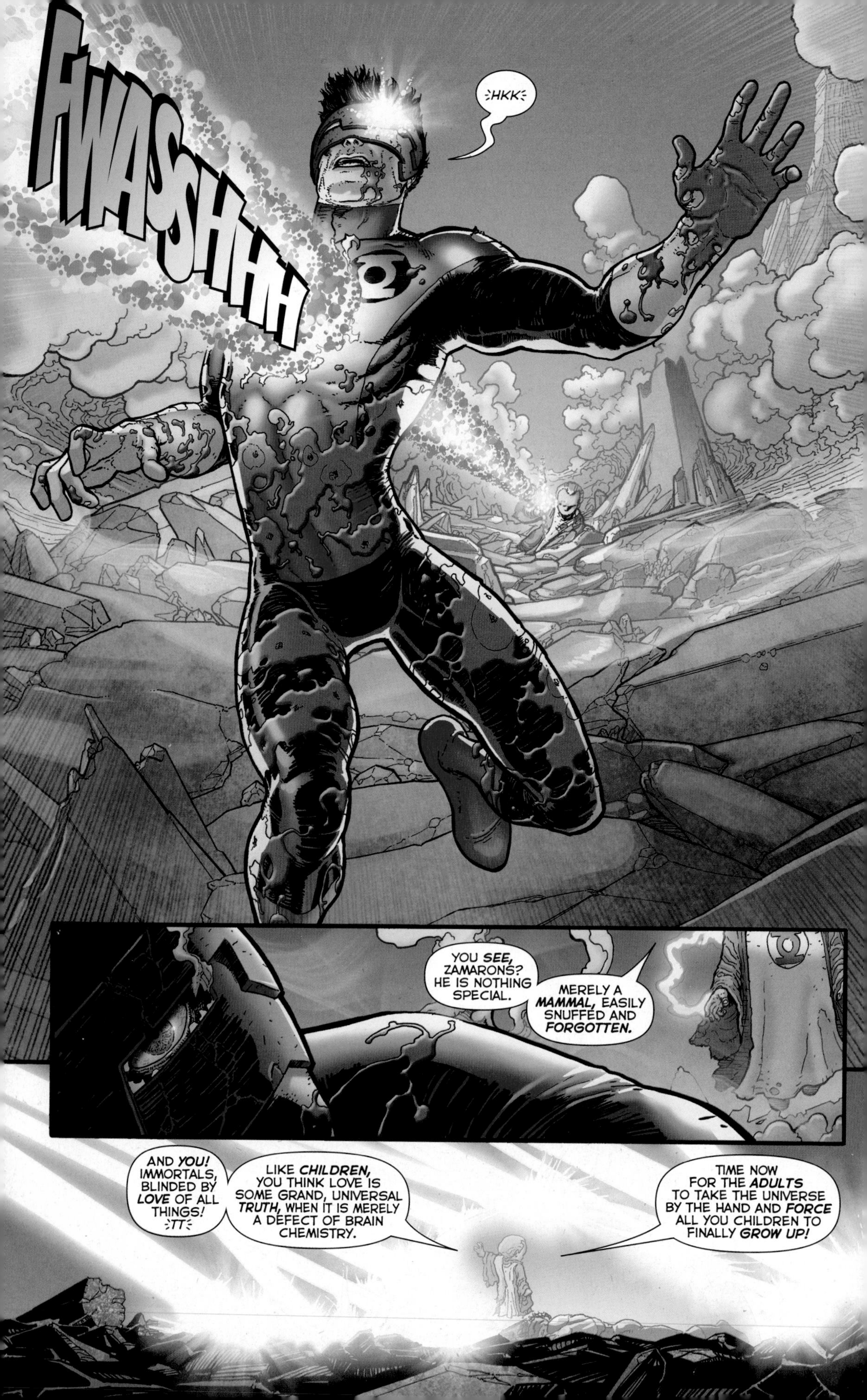
FWASHHH
HKK
YOU SEE, ZAMARONS? HE IS NOTHING SPECIAL.
MERELY A MAMMAL, EASILY SNUFFED AND FORGOTTEN.
AND YOU! IMMORTALS, BLINDED BY LOVE OF ALL THINGS! TT
LIKE CHILDREN, YOU THINK LOVE IS SOME GRAND, UNIVERSAL TRUTH, WHEN IT IS MERELY A DEFECT OF BRAIN CHEMISTRY.
TIME NOW FOR THE ADULTS TO TAKE THE UNIVERSE BY THE HAND AND FORCE ALL YOU CHILDREN TO FINALLY GROW UP!

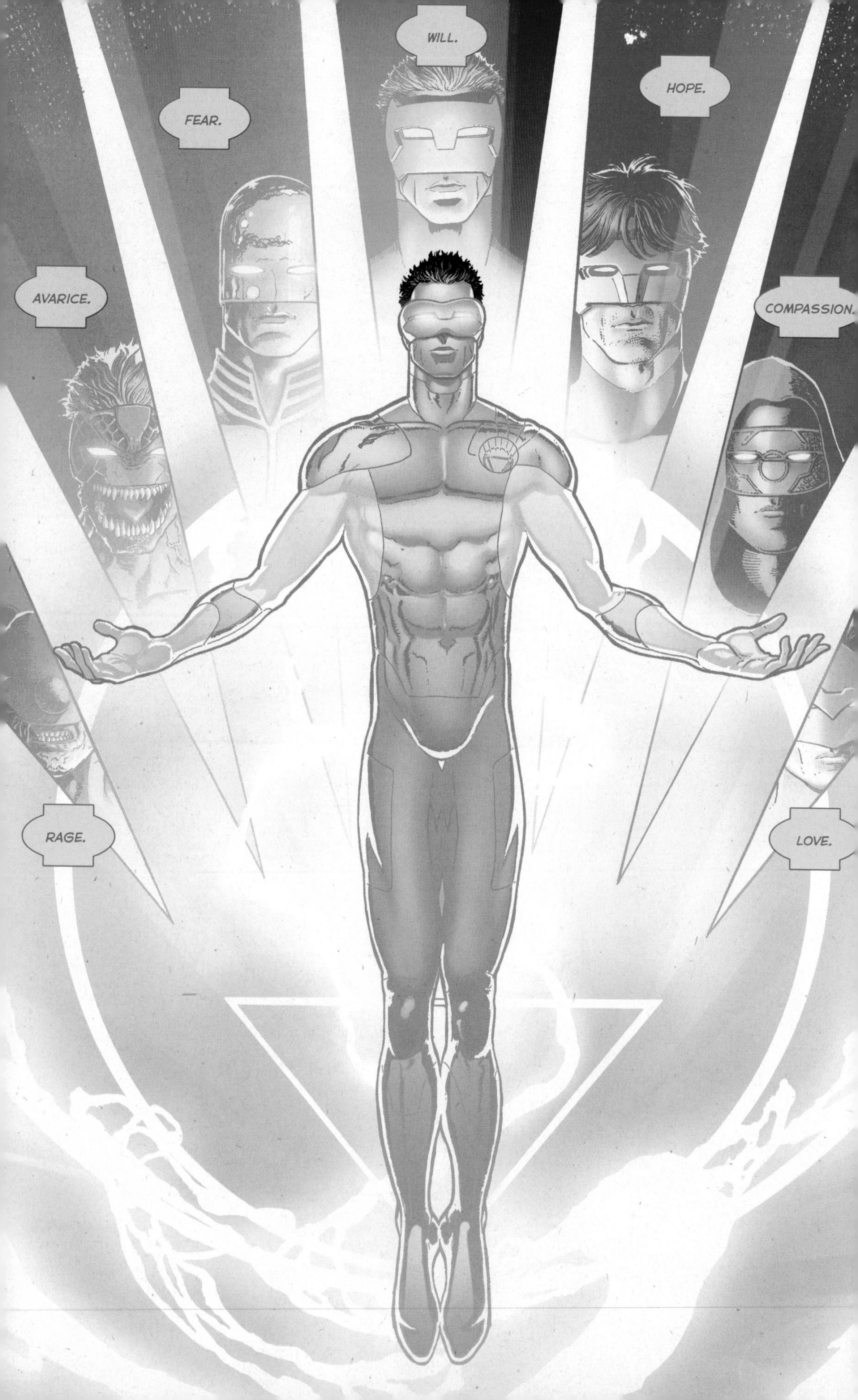
WILL.
FEAR.
HOPE.
AVARICE.
COMPASSION.
RAGE.
LOVE.

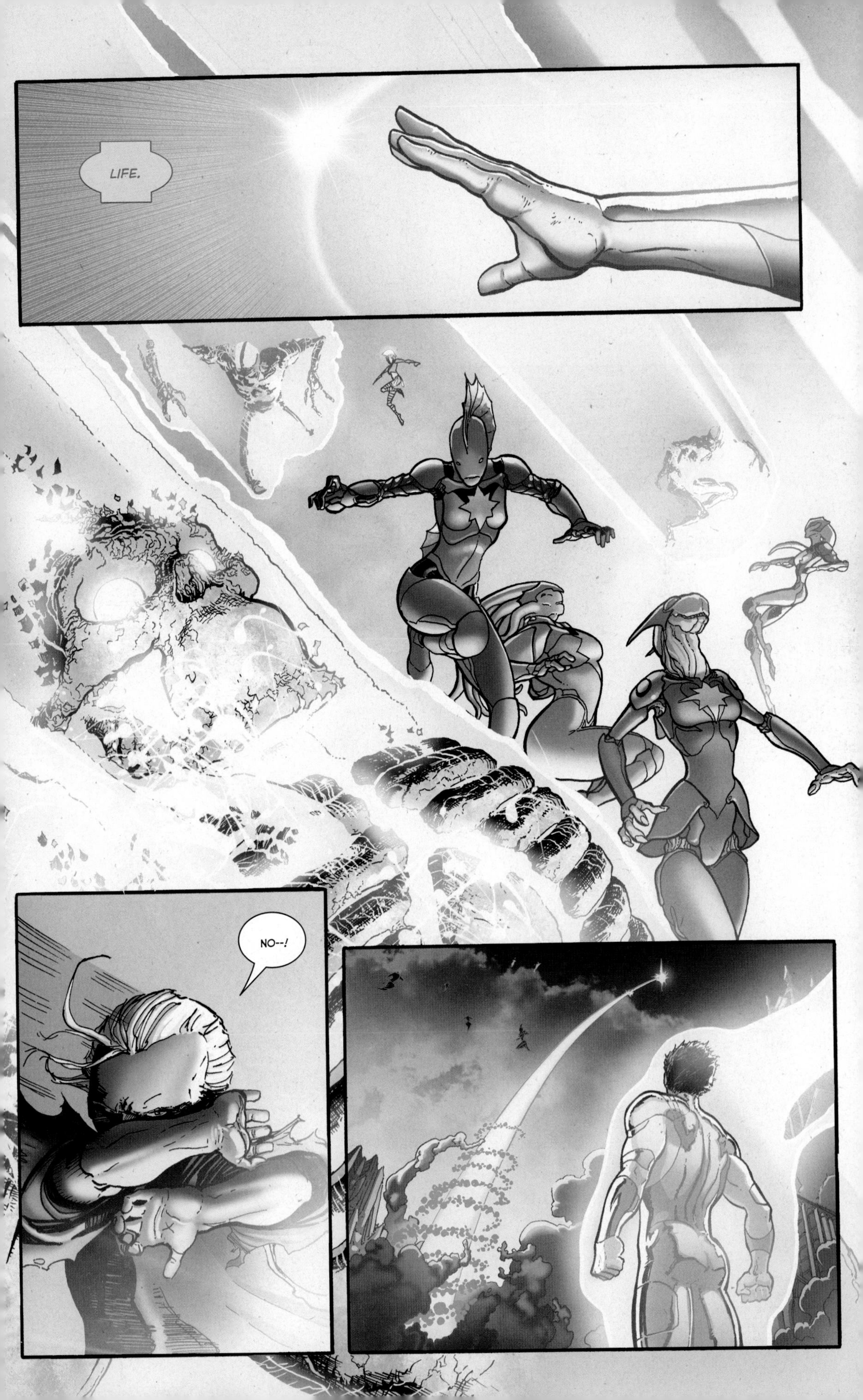
LIFE.
NO--!

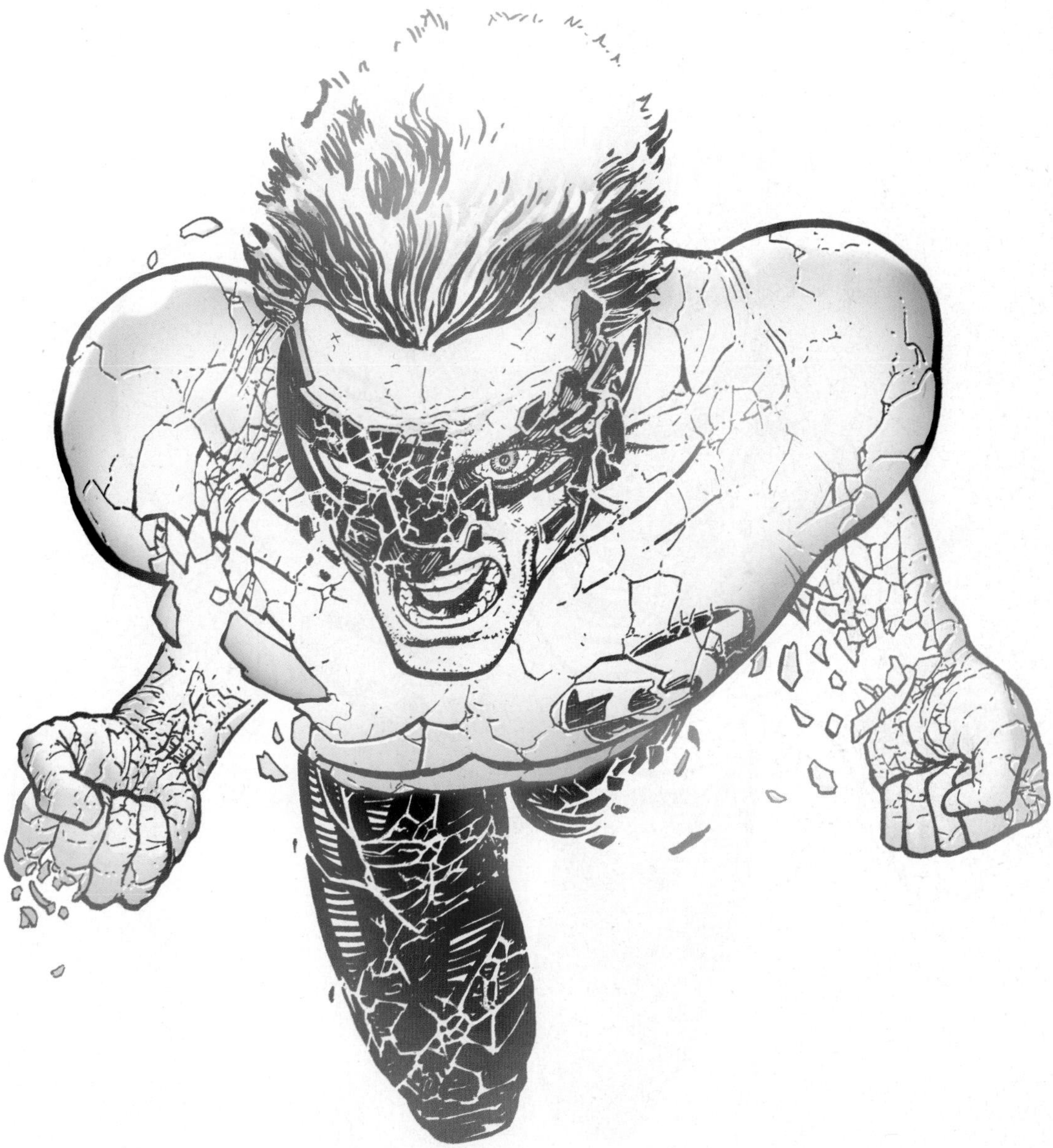

2 REUNIONS AND A FUNERAL

TONY BEDARD writer AARON KUDER artist
AARON KUDER & WIL QUINTANA cover

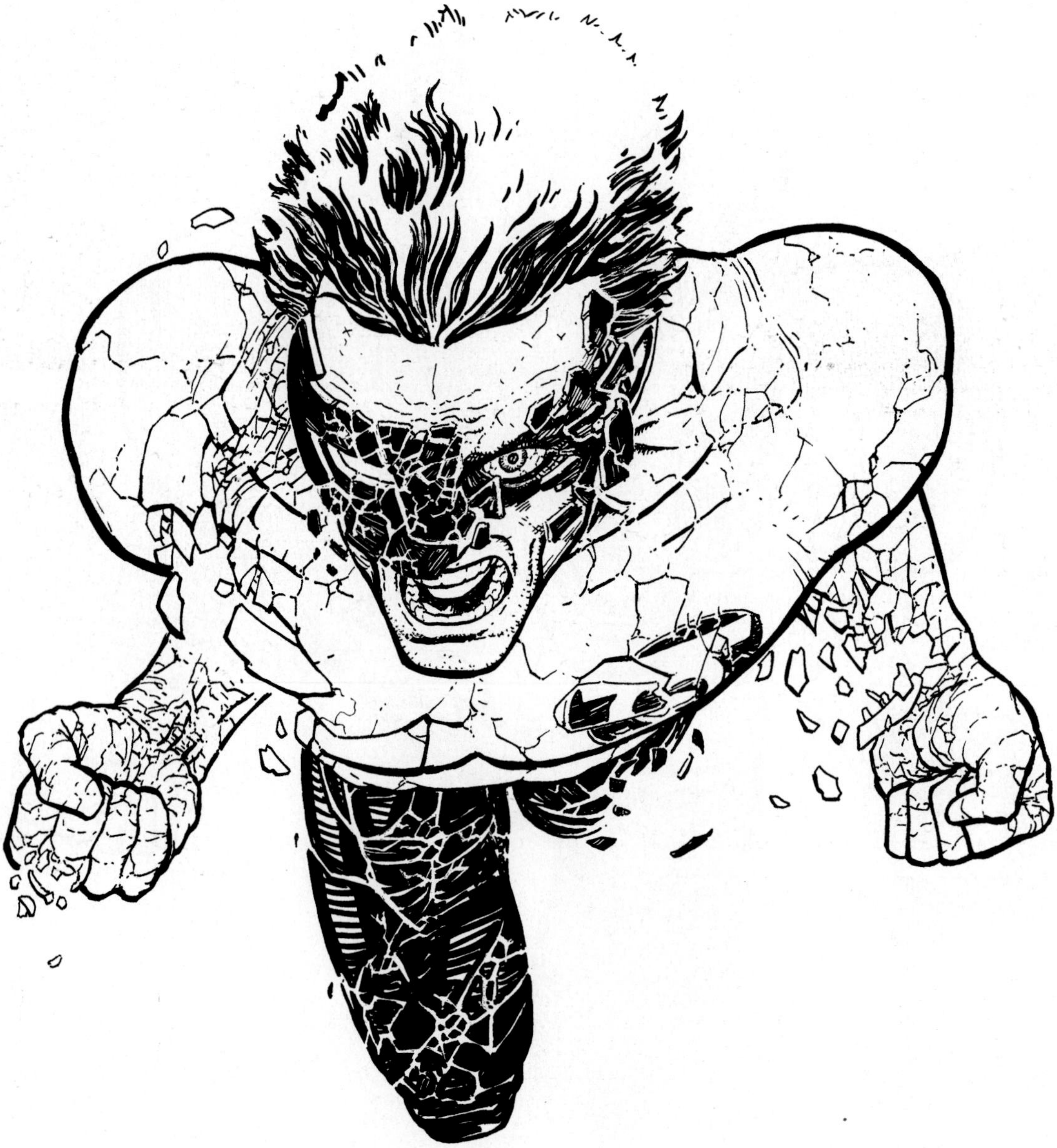

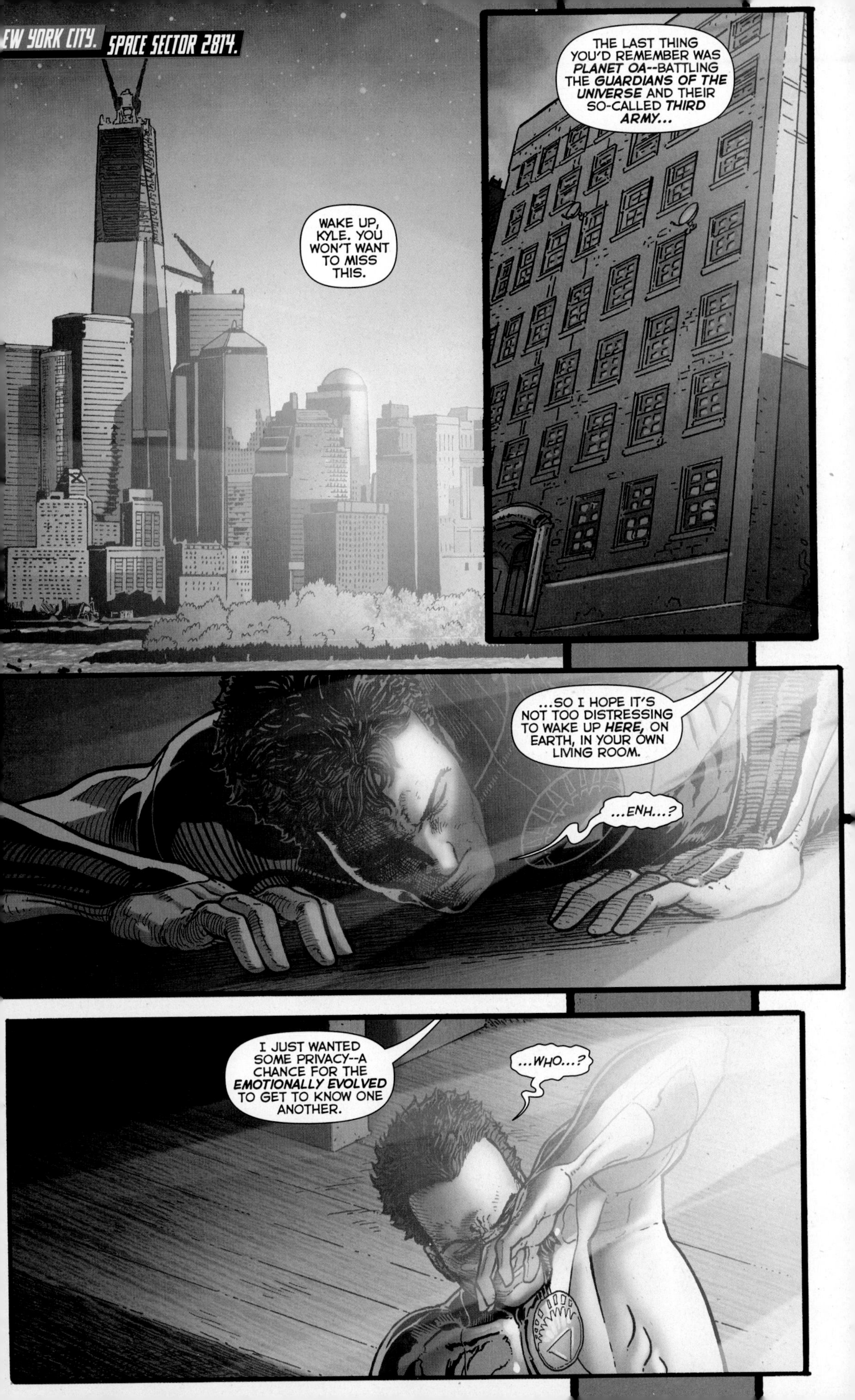

EW YORK CITY.
SPACE SECTOR 2814.
WAKE UP, KYLE. YOU WON'T WANT TO MISS THIS.
THE LAST THING YOU'D REMEMBER WAS PLANET OA--BATTLING THE GUARDIANS OF THE UNIVERSE AND THEIR SO-CALLED THIRD ARMY...
...SO I HOPE IT'S NOT TOO DISTRESSING TO WAKE UP HERE, ON EARTH, IN YOUR OWN LIVING ROOM.
...ENH...?
I JUST WANTED SOME PRIVACY--A CHANCE FOR THE EMOTIONALLY EVOLVED TO GET TO KNOW ONE ANOTHER.
...WHO...?

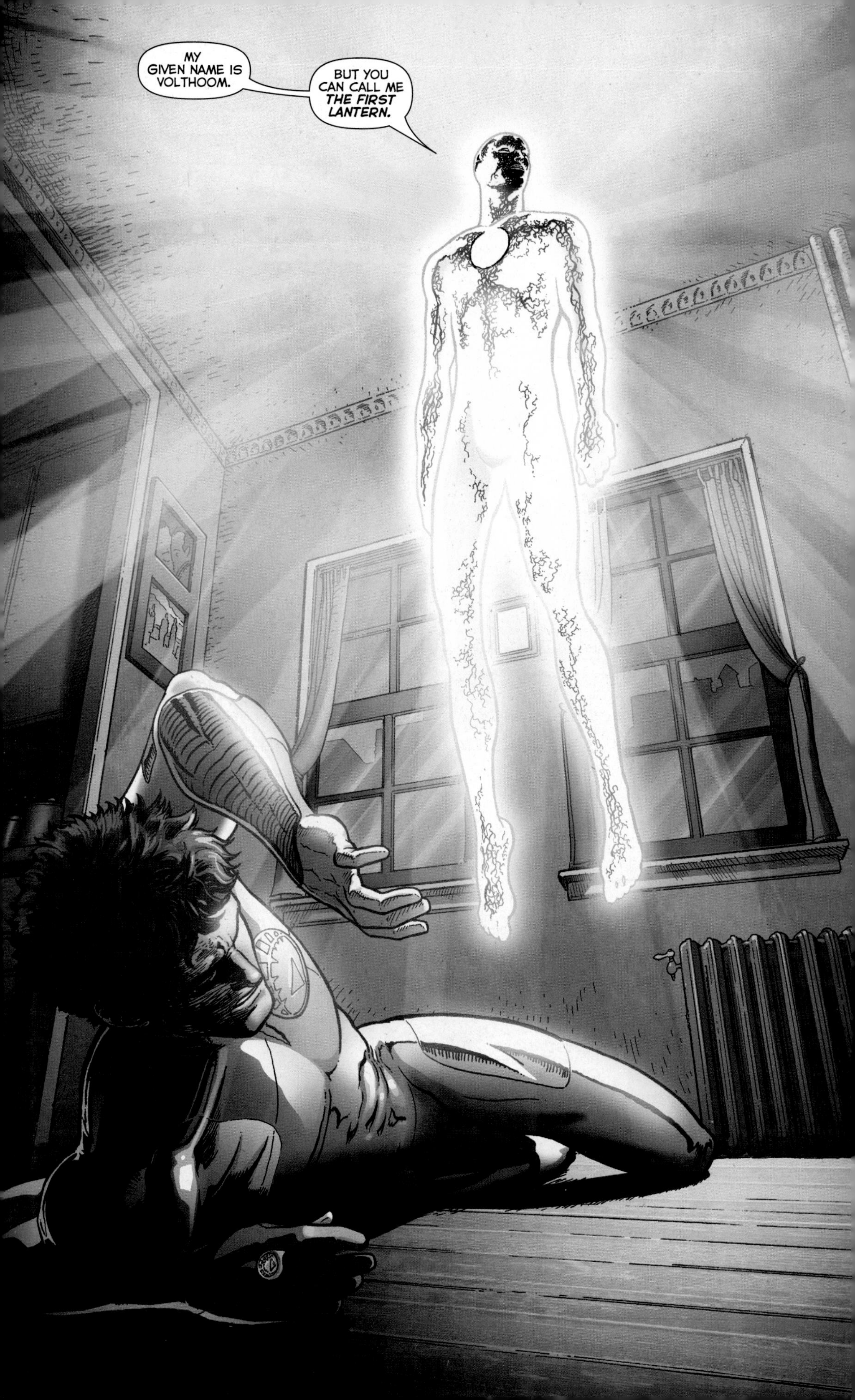
MY GIVEN NAME IS VOLTHOOM.
BUT YOU CAN CALL ME *THE FIRST LANTERN.*

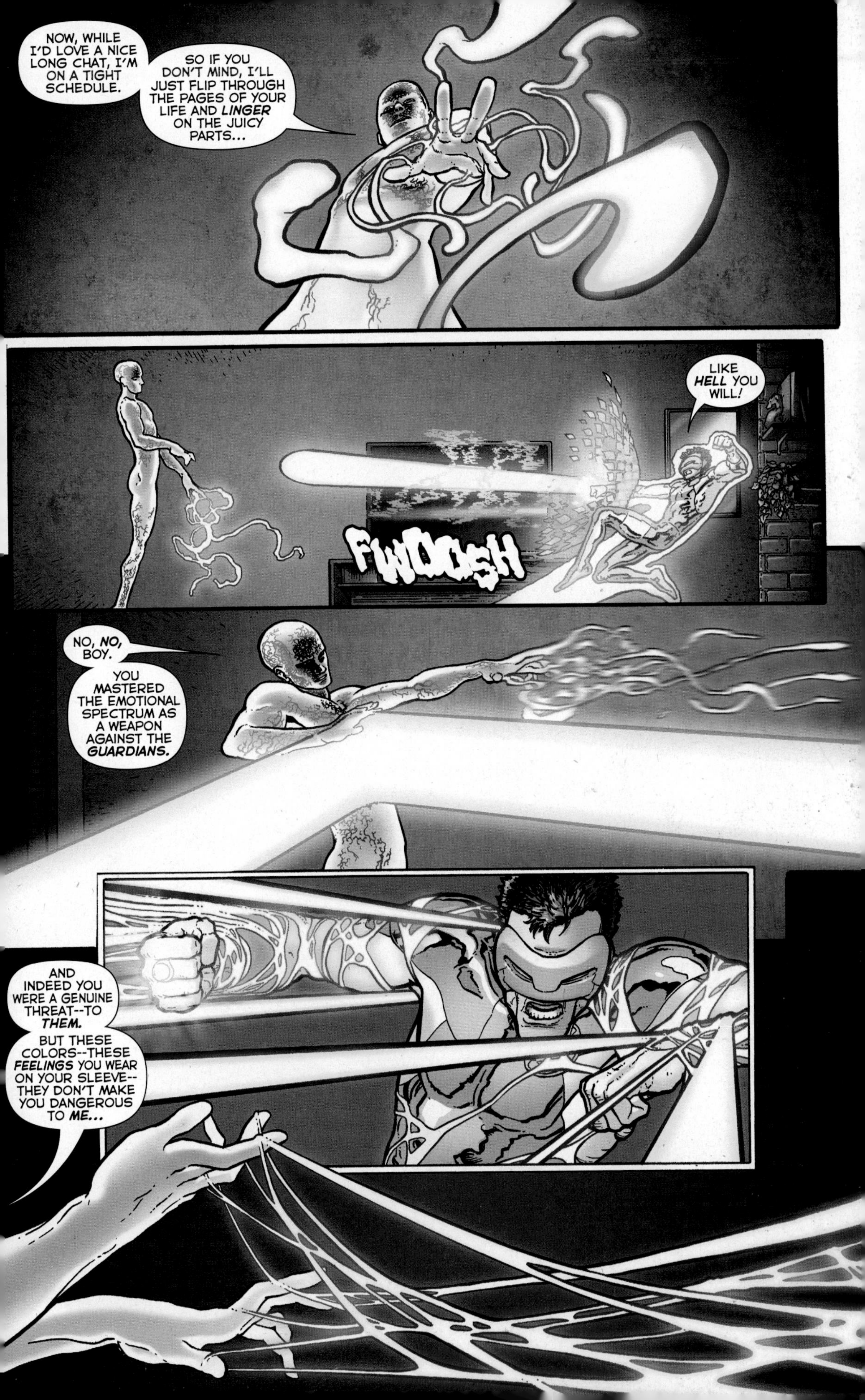
NOW, WHILE I'D LOVE A NICE LONG CHAT, I'M ON A TIGHT SCHEDULE.
SO IF YOU DON'T MIND, I'LL JUST FLIP THROUGH THE PAGES OF YOUR LIFE AND *LINGER* ON THE JUICY PARTS...
LIKE *HELL* YOU WILL!
FWOOSH
NO, *NO*, BOY.
YOU MASTERED THE EMOTIONAL SPECTRUM AS A WEAPON AGAINST THE *GUARDIANS.*
AND INDEED YOU WERE A GENUINE THREAT--TO *THEM.*
BUT THESE COLORS--THESE *FEELINGS* YOU WEAR ON YOUR SLEEVE--THEY DON'T MAKE YOU DANGEROUS TO *ME*...

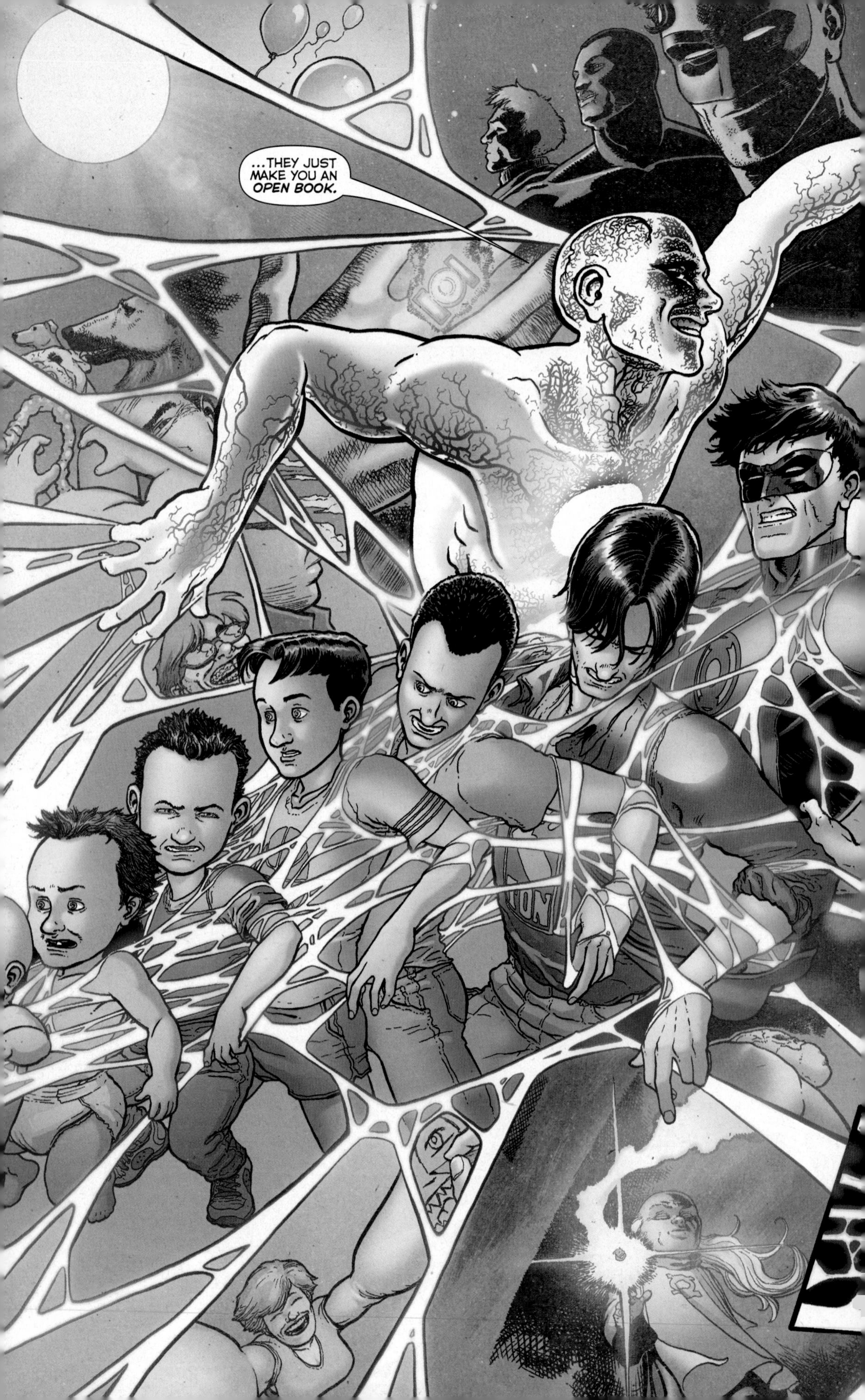
...THEY JUST MAKE YOU AN OPEN BOOK.

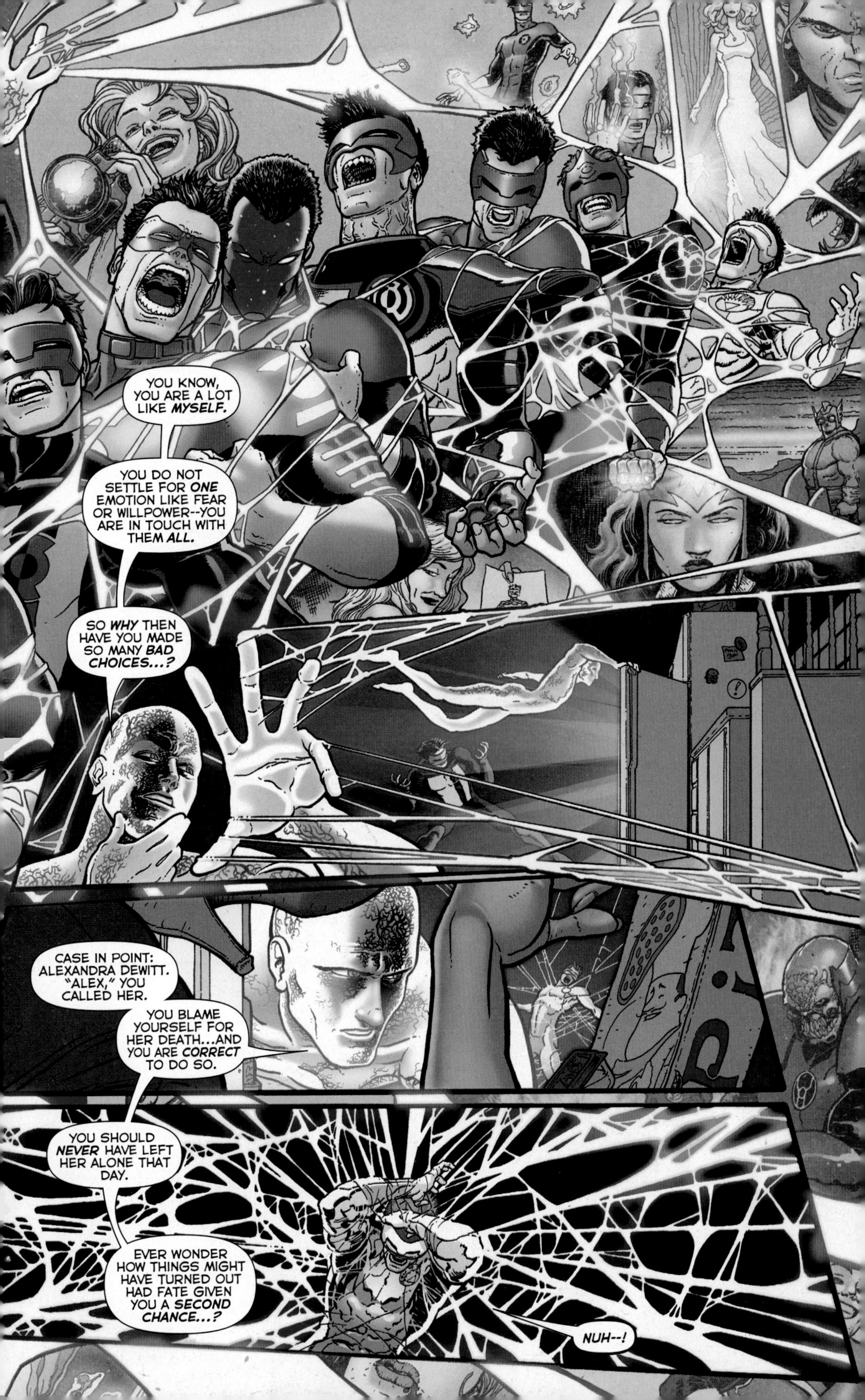
YOU KNOW, YOU ARE A LOT LIKE *MYSELF.*
YOU DO NOT SETTLE FOR *ONE* EMOTION LIKE FEAR OR WILLPOWER--YOU ARE IN TOUCH WITH THEM *ALL.*
SO *WHY* THEN HAVE YOU MADE SO MANY *BAD CHOICES...?*
CASE IN POINT: ALEXANDRA DEWITT. "ALEX," YOU CALLED HER.
YOU BLAME YOURSELF FOR HER DEATH...AND YOU ARE *CORRECT* TO DO SO.
YOU SHOULD *NEVER* HAVE LEFT HER ALONE THAT DAY.
EVER WONDER HOW THINGS MIGHT HAVE TURNED OUT HAD FATE GIVEN YOU A *SECOND CHANCE...?*
NUH--!

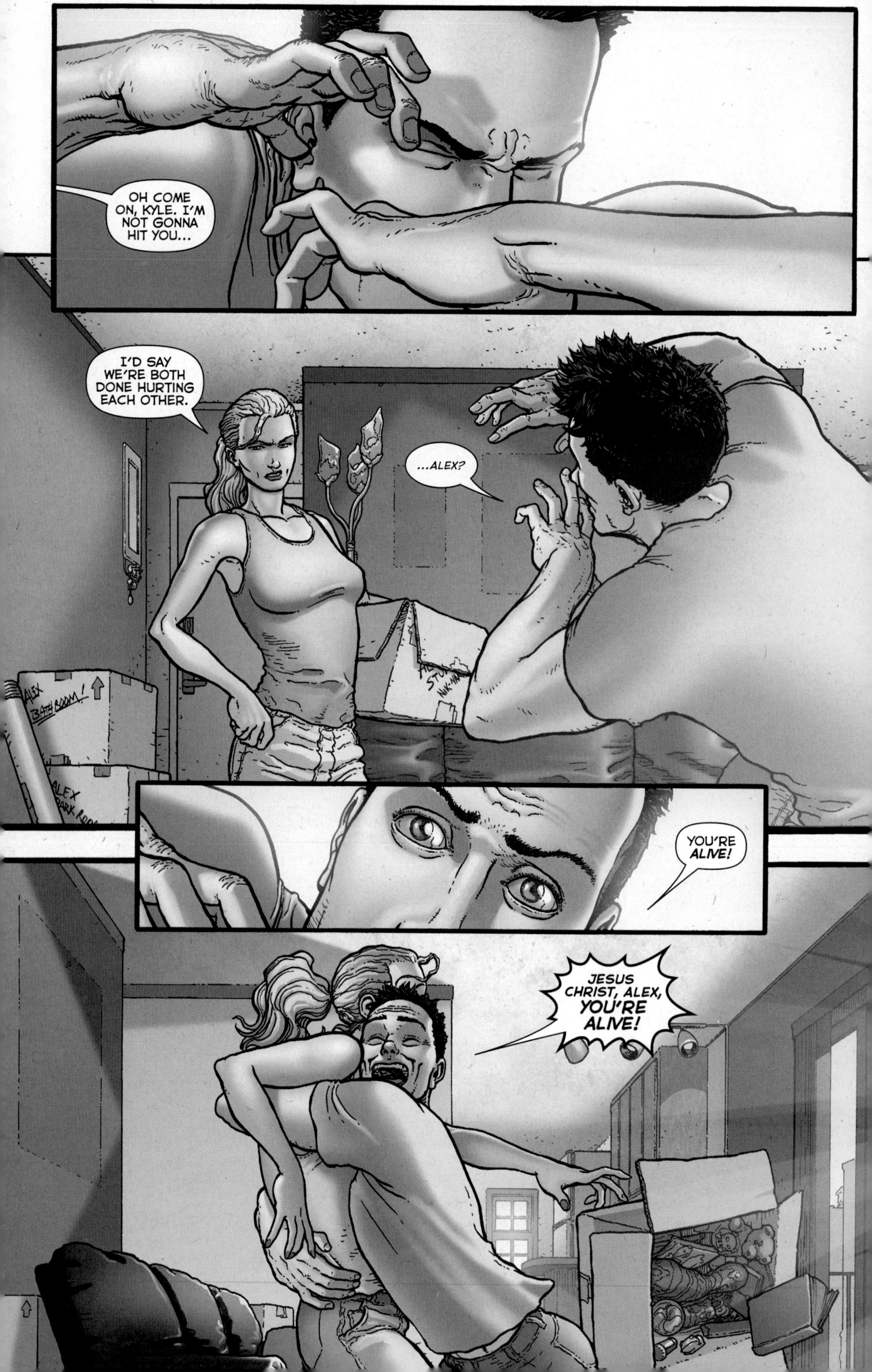
OH COME ON, KYLE. I'M NOT GONNA HIT YOU...
I'D SAY WE'RE BOTH DONE HURTING EACH OTHER.
...ALEX?
YOU'RE *ALIVE!*
JESUS CHRIST, ALEX, ***YOU'RE ALIVE!***

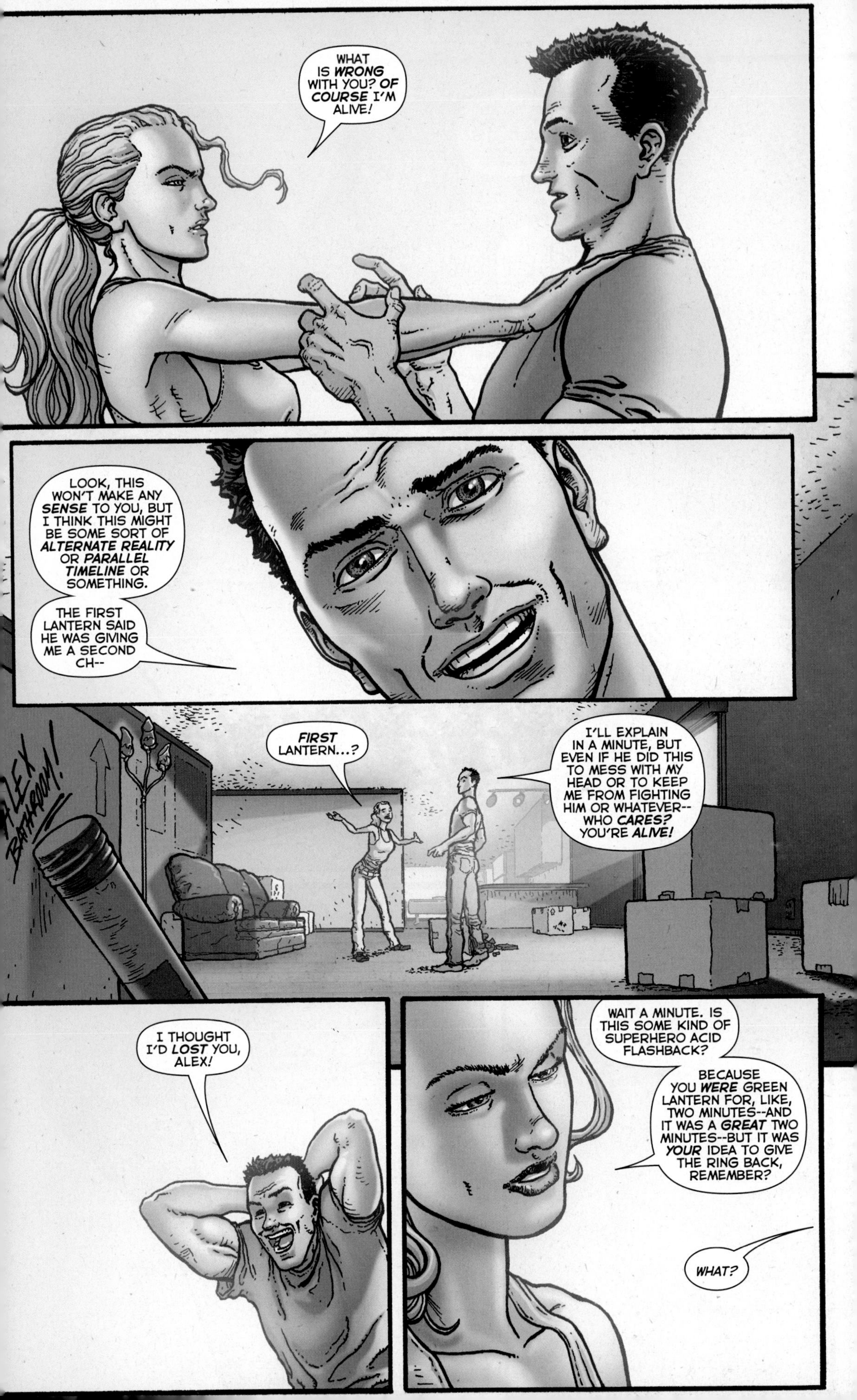
WHAT IS WRONG WITH YOU? OF COURSE I'M ALIVE!
LOOK, THIS WON'T MAKE ANY SENSE TO YOU, BUT I THINK THIS MIGHT BE SOME SORT OF ALTERNATE REALITY OR PARALLEL TIMELINE OR SOMETHING.
THE FIRST LANTERN SAID HE WAS GIVING ME A SECOND CH--
ALEX BATHROOM!
FIRST LANTERN...?
I'LL EXPLAIN IN A MINUTE, BUT EVEN IF HE DID THIS TO MESS WITH MY HEAD OR TO KEEP ME FROM FIGHTING HIM OR WHATEVER-- WHO CARES? YOU'RE ALIVE!
I THOUGHT I'D LOST YOU, ALEX!
WAIT A MINUTE. IS THIS SOME KIND OF SUPERHERO ACID FLASHBACK?
BECAUSE YOU WERE GREEN LANTERN FOR, LIKE, TWO MINUTES--AND IT WAS A GREAT TWO MINUTES--BUT IT WAS YOUR IDEA TO GIVE THE RING BACK, REMEMBER?
WHAT?

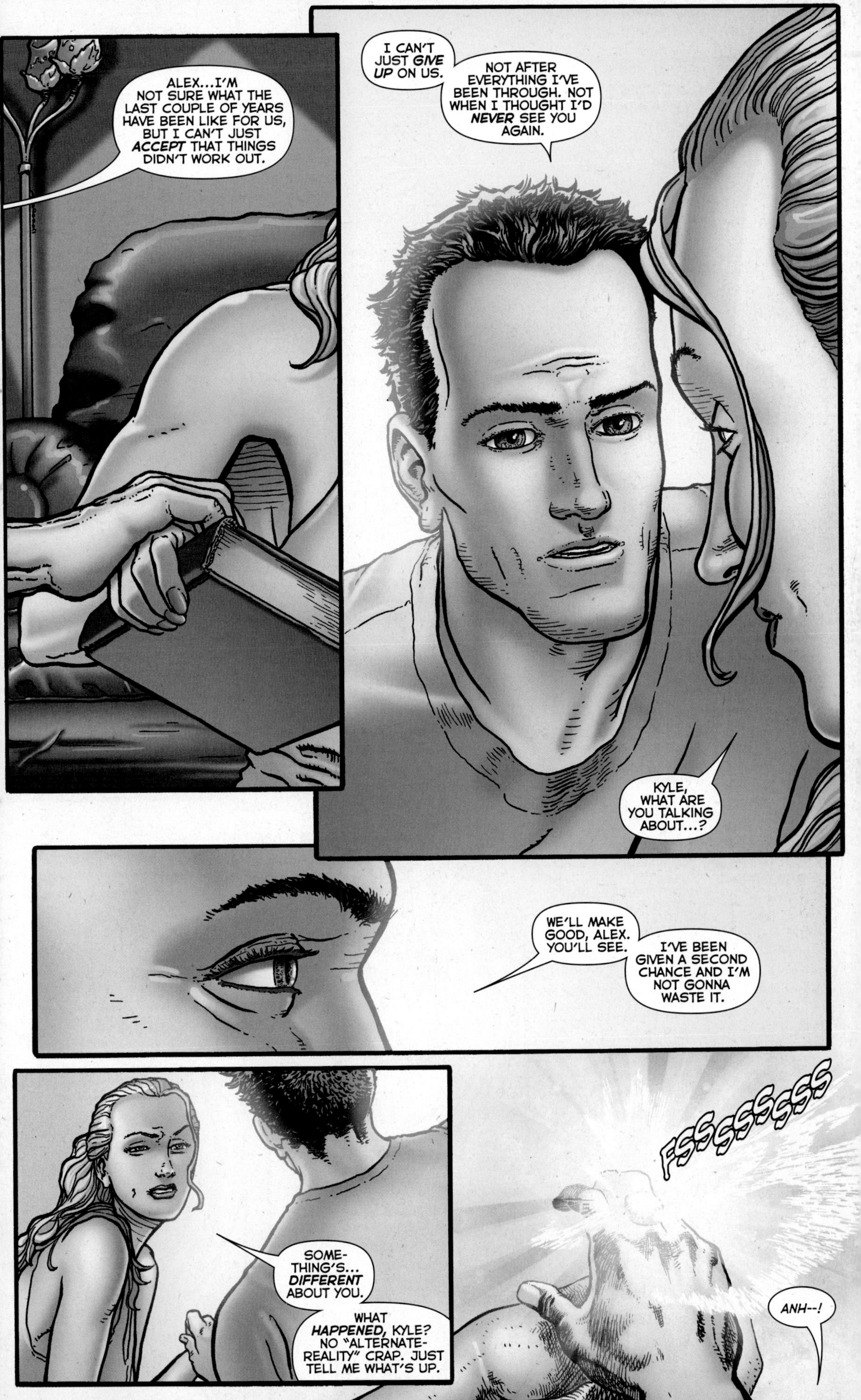
ALEX...I'M NOT SURE WHAT THE LAST COUPLE OF YEARS HAVE BEEN LIKE FOR US, BUT I CAN'T JUST ACCEPT THAT THINGS DIDN'T WORK OUT.
I CAN'T JUST GIVE UP ON US.
NOT AFTER EVERYTHING I'VE BEEN THROUGH. NOT WHEN I THOUGHT I'D NEVER SEE YOU AGAIN.
KYLE, WHAT ARE YOU TALKING ABOUT...?
WE'LL MAKE GOOD, ALEX. YOU'LL SEE.
I'VE BEEN GIVEN A SECOND CHANCE AND I'M NOT GONNA WASTE IT.
SOME-THING'S... DIFFERENT ABOUT YOU.
WHAT HAPPENED, KYLE? NO "ALTERNATE-REALITY" CRAP. JUST TELL ME WHAT'S UP.
FSSSSSSSS
ANH--!

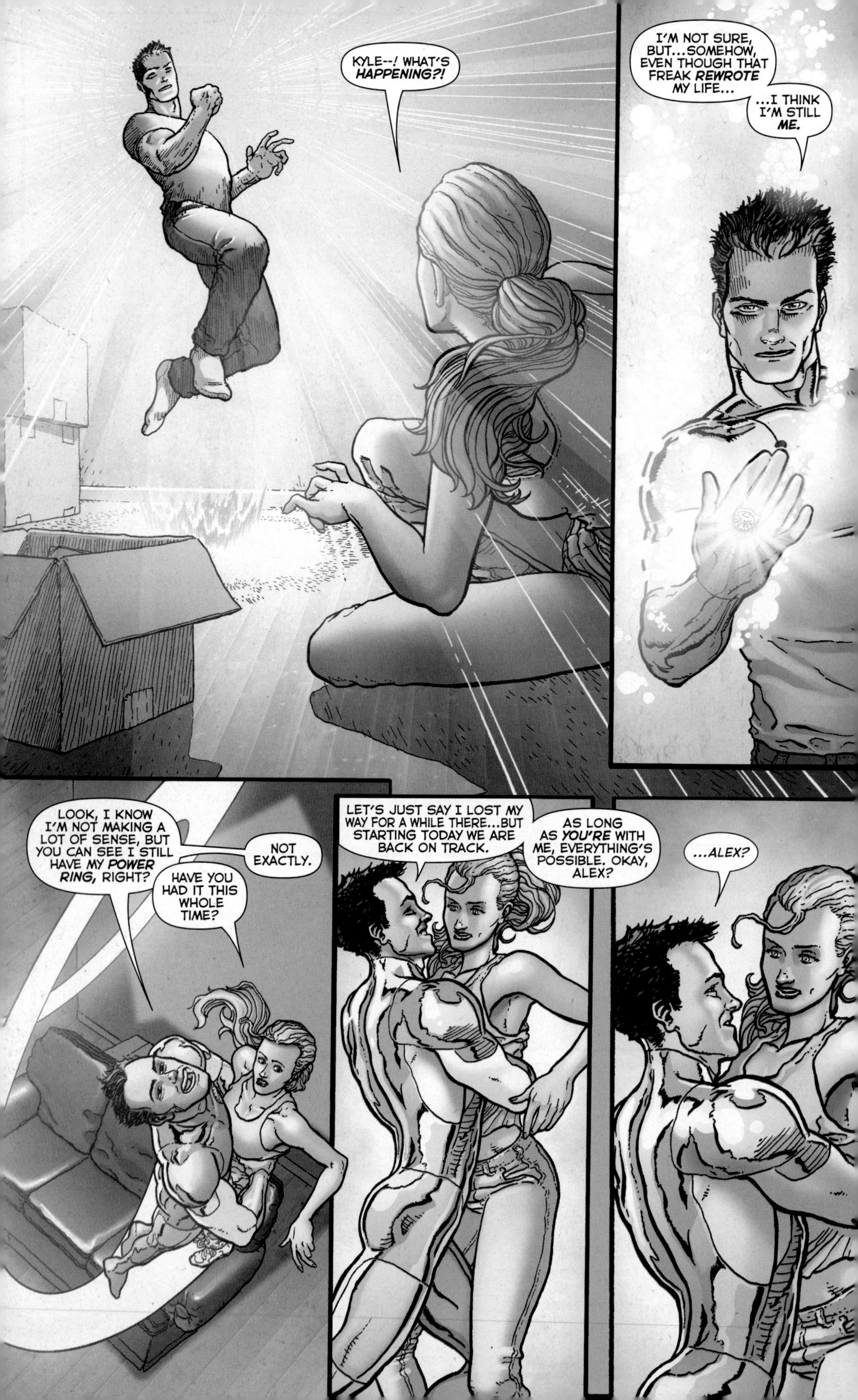
KYLE--! WHAT'S HAPPENING?!
I'M NOT SURE, BUT...SOMEHOW, EVEN THOUGH THAT FREAK REWROTE MY LIFE...
...I THINK I'M STILL ME.
LOOK, I KNOW I'M NOT MAKING A LOT OF SENSE, BUT YOU CAN SEE I STILL HAVE MY POWER RING, RIGHT?
NOT EXACTLY.
HAVE YOU HAD IT THIS WHOLE TIME?
LET'S JUST SAY I LOST MY WAY FOR A WHILE THERE...BUT STARTING TODAY WE ARE BACK ON TRACK.
AS LONG AS YOU'RE WITH ME, EVERYTHING'S POSSIBLE. OKAY, ALEX?
...ALEX?

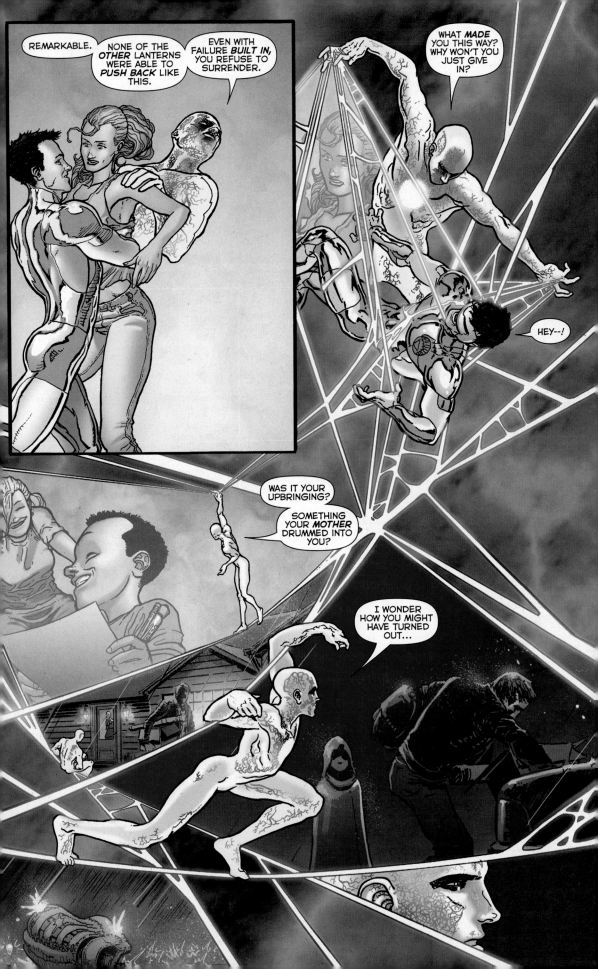

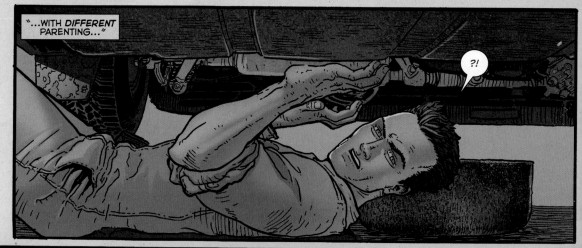

"...WITH *DIFFERENT* PARENTING..."

?!

WHAT JUST HAPPENED?

I WAS... *WITH SOMEONE...* SOMEONE *IMPORTANT...*

...SOMEONE... I *LOVE...*?

NO! I *WON'T* FORGET HER.

:NNH: WHATEVER'S GOING ON HERE... *SOME-ONE* WANTS ME TO FORGET...

...BLONDE... FUNNY...SMART... STRONG...

ALEX!

RAYNER'S AUTO

I WAS WITH ALEX. AND THEN THAT "FIRST LANTERN" CAME, AND--

"HANG ON. WHO'S THAT TALKING TO *JOHNNY LAW* IN THERE...?"

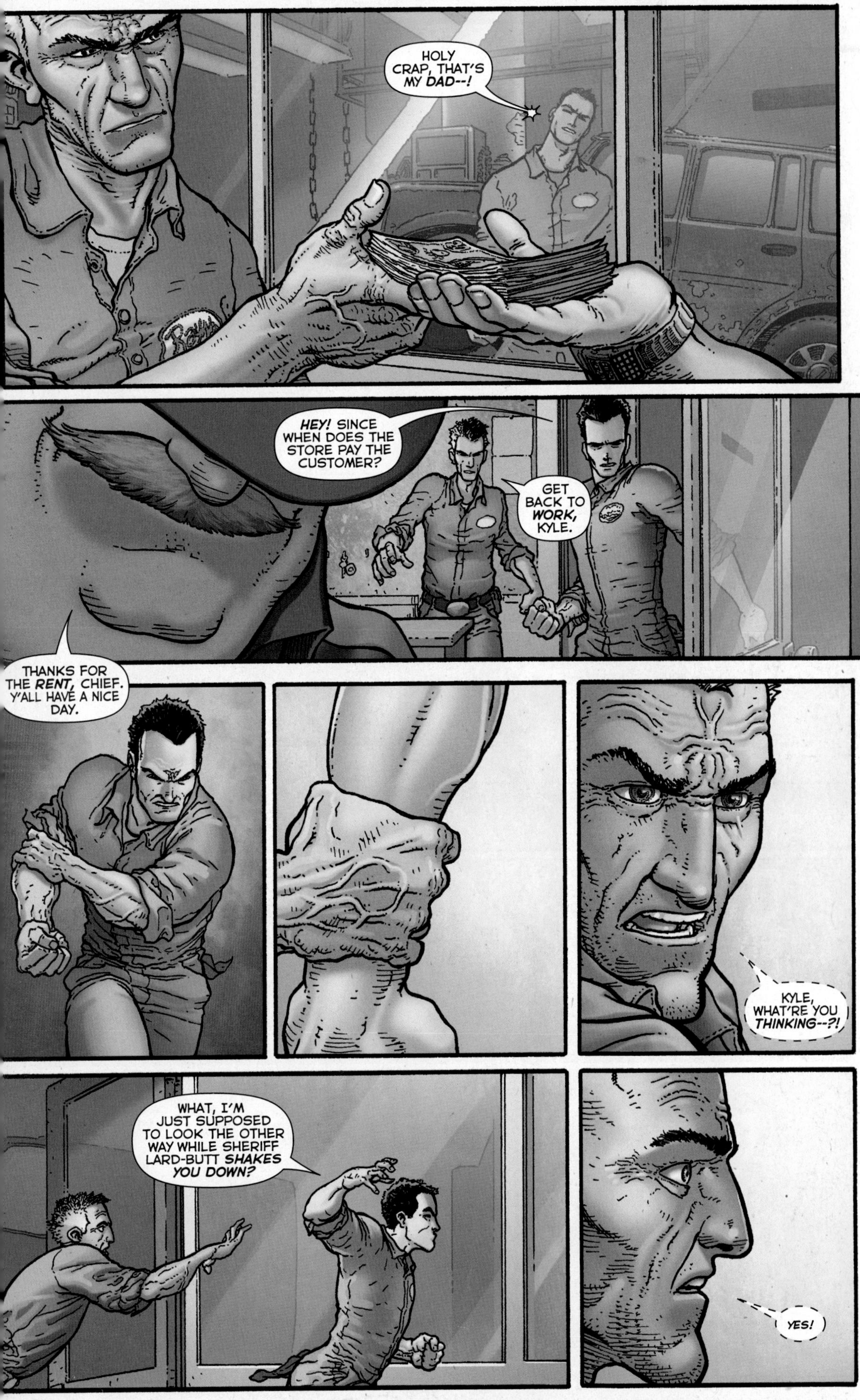
HOLY CRAP, THAT'S MY DAD--!
HEY! SINCE WHEN DOES THE STORE PAY THE CUSTOMER?
GET BACK TO WORK, KYLE.
THANKS FOR THE RENT, CHIEF. Y'ALL HAVE A NICE DAY.
KYLE, WHAT'RE YOU THINKING--?!
WHAT, I'M JUST SUPPOSED TO LOOK THE OTHER WAY WHILE SHERIFF LARD-BUTT SHAKES YOU DOWN?
YES!

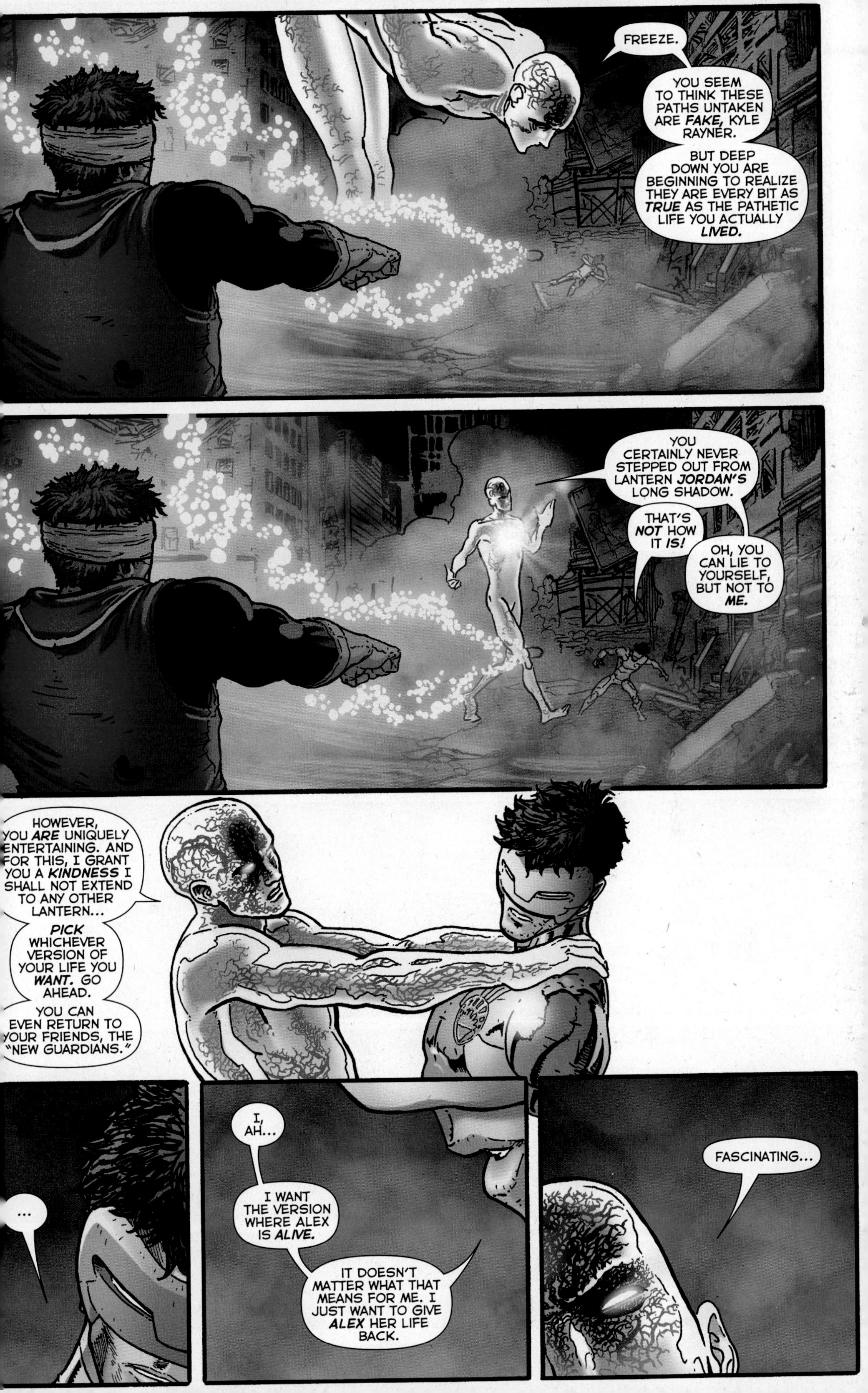
FREEZE.
YOU SEEM TO THINK THESE PATHS UNTAKEN ARE FAKE, KYLE RAYNER.
BUT DEEP DOWN YOU ARE BEGINNING TO REALIZE THEY ARE EVERY BIT AS TRUE AS THE PATHETIC LIFE YOU ACTUALLY LIVED.
YOU CERTAINLY NEVER STEPPED OUT FROM LANTERN JORDAN'S LONG SHADOW.
THAT'S NOT HOW IT IS!
OH, YOU CAN LIE TO YOURSELF, BUT NOT TO ME.
HOWEVER, YOU ARE UNIQUELY ENTERTAINING. AND FOR THIS, I GRANT YOU A KINDNESS I SHALL NOT EXTEND TO ANY OTHER LANTERN...
PICK WHICHEVER VERSION OF YOUR LIFE YOU WANT. GO AHEAD.
YOU CAN EVEN RETURN TO YOUR FRIENDS, THE "NEW GUARDIANS."
...
I, AH...
I WANT THE VERSION WHERE ALEX IS ALIVE.
IT DOESN'T MATTER WHAT THAT MEANS FOR ME. I JUST WANT TO GIVE ALEX HER LIFE BACK.
FASCINATING...

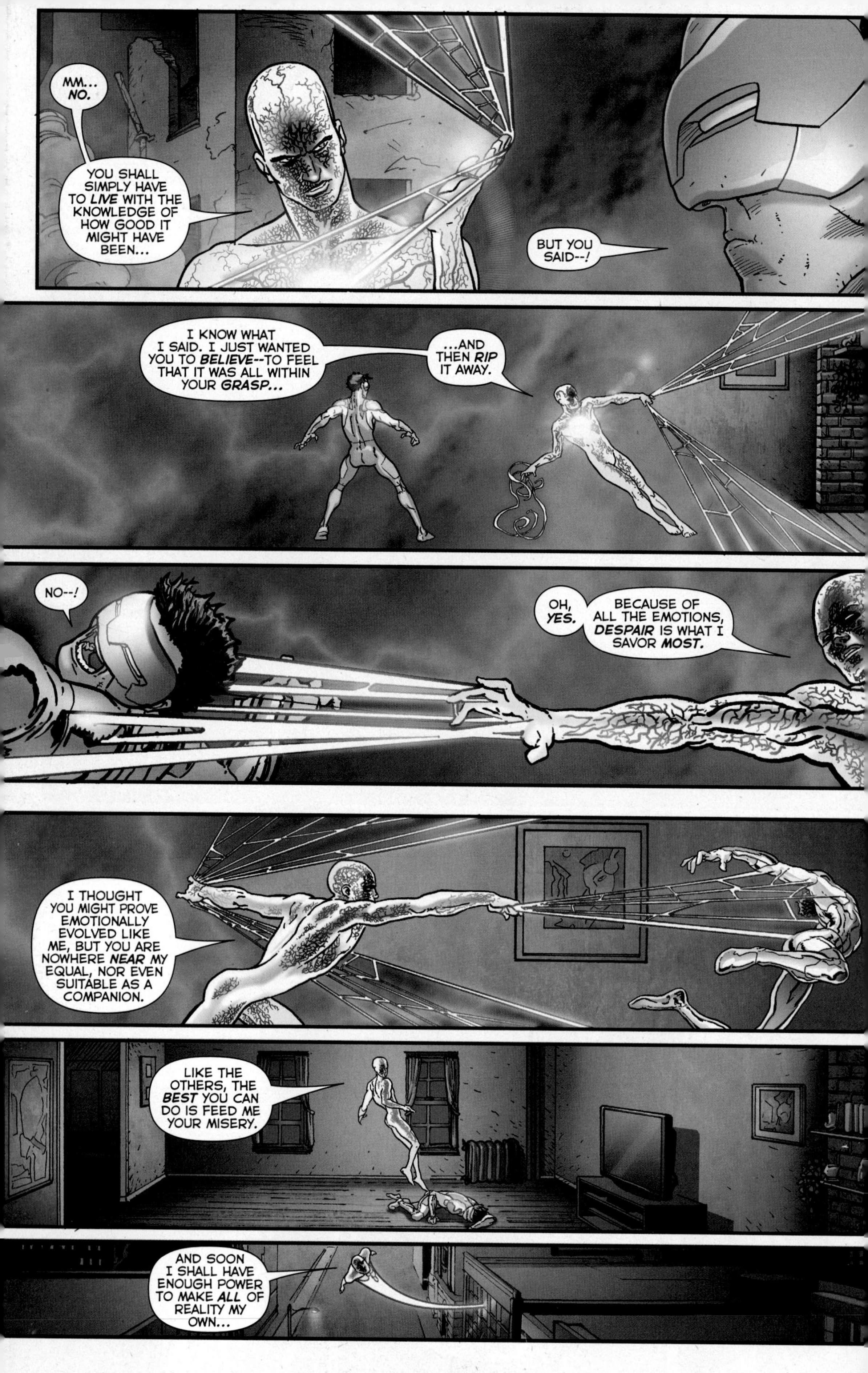
MM... NO.
YOU SHALL SIMPLY HAVE TO LIVE WITH THE KNOWLEDGE OF HOW GOOD IT MIGHT HAVE BEEN...
BUT YOU SAID--!
I KNOW WHAT I SAID. I JUST WANTED YOU TO BELIEVE--TO FEEL THAT IT WAS ALL WITHIN YOUR GRASP...
...AND THEN RIP IT AWAY.
NO--!
OH, YES.
BECAUSE OF ALL THE EMOTIONS, DESPAIR IS WHAT I SAVOR MOST.
I THOUGHT YOU MIGHT PROVE EMOTIONALLY EVOLVED LIKE ME, BUT YOU ARE NOWHERE NEAR MY EQUAL, NOR EVEN SUITABLE AS A COMPANION.
LIKE THE OTHERS, THE BEST YOU CAN DO IS FEED ME YOUR MISERY.
AND SOON I SHALL HAVE ENOUGH POWER TO MAKE ALL OF REALITY MY OWN...

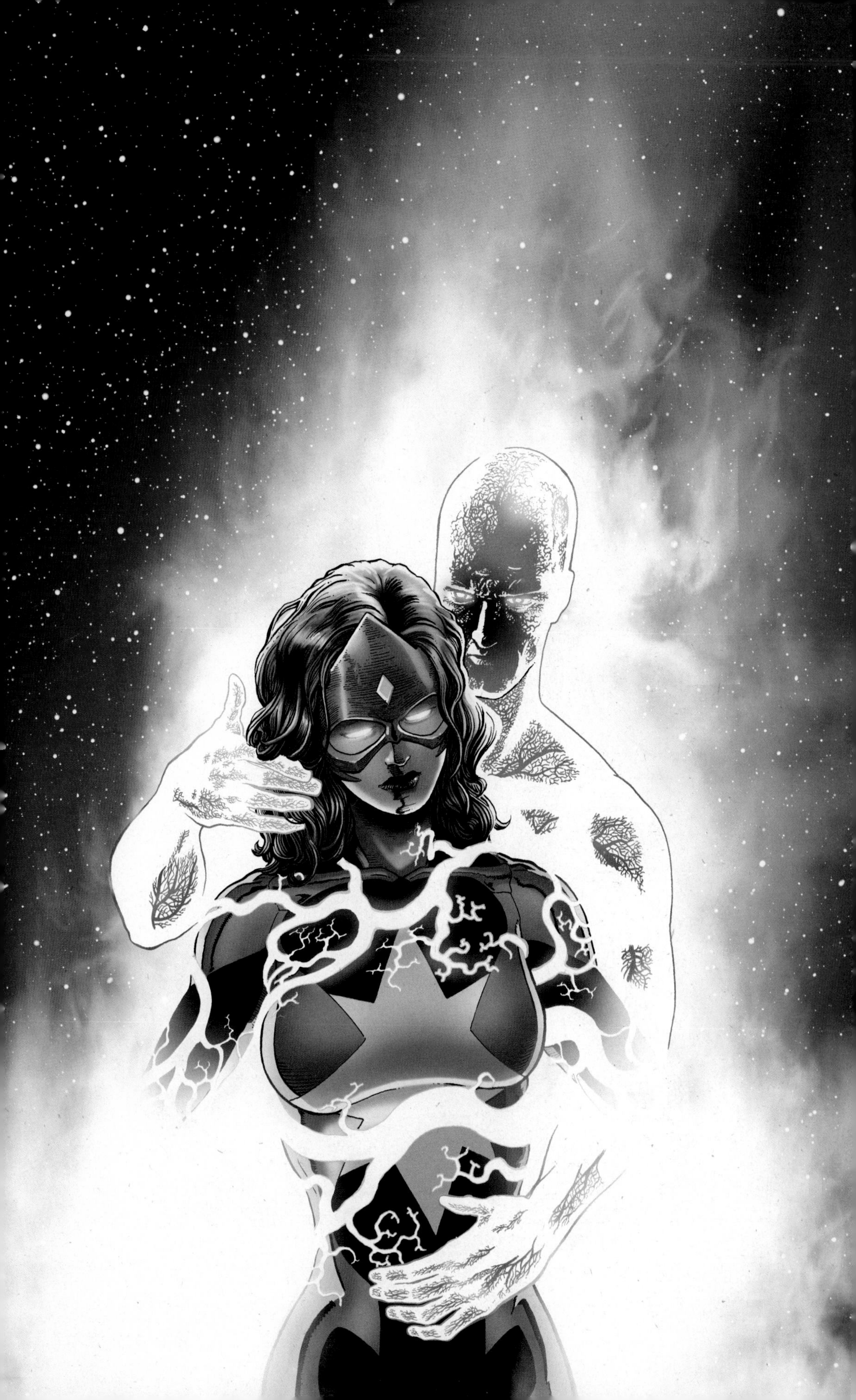

PATHS UNTAKEN

TONY BEDARD writer HENDRY PRASETYO, JIM CALAFIORE & JAVIER PULIDO artists

AARON KUDER & WIL QUINTANA cover

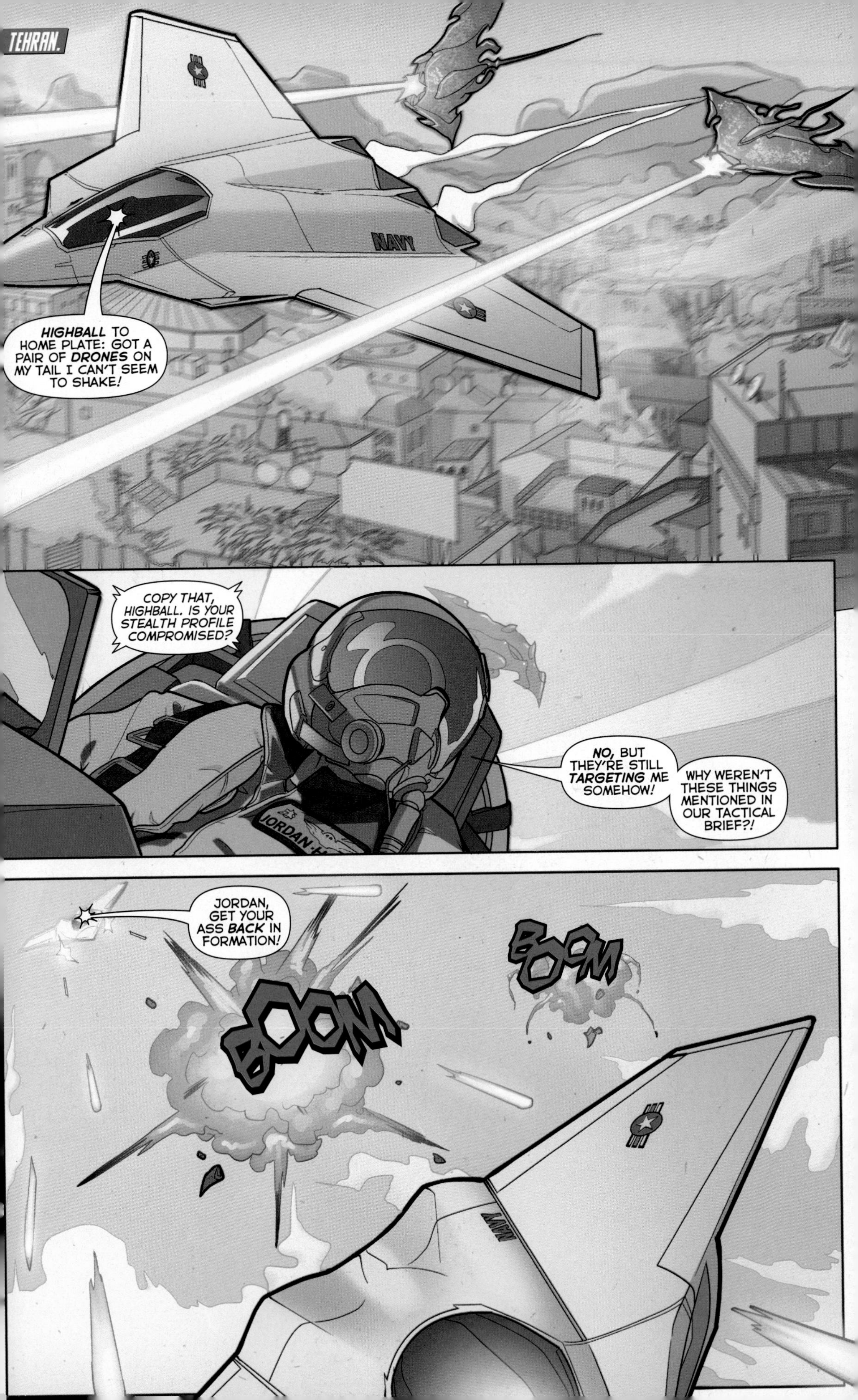
TEHRAN.
HIGHBALL TO HOME PLATE: GOT A PAIR OF DRONES ON MY TAIL I CAN'T SEEM TO SHAKE!
NAVY
COPY THAT, HIGHBALL. IS YOUR STEALTH PROFILE COMPROMISED?
NO, BUT THEY'RE STILL TARGETING ME SOMEHOW!
WHY WEREN'T THESE THINGS MENTIONED IN OUR TACTICAL BRIEF?!
JORDAN, GET YOUR ASS BACK IN FORMATION!
BOOM
BOOM

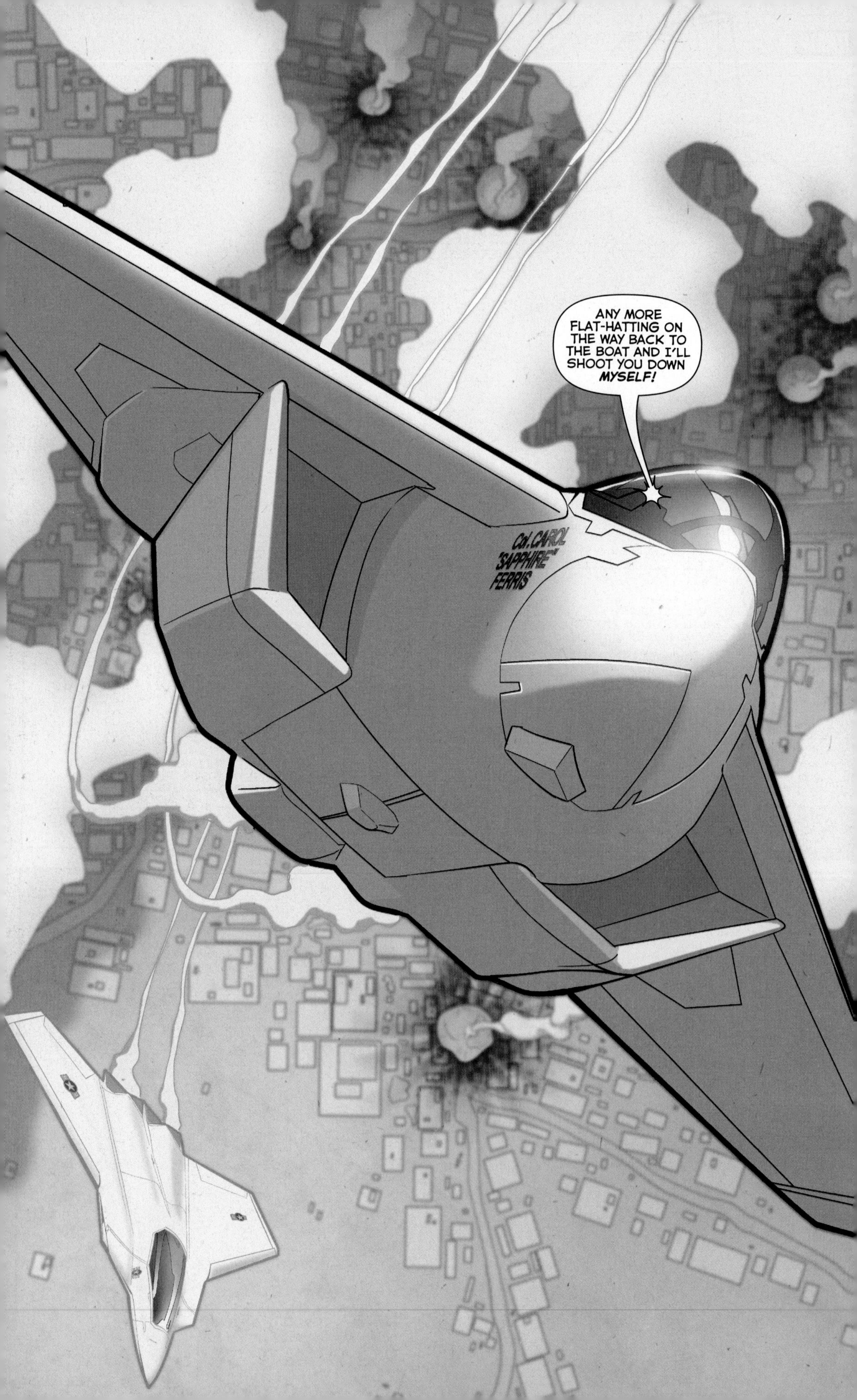
ANY MORE FLAT-HATTING ON THE WAY BACK TO THE BOAT AND I'LL SHOOT YOU DOWN *MYSELF!*
Col. CAROL "SAPPHIRE" FERRIS

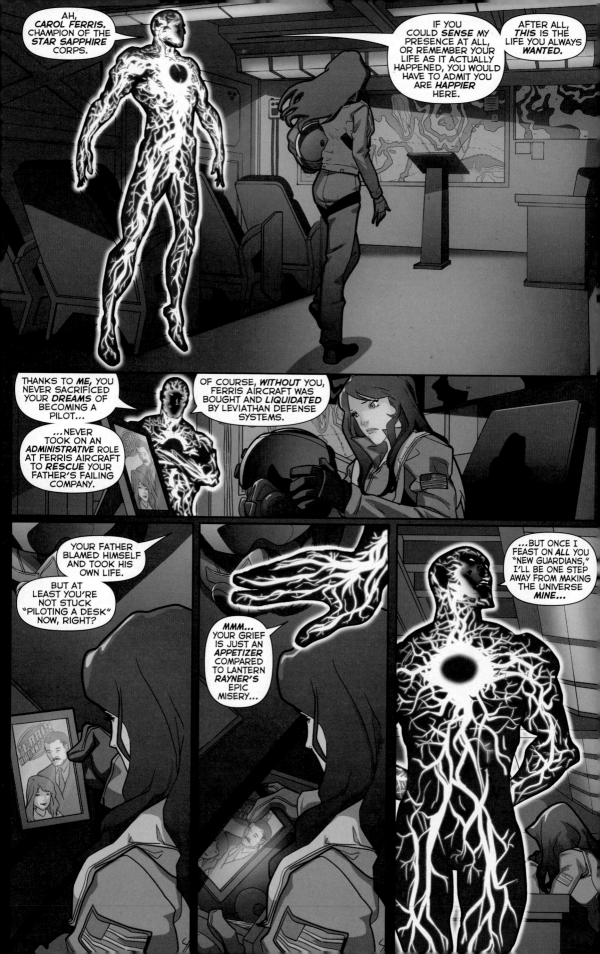

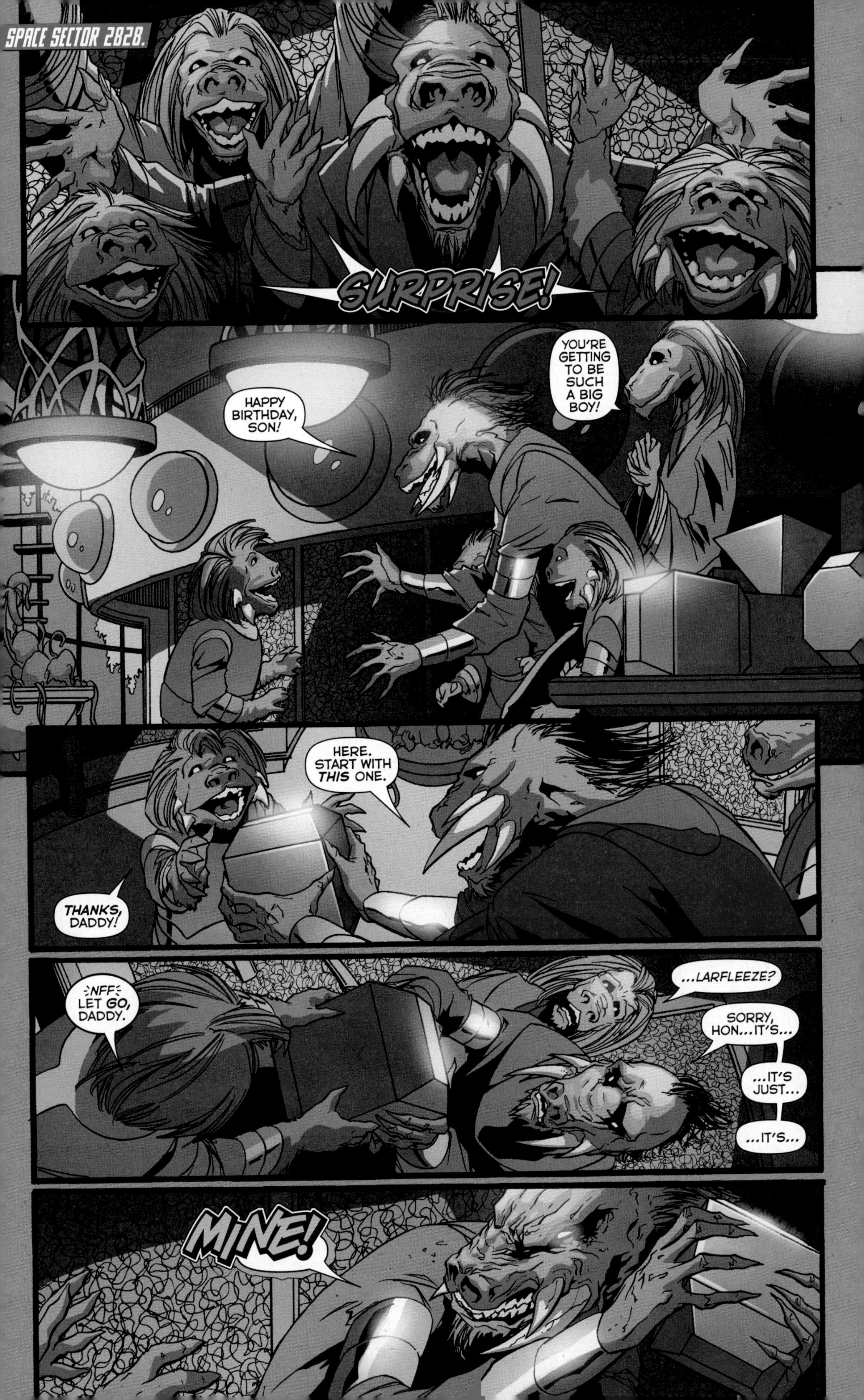
SPACE SECTOR 2828.
SURPRISE!
HAPPY BIRTHDAY, SON!
YOU'RE GETTING TO BE SUCH A BIG BOY!
HERE. START WITH THIS ONE.
THANKS, DADDY!
NFF LET GO, DADDY.
...LARFLEEZE?
SORRY, HON...IT'S...
...IT'S JUST...
...IT'S...
MINE!

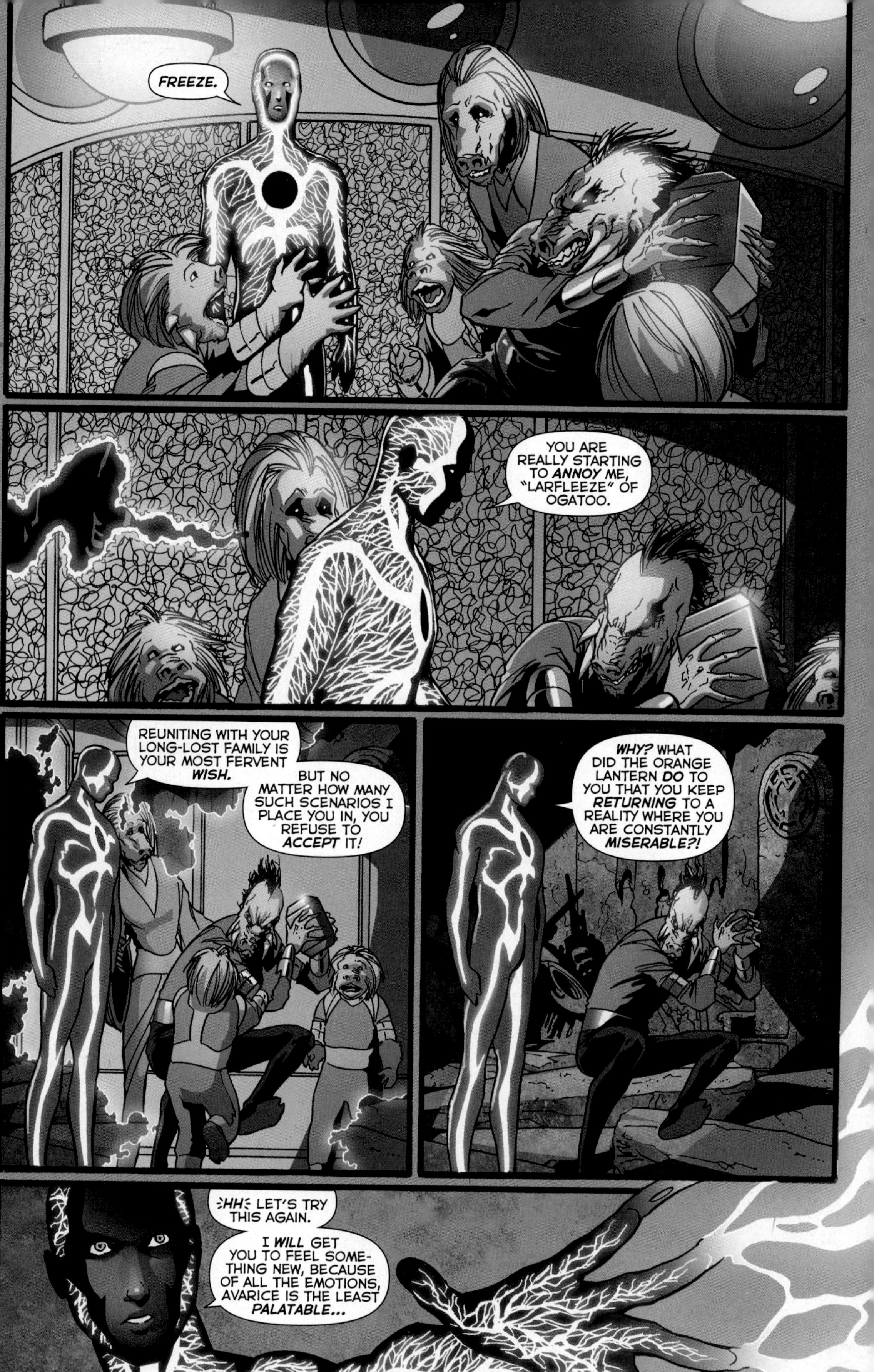
FREEZE.
YOU ARE REALLY STARTING TO ANNOY ME, "LARFLEEZE" OF OGATOO.
REUNITING WITH YOUR LONG-LOST FAMILY IS YOUR MOST FERVENT WISH.
BUT NO MATTER HOW MANY SUCH SCENARIOS I PLACE YOU IN, YOU REFUSE TO ACCEPT IT!
WHY? WHAT DID THE ORANGE LANTERN DO TO YOU THAT YOU KEEP RETURNING TO A REALITY WHERE YOU ARE CONSTANTLY MISERABLE?!
HH LET'S TRY THIS AGAIN.
I WILL GET YOU TO FEEL SOMETHING NEW, BECAUSE OF ALL THE EMOTIONS, AVARICE IS THE LEAST PALATABLE...

AT LEAST YOUR *BLUE* COMRADE ISN'T CAUSING AS MUCH TROUBLE.

FOR THE ONE YOU CALL *SAINT WALKER,* I ARRANGED A LIFE WHERE HE SERVES THE *GREEN* LANTERN CORPS, INSTEAD.

HIS COURAGE AND WILLPOWER ALLOWED HIM TO SAVE HIS HOMEWORLD OF ASTONIA...

...AND, MOST IMPORTANT TO *HIM,* THE LIVES OF HIS *FAMILY.*

JOY IS NOT QUITE SO SAVORY AS DESPAIR, BUT IN SUCH ABUNDANCE IT WILL DO.

DADDY! YOU'RE COMING TO MY SCHOOL PLAY, RIGHT?

WOULDN'T MISS IT FOR THE WORLD, JATT.

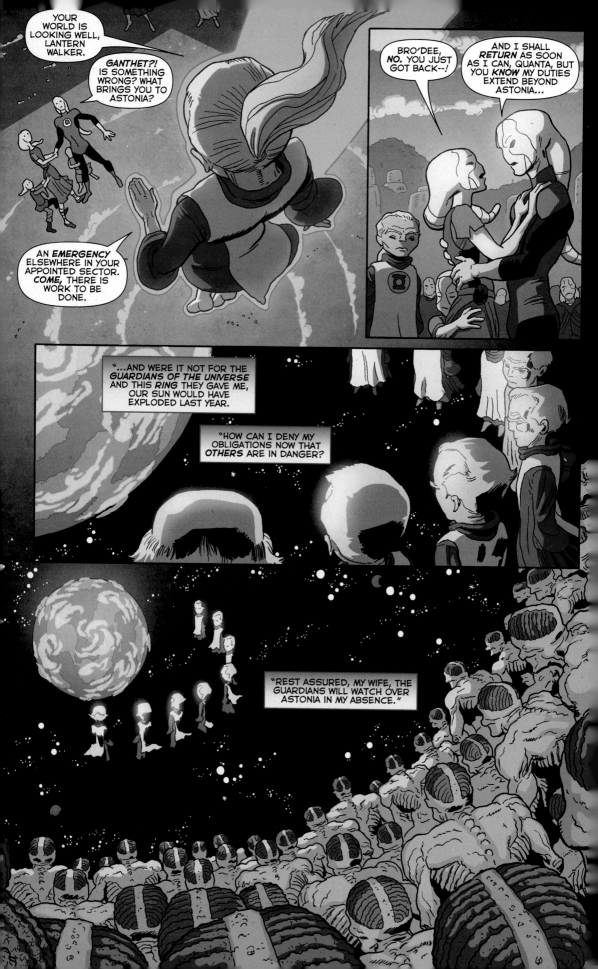

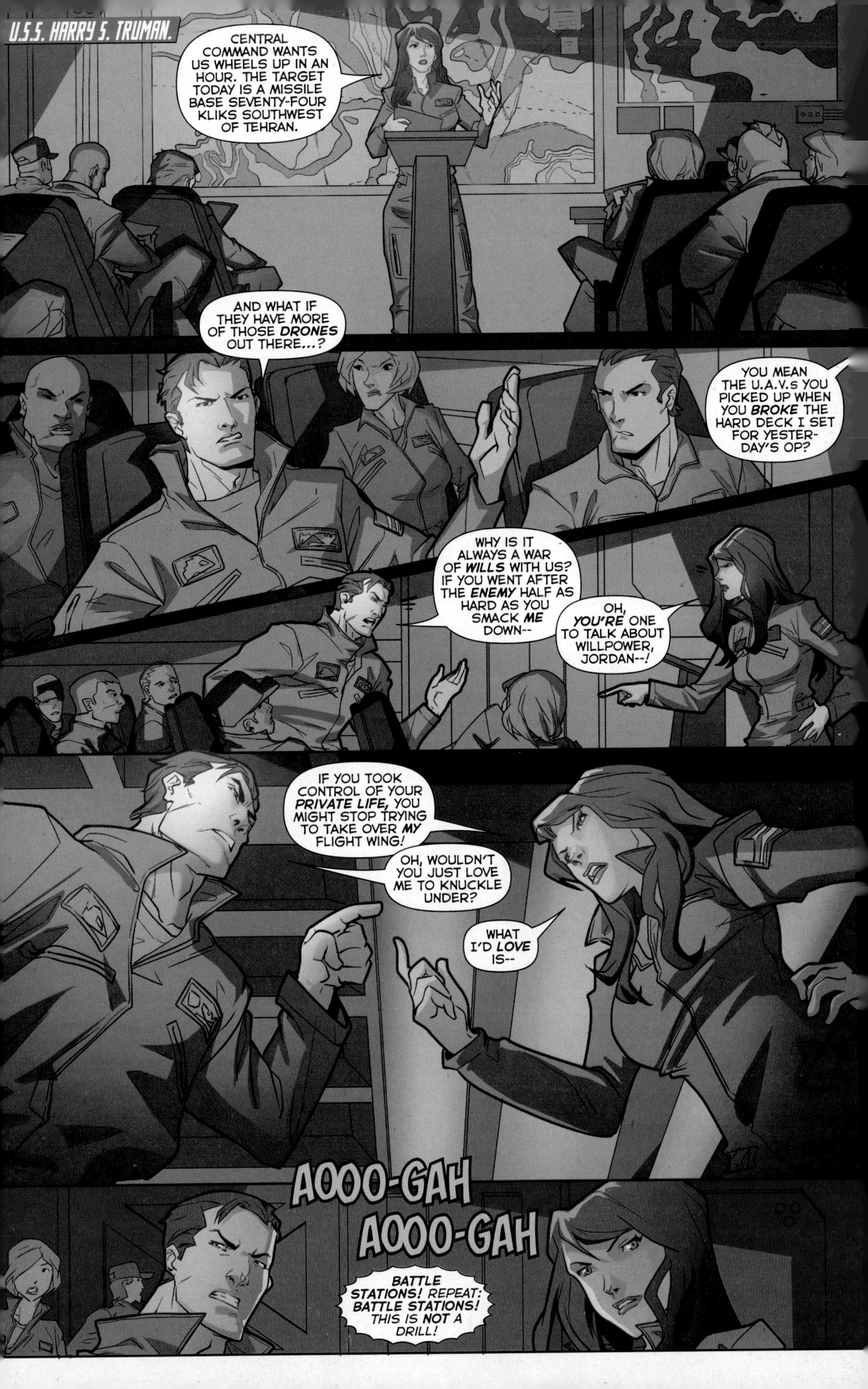
U.S.S. HARRY S. TRUMAN.
CENTRAL COMMAND WANTS US WHEELS UP IN AN HOUR. THE TARGET TODAY IS A MISSILE BASE SEVENTY-FOUR KLIKS SOUTHWEST OF TEHRAN.
AND WHAT IF THEY HAVE MORE OF THOSE *DRONES* OUT THERE...?
YOU MEAN THE U.A.V.s YOU PICKED UP WHEN YOU *BROKE* THE HARD DECK I SET FOR YESTER-DAY'S OP?
WHY IS IT ALWAYS A WAR OF *WILLS* WITH US? IF YOU WENT AFTER THE *ENEMY* HALF AS HARD AS YOU SMACK *ME* DOWN--
OH, *YOU'RE* ONE TO TALK ABOUT WILLPOWER, JORDAN--!
IF YOU TOOK CONTROL OF YOUR *PRIVATE LIFE,* YOU MIGHT STOP TRYING TO TAKE OVER *MY* FLIGHT WING!
OH, WOULDN'T YOU JUST LOVE ME TO KNUCKLE UNDER?
WHAT I'D *LOVE* IS--
AOOO-GAH
AOOO-GAH
BATTLE STATIONS! REPEAT: *BATTLE STATIONS!* THIS IS *NOT* A DRILL!

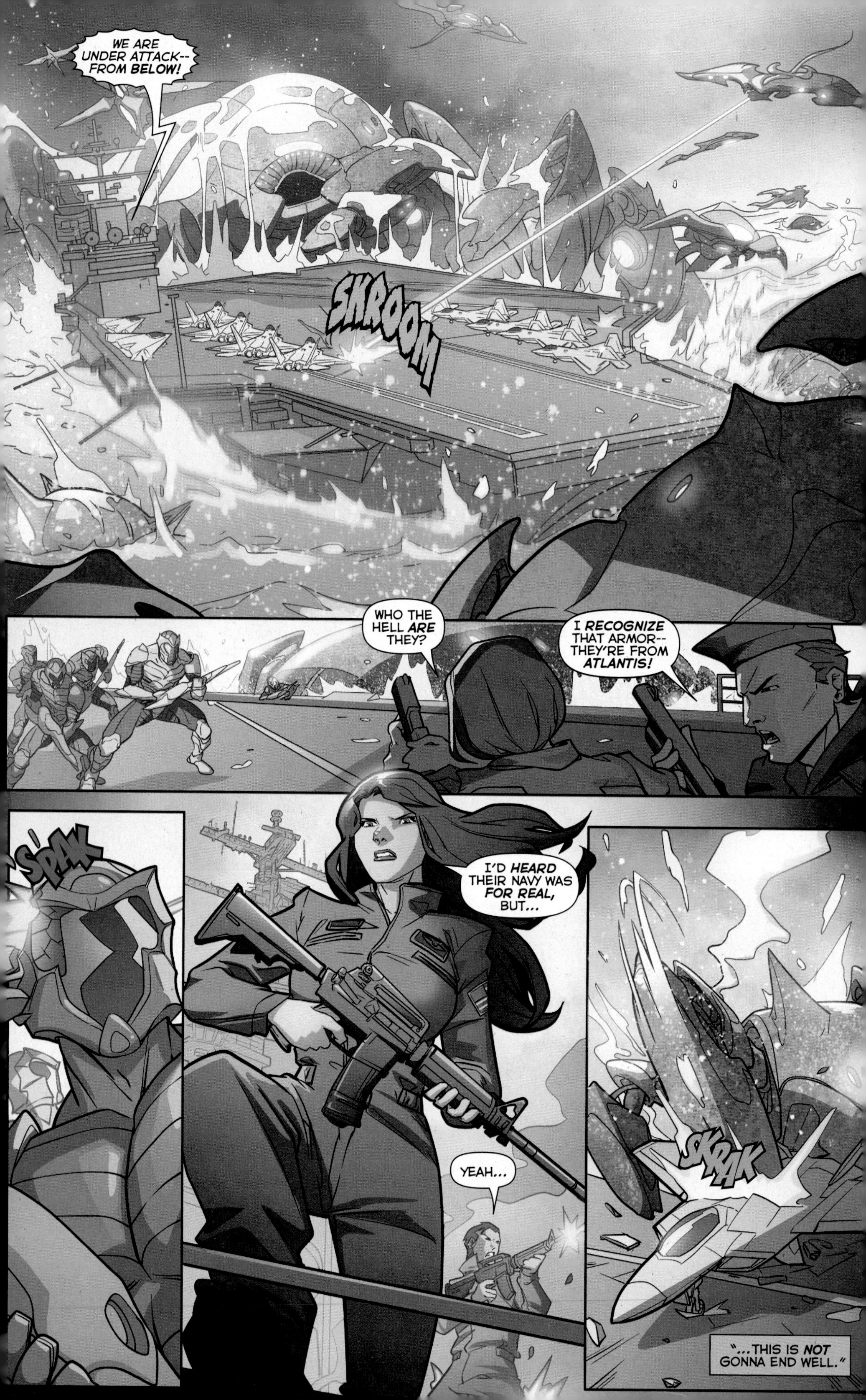
WE ARE UNDER ATTACK-- FROM BELOW!
SKROOM
WHO THE HELL ARE THEY?
I RECOGNIZE THAT ARMOR-- THEY'RE FROM ATLANTIS!
SPAK
I'D HEARD THEIR NAVY WAS FOR REAL, BUT...
YEAH...
SKRAK
"...THIS IS NOT GONNA END WELL."

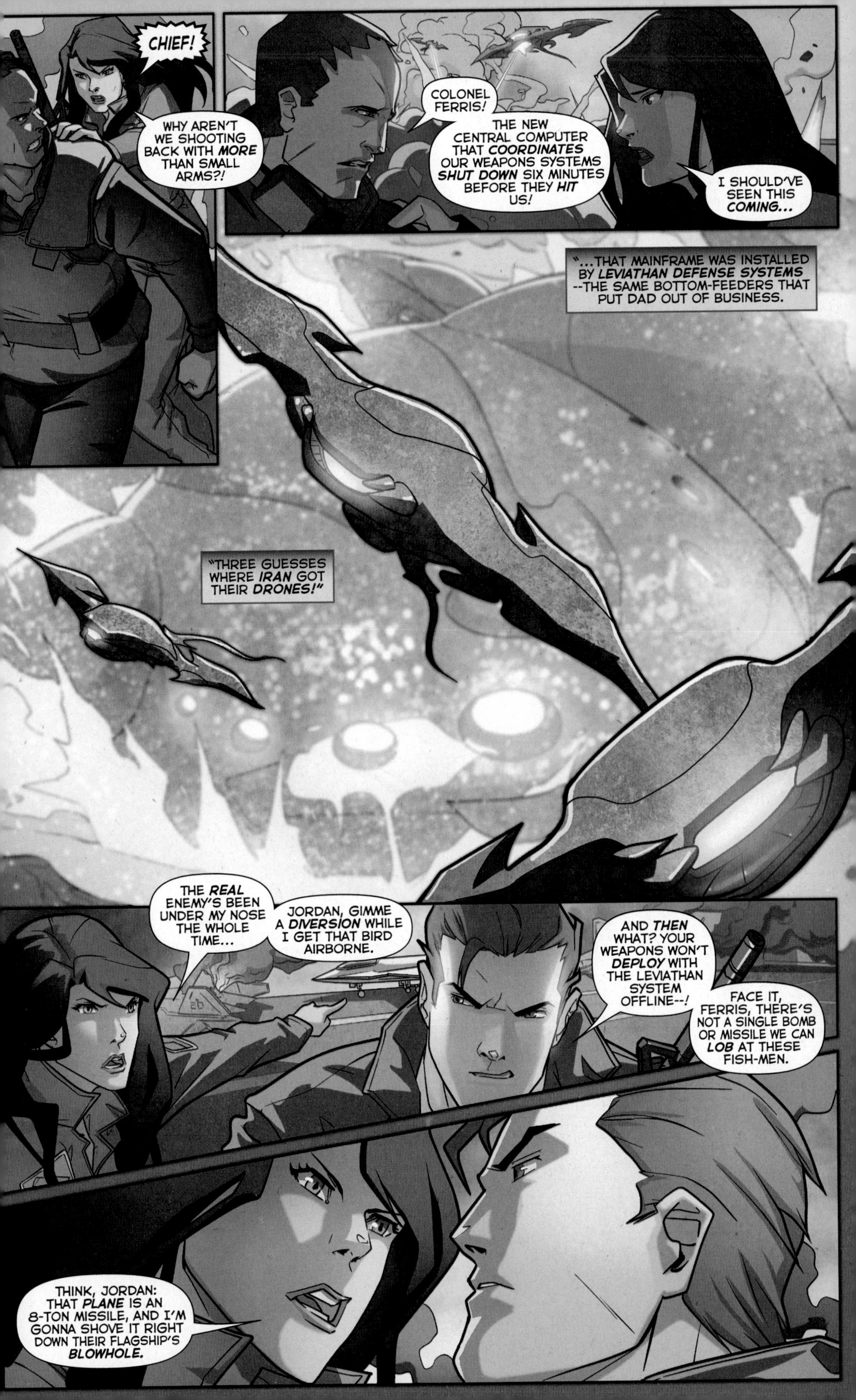
CHIEF!
WHY AREN'T WE SHOOTING BACK WITH MORE THAN SMALL ARMS?!
COLONEL FERRIS!
THE NEW CENTRAL COMPUTER THAT COORDINATES OUR WEAPONS SYSTEMS SHUT DOWN SIX MINUTES BEFORE THEY HIT US!
I SHOULD'VE SEEN THIS COMING...
"...THAT MAINFRAME WAS INSTALLED BY LEVIATHAN DEFENSE SYSTEMS --THE SAME BOTTOM-FEEDERS THAT PUT DAD OUT OF BUSINESS.
"THREE GUESSES WHERE IRAN GOT THEIR DRONES!"
THE REAL ENEMY'S BEEN UNDER MY NOSE THE WHOLE TIME...
JORDAN, GIMME A DIVERSION WHILE I GET THAT BIRD AIRBORNE.
AND THEN WHAT? YOUR WEAPONS WON'T DEPLOY WITH THE LEVIATHAN SYSTEM OFFLINE--!
FACE IT, FERRIS, THERE'S NOT A SINGLE BOMB OR MISSILE WE CAN LOB AT THESE FISH-MEN.
THINK, JORDAN: THAT PLANE IS AN 8-TON MISSILE, AND I'M GONNA SHOVE IT RIGHT DOWN THEIR FLAGSHIP'S BLOWHOLE.

WHY COME ALL THIS WAY IN PERSON, GANTHET? WHY NOT CONTACT ME THROUGH MY *RING*?

BUT THAT IS HALFWAY ACROSS THE GALAXY. I MAY NOT SEE MY FAMILY FOR *WEEKS*--!

I PROMISED MY SON I WOULD BE HERE FOR HIM TONIGHT. LET ME JUST *EXPLAIN* BEFORE I DEPART.

OUT OF THE QUESTION. YOUR DUTY TRUMPS SUCH TRIVIAL CONCERNS.

FAMILY IS ANYTHING BUT *TRIVIAL*!

THIS WILL ONLY TAKE A MOMENT!

ENOUGH QUESTIONS, LANTERN WALKER. GO TO PLANET KALVAX *AT ONCE* AND QUELL THE CIVIL WAR THERE.

WHAT IS *THIS*?

RING: WHERE DID THESE CREATURES *COME* FROM?

SCANNING.

D.N.A. PARTIAL MATCH FOR *GUARDIANS OF THE UNIVERSE*.

WHAT? THE GUARDIANS *SPAWNED* THEM?

BUT... THAT WOULD MEAN GANTHET WAS LURING ME *AWAY*!

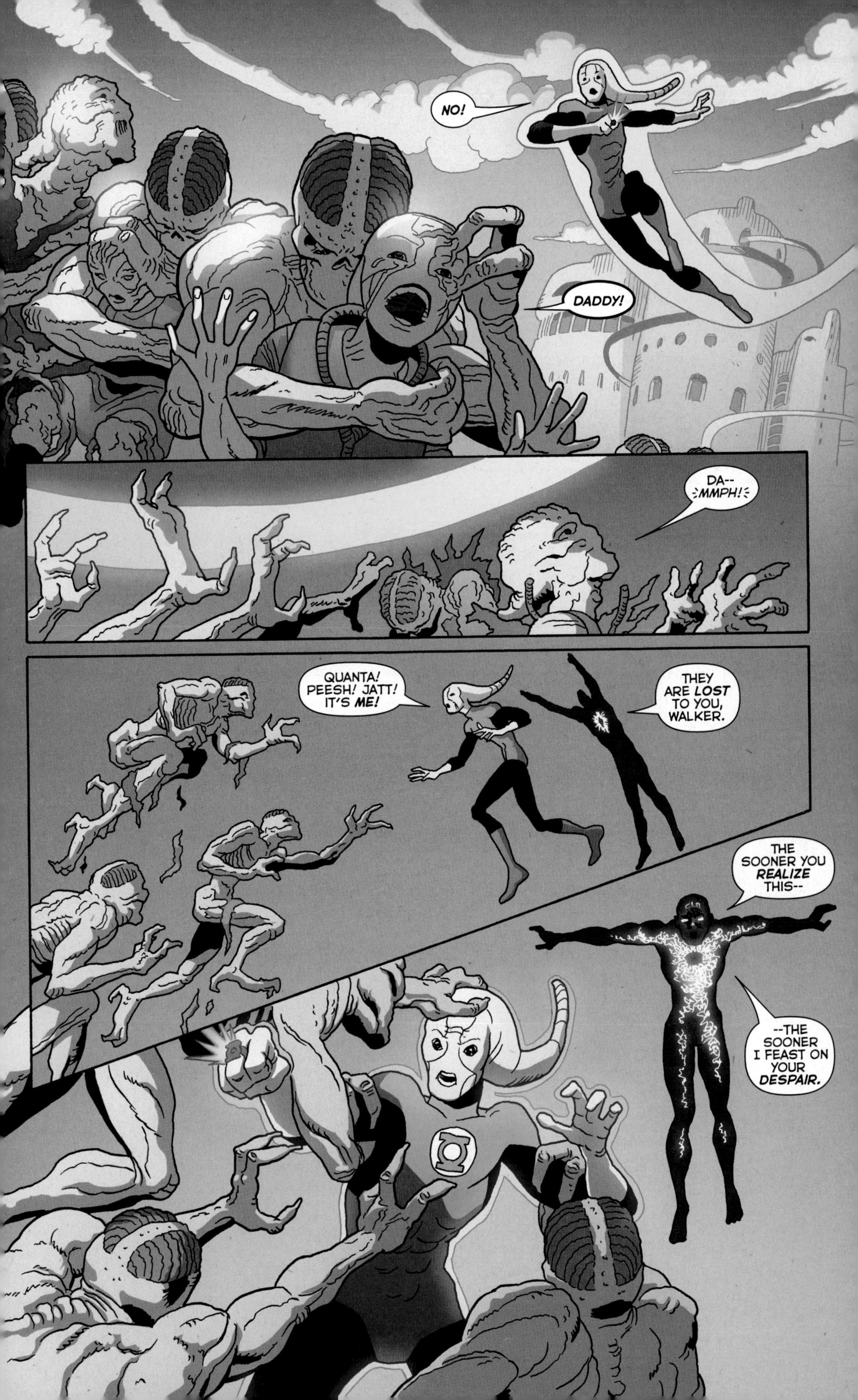
NO!
DADDY!
DA--
MMPH!
QUANTA! PEESH! JATT! IT'S ME!
THEY ARE LOST TO YOU, WALKER.
THE SOONER YOU REALIZE THIS--
--THE SOONER I FEAST ON YOUR DESPAIR.

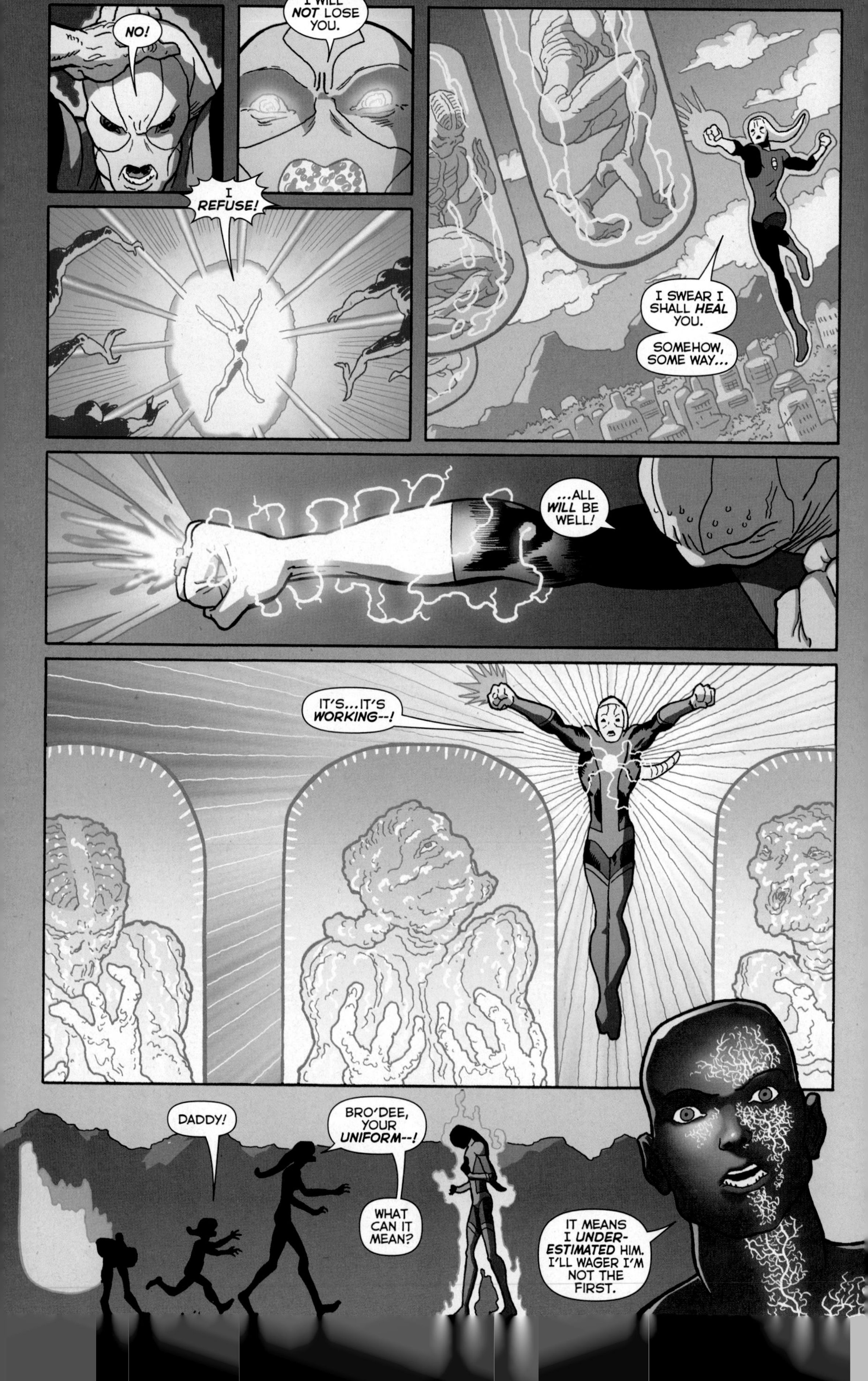
NO!
I WILL NOT LOSE YOU.
I REFUSE!
I SWEAR I SHALL HEAL YOU.
SOMEHOW, SOME WAY...
...ALL WILL BE WELL!
IT'S...IT'S WORKING--!
DADDY!
BRO'DEE, YOUR UNIFORM--!
WHAT CAN IT MEAN?
IT MEANS I UNDER-ESTIMATED HIM. I'LL WAGER I'M NOT THE FIRST.

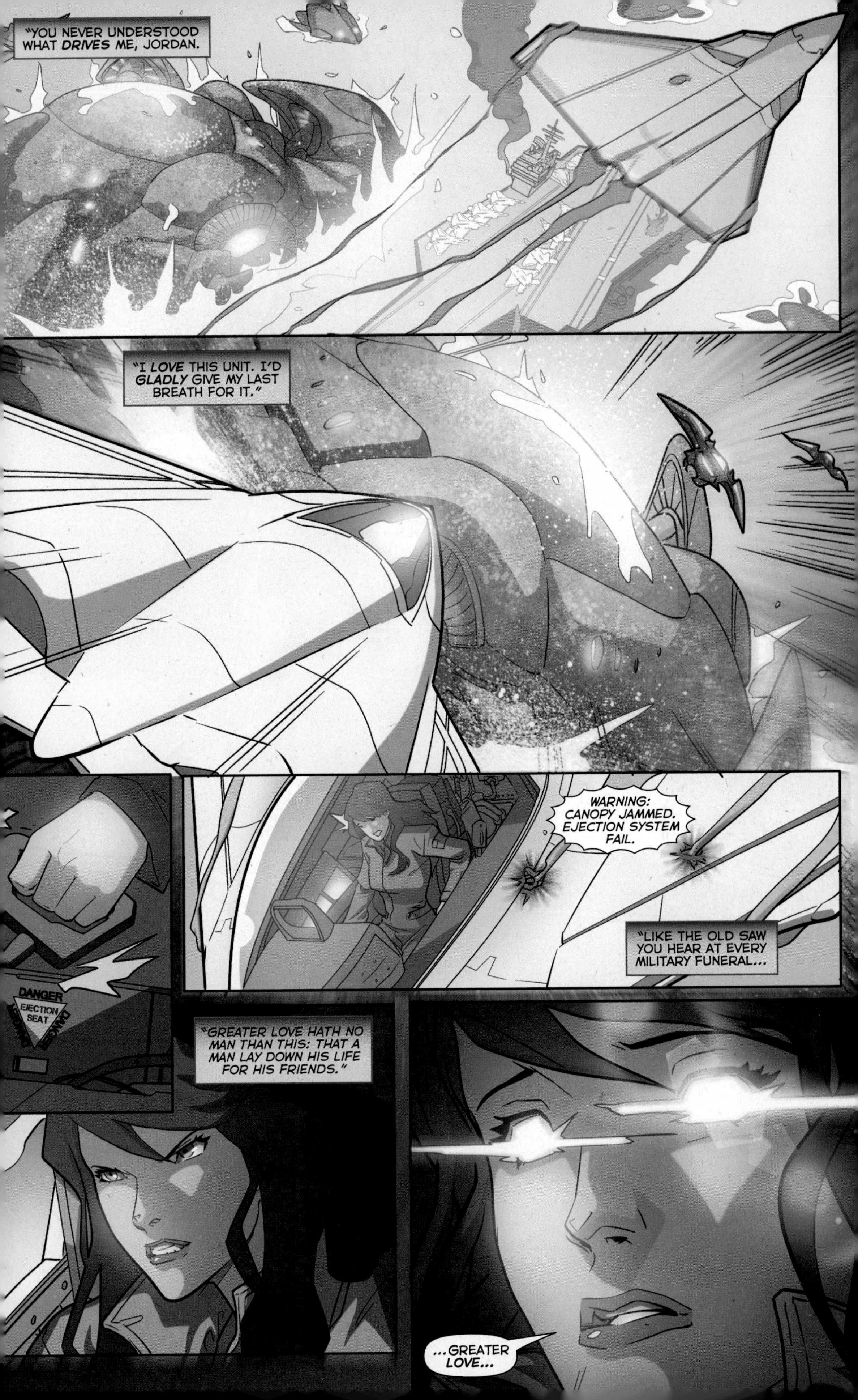
"YOU NEVER UNDERSTOOD WHAT DRIVES ME, JORDAN.
"I LOVE THIS UNIT. I'D GLADLY GIVE MY LAST BREATH FOR IT."
DANGER
EJECTION SEAT
DANGER
WARNING: CANOPY JAMMED. EJECTION SYSTEM FAIL.
"LIKE THE OLD SAW YOU HEAR AT EVERY MILITARY FUNERAL...
"GREATER LOVE HATH NO MAN THAN THIS: THAT A MAN LAY DOWN HIS LIFE FOR HIS FRIENDS."
...GREATER LOVE...

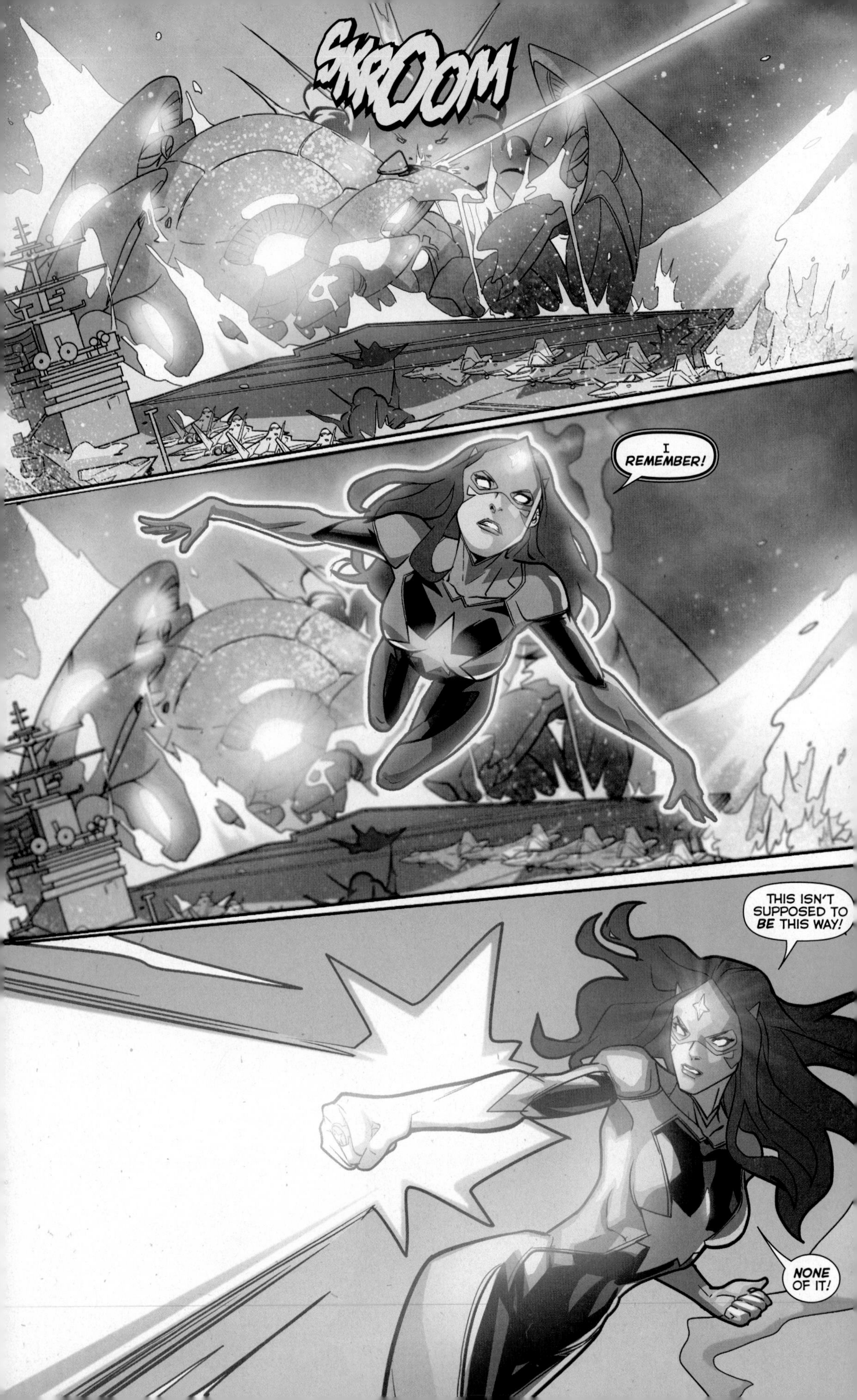
SKROOM
I REMEMBER!
THIS ISN'T SUPPOSED TO BE THIS WAY!
NONE OF IT!

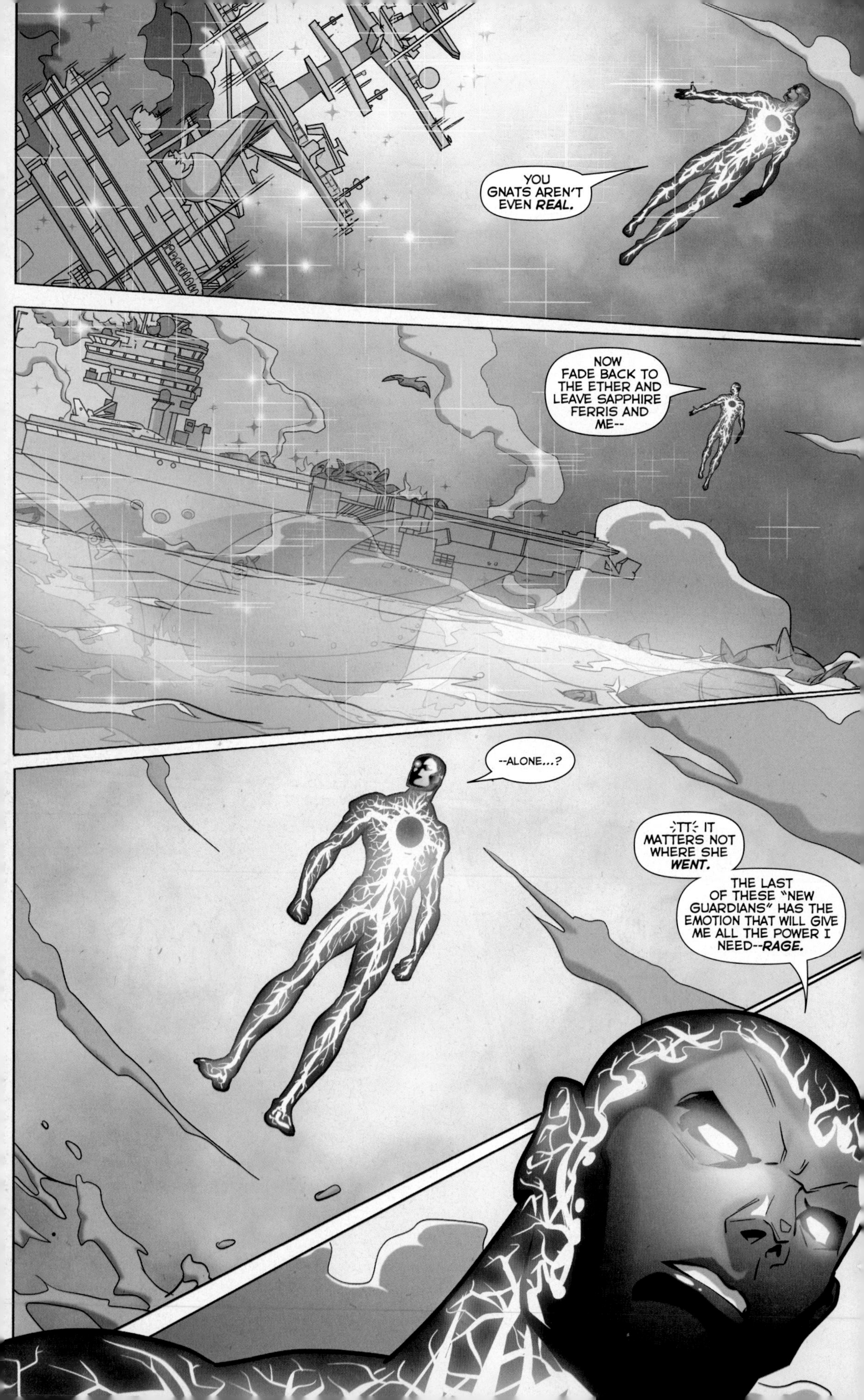
YOU GNATS AREN'T EVEN *REAL.*
NOW FADE BACK TO THE ETHER AND LEAVE SAPPHIRE FERRIS AND ME--
--ALONE...?
-TT- IT MATTERS NOT WHERE SHE *WENT.*
THE LAST OF THESE "NEW GUARDIANS" HAS THE EMOTION THAT WILL GIVE ME ALL THE POWER I NEED--*RAGE.*

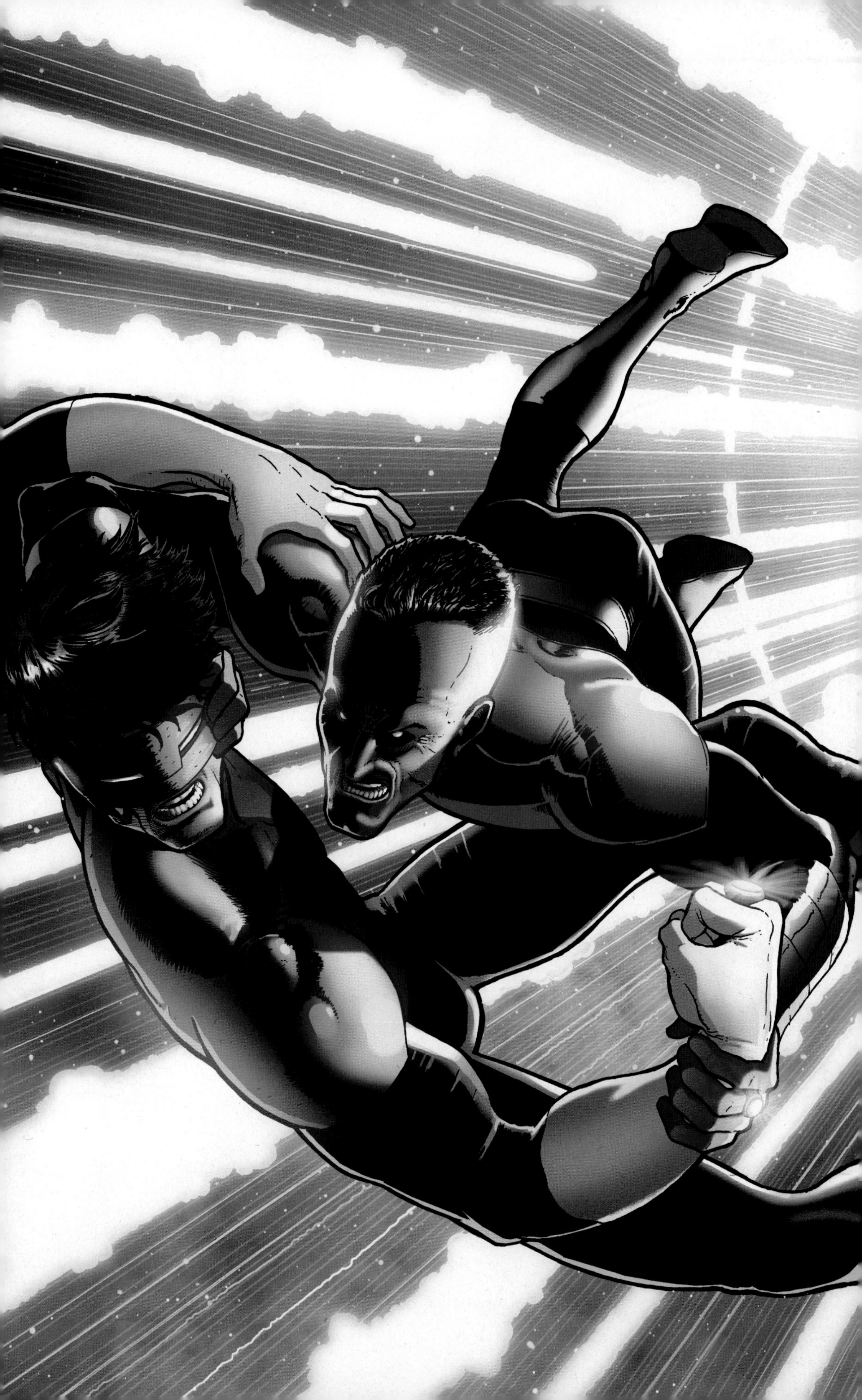

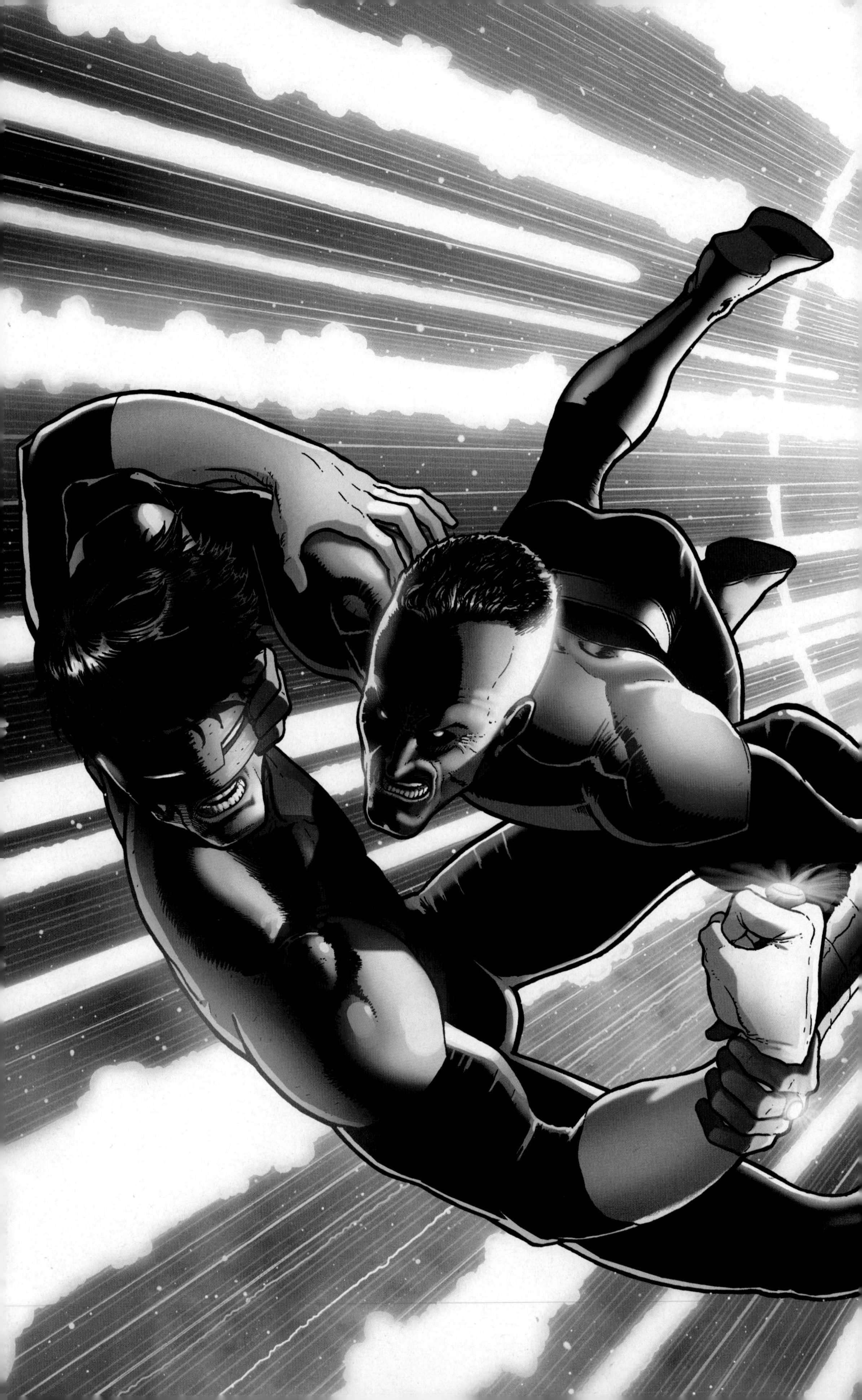

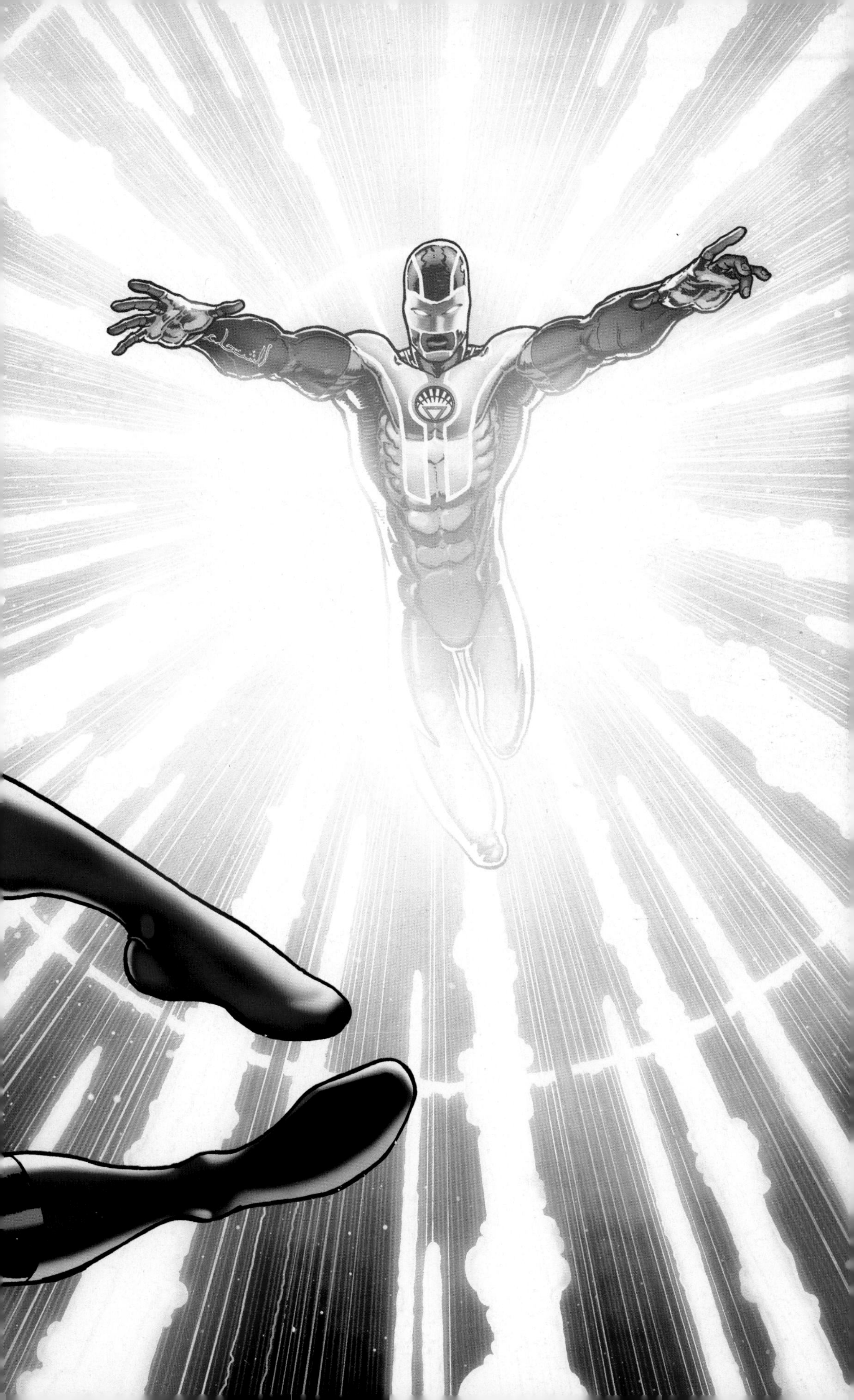

SHADOW OF DEATH

TONY BEDARD writer ANDRES GUINALDO penciller RAUL FERNANDEZ inker
AARON KUDER & WIL QUINTANA cover

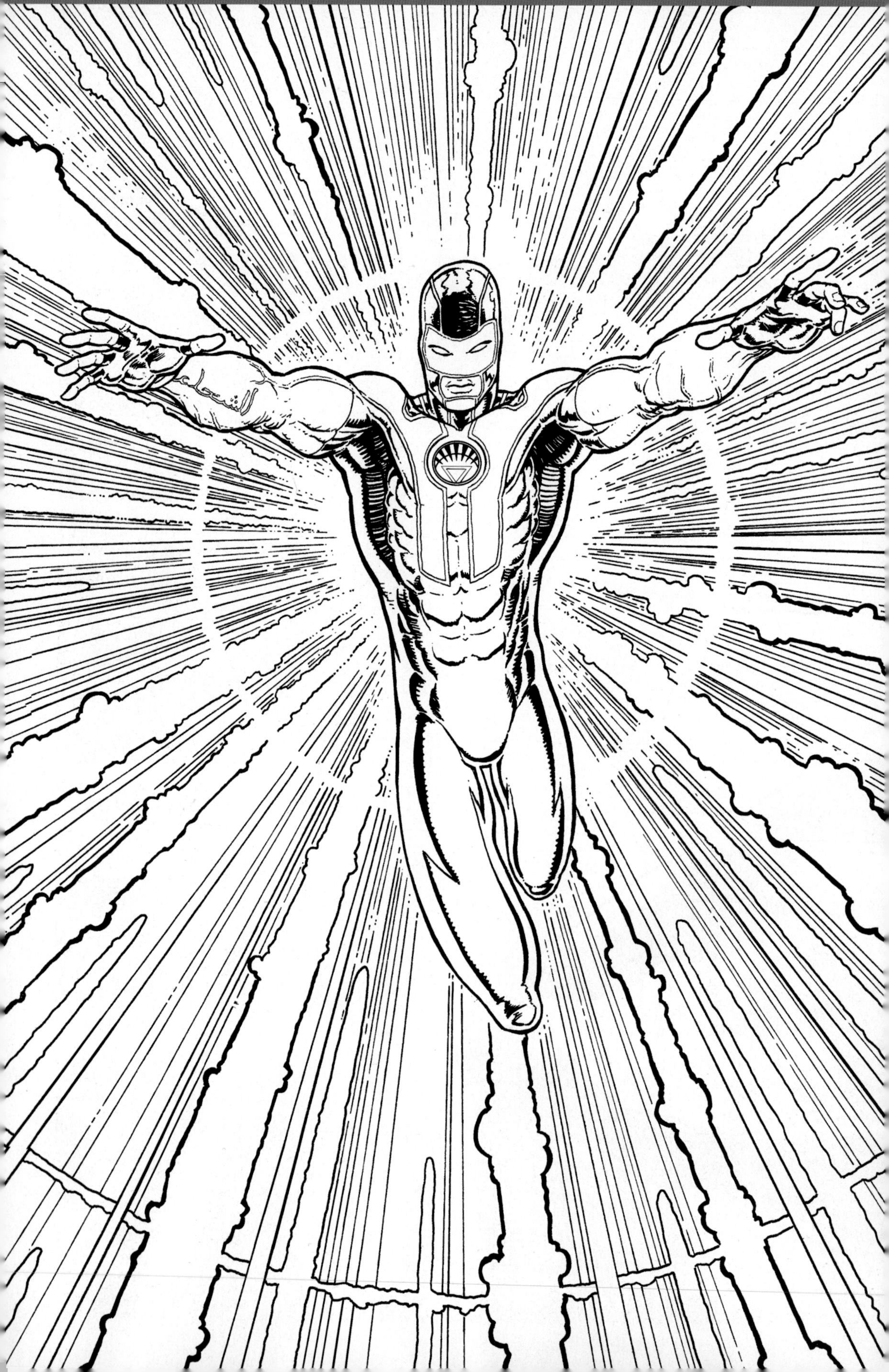

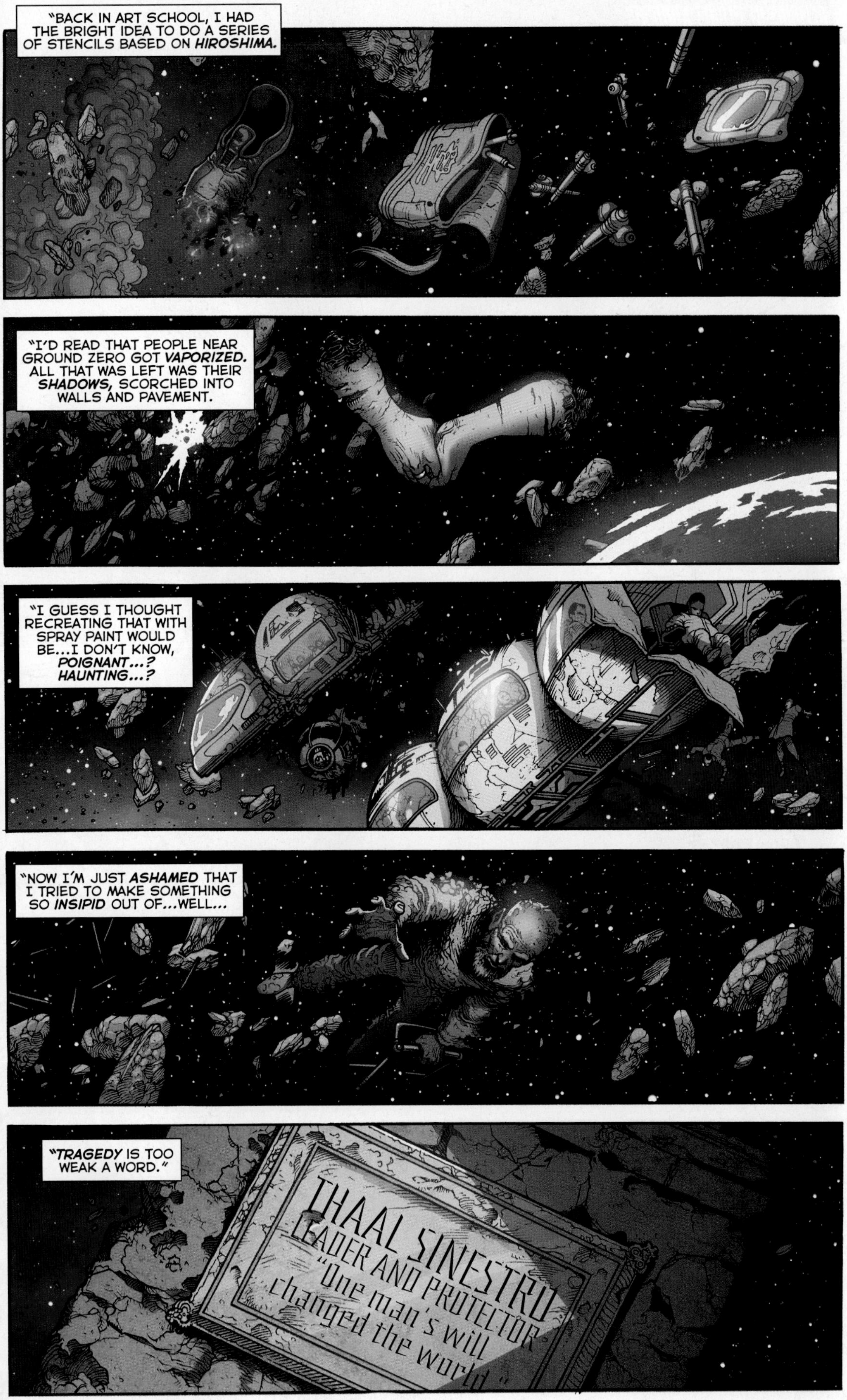
"BACK IN ART SCHOOL, I HAD THE BRIGHT IDEA TO DO A SERIES OF STENCILS BASED ON HIROSHIMA.
"I'D READ THAT PEOPLE NEAR GROUND ZERO GOT VAPORIZED. ALL THAT WAS LEFT WAS THEIR SHADOWS, SCORCHED INTO WALLS AND PAVEMENT.
"I GUESS I THOUGHT RECREATING THAT WITH SPRAY PAINT WOULD BE...I DON'T KNOW, POIGNANT...? HAUNTING...?
"NOW I'M JUST ASHAMED THAT I TRIED TO MAKE SOMETHING SO INSIPID OUT OF...WELL...
"TRAGEDY IS TOO WEAK A WORD."
THAAL SINESTRO
LEADER AND PROTECTOR
"One man's will changed the world."

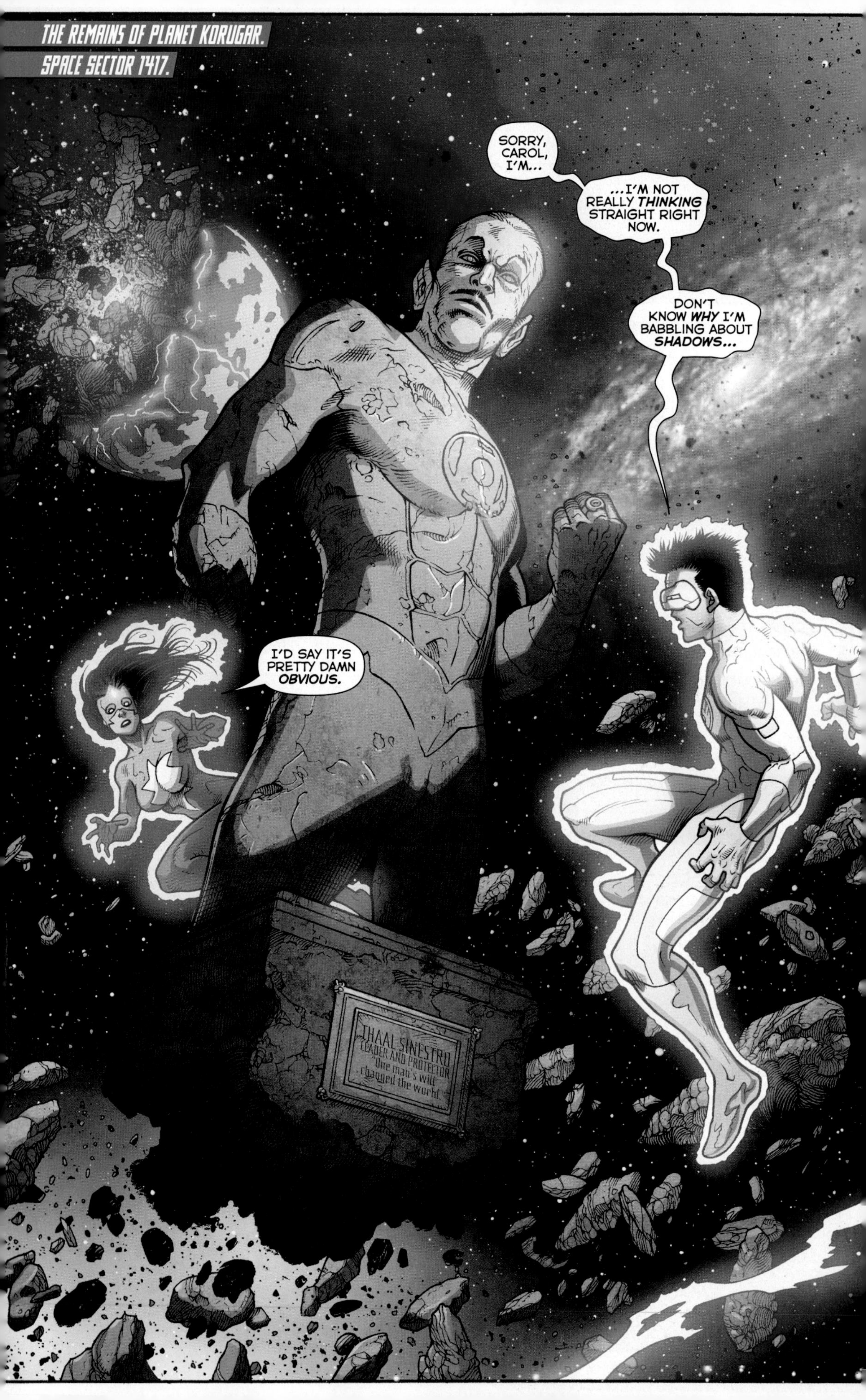
THE REMAINS OF PLANET KORUGAR.
SPACE SECTOR 1417.
SORRY, CAROL, I'M...
...I'M NOT REALLY *THINKING* STRAIGHT RIGHT NOW.
DON'T KNOW *WHY* I'M BABBLING ABOUT *SHADOWS*...
I'D SAY IT'S PRETTY DAMN *OBVIOUS.*
THAAL SINESTRO
LEADER AND PROTECTOR
"One man's will changed the world."

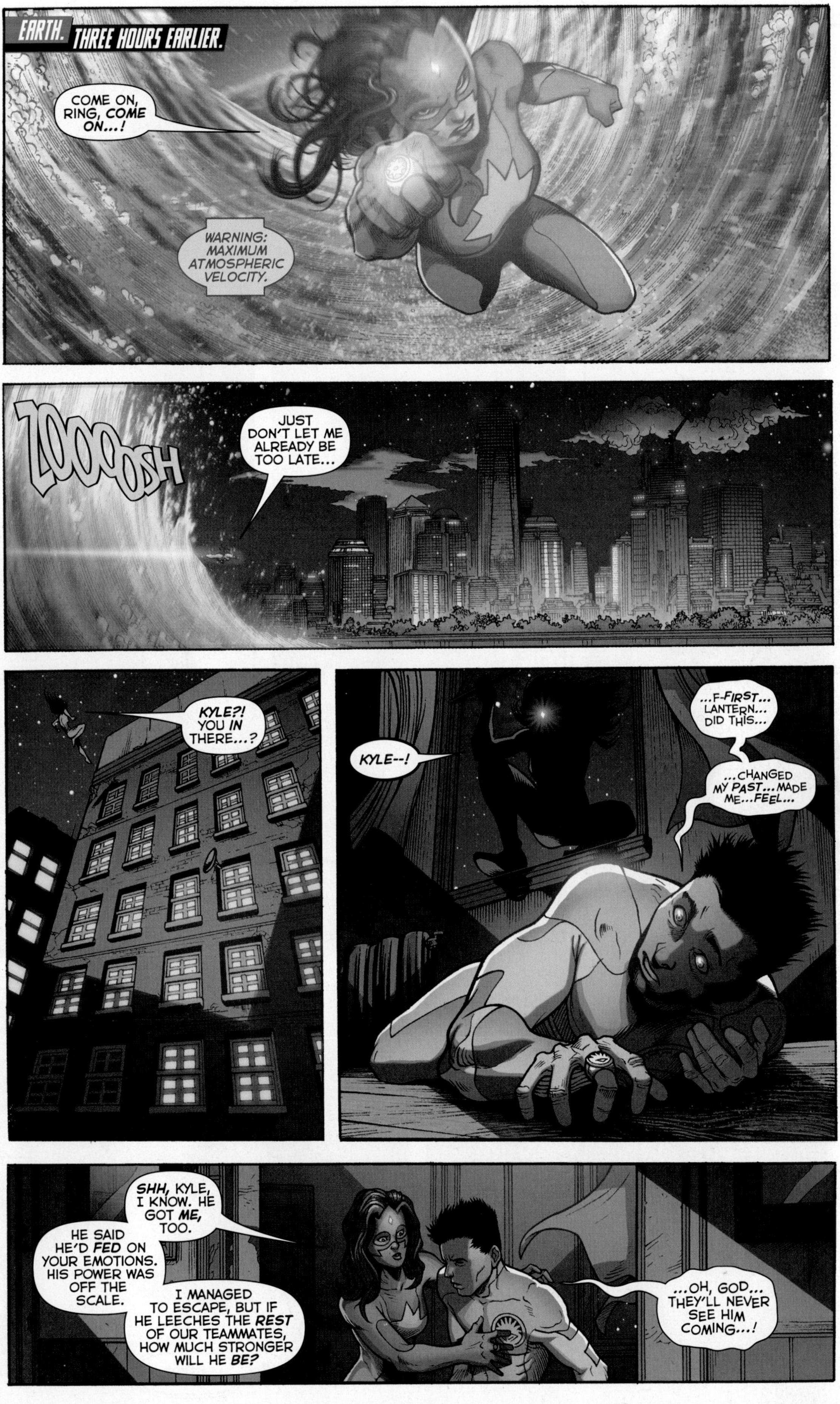
EARTH. THREE HOURS EARLIER.
COME ON, RING, COME ON...!
WARNING: MAXIMUM ATMOSPHERIC VELOCITY.
ZOOOOSH
JUST DON'T LET ME ALREADY BE TOO LATE...
KYLE?! YOU IN THERE...?
KYLE--!
...F-FIRST... LANTERN... DID THIS...
...CHANGED MY PAST... MADE ME...FEEL...
SHH, KYLE, I KNOW. HE GOT ME, TOO.
HE SAID HE'D FED ON YOUR EMOTIONS. HIS POWER WAS OFF THE SCALE.
I MANAGED TO ESCAPE, BUT IF HE LEECHES THE REST OF OUR TEAMMATES, HOW MUCH STRONGER WILL HE BE?
...OH, GOD... THEY'LL NEVER SEE HIM COMING...!

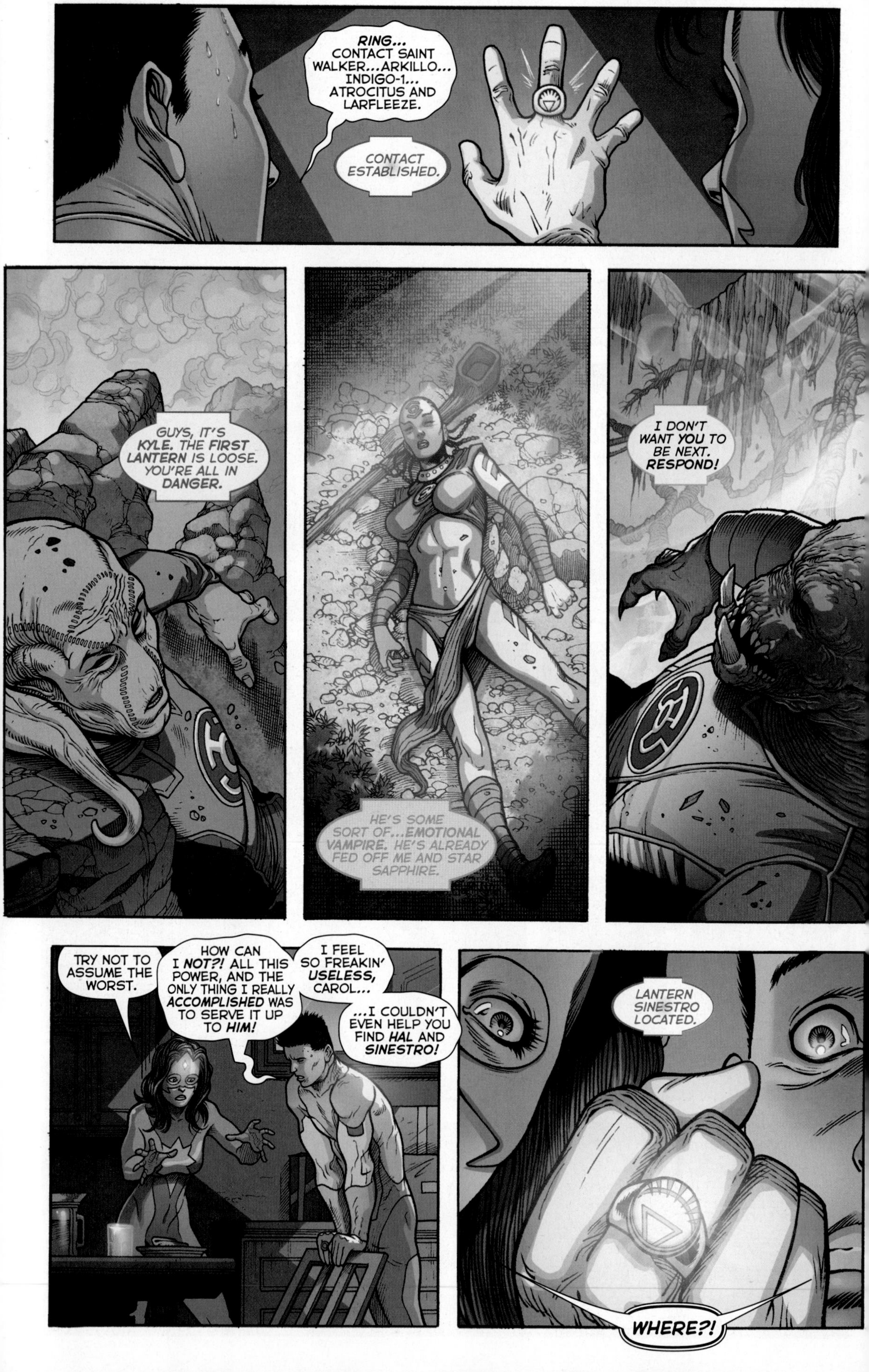
RING... CONTACT SAINT WALKER...ARKILLO... INDIGO-1... ATROCITUS AND LARFLEEZE.
CONTACT ESTABLISHED.
GUYS, IT'S KYLE. THE FIRST LANTERN IS LOOSE. YOU'RE ALL IN DANGER.
HE'S SOME SORT OF...EMOTIONAL VAMPIRE. HE'S ALREADY FED OFF ME AND STAR SAPPHIRE.
I DON'T WANT YOU TO BE NEXT. RESPOND!
TRY NOT TO ASSUME THE WORST.
HOW CAN I NOT?! ALL THIS POWER, AND THE ONLY THING I REALLY ACCOMPLISHED WAS TO SERVE IT UP TO HIM!
I FEEL SO FREAKIN' USELESS, CAROL...
...I COULDN'T EVEN HELP YOU FIND HAL AND SINESTRO!
LANTERN SINESTRO LOCATED.
WHERE?!

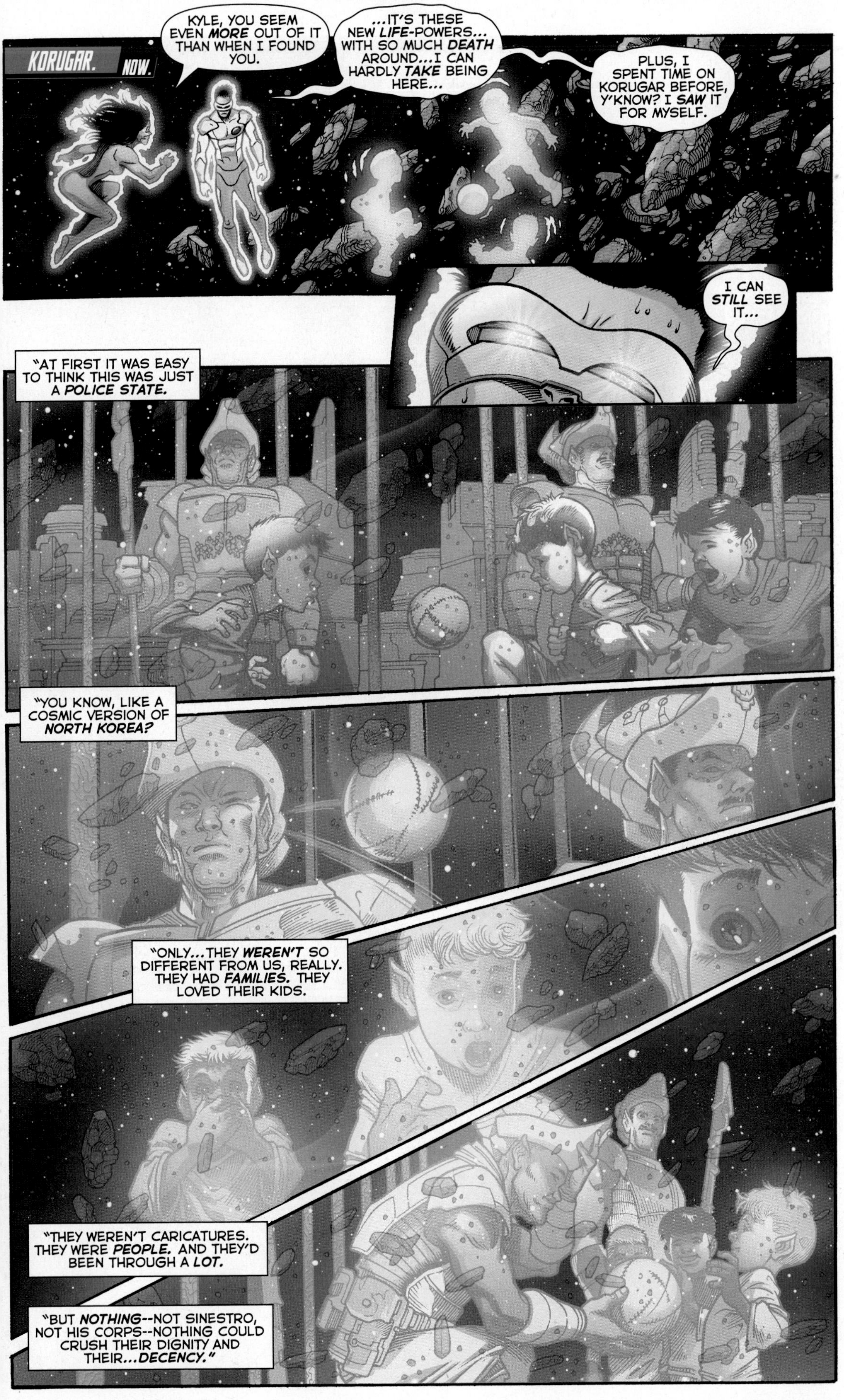
KORUGAR. NOW.
KYLE, YOU SEEM EVEN MORE OUT OF IT THAN WHEN I FOUND YOU.
...IT'S THESE NEW LIFE-POWERS... WITH SO MUCH DEATH AROUND...I CAN HARDLY TAKE BEING HERE...
PLUS, I SPENT TIME ON KORUGAR BEFORE, Y'KNOW? I SAW IT FOR MYSELF.
I CAN STILL SEE IT...
"AT FIRST IT WAS EASY TO THINK THIS WAS JUST A POLICE STATE.
"YOU KNOW, LIKE A COSMIC VERSION OF NORTH KOREA?
"ONLY...THEY WEREN'T SO DIFFERENT FROM US, REALLY. THEY HAD FAMILIES. THEY LOVED THEIR KIDS.
"THEY WEREN'T CARICATURES. THEY WERE PEOPLE. AND THEY'D BEEN THROUGH A LOT.
"BUT NOTHING--NOT SINESTRO, NOT HIS CORPS--NOTHING COULD CRUSH THEIR DIGNITY AND THEIR...DECENCY."

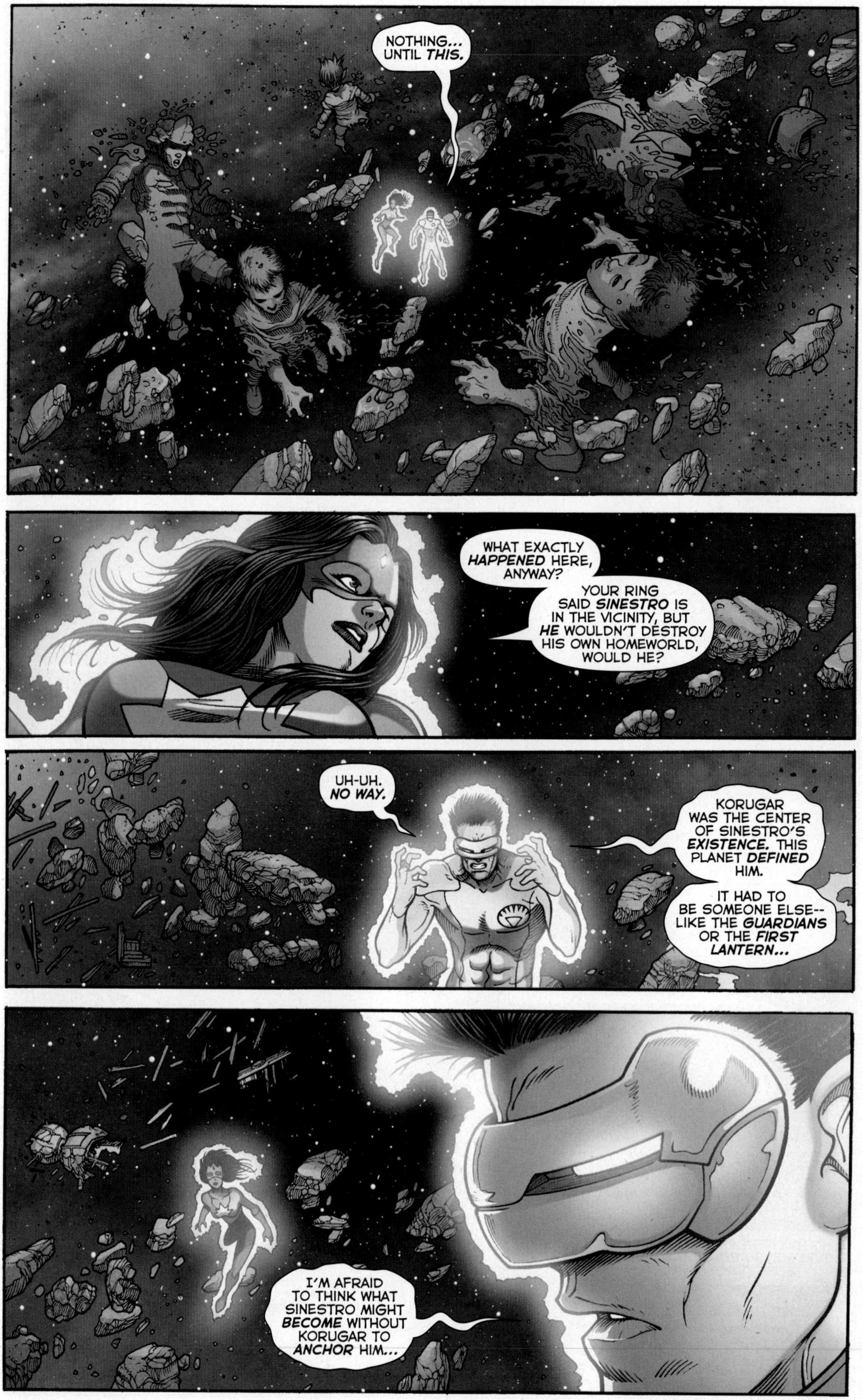
NOTHING... UNTIL *THIS.*
WHAT EXACTLY *HAPPENED* HERE, ANYWAY?
YOUR RING SAID *SINESTRO* IS IN THE VICINITY, BUT *HE* WOULDN'T DESTROY HIS OWN HOMEWORLD, WOULD HE?
UH-UH. *NO WAY.*
KORUGAR WAS THE CENTER OF SINESTRO'S *EXISTENCE.* THIS PLANET *DEFINED* HIM.
IT HAD TO BE SOMEONE ELSE-- LIKE THE *GUARDIANS* OR THE *FIRST LANTERN...*
I'M AFRAID TO THINK WHAT SINESTRO MIGHT *BECOME* WITHOUT KORUGAR TO *ANCHOR* HIM...

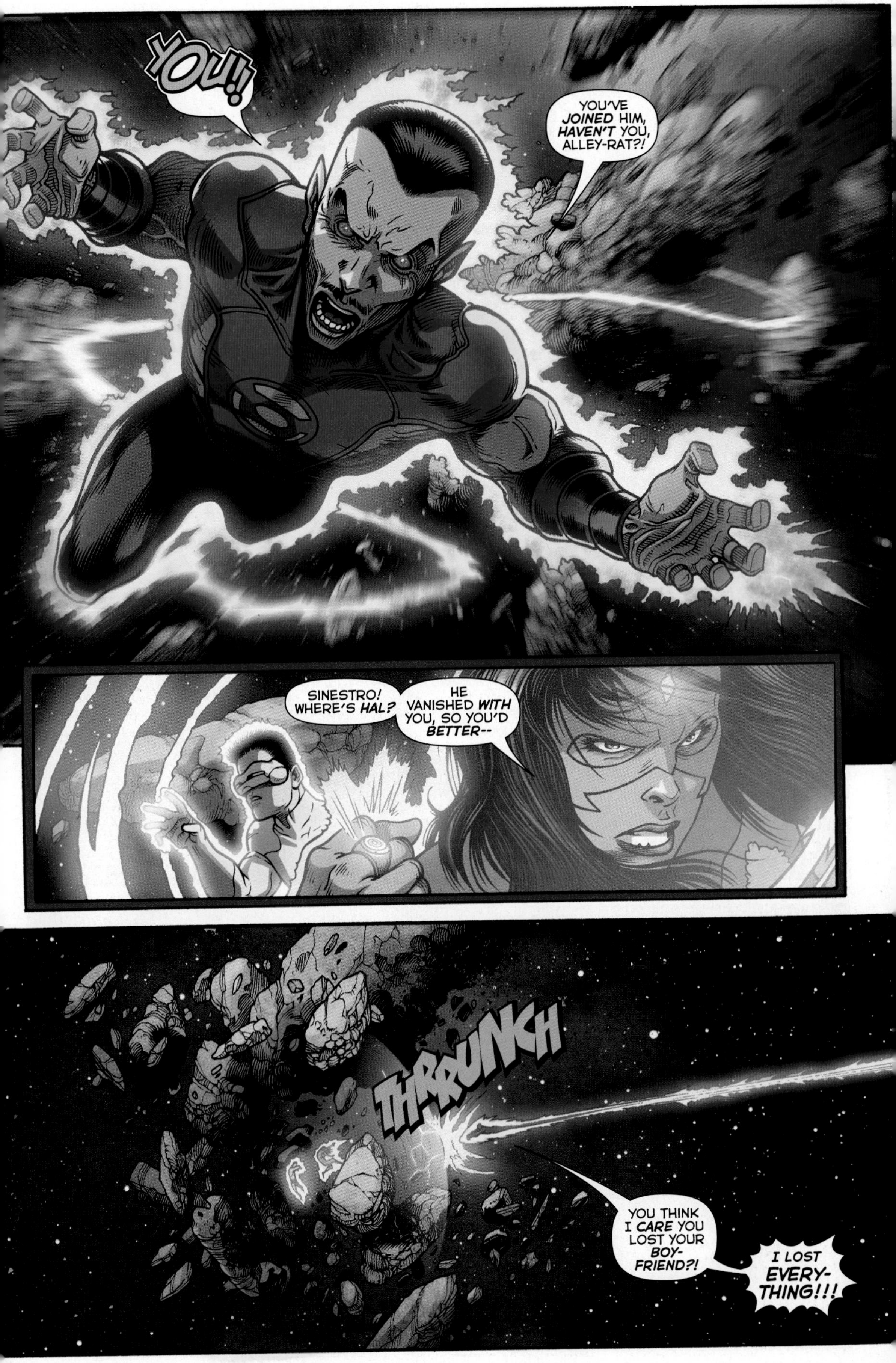
YOU!!
YOU'VE JOINED HIM, HAVEN'T YOU, ALLEY-RAT?!
SINESTRO! WHERE'S HAL?
HE VANISHED WITH YOU, SO YOU'D BETTER--
THRRUNCH
YOU THINK I CARE YOU LOST YOUR BOY-FRIEND?!
I LOST EVERY-THING!!!

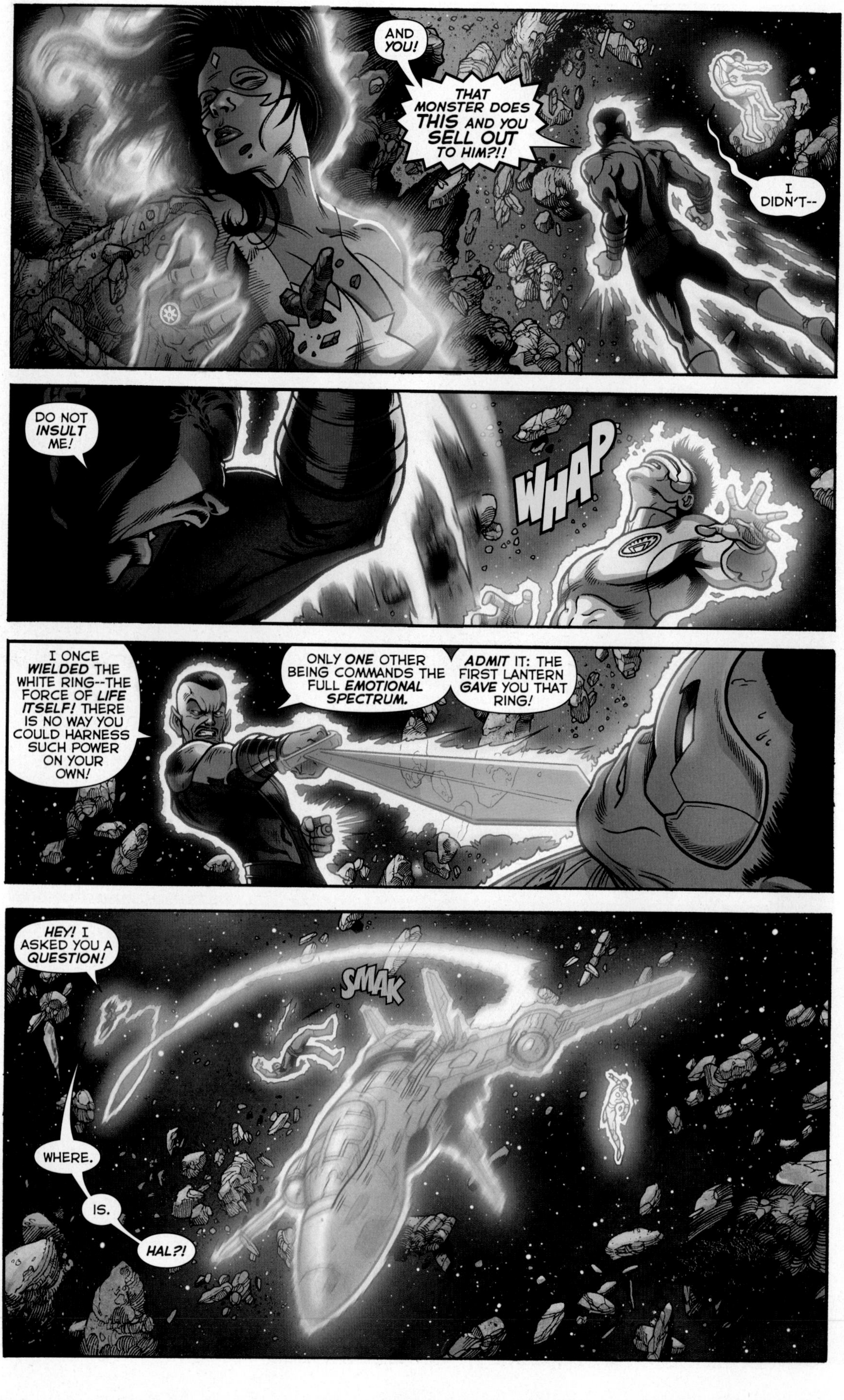
AND YOU!
THAT MONSTER DOES THIS AND YOU SELL OUT TO HIM?!!
I DIDN'T--
DO NOT INSULT ME!
WHAP
I ONCE WIELDED THE WHITE RING--THE FORCE OF LIFE ITSELF! THERE IS NO WAY YOU COULD HARNESS SUCH POWER ON YOUR OWN!
ONLY ONE OTHER BEING COMMANDS THE FULL EMOTIONAL SPECTRUM.
ADMIT IT: THE FIRST LANTERN GAVE YOU THAT RING!
HEY! I ASKED YOU A QUESTION!
SMAK
WHERE.
IS.
HAL?!

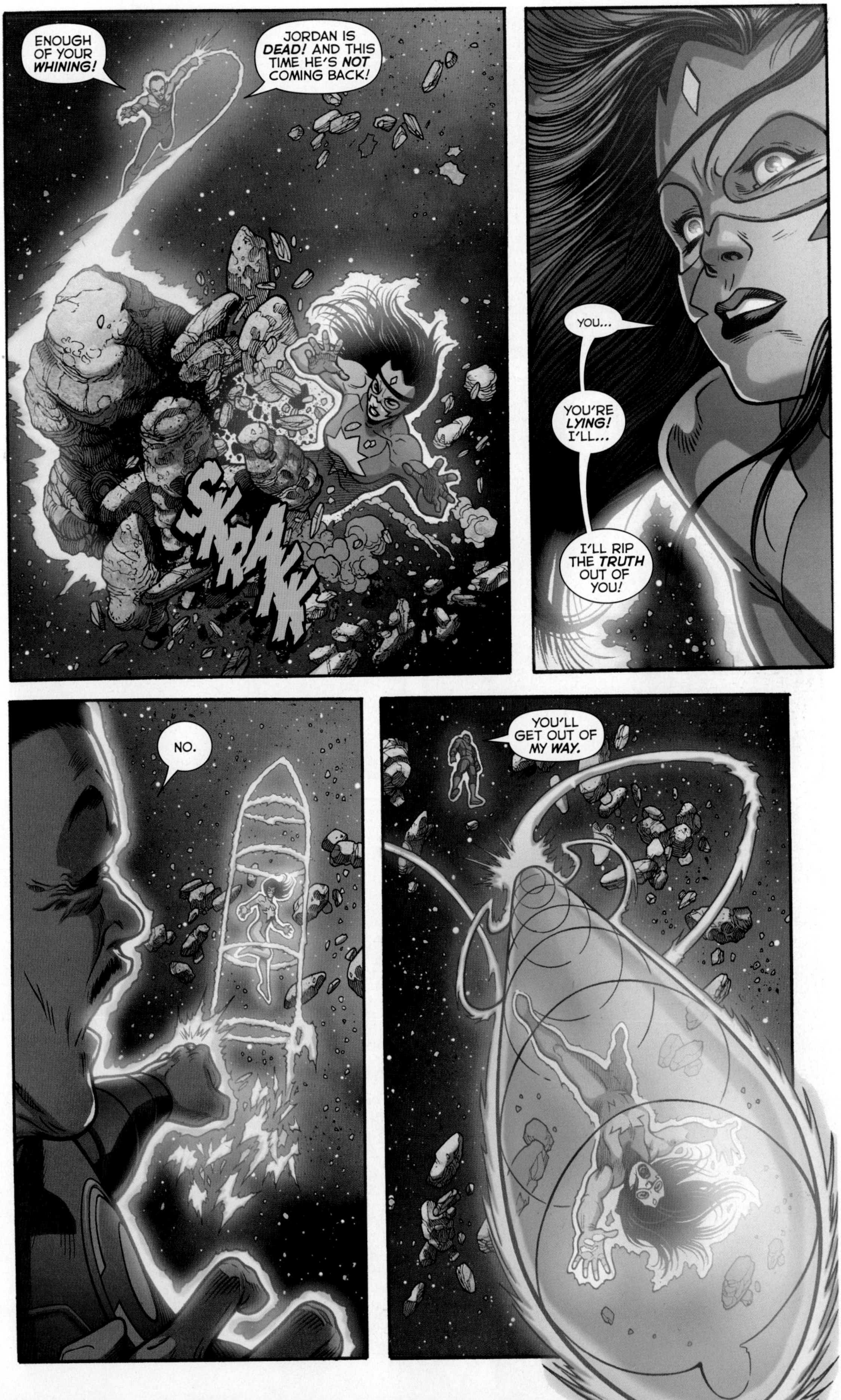
ENOUGH OF YOUR WHINING!
JORDAN IS DEAD! AND THIS TIME HE'S NOT COMING BACK!
SKRAKK
YOU...
YOU'RE LYING! I'LL...
I'LL RIP THE TRUTH OUT OF YOU!
NO.
YOU'LL GET OUT OF MY WAY.

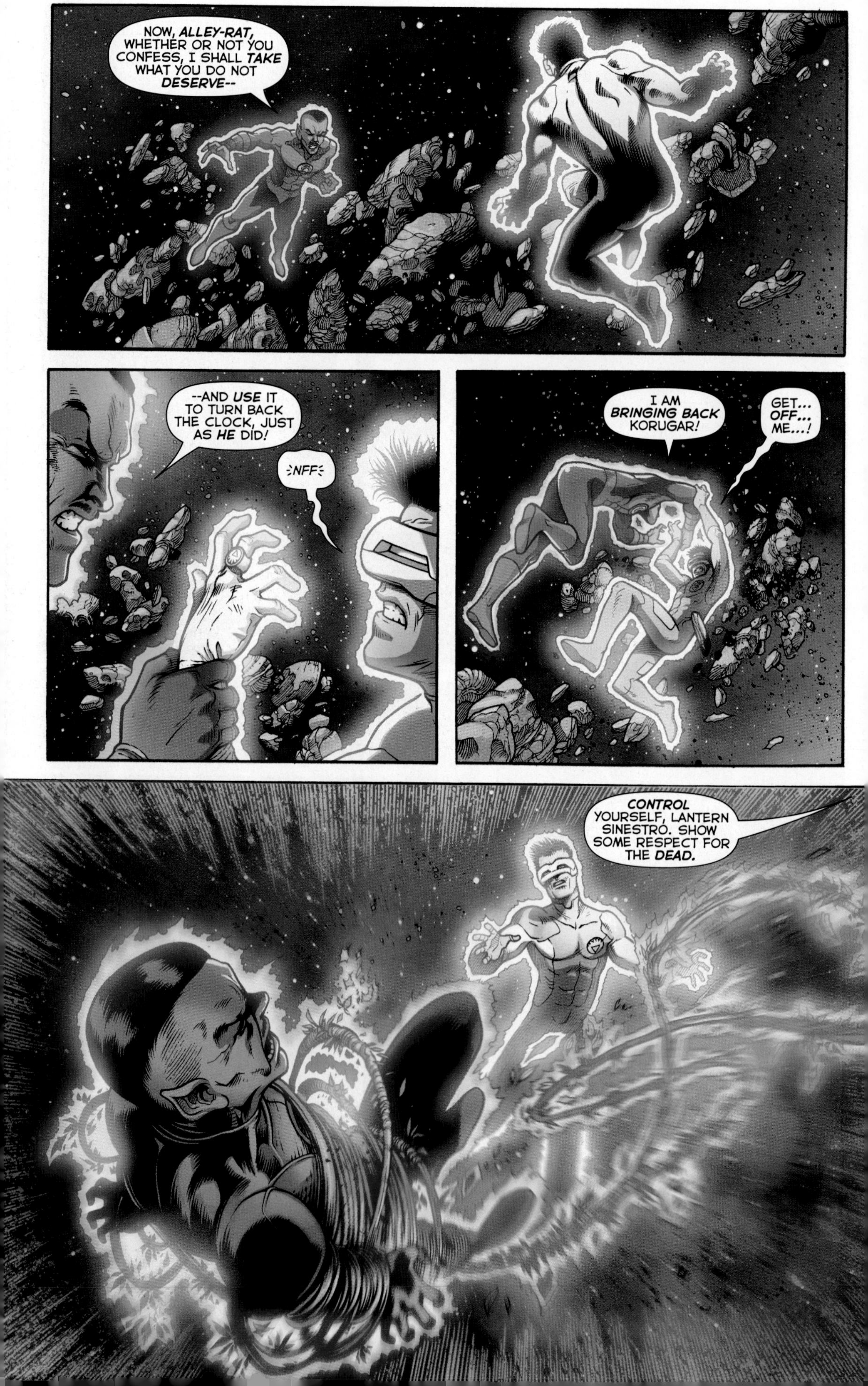
NOW, ALLEY-RAT, WHETHER OR NOT YOU CONFESS, I SHALL TAKE WHAT YOU DO NOT DESERVE--
--AND USE IT TO TURN BACK THE CLOCK, JUST AS HE DID!
NFF
I AM BRINGING BACK KORUGAR!
GET... OFF... ME...!
CONTROL YOURSELF, LANTERN SINESTRO. SHOW SOME RESPECT FOR THE DEAD.

SORRY, B'DG, WISH I COULD HELP, BUT--

YOUR RING CANNOT FUNCTION *AGAINST* HIM, I KNOW.

BUT WE DID NOT COME TO *FIGHT* LANTERN SINESTRO...

"...NOT WHILE WE *ALL* HAVE A COMMON ENEMY IN THE *FIRST LANTERN.*"

I'VE SEEN THE *SQUIRREL-LANTERN* BEFORE, BUT WHO'S THE OTHER GUY?

NO IDEA.

ALLOW ME TO PRESENT *SIMON BAZ* OF EARTH...

...NEWEST PROTECTOR OF SECTOR 2814 AND, AH...

...HAL JORDAN'S *REPLACEMENT.*

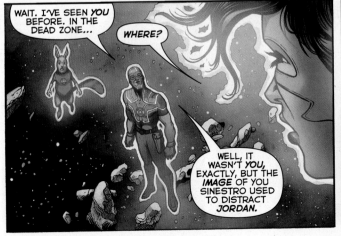

WAIT. I'VE SEEN *YOU* BEFORE. IN THE DEAD ZONE...

WHERE?

WELL, IT WASN'T *YOU,* EXACTLY, BUT THE *IMAGE* OF YOU SINESTRO USED TO DISTRACT *JORDAN.*

YOU FOUND *HAL?!*

IS HE *OKAY?!*

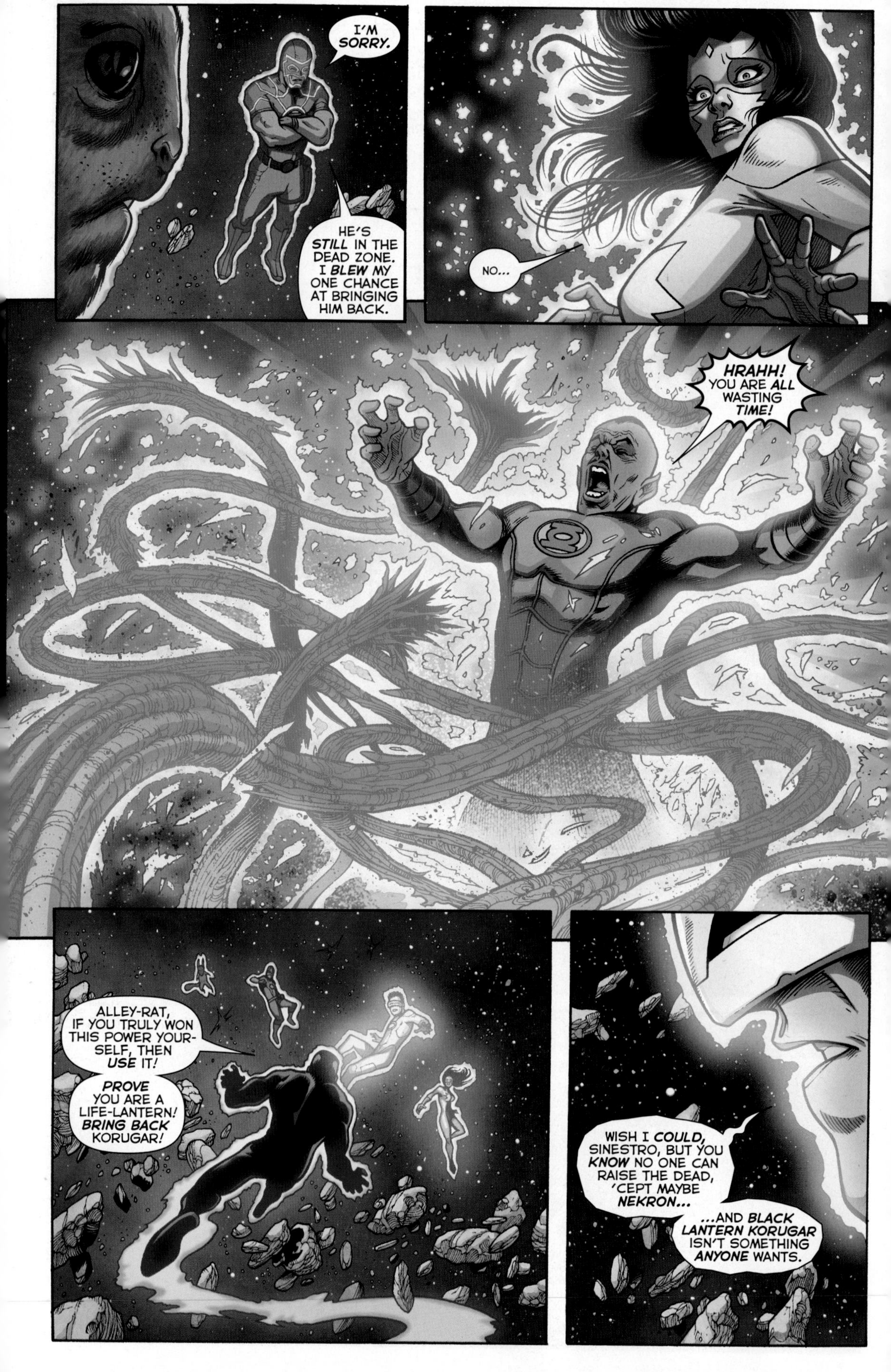
I'M SORRY.
HE'S STILL IN THE DEAD ZONE. I BLEW MY ONE CHANCE AT BRINGING HIM BACK.
NO...
HRAHH! YOU ARE ALL WASTING TIME!
ALLEY-RAT, IF YOU TRULY WON THIS POWER YOURSELF, THEN USE IT!
PROVE YOU ARE A LIFE-LANTERN! BRING BACK KORUGAR!
WISH I COULD, SINESTRO, BUT YOU KNOW NO ONE CAN RAISE THE DEAD, 'CEPT MAYBE NEKRON...
...AND BLACK LANTERN KORUGAR ISN'T SOMETHING ANYONE WANTS.

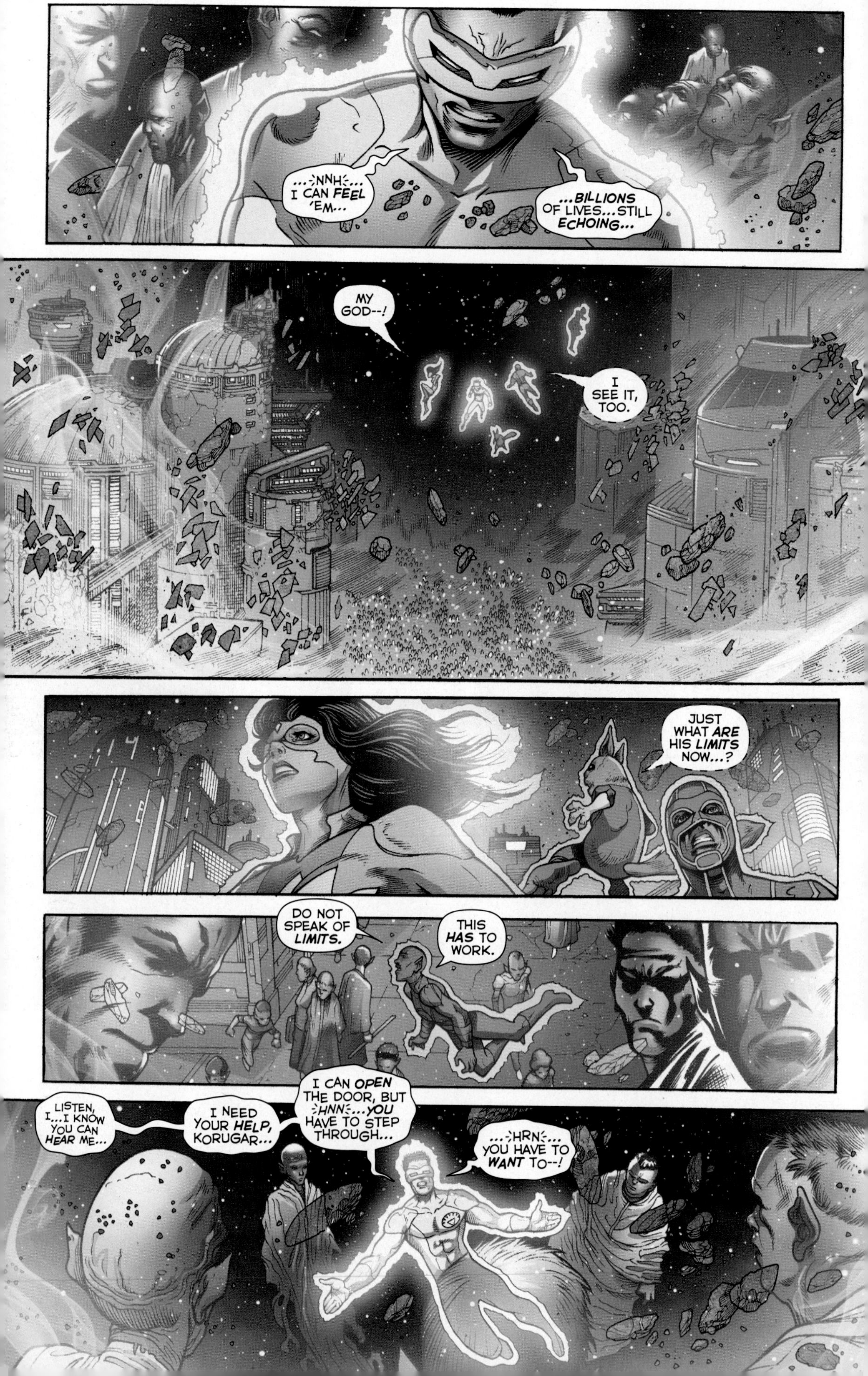
...NNH...
I CAN FEEL 'EM...
...BILLIONS OF LIVES...STILL ECHOING...
MY GOD--!
I SEE IT, TOO.
JUST WHAT ARE HIS LIMITS NOW...?
DO NOT SPEAK OF LIMITS.
THIS HAS TO WORK.
LISTEN, I...I KNOW YOU CAN HEAR ME...
I NEED YOUR HELP, KORUGAR...
I CAN OPEN THE DOOR, BUT HNN...YOU HAVE TO STEP THROUGH...
...HRN... YOU HAVE TO WANT TO--!

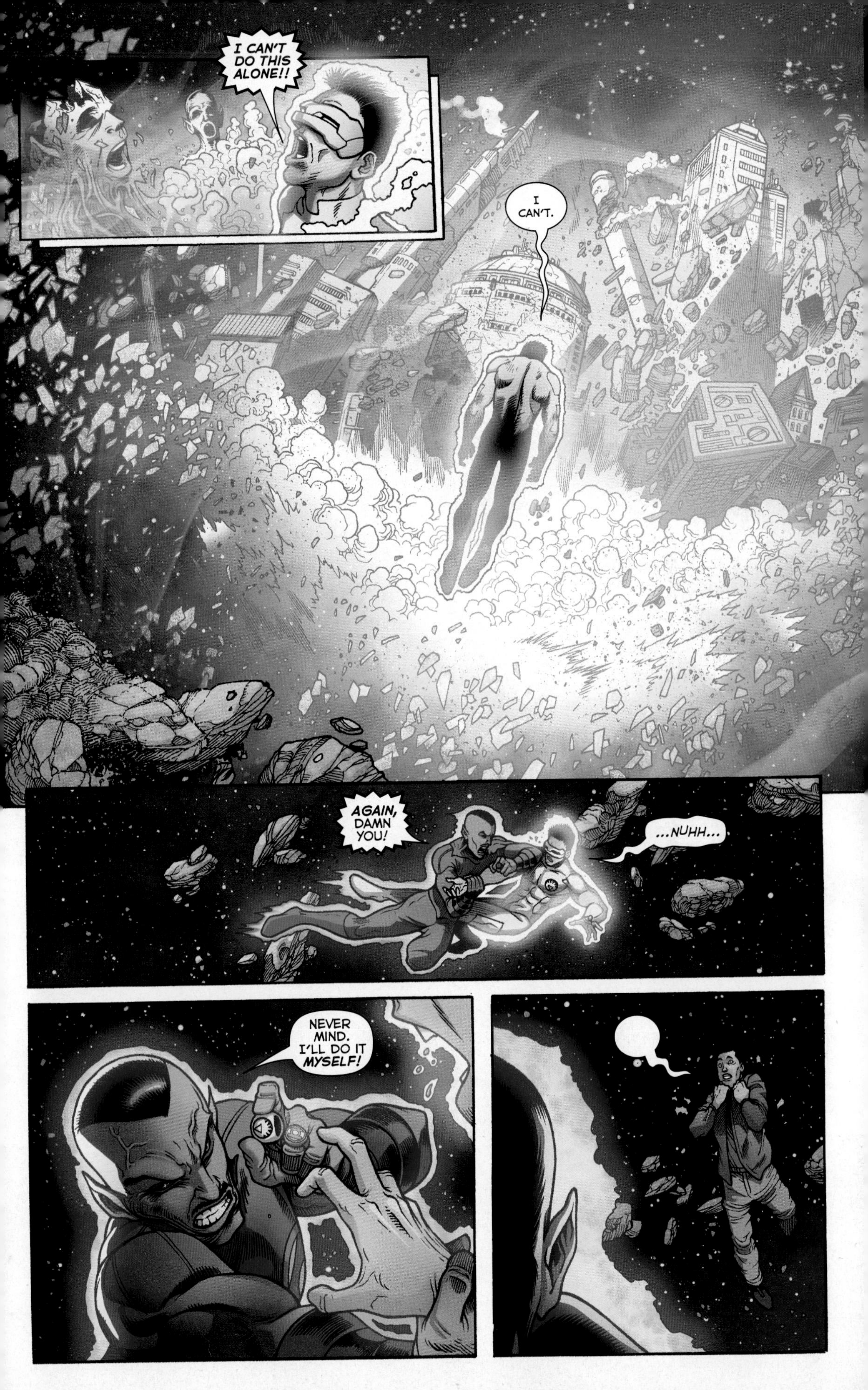
I CAN'T DO THIS ALONE!!
I CAN'T.
AGAIN, DAMN YOU!
...NUHH...
NEVER MIND. I'LL DO IT *MYSELF!*

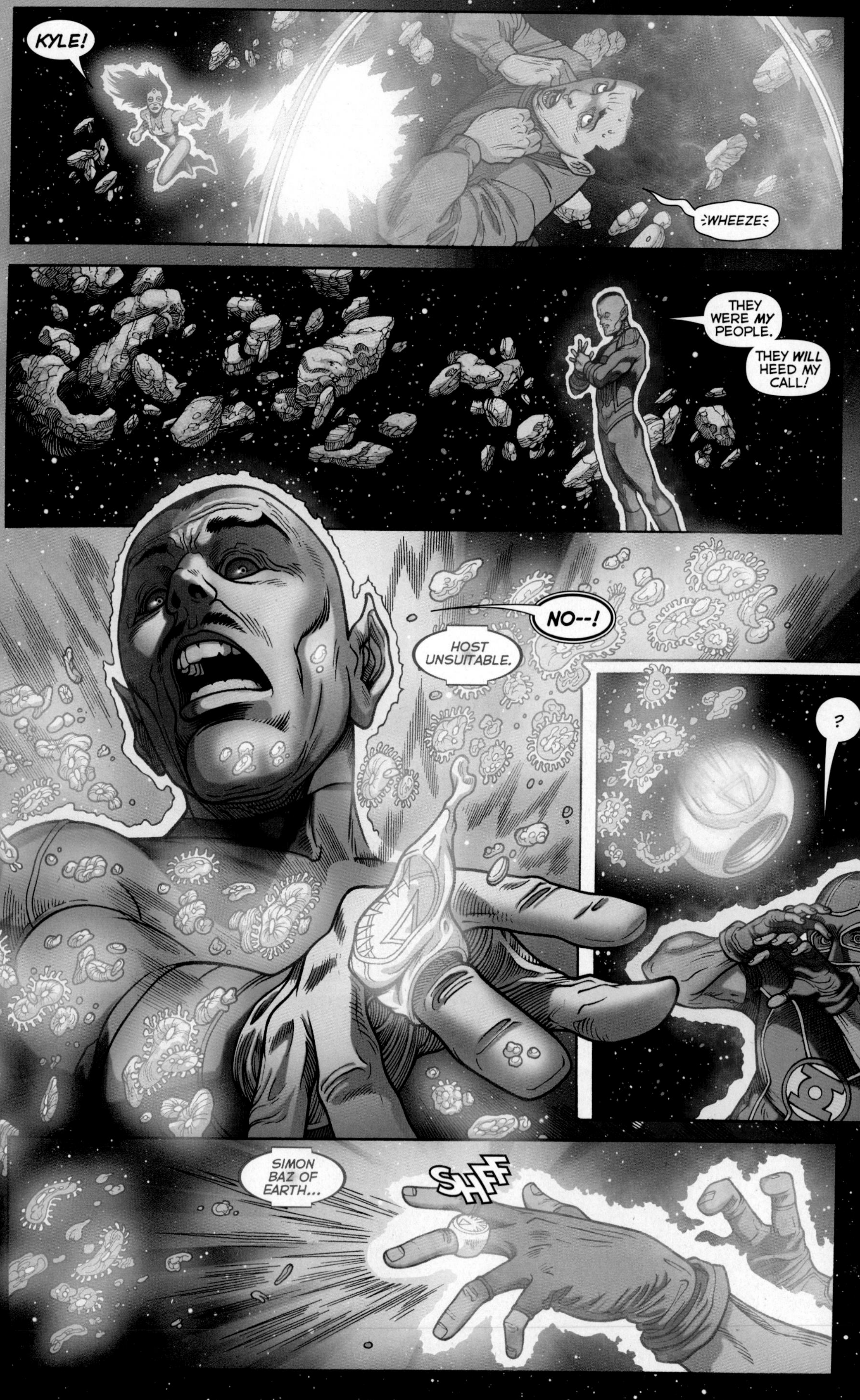
KYLE!
WHEEZE
THEY WERE MY PEOPLE.
THEY WILL HEED MY CALL!
NO--!
HOST UNSUITABLE.
?
SIMON BAZ OF EARTH...
SHFF

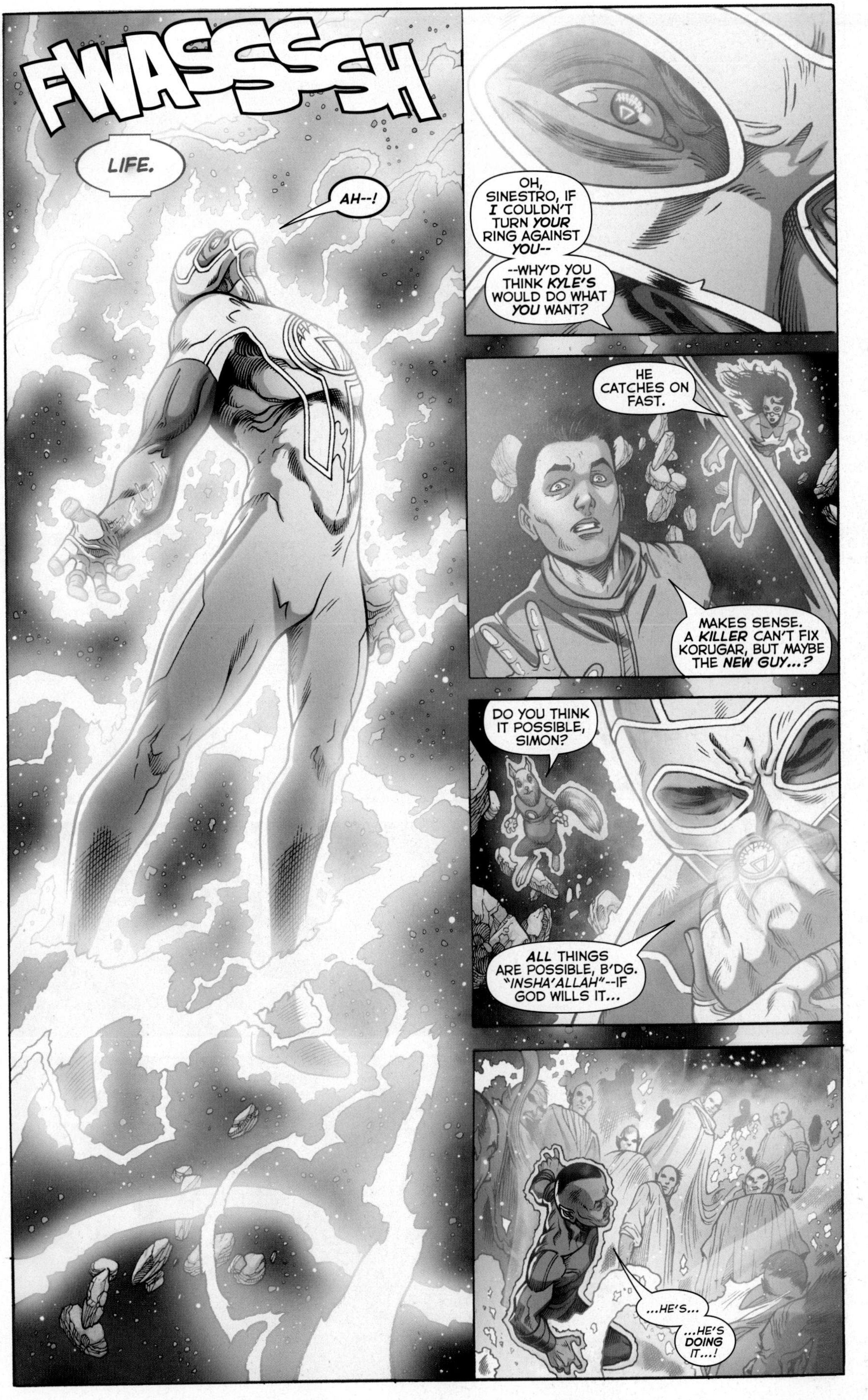
FWASSSSH
LIFE.
AH--!
OH, SINESTRO, IF I COULDN'T TURN YOUR RING AGAINST YOU--
--WHY'D YOU THINK KYLE'S WOULD DO WHAT YOU WANT?
HE CATCHES ON FAST.
MAKES SENSE. A KILLER CAN'T FIX KORUGAR, BUT MAYBE THE NEW GUY...?
DO YOU THINK IT POSSIBLE, SIMON?
ALL THINGS ARE POSSIBLE, B'DG. "INSHA'ALLAH"--IF GOD WILLS IT...
...HE'S...
...HE'S DOING IT...!

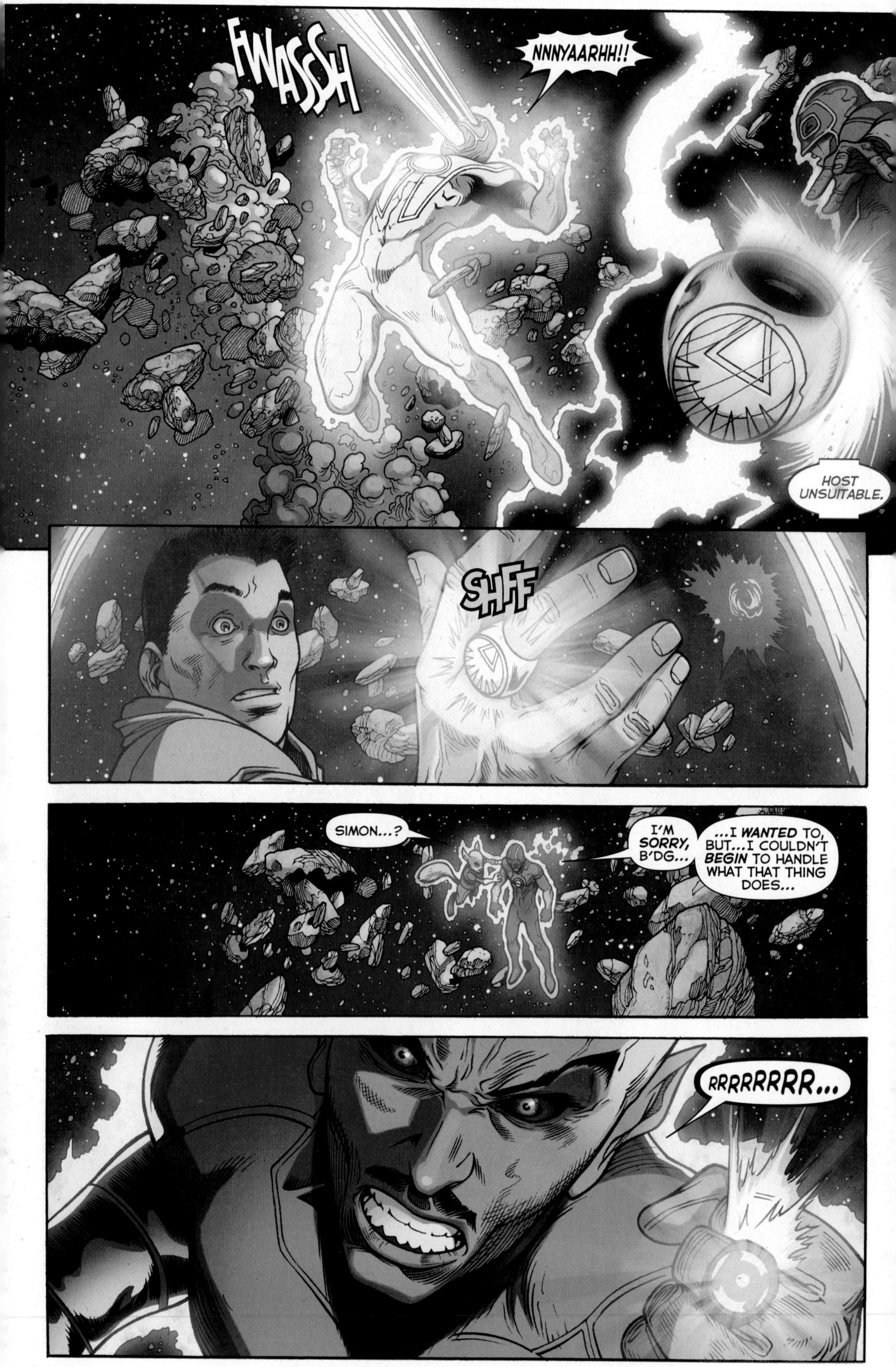
FWASSSH
NNNYAARHH!!
HOST UNSUITABLE.
SHFF
SIMON...?
I'M SORRY, B'DG...
...I WANTED TO, BUT...I COULDN'T BEGIN TO HANDLE WHAT THAT THING DOES...
RRRRRRRR...

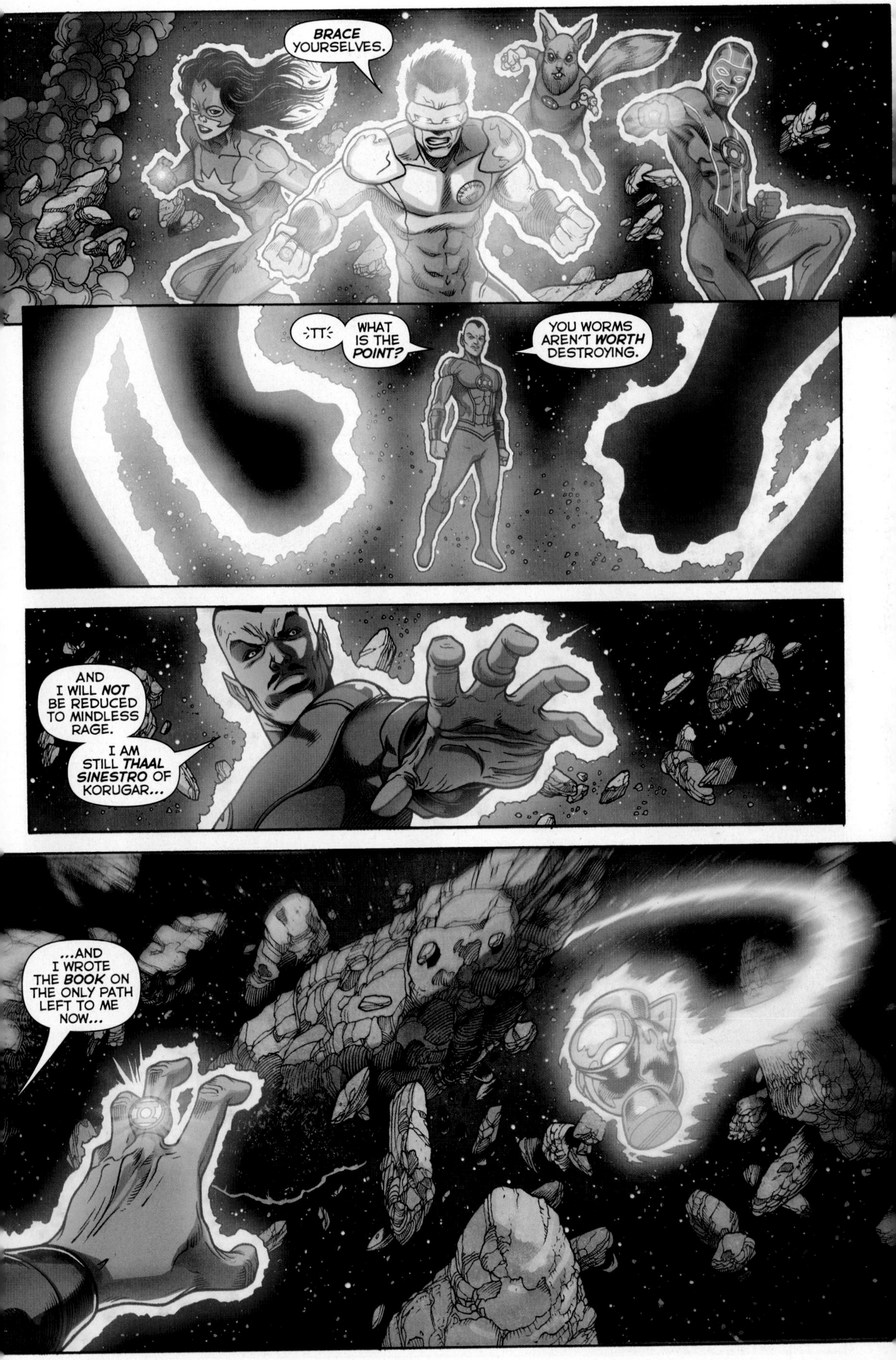

BRACE YOURSELVES.
TT
WHAT IS THE POINT?
YOU WORMS AREN'T WORTH DESTROYING.
AND I WILL NOT BE REDUCED TO MINDLESS RAGE.
I AM STILL THAAL SINESTRO OF KORUGAR...
...AND I WROTE THE BOOK ON THE ONLY PATH LEFT TO ME NOW...

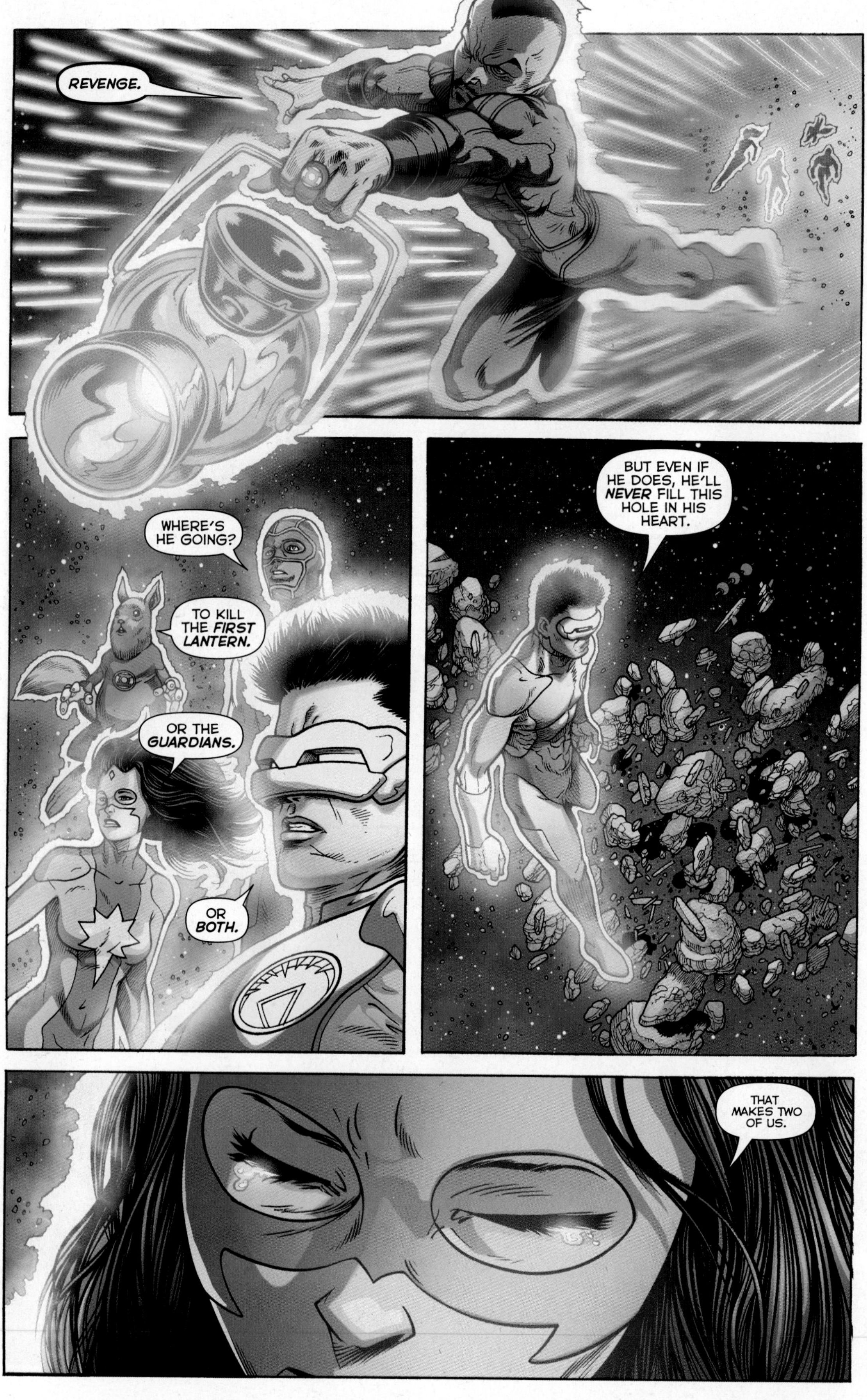
REVENGE.
WHERE'S HE GOING?
TO KILL THE FIRST LANTERN.
OR THE GUARDIANS.
OR BOTH.
BUT EVEN IF HE DOES, HE'LL NEVER FILL THIS HOLE IN HIS HEART.
THAT MAKES TWO OF US.

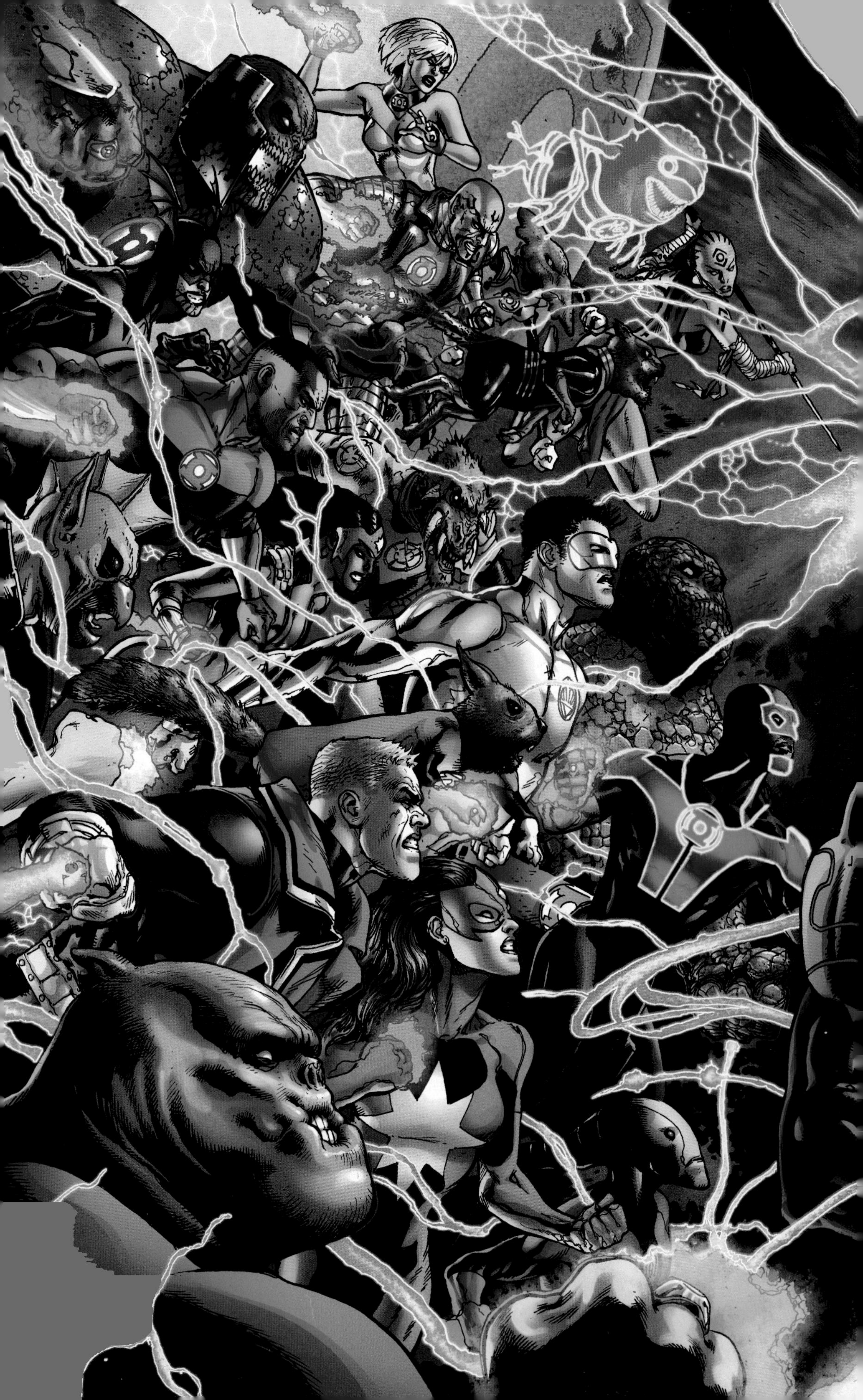

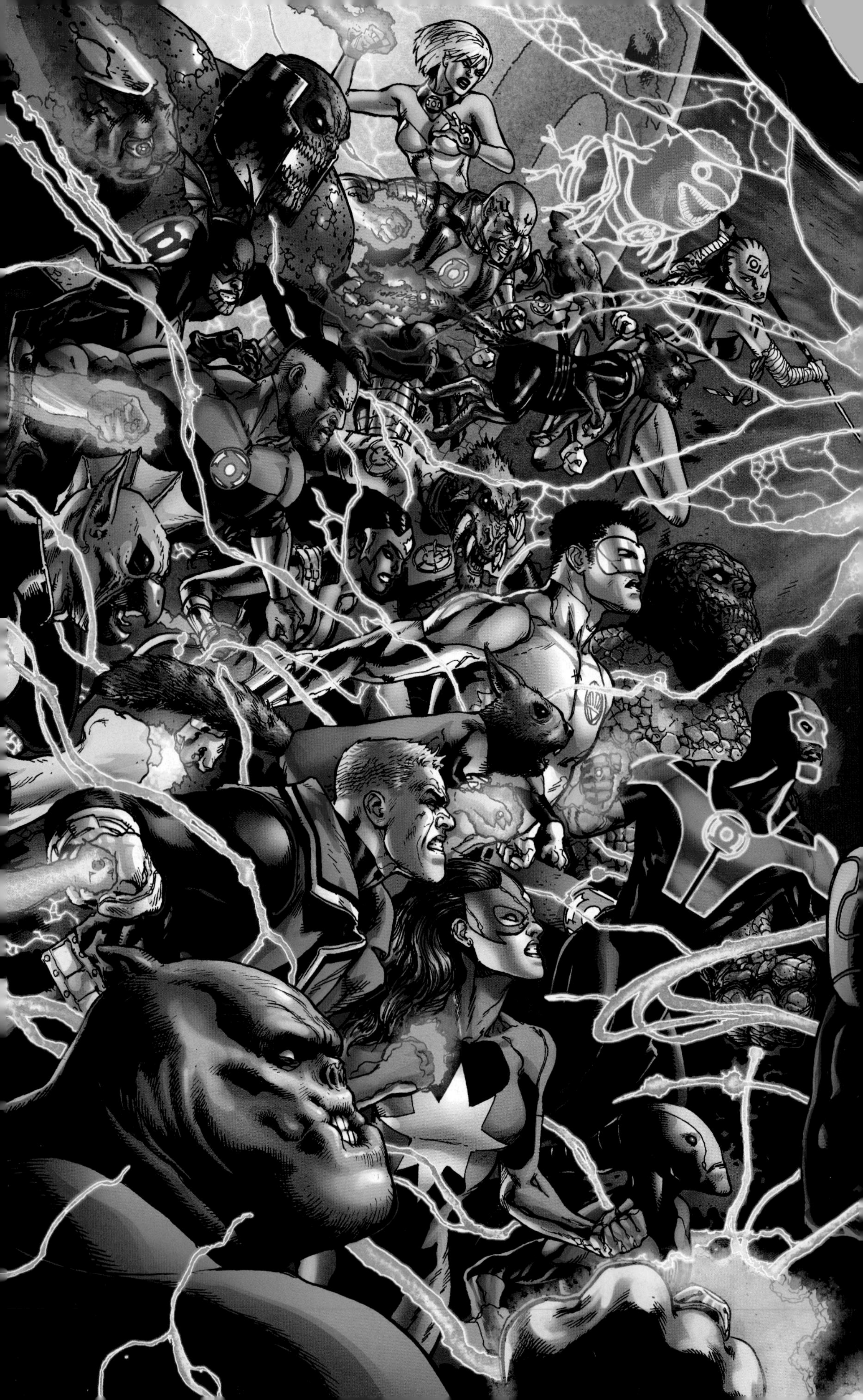

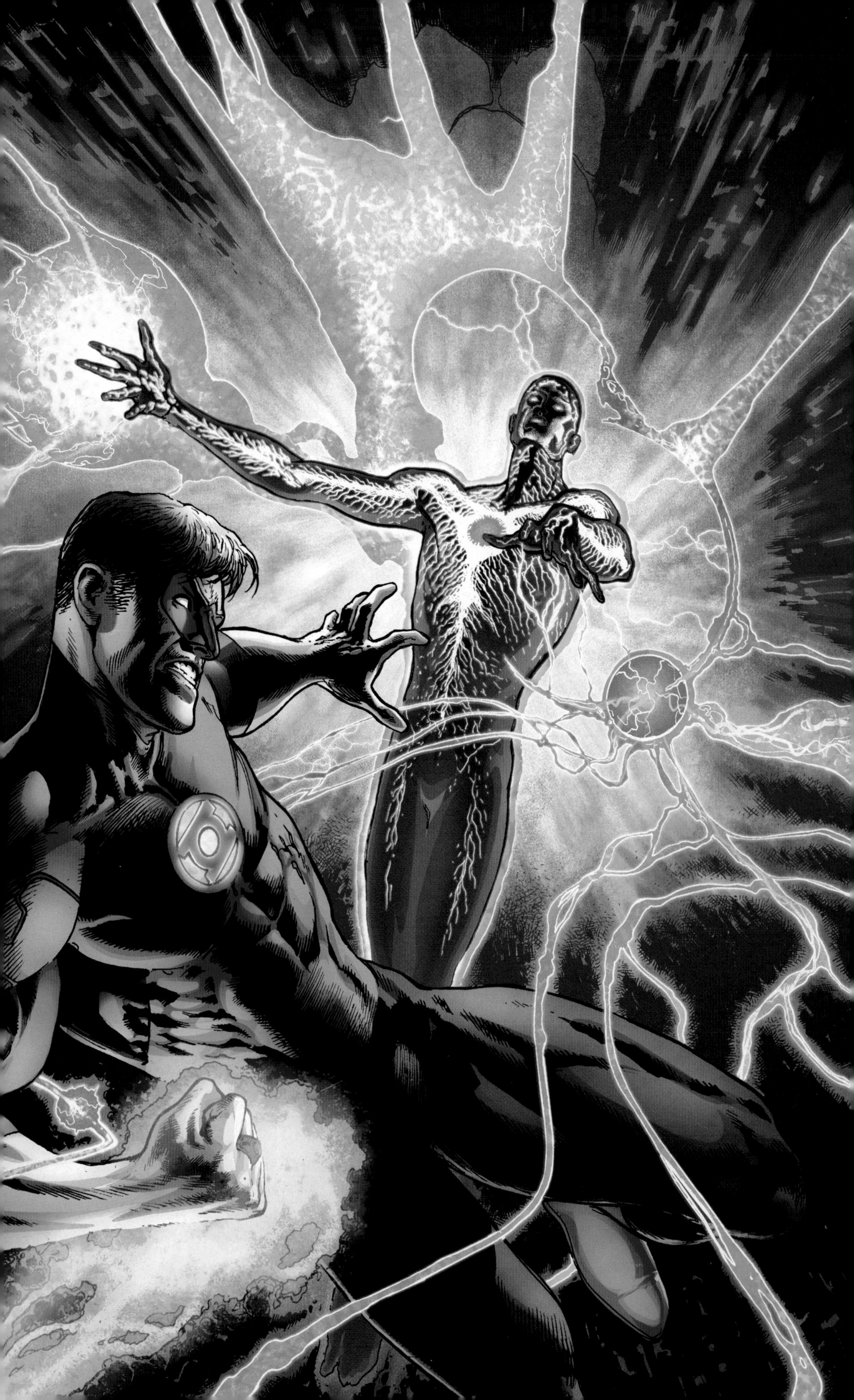

THE END

GEOFF JOHNS writer DOUG MAHNKE, PATRICK GLEASON, CULLY HAMNER, AARON KUDER, JERRY ORDWAY, ETHAN VAN SCIVER, IVAN REIS with OCLAIR ALBERT & JOE PRADO artists CHRISTIAN ALAMY, KEITH CHAMPAGNE, MARC DEERING, MARK IRWIN, WADE VON GRAWBADGER, TOM NGUYEN & DOUG MAHNKE inkers DOUG MAHNKE with ALEX SINCLAIR cover

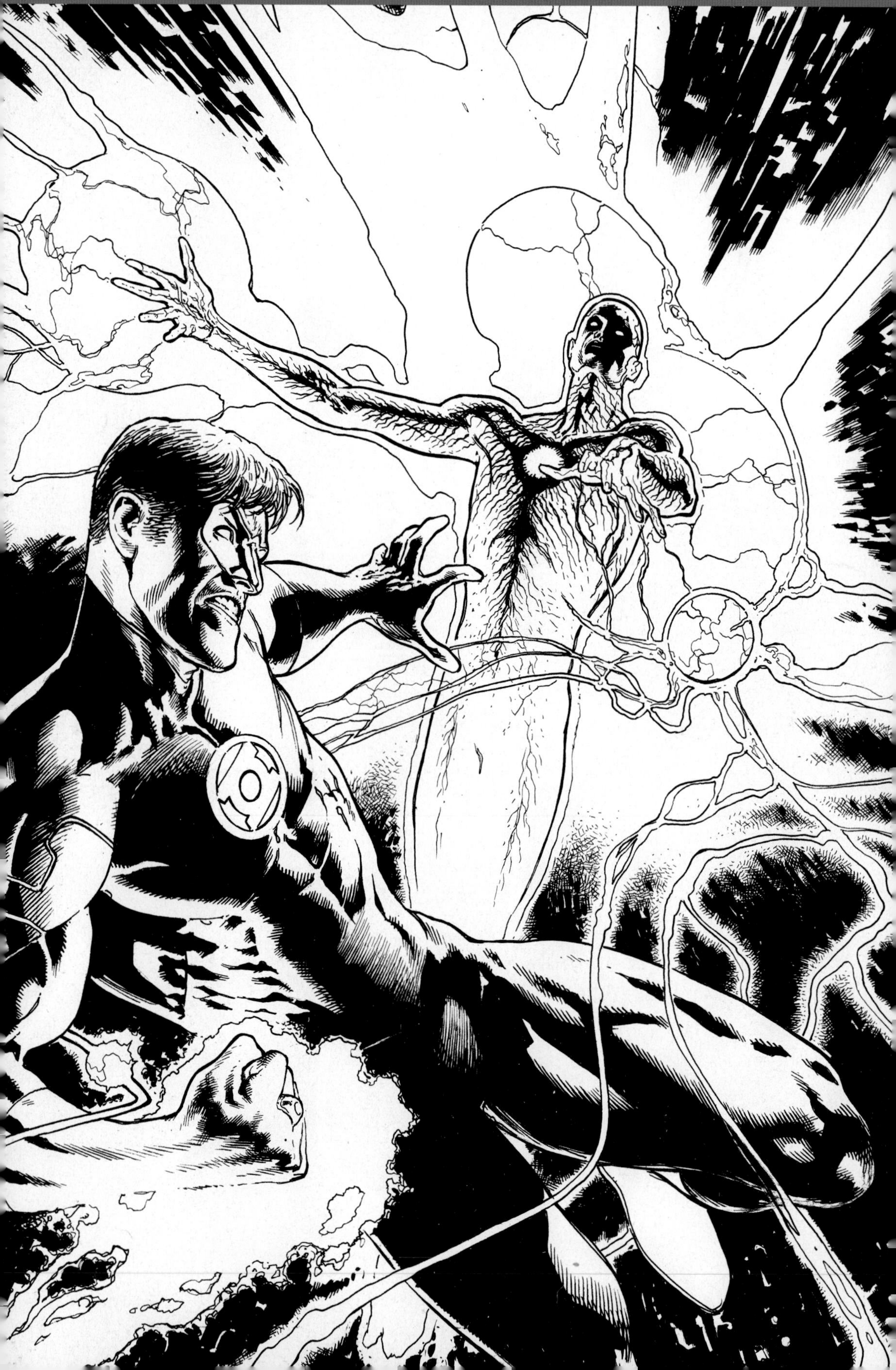

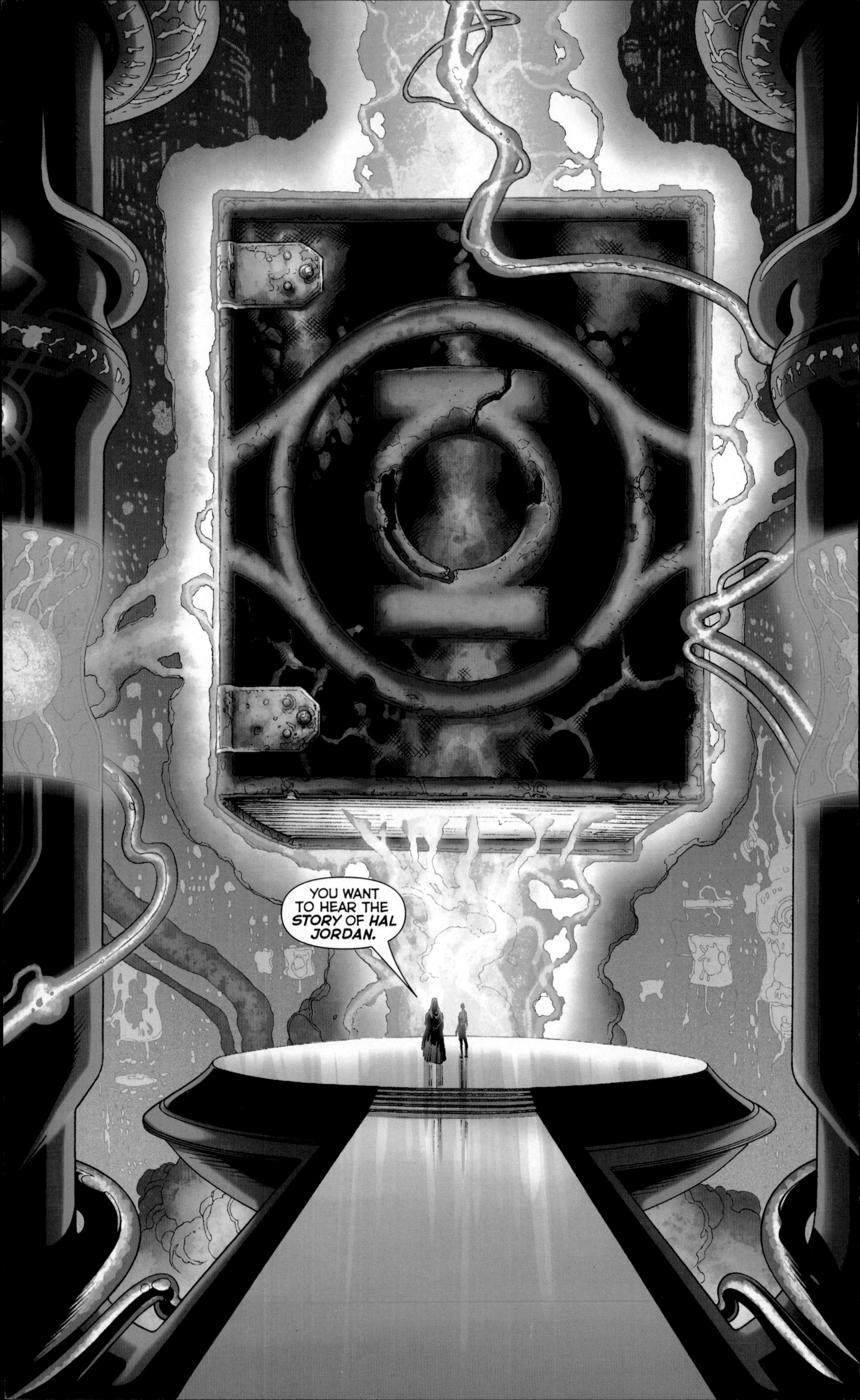
YOU WANT TO HEAR THE STORY OF HAL JORDAN.

THE BOOK GROWS *OLD.* KEPT ALIVE BY A *TALE* THAT WILL *NEVER* DIE, BUT *FEW* TRULY KNOW.

KRAKKKLL

I AM HONORED, BOOKKEEPER.

LET ME BEGIN WHERE IT BEGAN... THE MOMENT THE LEGENDARY *ABIN SUR* CRASHED AND DIED ON THE PLANET EARTH, HAL JORDAN BECAME THE *FIRST HUMAN* TO EVER BE INDUCTED INTO THE GREEN LANTERN CORPS.

AND HIS *GREATEST TRIALS* WERE BOOKENDED BY THE MIRACLE OF *REBIRTH.*

"FOR YEARS, HAL SERVED THE CORPS FAIRLY WELL, IF NOT UNORTHODOXLY."

HAL, WILL YOU PLEASE STAY *OUT* OF MY FLIGHT PATH.

ONLY IF YOU SAY *YES* TO A WEEKEND IN CABO.

"BUT THESE FIRST YEARS OF SERVICE ENDED WHEN HAL FAILED HIS OATH.

"IN THE WAKE OF A HORRIFIC ATTACK ON THE CITY HE CALLED HOME, HAL JORDAN WAS OVER-WHELMED WITH ANGER, DESPAIR, AND ABOVE ALL, FEAR.

"HE ALLOWED THAT FEAR TO BLIND HIM... AND EVIL ESCAPED HIS SIGHT.

"IN A MOMENT OF *WEAKNESS,* THE LIVING EMBODIMENT OF *FEAR*--AN ENTITY KNOWN AS *PARALLAX*--TOOK HOLD OF HAL'S SOUL.

"FOR ALL INTENTS AND PURPOSES, THE GREEN LANTERN *DIED.*

"AND A *MONSTER* WAS BORN.

"IN THE AFTERMATH, HAL JORDAN FOUND HIMSELF AN UNLIKELY PARTNER TO SINESTRO, WHO HAD CONTROVERSIALLY REGAINED HIS STATUS AS A *GREEN LANTERN*.

"...AND UNCOVERED THE GUARDIANS' PLANS TO *DESTROY* THE GREEN LANTERN CORPS.

"A *NEW* LANTERN OF EARTH-- *SIMON BAZ*-- ATTEMPTED TO *RESCUE* HAL.

"...SO HE *JUMPED*.

"DRIVEN *MAD* BY *EMPTY HEARTS*, THE GUARDIANS USED THE UNDEAD LANTERN *BLACK HAND* TO *KILL* HAL AND SINESTRO...

"WHEN HAL LEARNED OF *KORUGAR'S DESTRUCTION* AT THE HANDS OF THE FIRST LANTERN, HE REFUSED TO WAIT FOR HELP ANY LONGER...

"BUT USING SIMON BAZ, SINESTRO ESCAPED INSTEAD.

"FOLLOWING THE WAR OF LIGHT, THE *DEAD* ROSE FROM THEIR GRAVES.

I HAVE NO OTHER OPTION.

"THEY BATTLED AGAINST SINESTRO'S VERY OWN CORPS, WHO HAD *ENSLAVED* THE ONLY THING SINESTRO EVER CARED ABOUT--HIS HOMEWORLD OF *KORUGAR*.

"DRAWN INTO BLACK HAND'S *RING*, THEIR SOULS WERE *LOST* IN THE *DEAD ZONE*.

"THE LOVE- SPREADING *STAR SAPPHIRES*, HOPEFUL *BLUE LANTERNS* AND ENIGMATIC *INDIGO TRIBE* FOUGHT ALONGSIDE HAL AGAINST *NEKRON* AND HIS UNDEAD *BLACK LANTERNS*.

"TOGETHER, HAL AND SINESTRO FREED *KORUGAR*...

"WHILE HAL SOUGHT ANOTHER WAY OUT, THE UNIVERSE FACED THE *WRATH* OF THE *FIRST LANTERN*-- A MYSTERIOUS BEING NAMED *VOLTHOOM*.

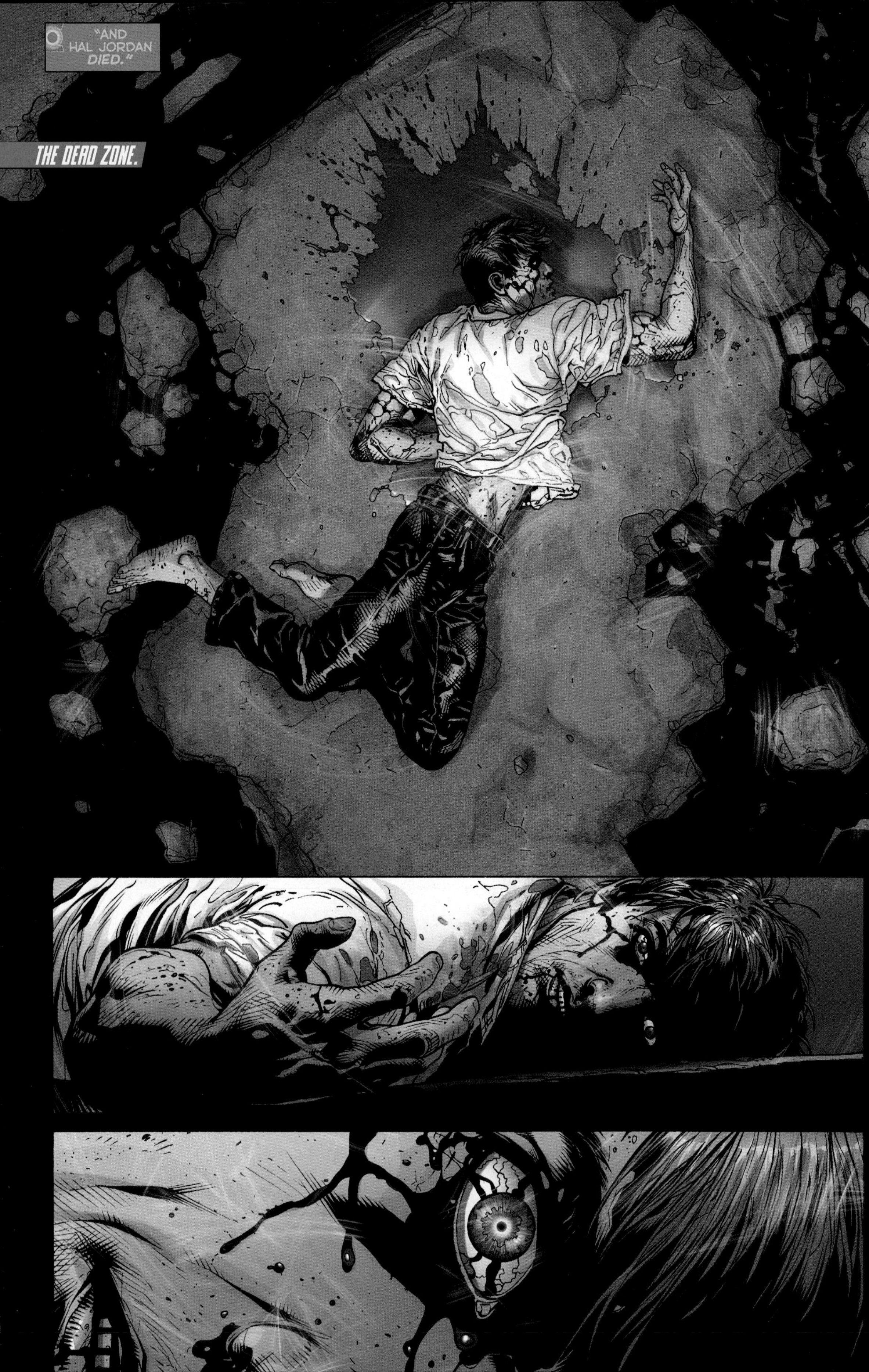
"AND HAL JORDAN DIED."
THE DEAD ZONE.

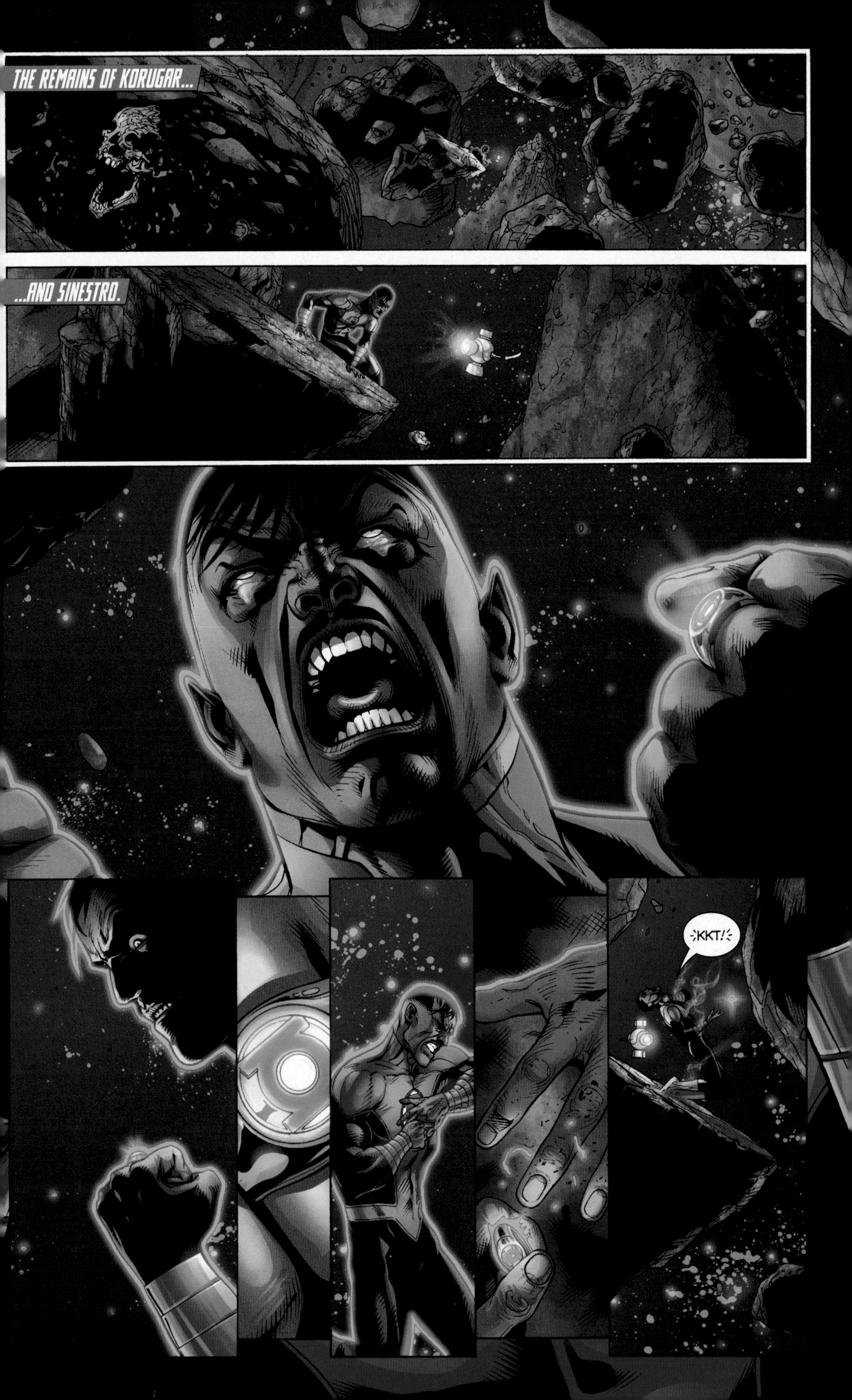
THE REMAINS OF KORUGAR...
...AND SINESTRO.
KKT!

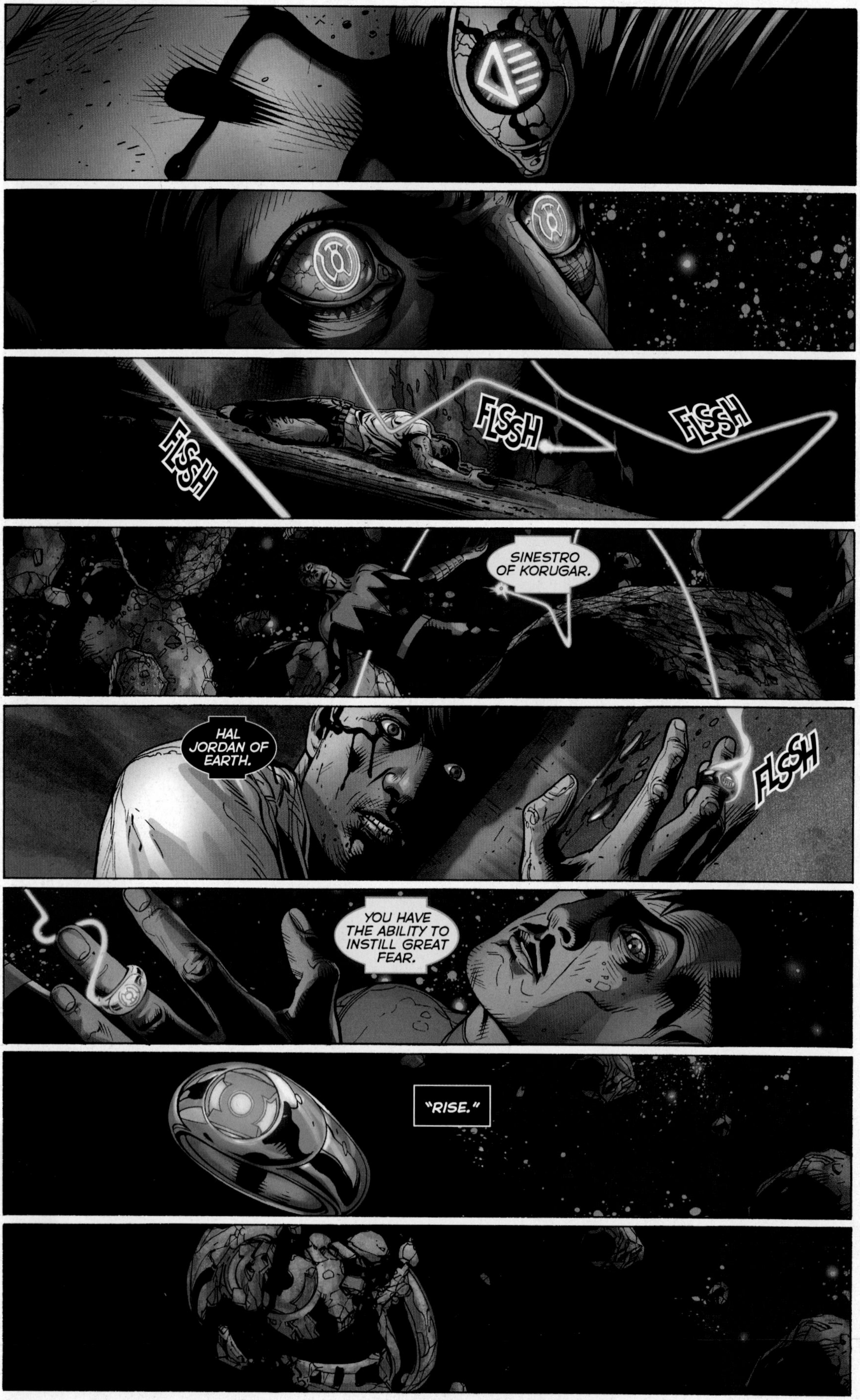
FLSSH
FLSSH
FLSSH
SINESTRO OF KORUGAR.
HAL JORDAN OF EARTH.
FLSSH
YOU HAVE THE ABILITY TO INSTILL GREAT FEAR.
"RISE."

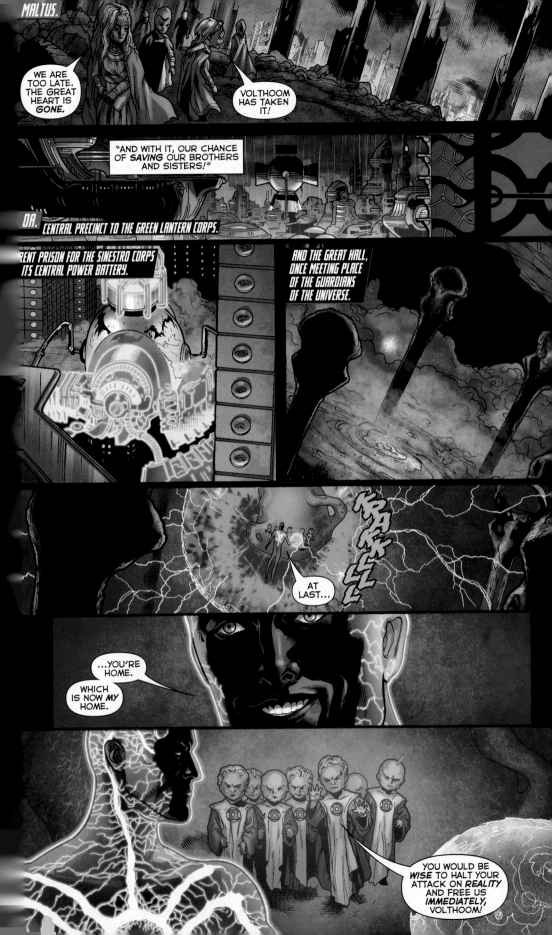

MALTUS.

WE ARE TOO LATE. THE GREAT HEART IS GONE.

VOLTHOOM HAS TAKEN IT!

"AND WITH IT, OUR CHANCE OF SAVING OUR BROTHERS AND SISTERS!"

OA. CENTRAL PRECINCT TO THE GREEN LANTERN CORPS.

RENT PRISON FOR THE SINESTRO CORPS ITS CENTRAL POWER BATTERY.

AND THE GREAT HALL, ONCE MEETING PLACE OF THE GUARDIANS OF THE UNIVERSE.

KRAKKLL

AT LAST...

...YOU'RE HOME.

WHICH IS NOW MY HOME.

YOU WOULD BE WISE TO HALT YOUR ATTACK ON REALITY AND FREE US IMMEDIATELY, VOLTHOOM!

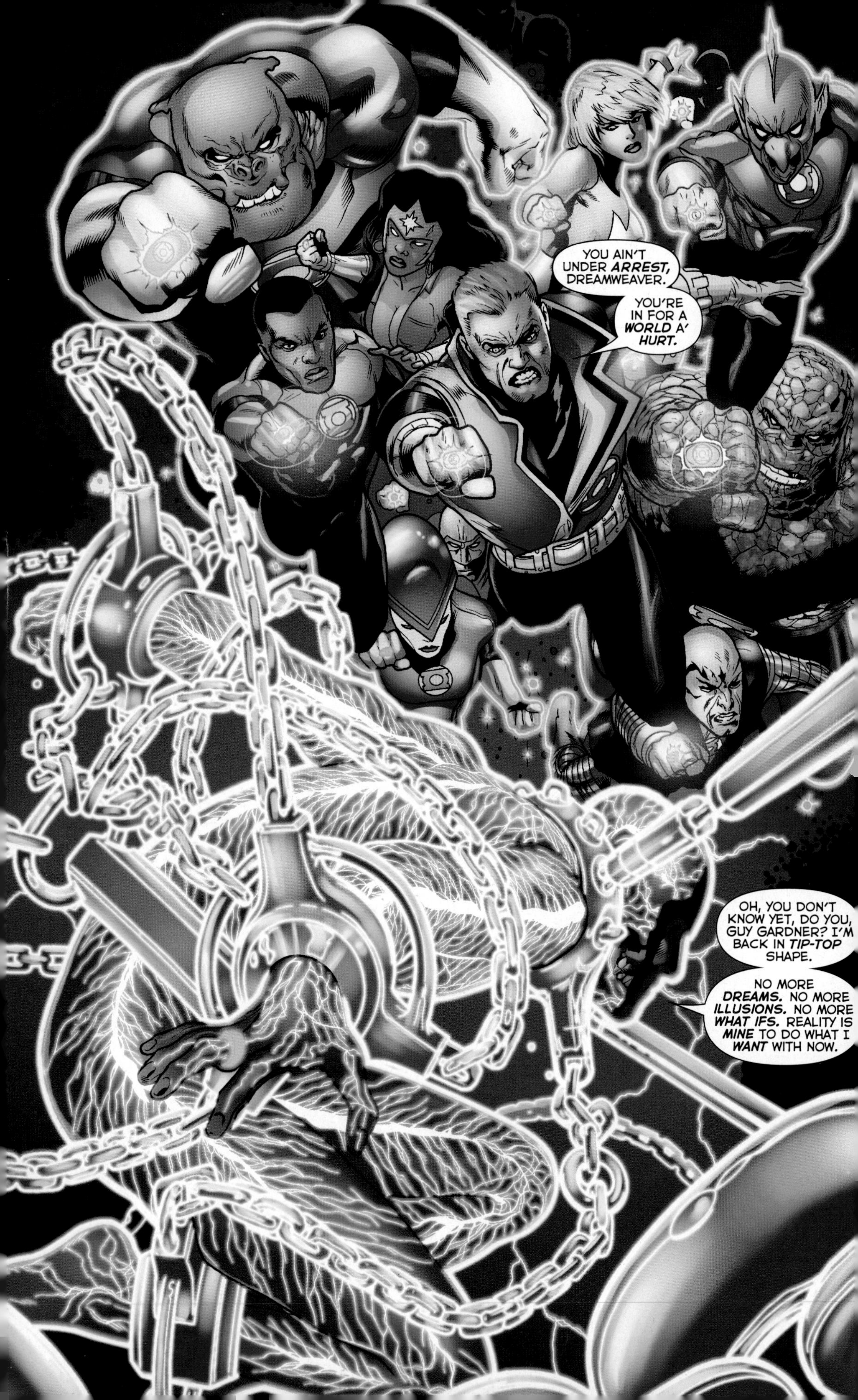
YOU AIN'T UNDER ARREST, DREAMWEAVER.
YOU'RE IN FOR A WORLD A' HURT.
OH, YOU DON'T KNOW YET, DO YOU, GUY GARDNER? I'M BACK IN TIP-TOP SHAPE.
NO MORE DREAMS. NO MORE ILLUSIONS. NO MORE WHAT IFS. REALITY IS MINE TO DO WHAT I WANT WITH NOW.

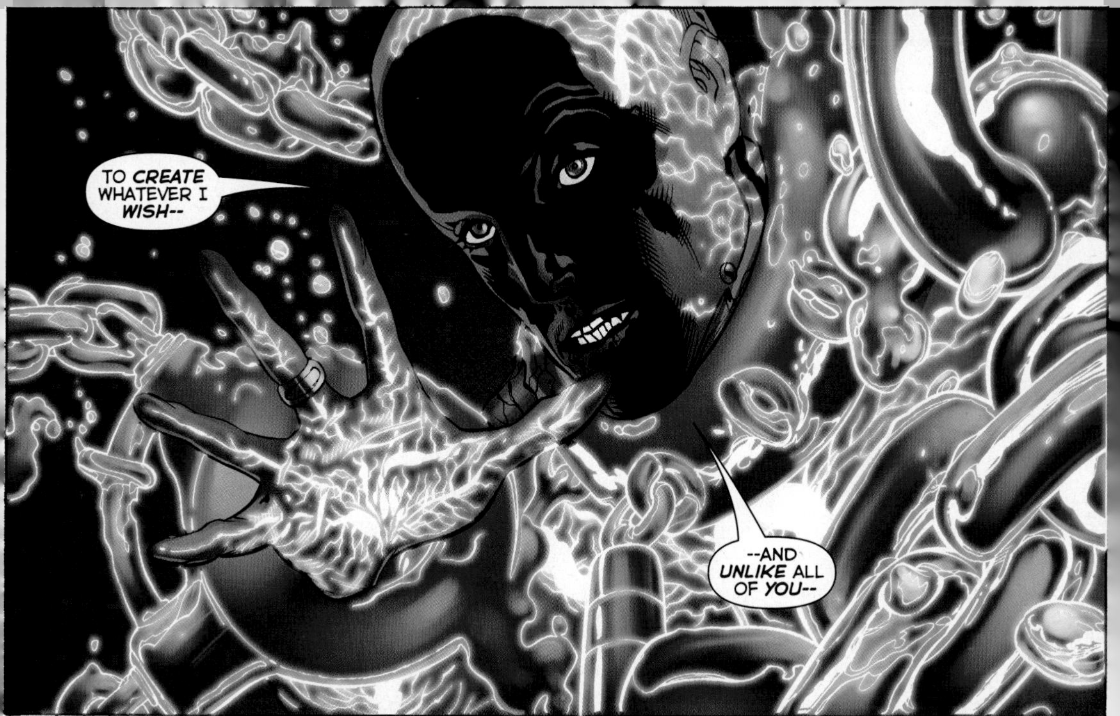
TO CREATE WHATEVER I WISH--
--AND UNLIKE ALL OF YOU--
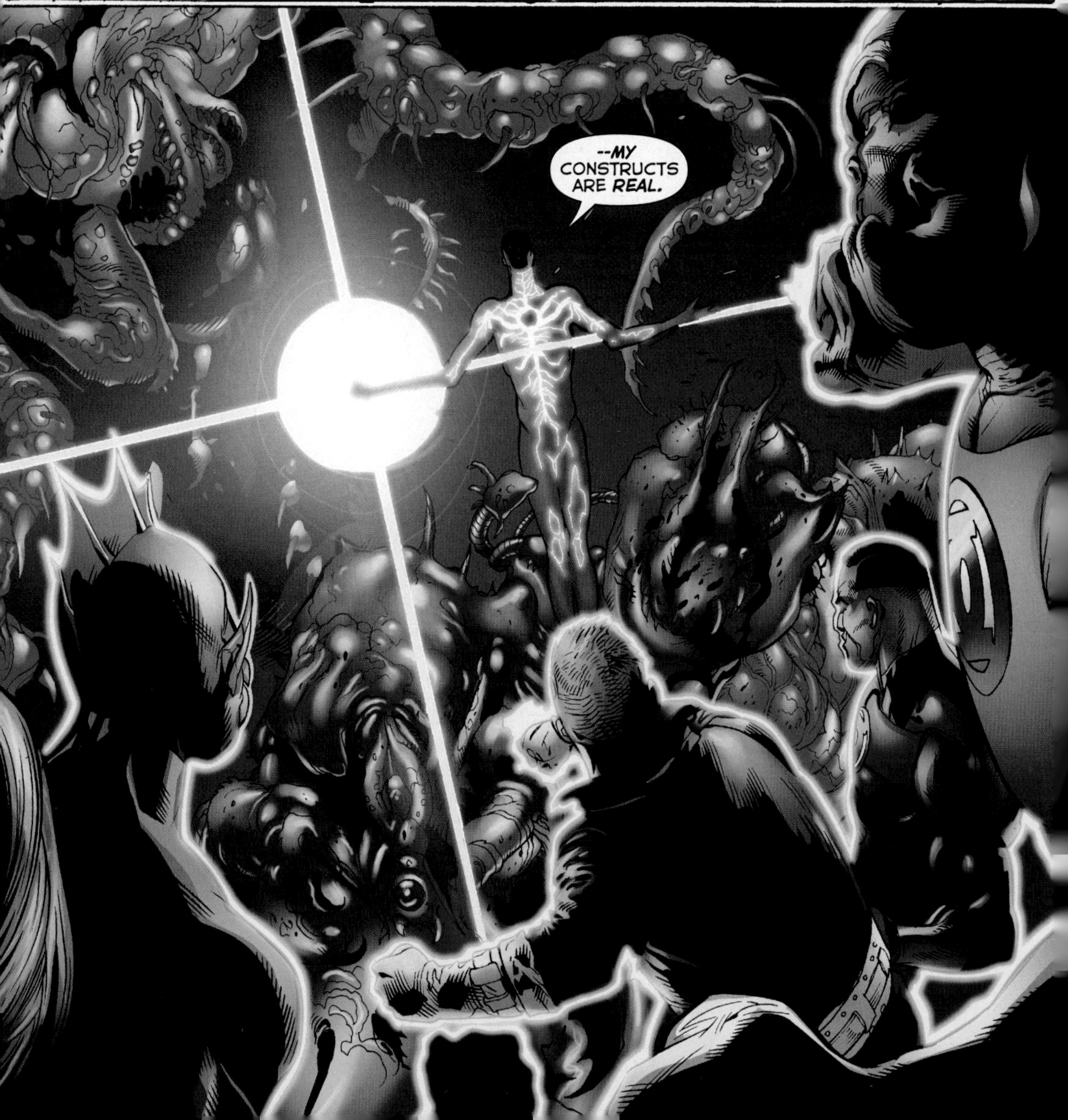
--MY CONSTRUCTS ARE REAL.

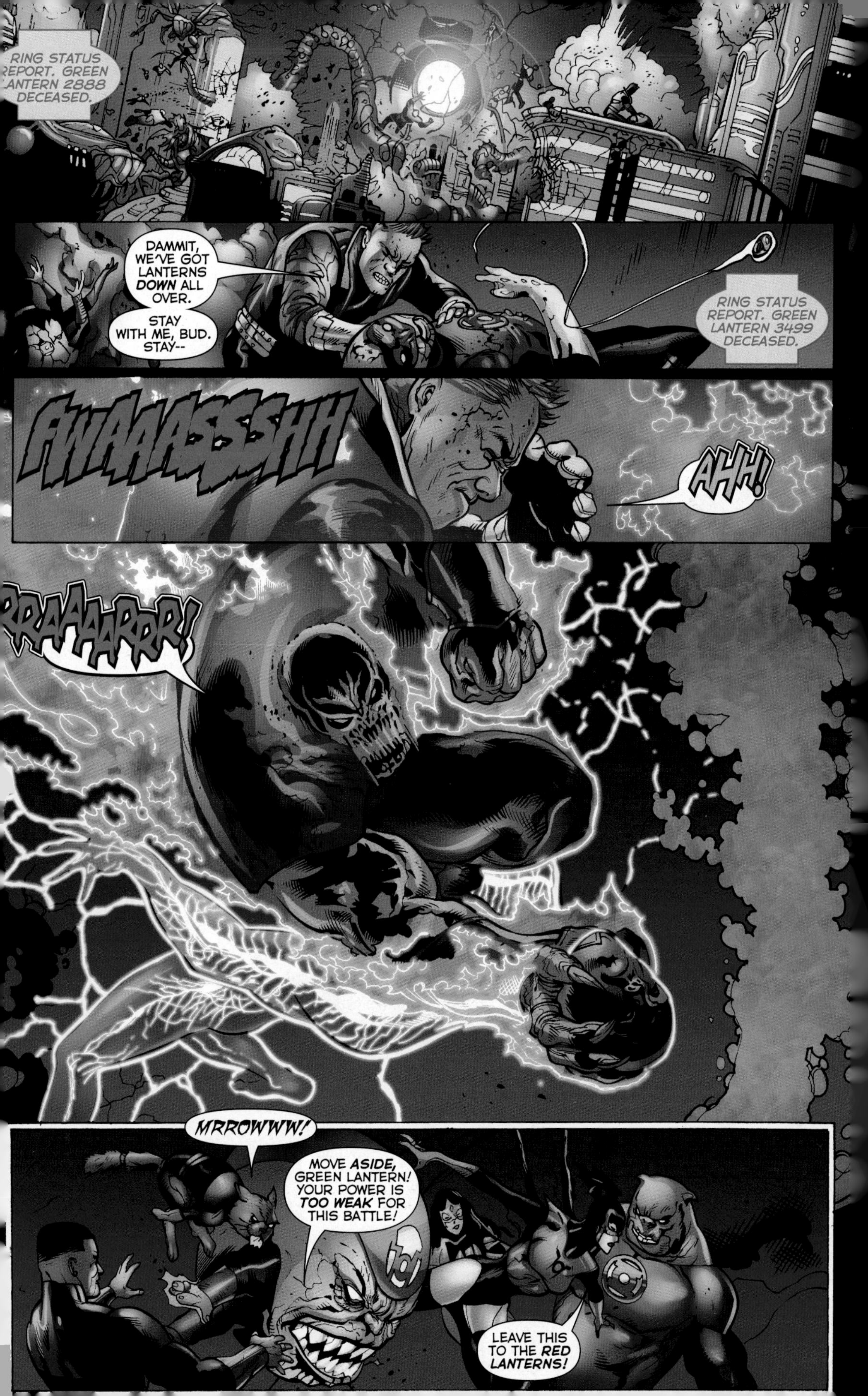
RING STATUS REPORT. GREEN LANTERN 2888 DECEASED.
DAMMIT, WE'VE GOT LANTERNS DOWN ALL OVER.
STAY WITH ME, BUD. STAY--
RING STATUS REPORT. GREEN LANTERN 3499 DECEASED.
FWAAAASSSHH
AHH!
RRAAAARRR!
MRROWWW!
MOVE ASIDE, GREEN LANTERN! YOUR POWER IS TOO WEAK FOR THIS BATTLE!
LEAVE THIS TO THE RED LANTERNS!

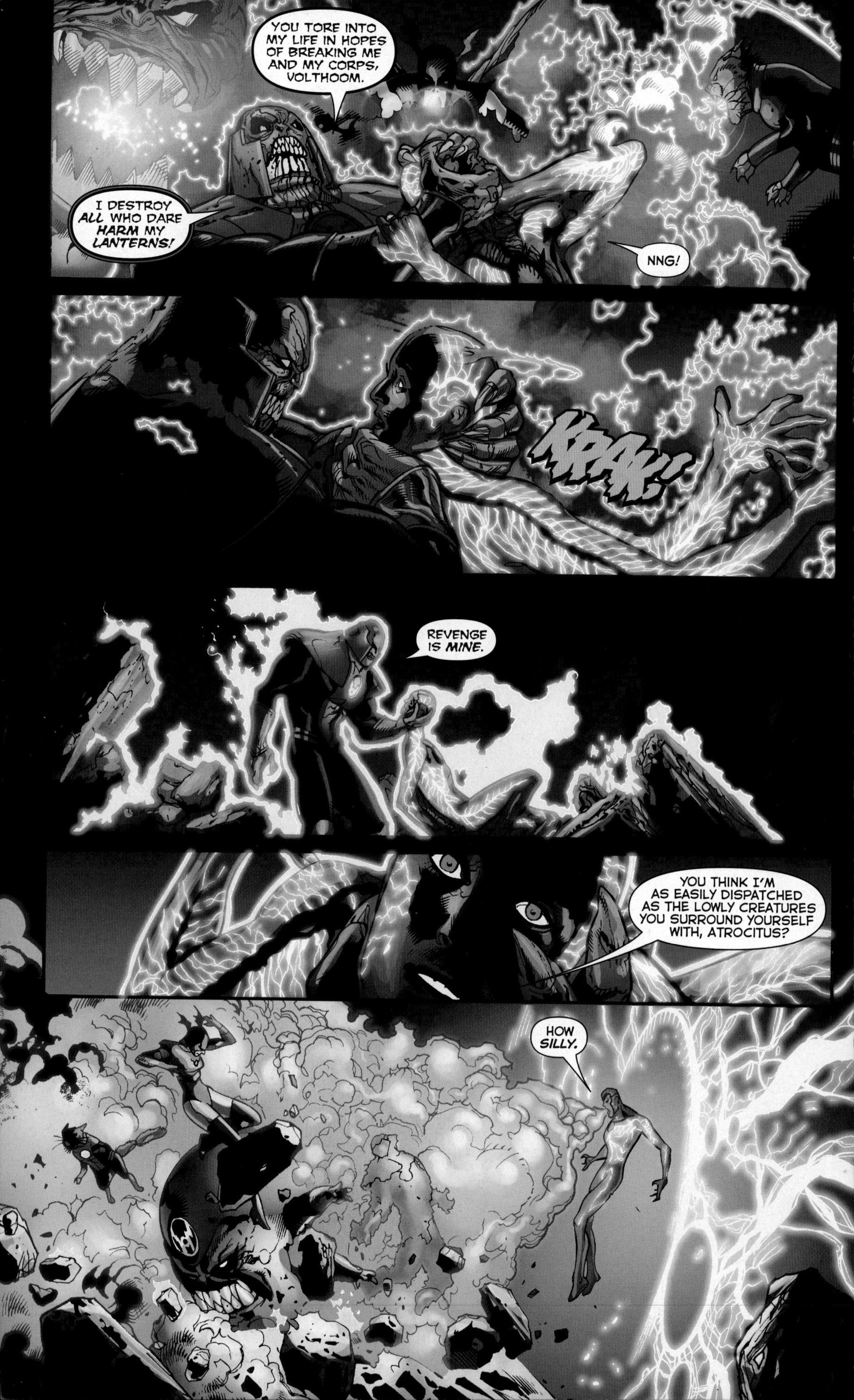
YOU TORE INTO MY LIFE IN HOPES OF BREAKING ME AND MY CORPS, VOLTHOOM.
I DESTROY ALL WHO DARE HARM MY LANTERNS!
NNG!
KRAK!
REVENGE IS MINE.
YOU THINK I'M AS EASILY DISPATCHED AS THE LOWLY CREATURES YOU SURROUND YOURSELF WITH, ATROCITUS?
HOW SILLY.

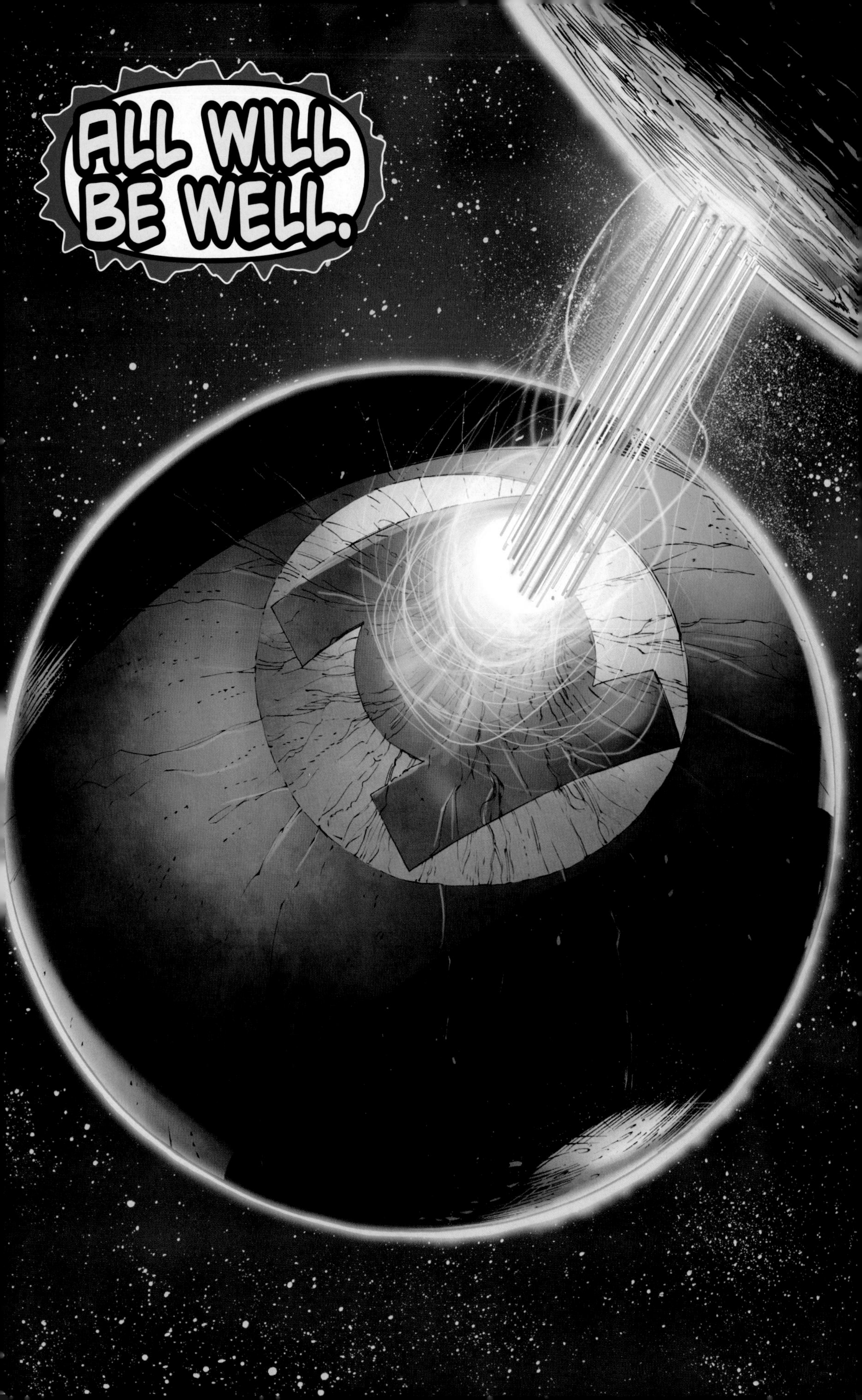
ALL WILL
BE WELL.

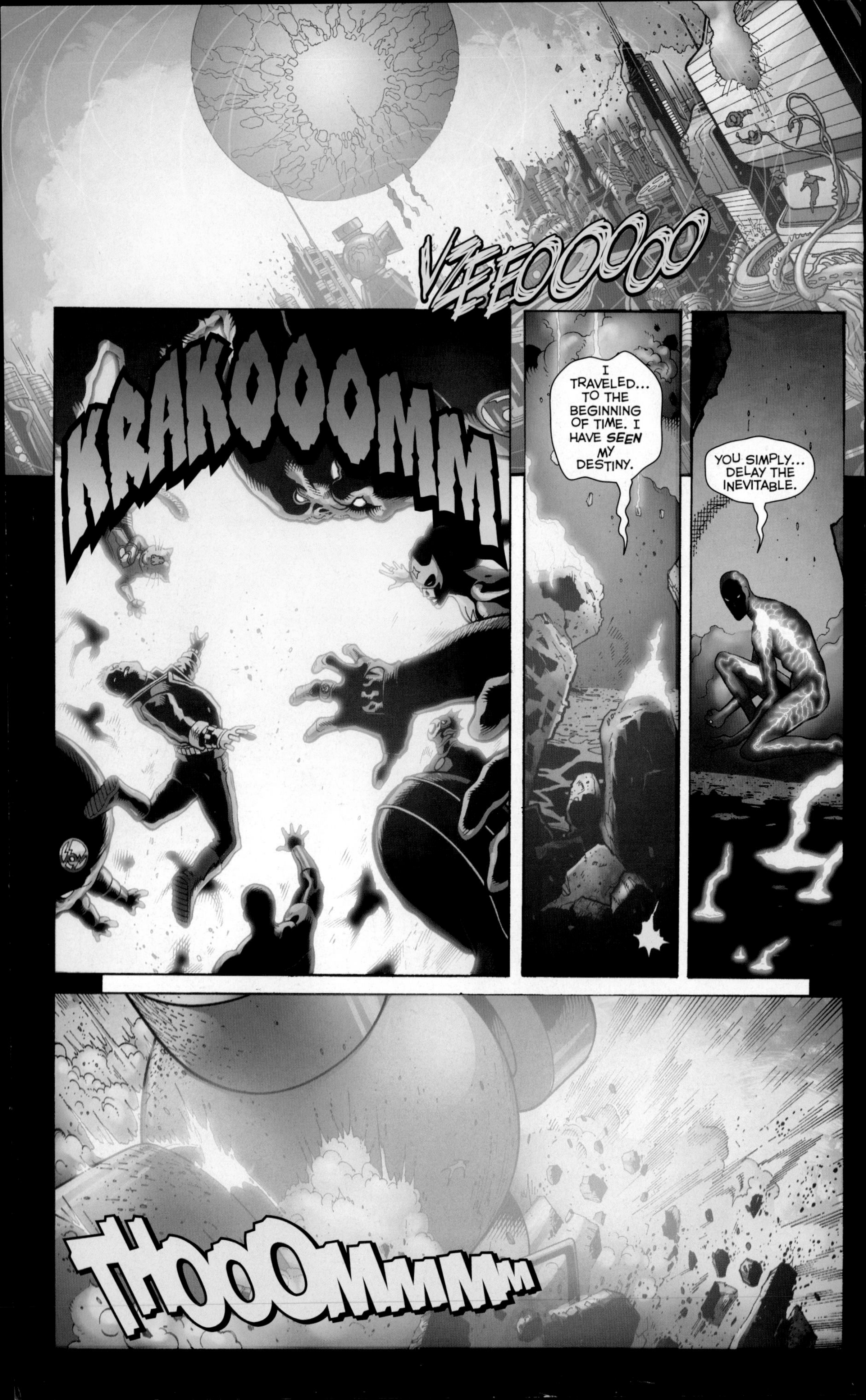
VZEEOOOOO
KRAKOOOMMM
I TRAVELED... TO THE BEGINNING OF TIME. I HAVE SEEN MY DESTINY.
YOU SIMPLY... DELAY THE INEVITABLE.
THOOOMMMM

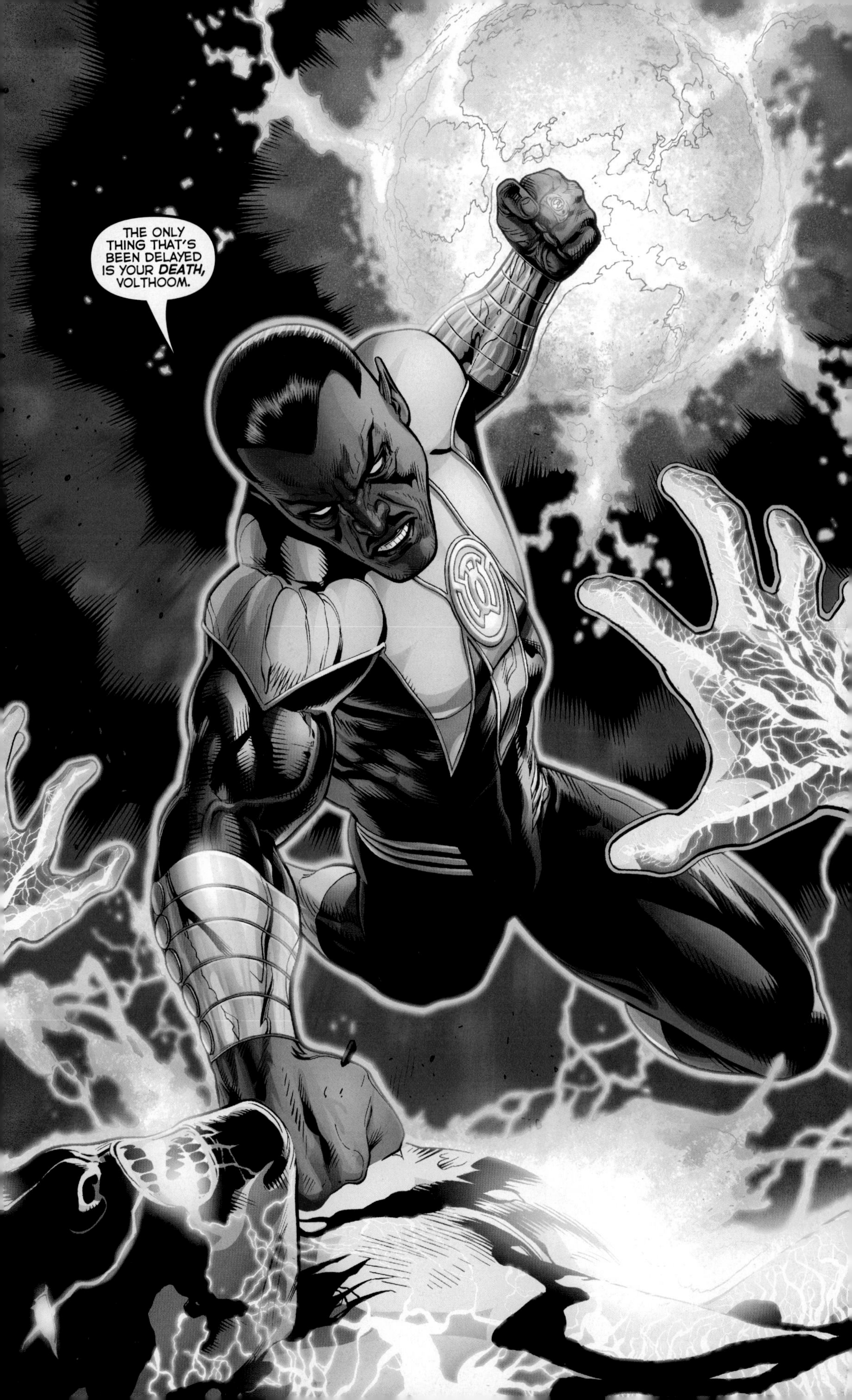
THE ONLY THING THAT'S BEEN DELAYED IS YOUR *DEATH,* VOLTHOOM.

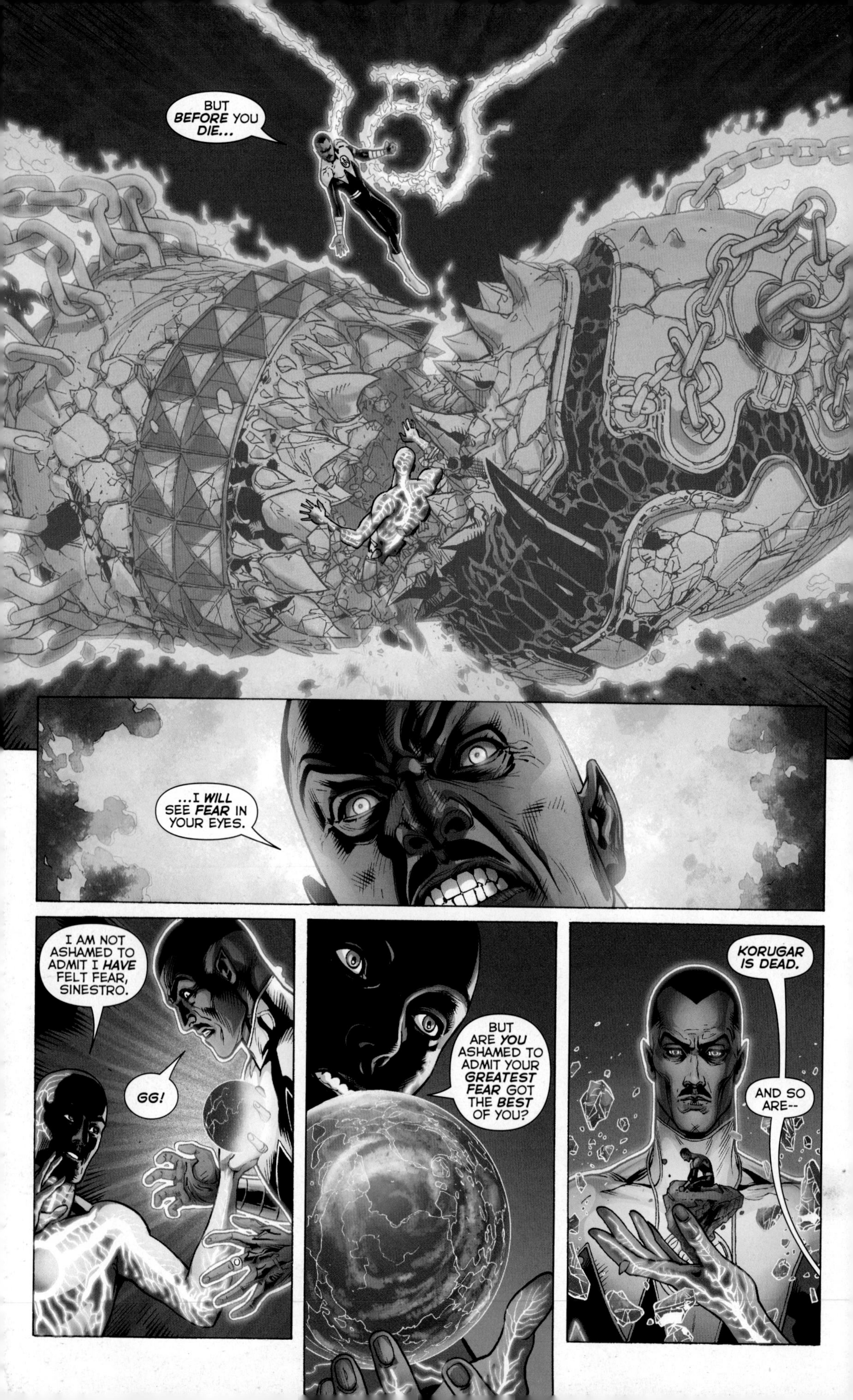
BUT BEFORE YOU DIE...
...I WILL SEE FEAR IN YOUR EYES.
I AM NOT ASHAMED TO ADMIT I HAVE FELT FEAR, SINESTRO.
GG!
BUT ARE YOU ASHAMED TO ADMIT YOUR GREATEST FEAR GOT THE BEST OF YOU?
KORUGAR IS DEAD.
AND SO ARE--

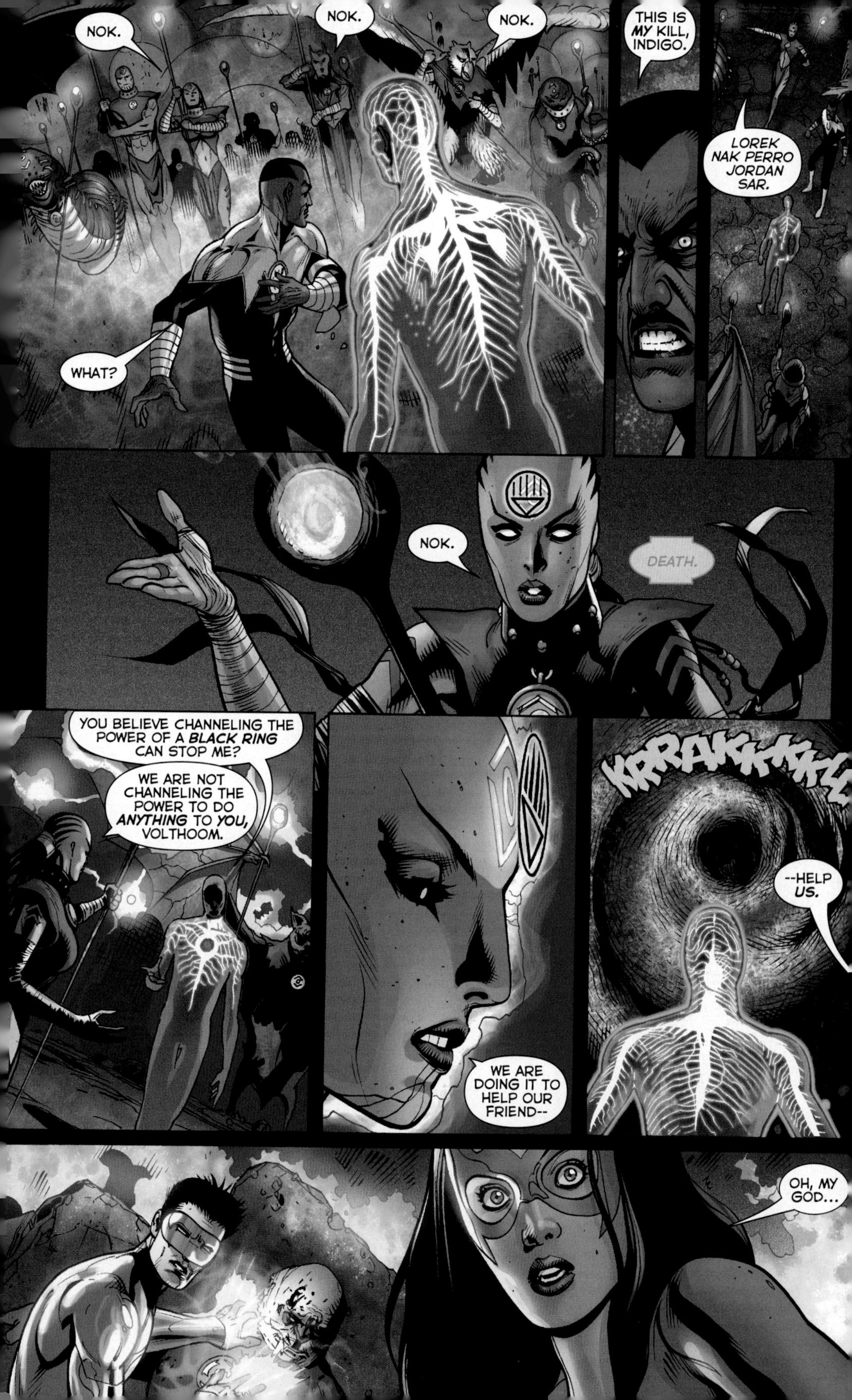
NOK.
NOK.
NOK.
WHAT?
THIS IS MY KILL, INDIGO.
LOREK NAK PERRO JORDAN SAR.
NOK.
DEATH.
YOU BELIEVE CHANNELING THE POWER OF A BLACK RING CAN STOP ME?
WE ARE NOT CHANNELING THE POWER TO DO ANYTHING TO YOU, VOLTHOOM.
WE ARE DOING IT TO HELP OUR FRIEND--
KRRAKKKKK
--HELP US.
OH, MY GOD...

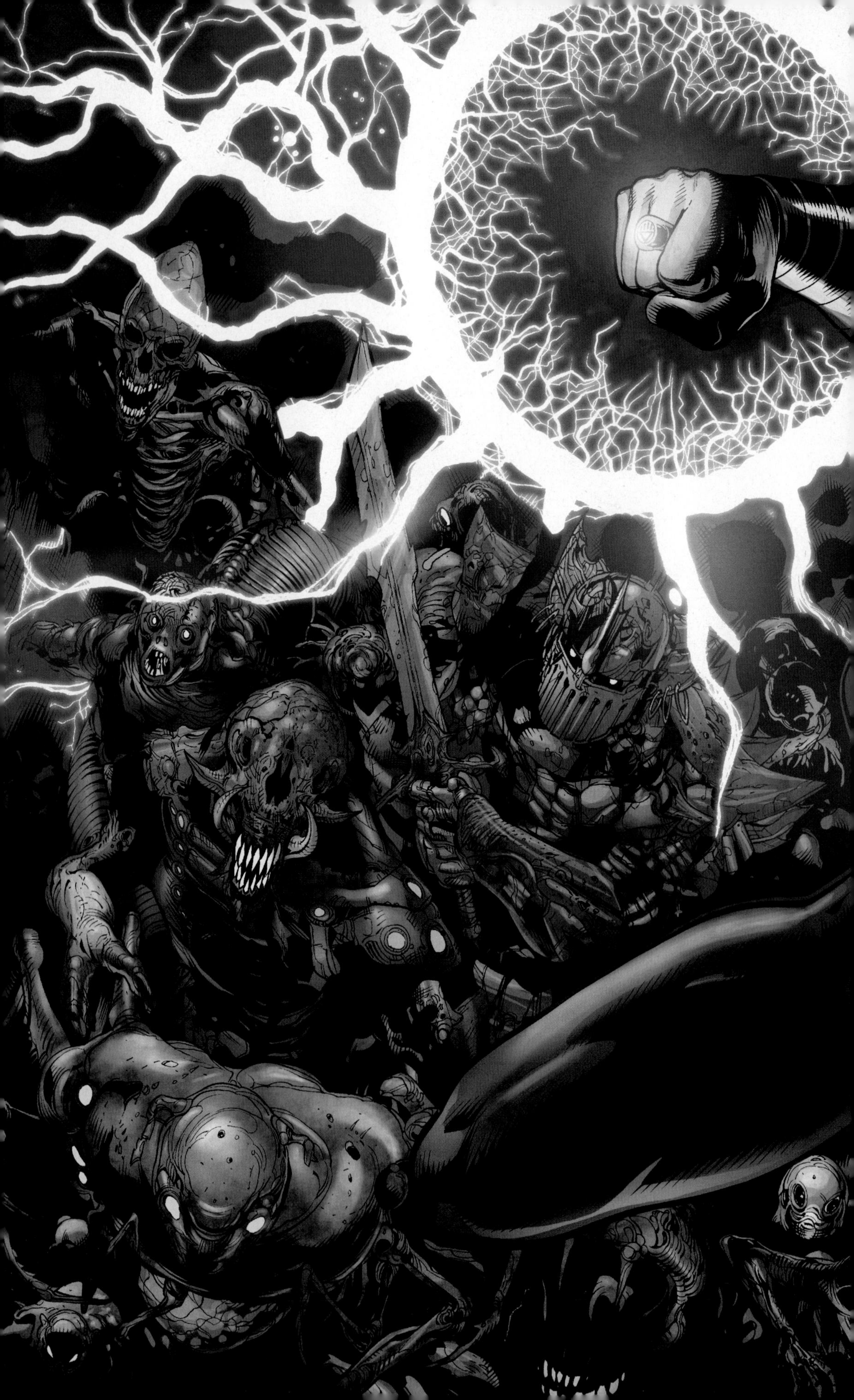

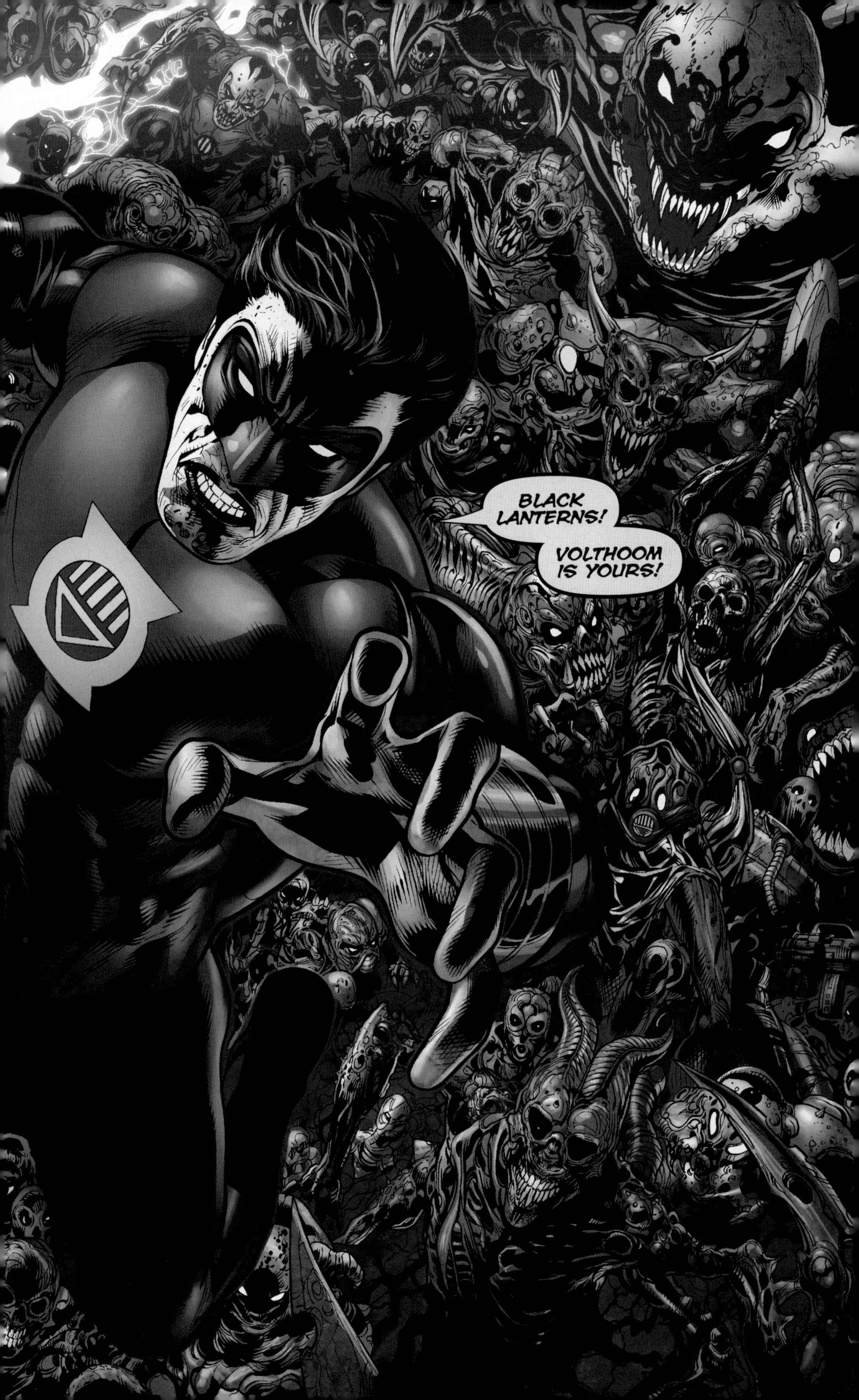
BLACK LANTERNS!
VOLTHOOM IS YOURS!

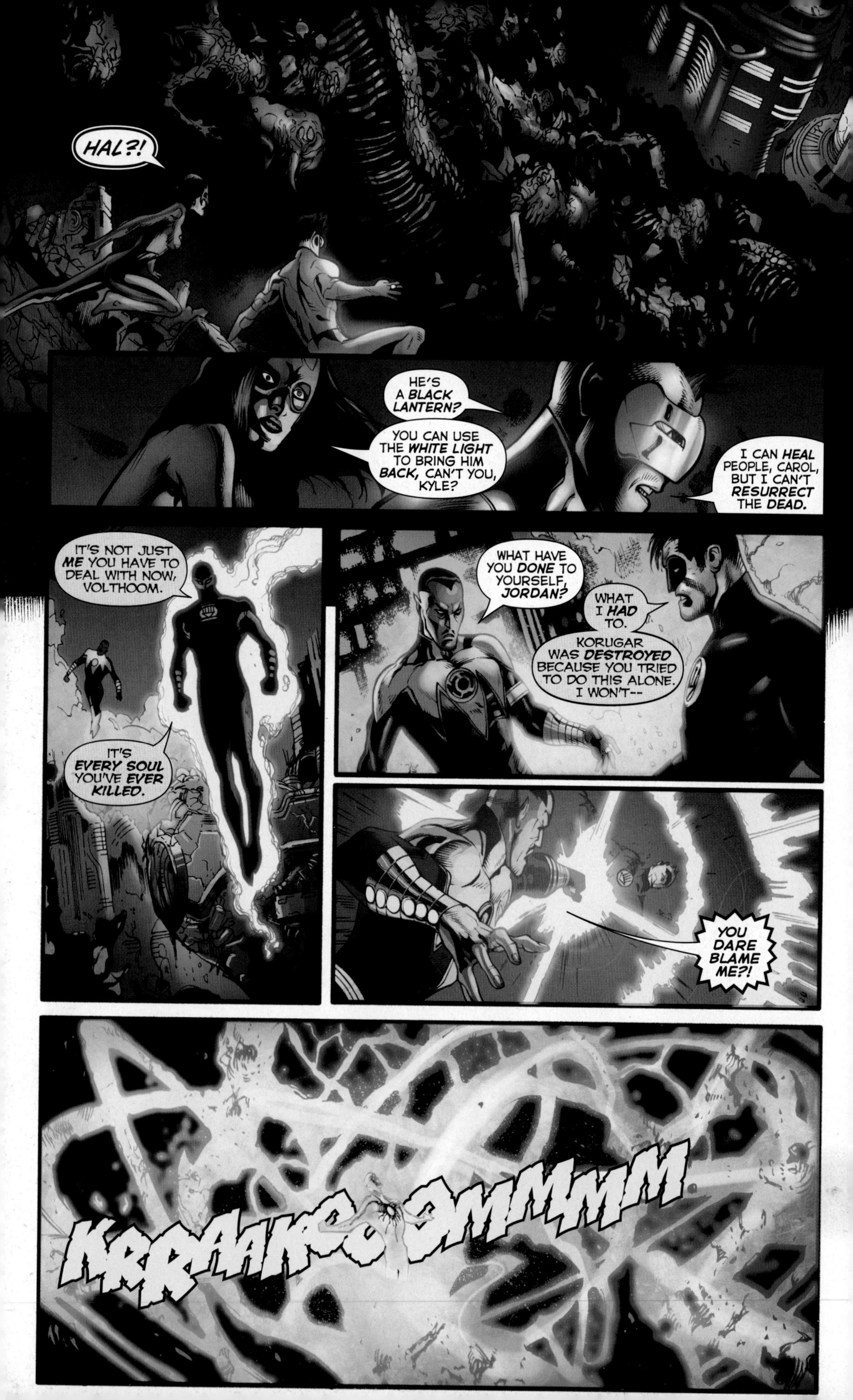
HAL?!
HE'S A BLACK LANTERN?
YOU CAN USE THE WHITE LIGHT TO BRING HIM BACK, CAN'T YOU, KYLE?
I CAN HEAL PEOPLE, CAROL, BUT I CAN'T RESURRECT THE DEAD.
IT'S NOT JUST ME YOU HAVE TO DEAL WITH NOW, VOLTHOOM.
IT'S EVERY SOUL YOU'VE EVER KILLED.
WHAT HAVE YOU DONE TO YOURSELF, JORDAN?
WHAT I HAD TO.
KORUGAR WAS DESTROYED BECAUSE YOU TRIED TO DO THIS ALONE. I WON'T--
YOU DARE BLAME ME?!
KRRAAKOOOMMMMM

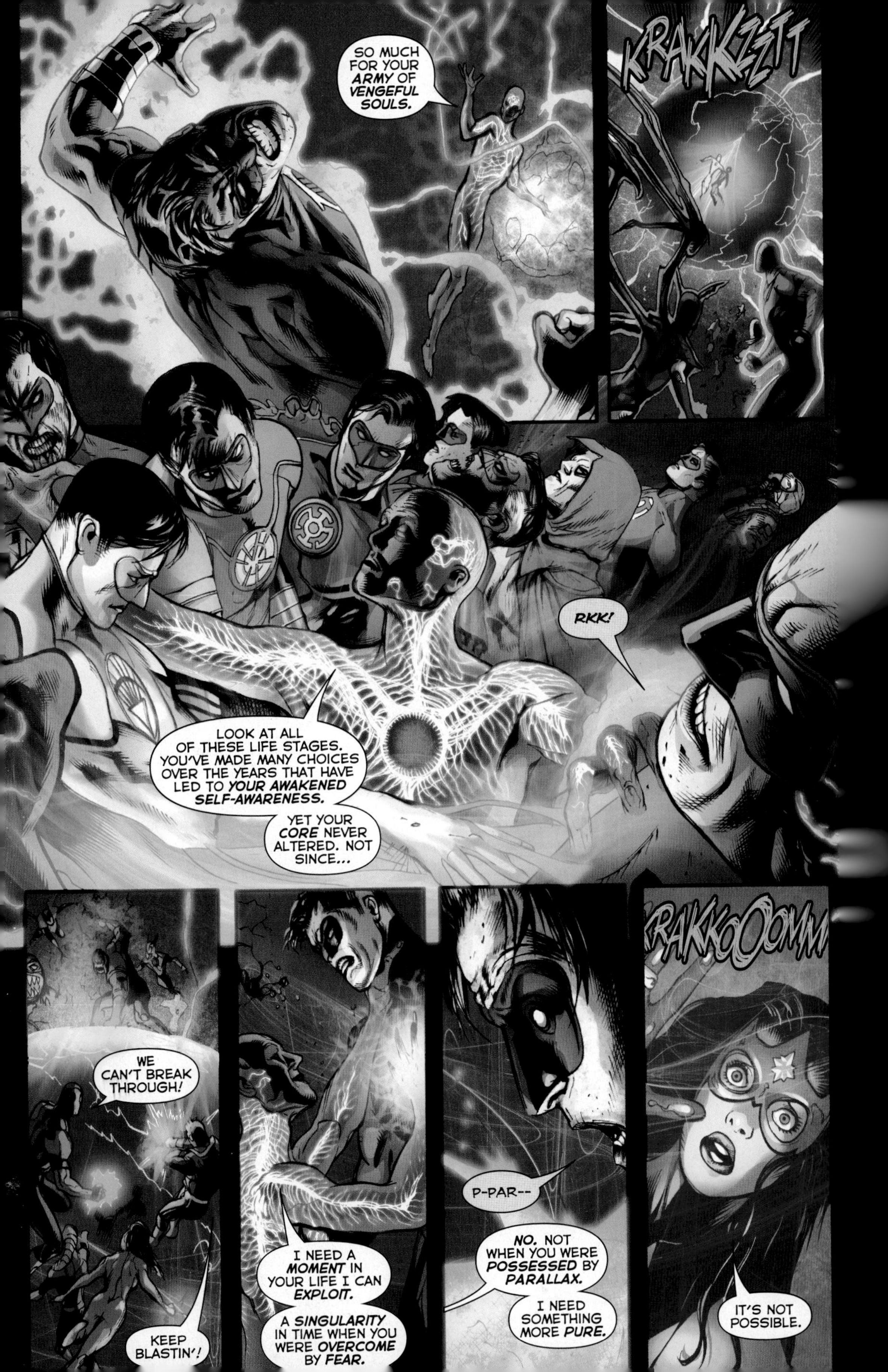
SO MUCH FOR YOUR ARMY OF VENGEFUL SOULS.
KRAKKZZTT
RKK!
LOOK AT ALL OF THESE LIFE STAGES. YOU'VE MADE MANY CHOICES OVER THE YEARS THAT HAVE LED TO YOUR AWAKENED SELF-AWARENESS.
YET YOUR CORE NEVER ALTERED. NOT SINCE...
WE CAN'T BREAK THROUGH!
KEEP BLASTIN'!
I NEED A MOMENT IN YOUR LIFE I CAN EXPLOIT.
A SINGULARITY IN TIME WHEN YOU WERE OVERCOME BY FEAR.
P-PAR--
NO. NOT WHEN YOU WERE POSSESSED BY PARALLAX.
I NEED SOMETHING MORE PURE.
KRAKKOOOMM
IT'S NOT POSSIBLE.

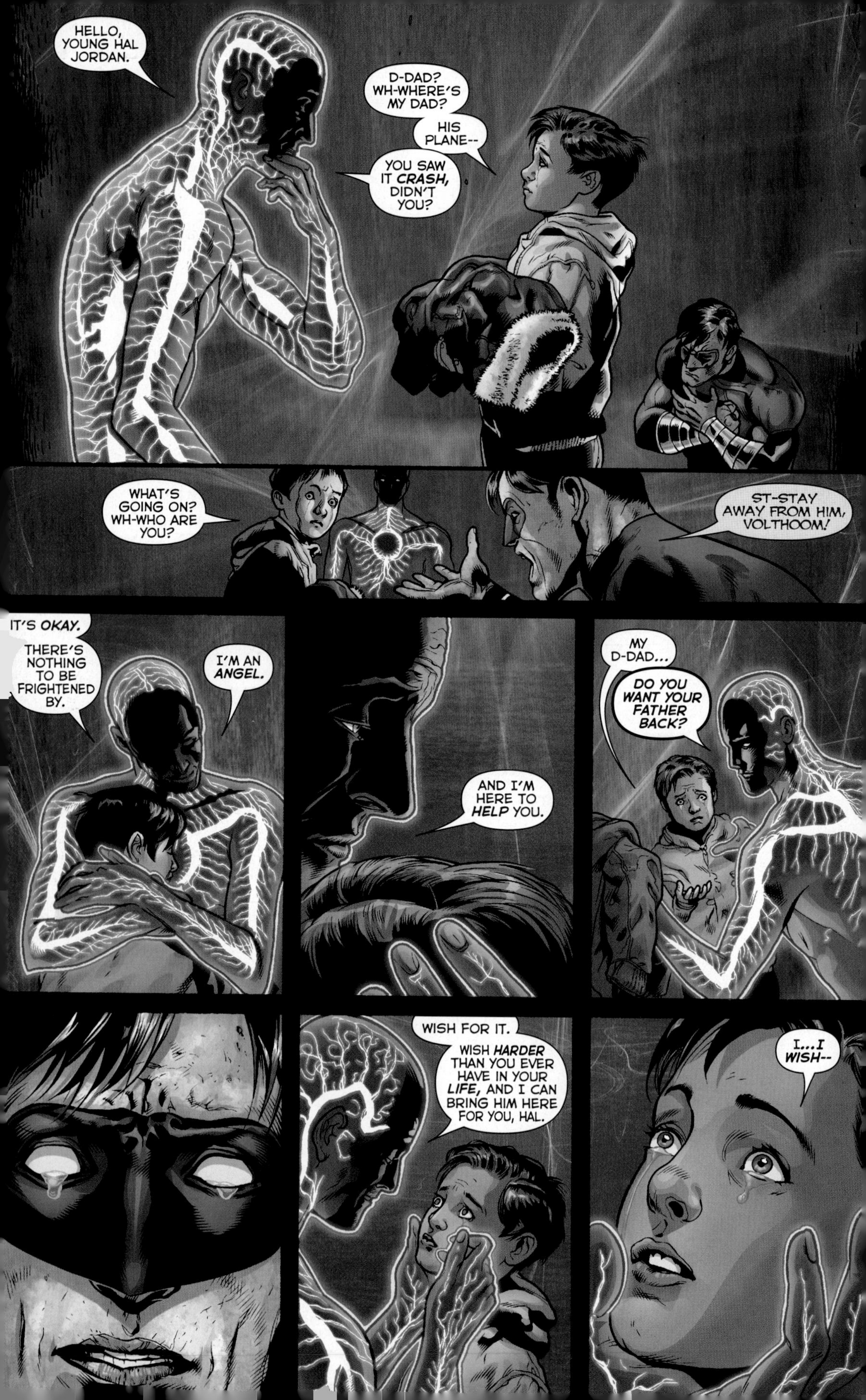
HELLO, YOUNG HAL JORDAN.
D-DAD? WH-WHERE'S MY DAD?
HIS PLANE--
YOU SAW IT *CRASH,* DIDN'T YOU?
WHAT'S GOING ON? WH-WHO ARE YOU?
ST-STAY AWAY FROM HIM, VOLTHOOM!
IT'S *OKAY.*
THERE'S NOTHING TO BE FRIGHTENED BY.
I'M AN *ANGEL.*
AND I'M HERE TO *HELP* YOU.
MY D-DAD...
DO YOU WANT YOUR FATHER BACK?
WISH FOR IT.
WISH *HARDER* THAN YOU EVER HAVE IN YOUR *LIFE,* AND I CAN BRING HIM HERE FOR YOU, HAL.
I...I WISH--

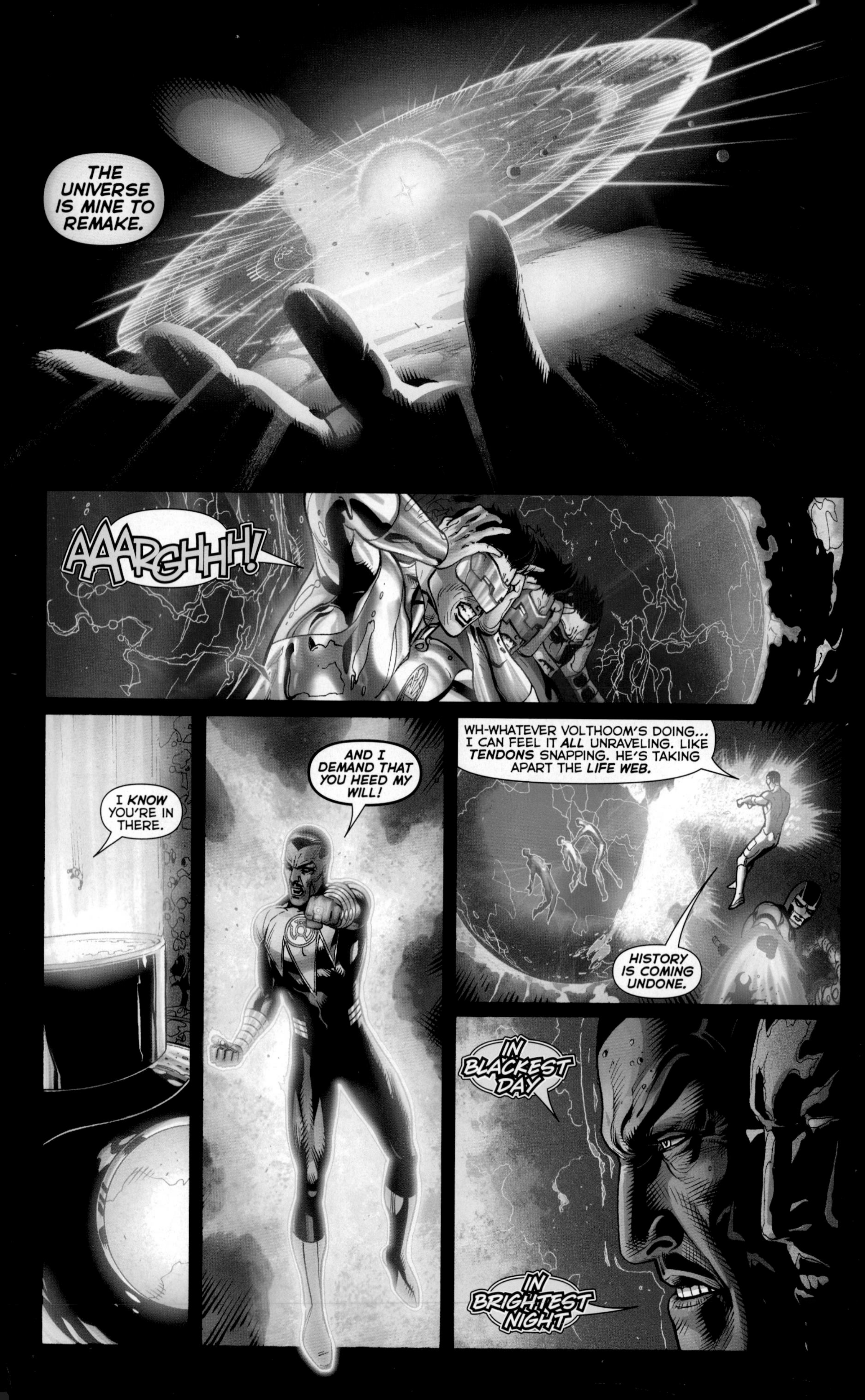
THE UNIVERSE IS MINE TO REMAKE.
AAARGHHH!
I KNOW YOU'RE IN THERE.
AND I DEMAND THAT YOU HEED MY WILL!
WH-WHATEVER VOLTHOOM'S DOING... I CAN FEEL IT ALL UNRAVELING. LIKE TENDONS SNAPPING. HE'S TAKING APART THE LIFE WEB.
HISTORY IS COMING UNDONE.
IN BLACKEST DAY
IN BRIGHTEST NIGHT

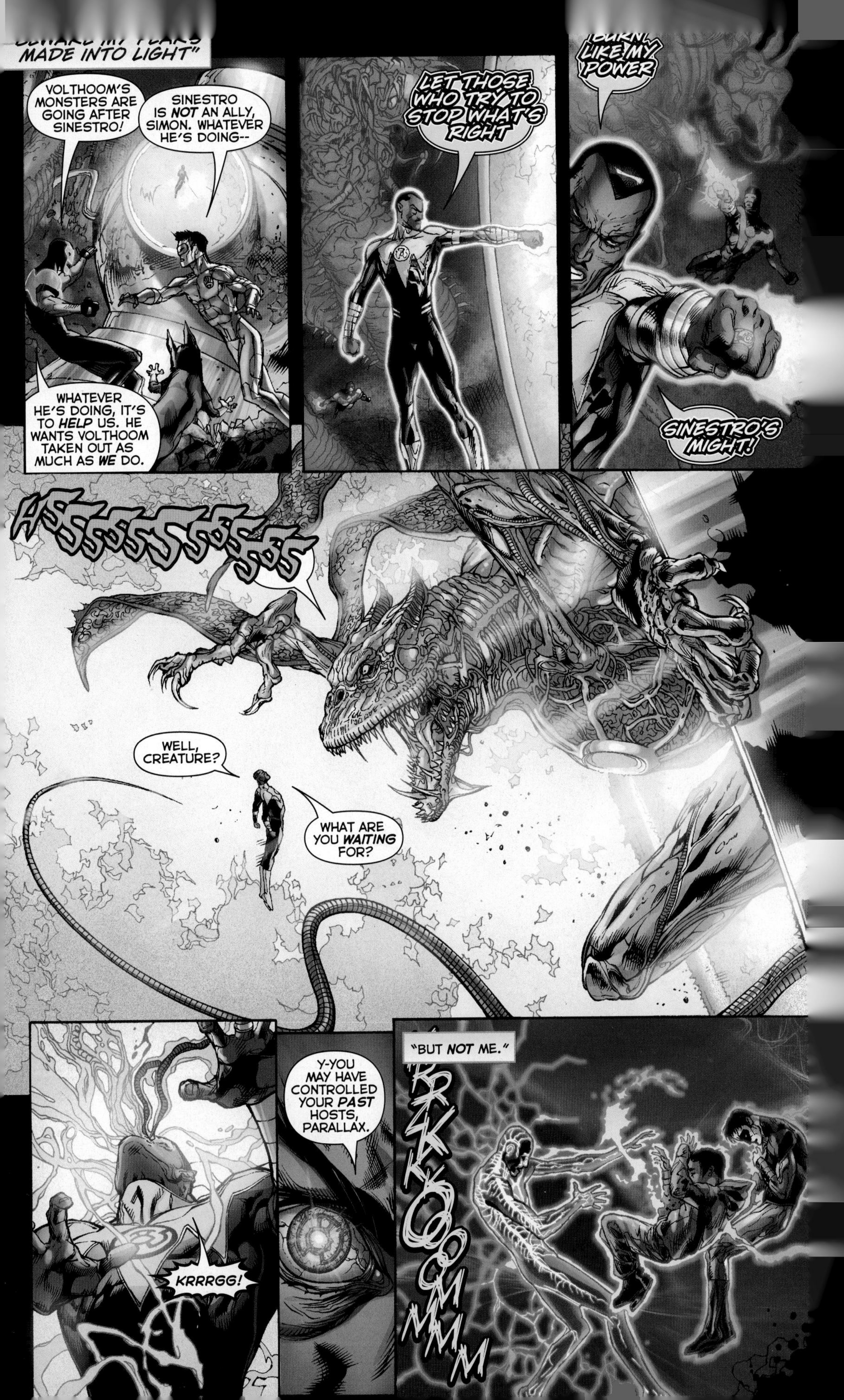
"...MADE INTO LIGHT"
VOLTHOOM'S MONSTERS ARE GOING AFTER SINESTRO!
SINESTRO IS NOT AN ALLY, SIMON. WHATEVER HE'S DOING--
WHATEVER HE'S DOING, IT'S TO HELP US. HE WANTS VOLTHOOM TAKEN OUT AS MUCH AS WE DO.
LET THOSE WHO TRY TO STOP WHAT'S RIGHT
BURN, LIKE MY POWER
SINESTRO'S MIGHT!
HSSSSSSSSSS
WELL, CREATURE?
WHAT ARE YOU WAITING FOR?
Y-YOU MAY HAVE CONTROLLED YOUR PAST HOSTS, PARALLAX.
KRRRGG!
"BUT NOT ME."
KRRKOOOOMMMM

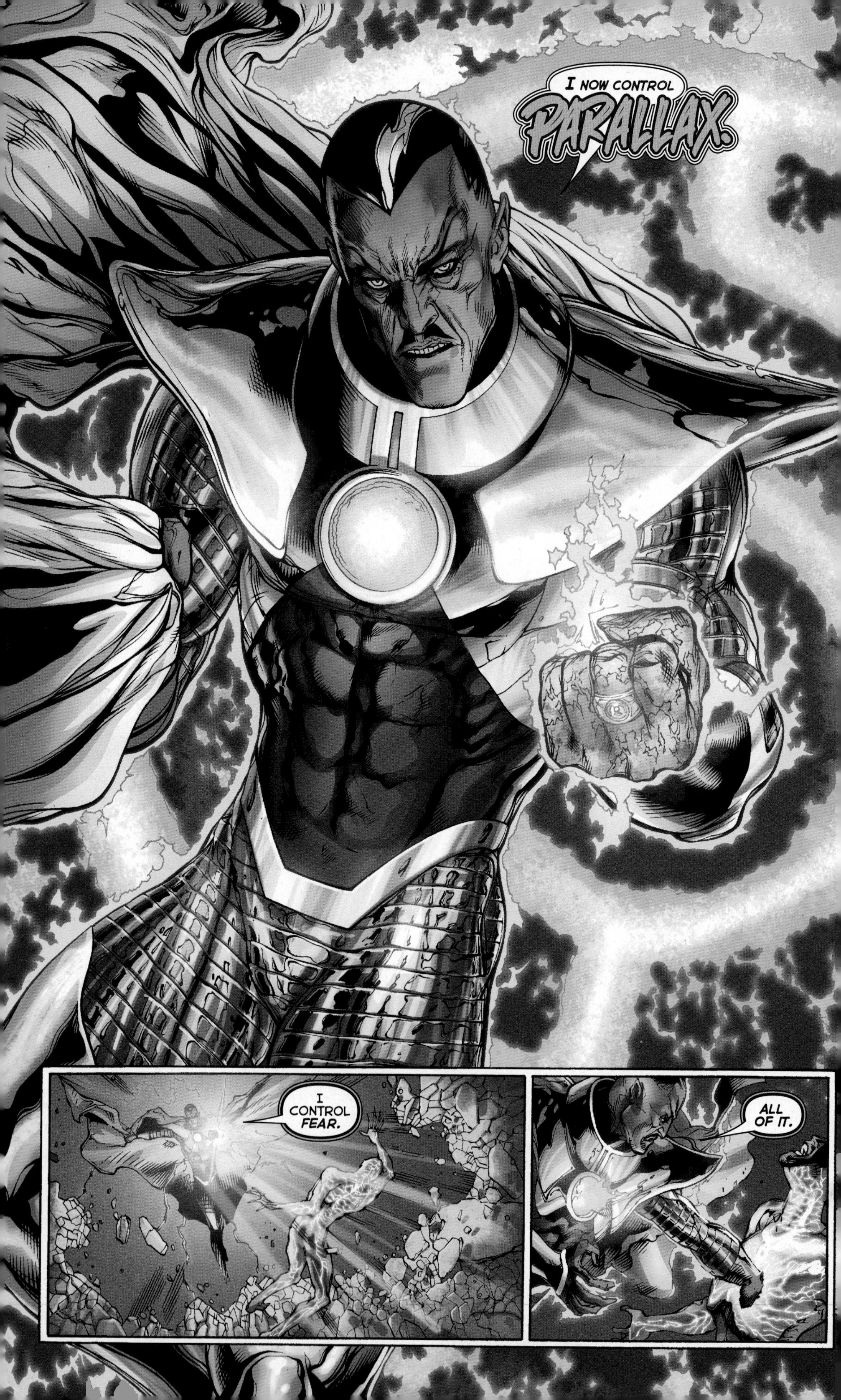
I NOW CONTROL
PARALLAX.
I CONTROL FEAR.
ALL OF IT.

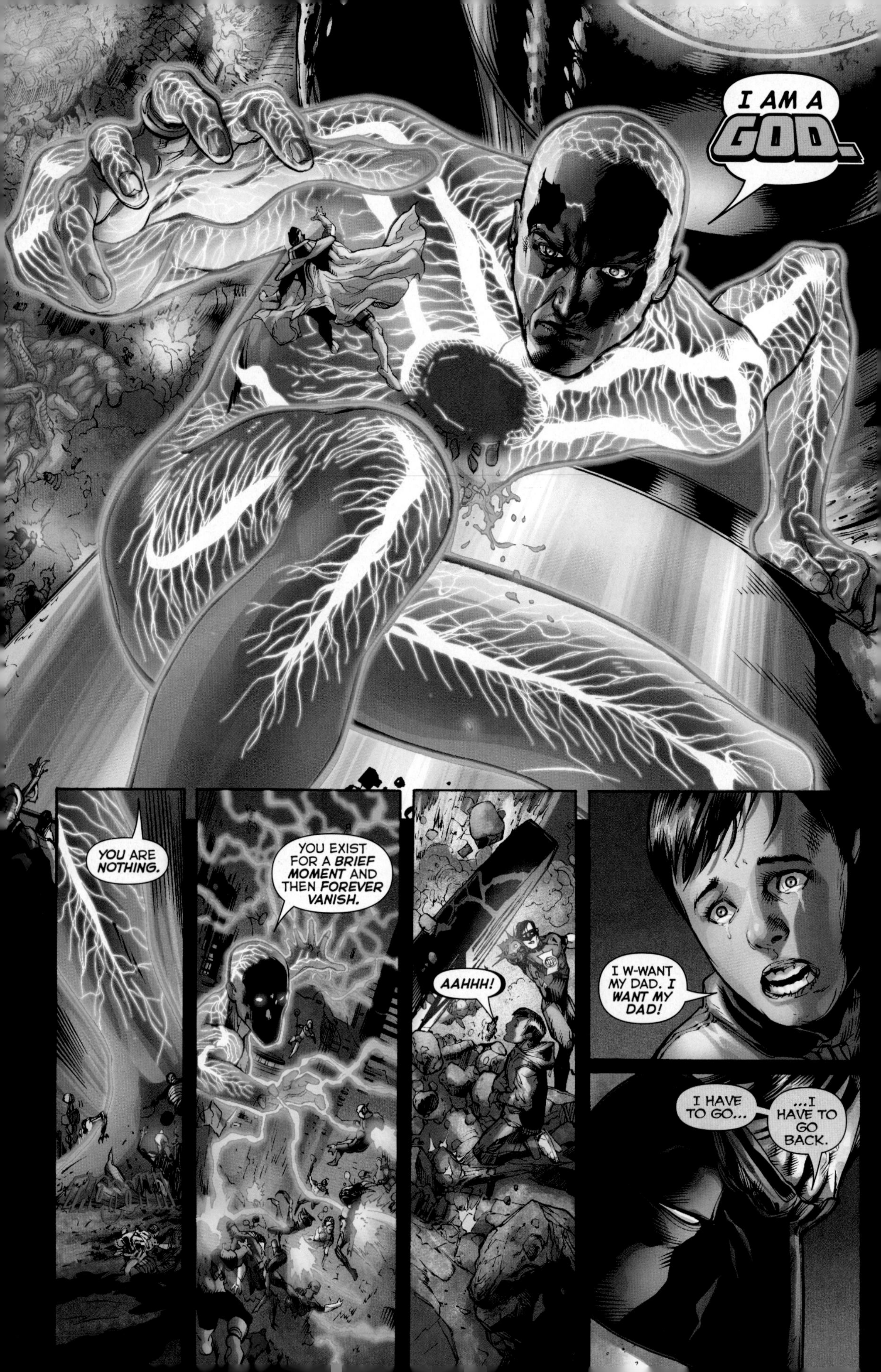
I AM A GOD.
YOU ARE NOTHING.
YOU EXIST FOR A BRIEF MOMENT AND THEN FOREVER VANISH.
AAHHH!
I W-WANT MY DAD. I WANT MY DAD!
I HAVE TO GO...
...I HAVE TO GO BACK.

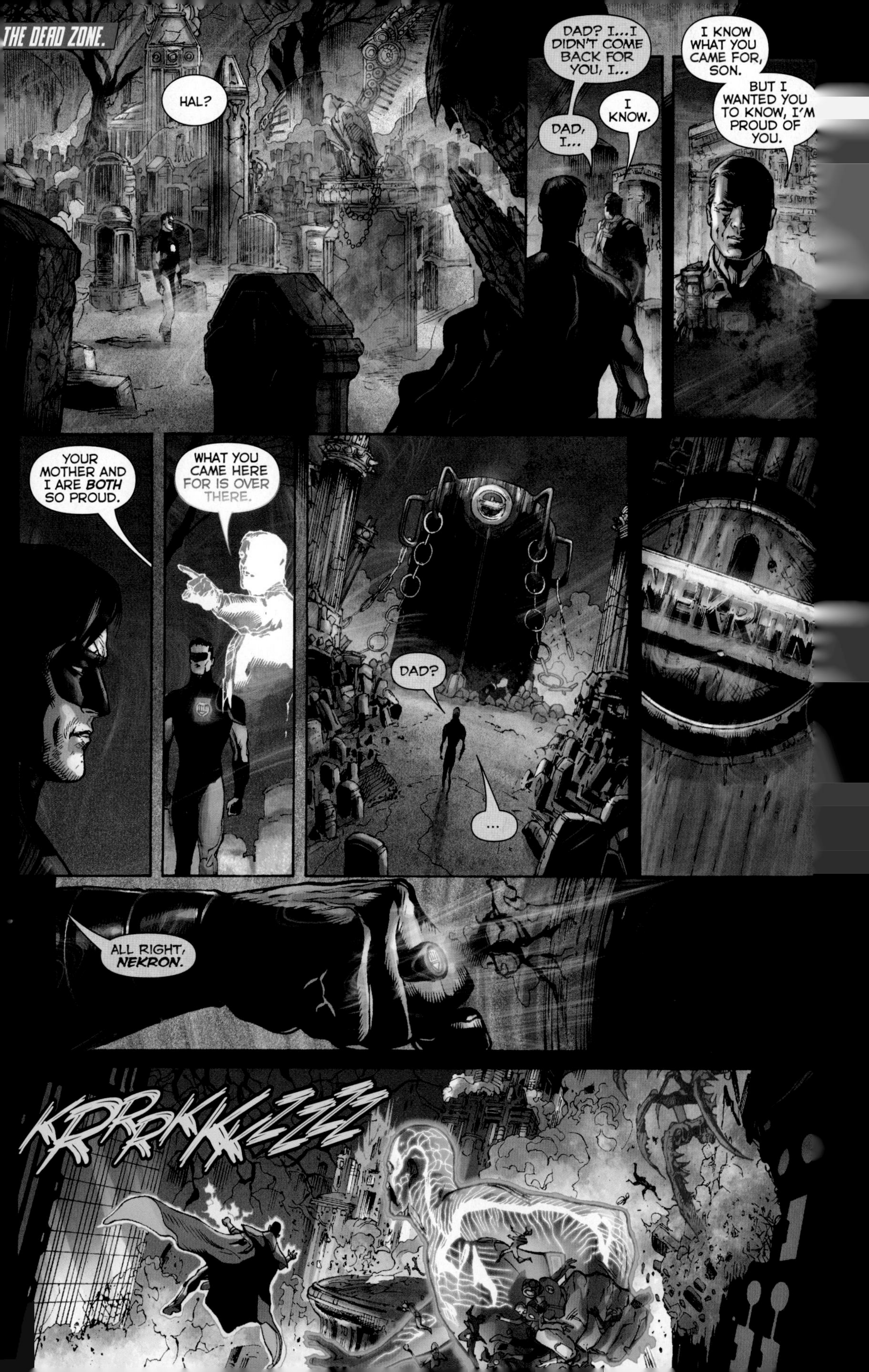
THE DEAD ZONE.
HAL?
DAD? I...I DIDN'T COME BACK FOR YOU, I...
DAD, I...
I KNOW.
I KNOW WHAT YOU CAME FOR, SON.
BUT I WANTED YOU TO KNOW, I'M PROUD OF YOU.
YOUR MOTHER AND I ARE BOTH SO PROUD.
WHAT YOU CAME HERE FOR IS OVER THERE.
DAD?
...
NEKRON
ALL RIGHT, NEKRON.
KRRRKKKZZZZZ

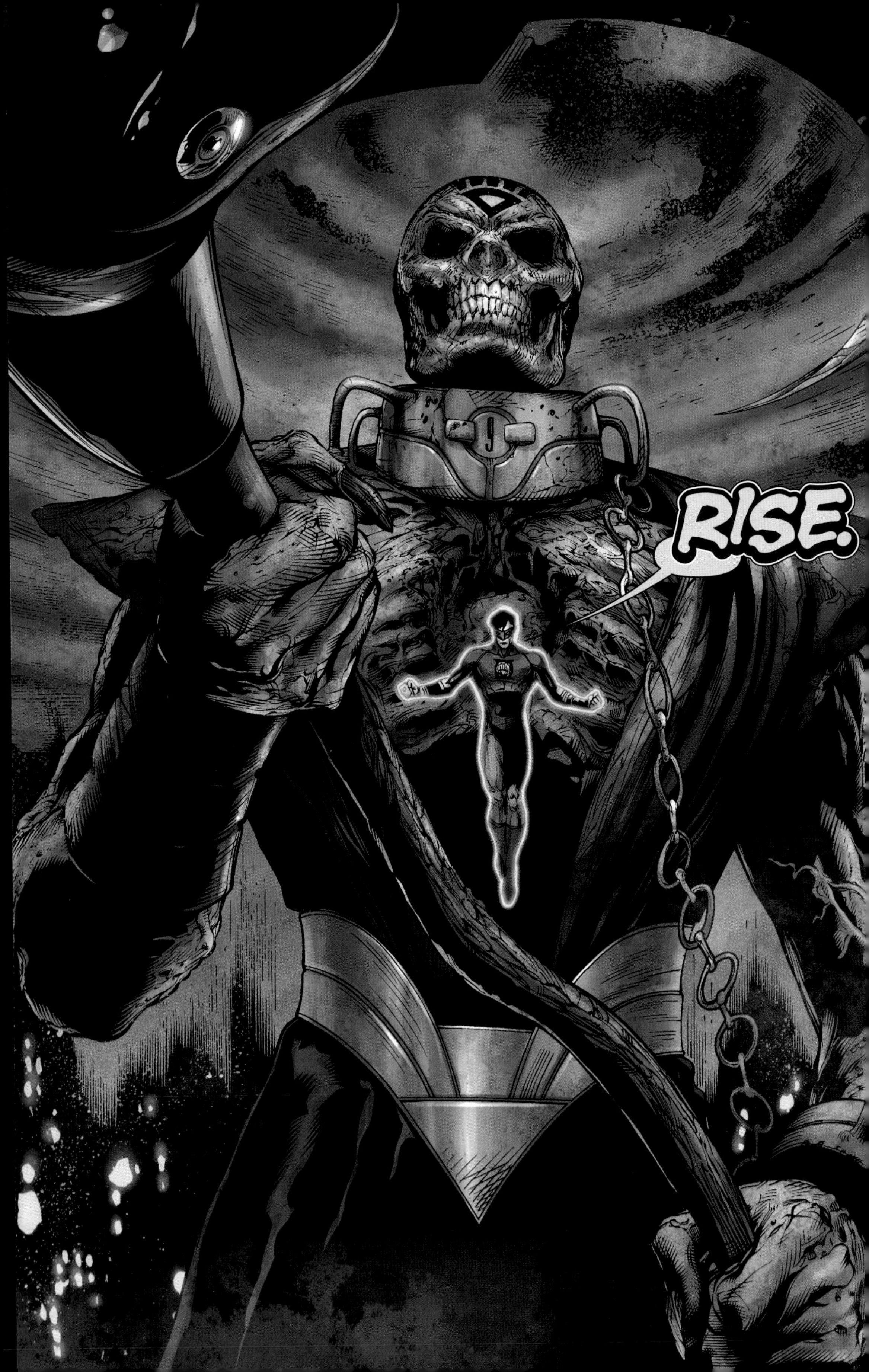
RISE.

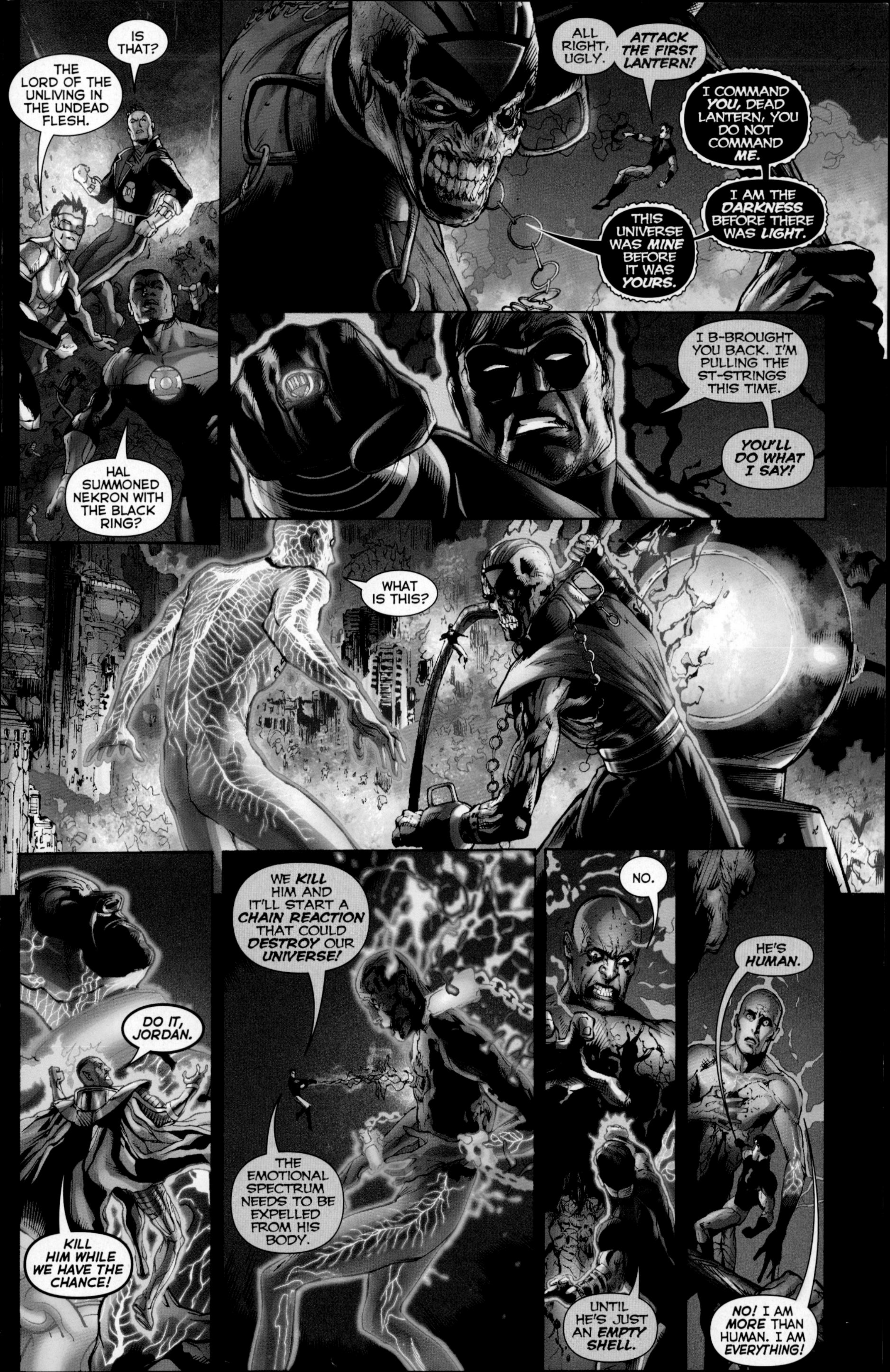
IS THAT?
THE LORD OF THE UNLIVING IN THE UNDEAD FLESH.
HAL SUMMONED NEKRON WITH THE BLACK RING?
ALL RIGHT, UGLY.
ATTACK THE FIRST LANTERN!
I COMMAND YOU, DEAD LANTERN, YOU DO NOT COMMAND ME.
I AM THE DARKNESS BEFORE THERE WAS LIGHT.
THIS UNIVERSE WAS MINE BEFORE IT WAS YOURS.
I B-BROUGHT YOU BACK. I'M PULLING THE ST-STRINGS THIS TIME.
YOU'LL DO WHAT I SAY!
WHAT IS THIS?
DO IT, JORDAN.
KILL HIM WHILE WE HAVE THE CHANCE!
WE KILL HIM AND IT'LL START A CHAIN REACTION THAT COULD DESTROY OUR UNIVERSE!
THE EMOTIONAL SPECTRUM NEEDS TO BE EXPELLED FROM HIS BODY.
NO.
UNTIL HE'S JUST AN EMPTY SHELL.
HE'S HUMAN.
NO! I AM MORE THAN HUMAN. I AM EVERYTHING!

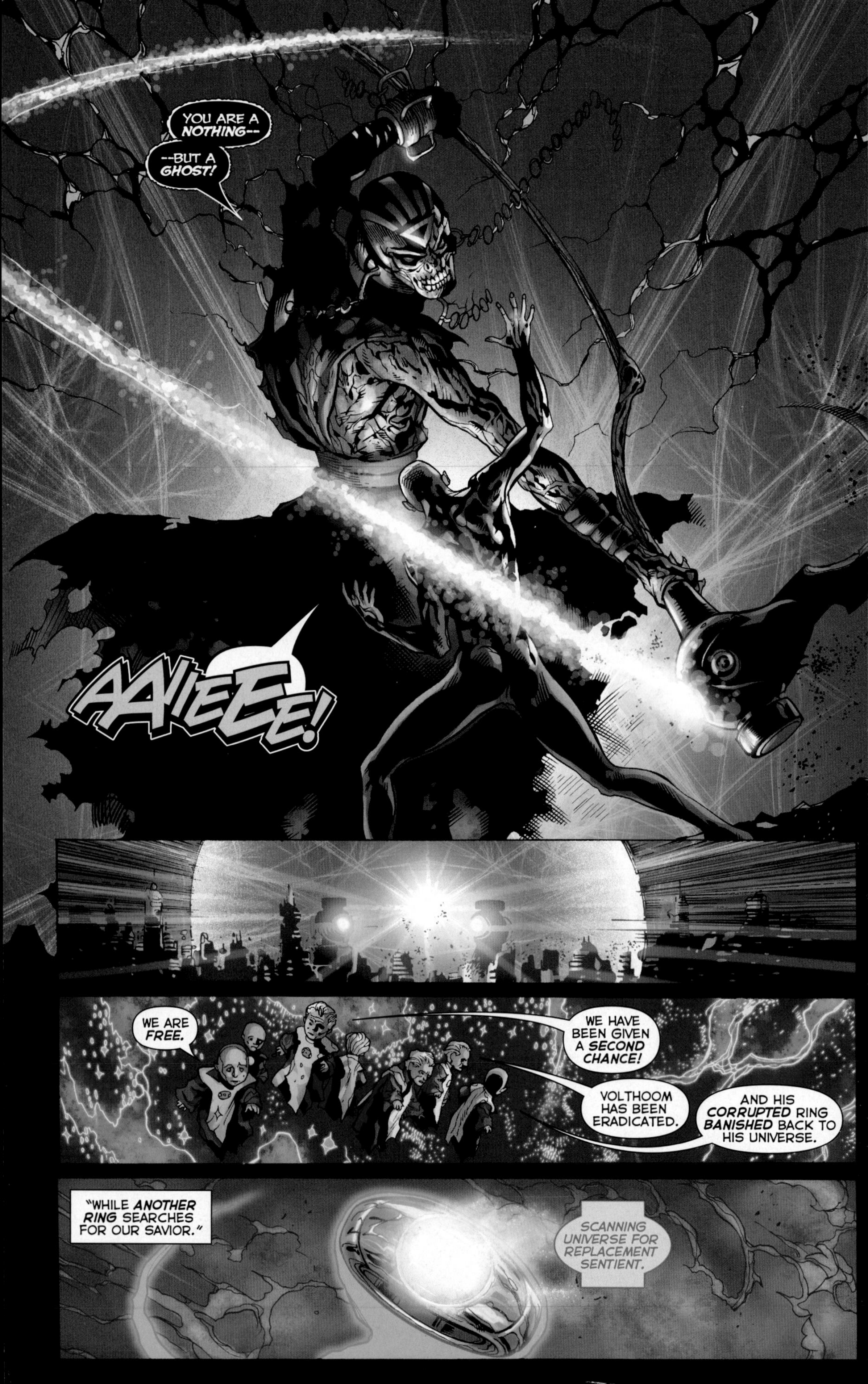

YOU ARE A NOTHING--
--BUT A GHOST!
AAIIEEEE!
WE ARE FREE.
WE HAVE BEEN GIVEN A SECOND CHANCE!
VOLTHOOM HAS BEEN ERADICATED.
AND HIS CORRUPTED RING BANISHED BACK TO HIS UNIVERSE.
"WHILE ANOTHER RING SEARCHES FOR OUR SAVIOR."
SCANNING UNIVERSE FOR REPLACEMENT SENTIENT.

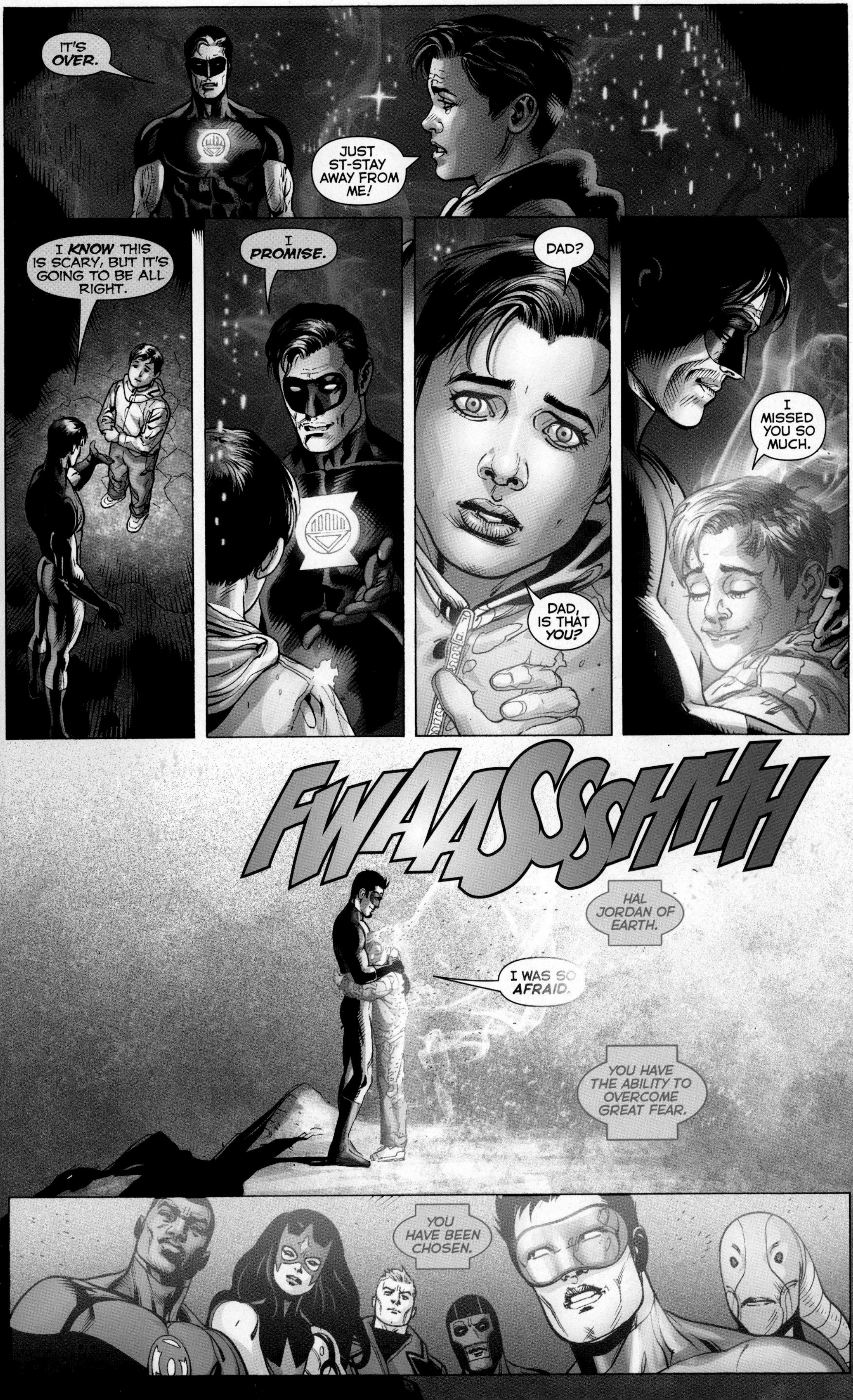
IT'S OVER.
JUST ST-STAY AWAY FROM ME!
I KNOW THIS IS SCARY, BUT IT'S GOING TO BE ALL RIGHT.
I PROMISE.
DAD?
DAD, IS THAT YOU?
I MISSED YOU SO MUCH.
FWAASSHHH
HAL JORDAN OF EARTH.
I WAS SO AFRAID.
YOU HAVE THE ABILITY TO OVERCOME GREAT FEAR.
YOU HAVE BEEN CHOSEN.

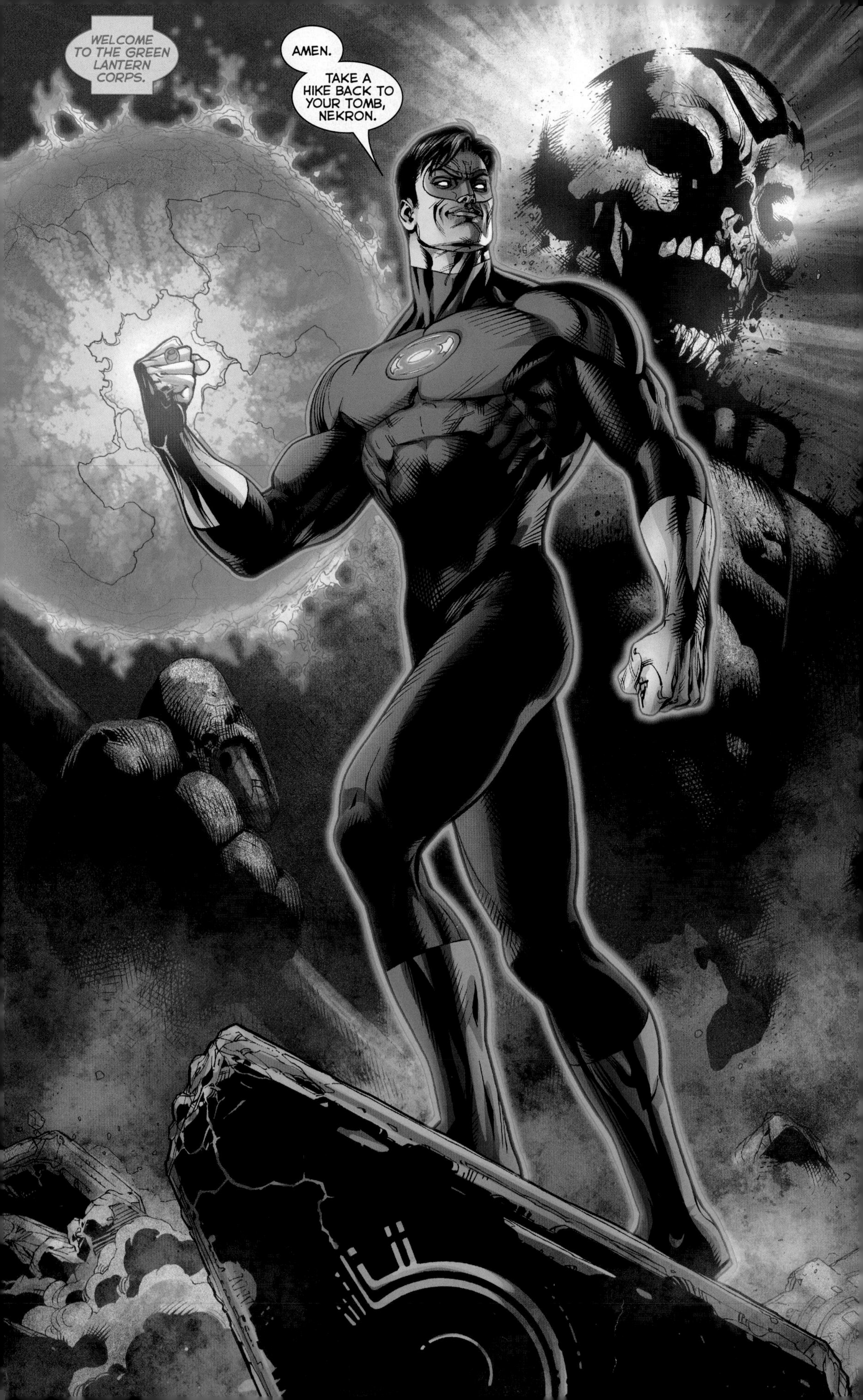
WELCOME TO THE GREEN LANTERN CORPS.
AMEN.
TAKE A HIKE BACK TO YOUR TOMB, NEKRON.

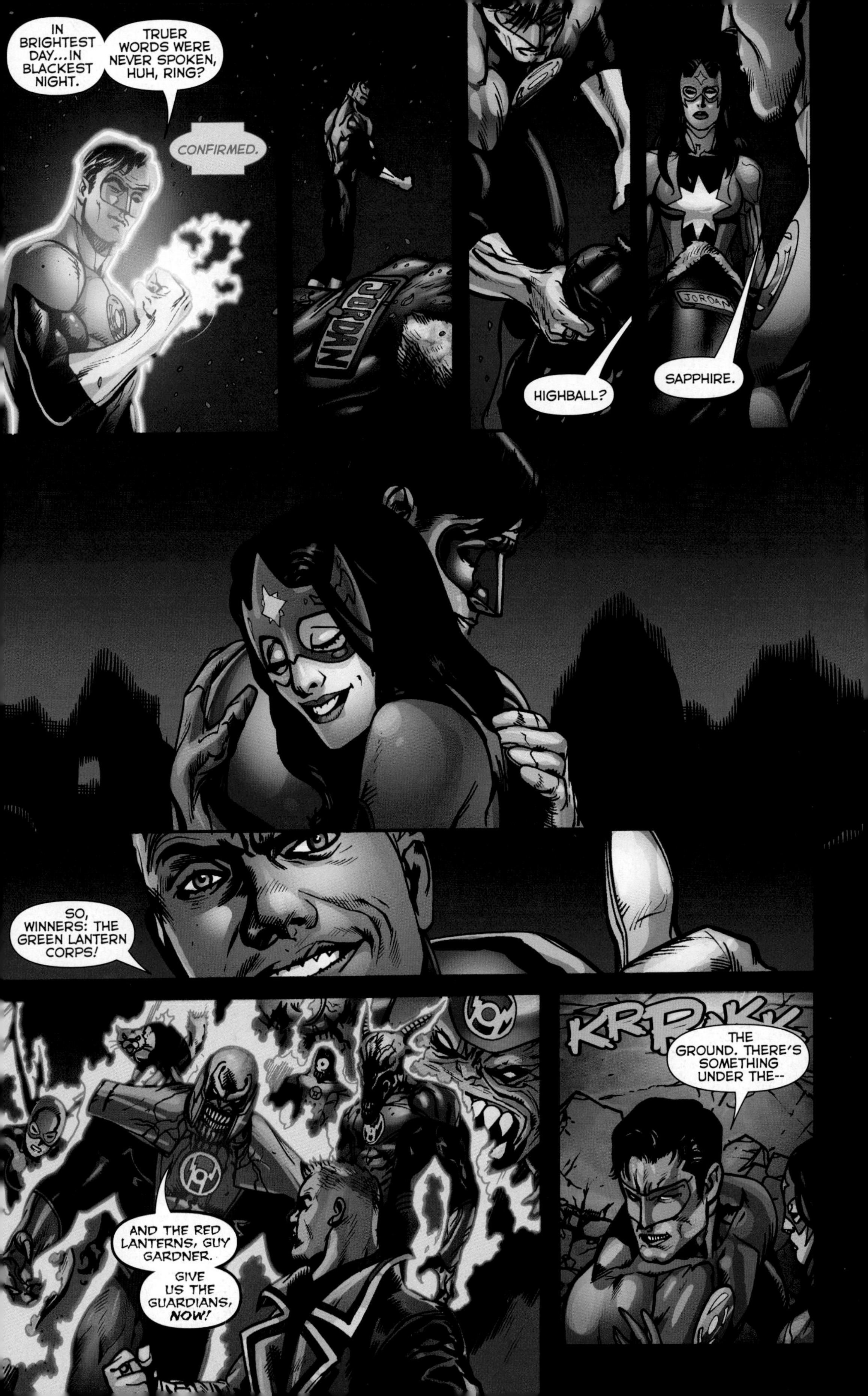
IN BRIGHTEST DAY...IN BLACKEST NIGHT.
TRUER WORDS WERE NEVER SPOKEN, HUH, RING?
CONFIRMED.
JORDAN
JORDAN
HIGHBALL?
SAPPHIRE.
SO, WINNERS: THE GREEN LANTERN CORPS!
AND THE RED LANTERNS, GUY GARDNER.
GIVE US THE GUARDIANS, NOW!
KRP KYL
THE GROUND. THERE'S SOMETHING UNDER THE--

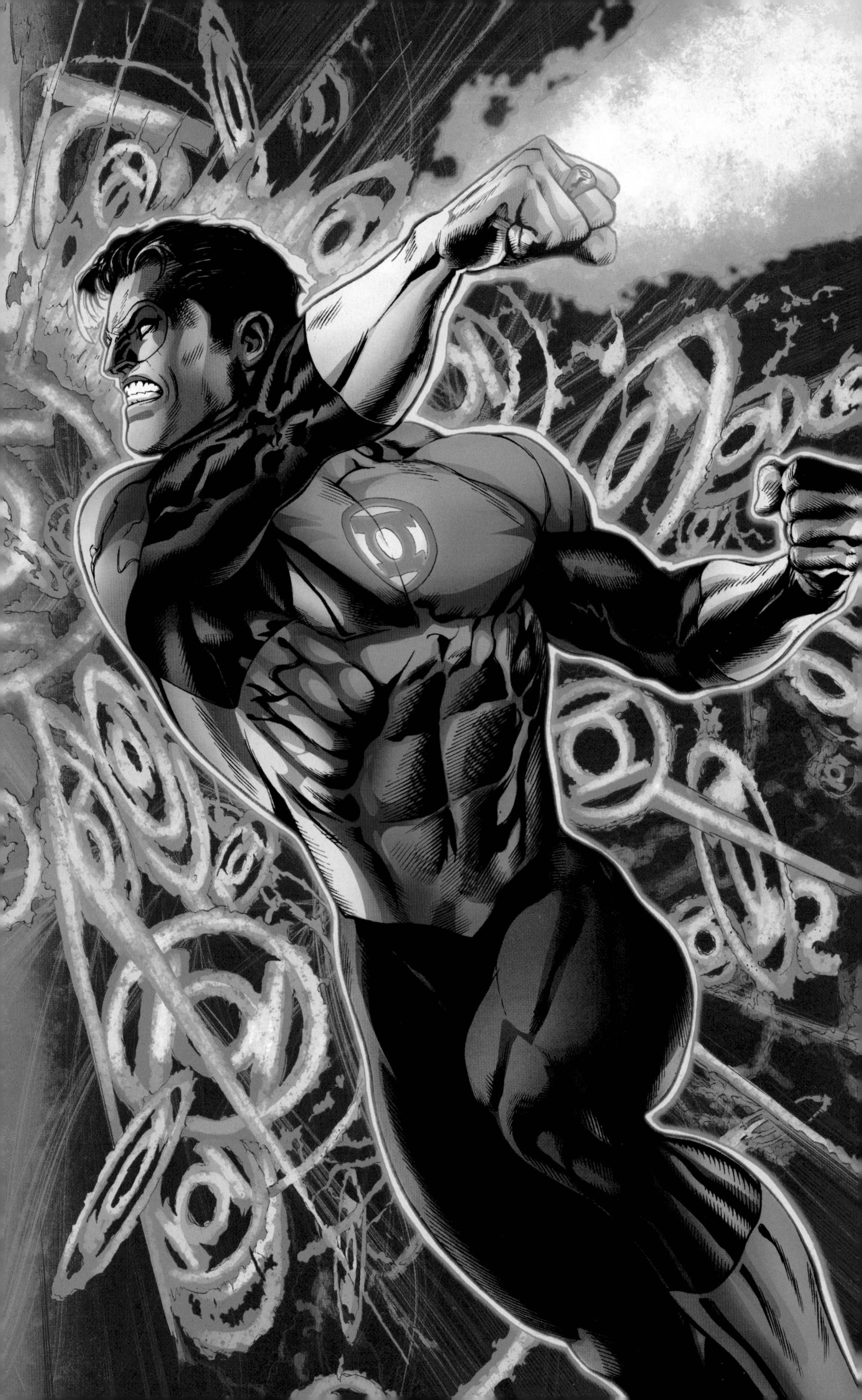

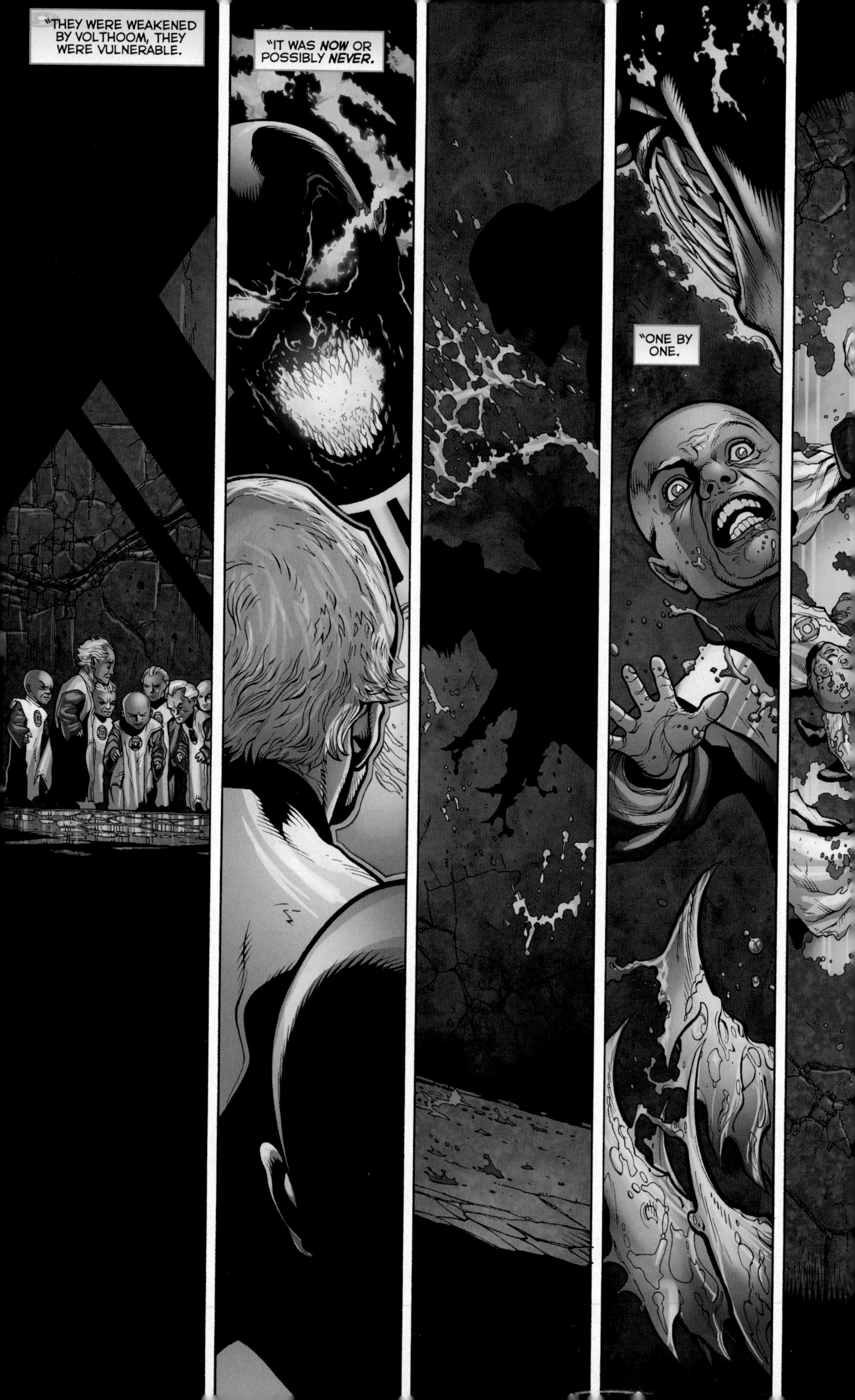
"THEY WERE WEAKENED BY VOLTHOOM, THEY WERE VULNERABLE.
"IT WAS *NOW* OR POSSIBLY *NEVER*.
"ONE BY ONE.

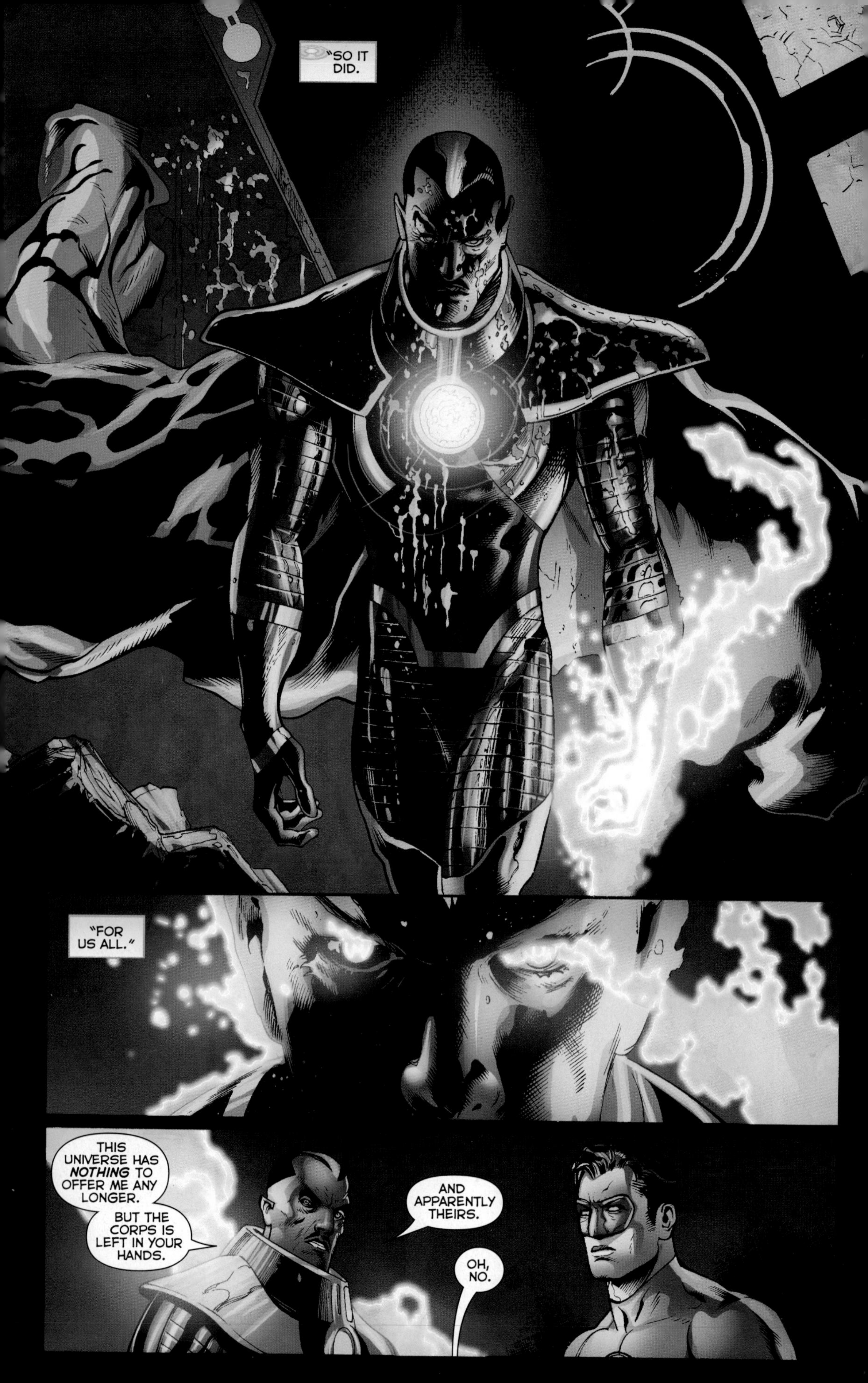
"SO IT DID.
"FOR US ALL."
THIS UNIVERSE HAS *NOTHING* TO OFFER ME ANY LONGER.
BUT THE CORPS IS LEFT IN YOUR HANDS.
AND APPARENTLY THEIRS.
OH, NO.

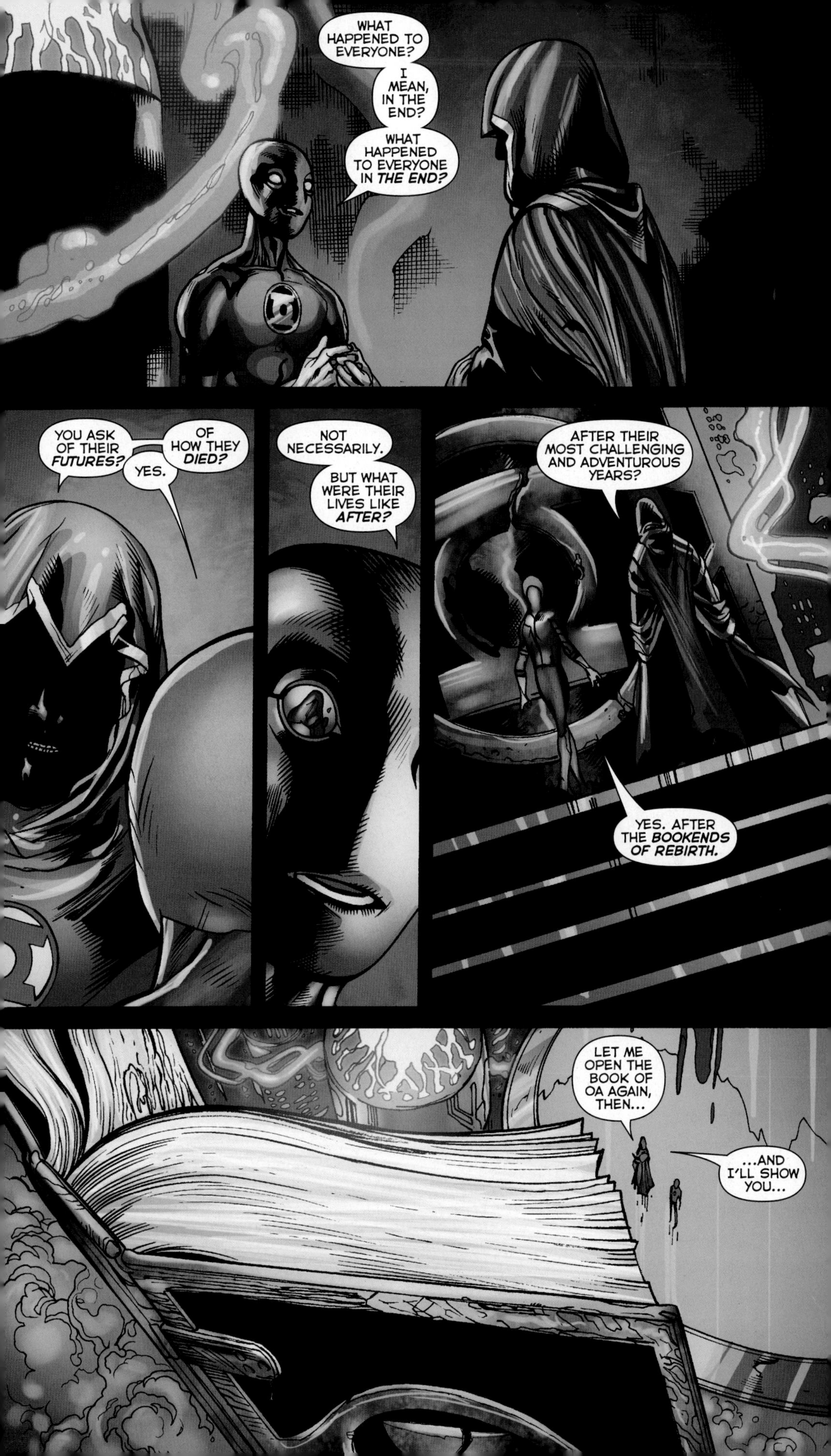

WHAT HAPPENED TO EVERYONE?
I MEAN, IN THE END?
WHAT HAPPENED TO EVERYONE IN *THE END?*
YOU ASK OF THEIR *FUTURES?*
OF HOW THEY *DIED?*
YES.
NOT NECESSARILY.
BUT WHAT WERE THEIR LIVES LIKE *AFTER?*
AFTER THEIR MOST CHALLENGING AND ADVENTUROUS YEARS?
YES. AFTER THE *BOOKENDS OF REBIRTH.*
LET ME OPEN THE BOOK OF OA AGAIN, THEN...
...AND I'LL SHOW YOU...

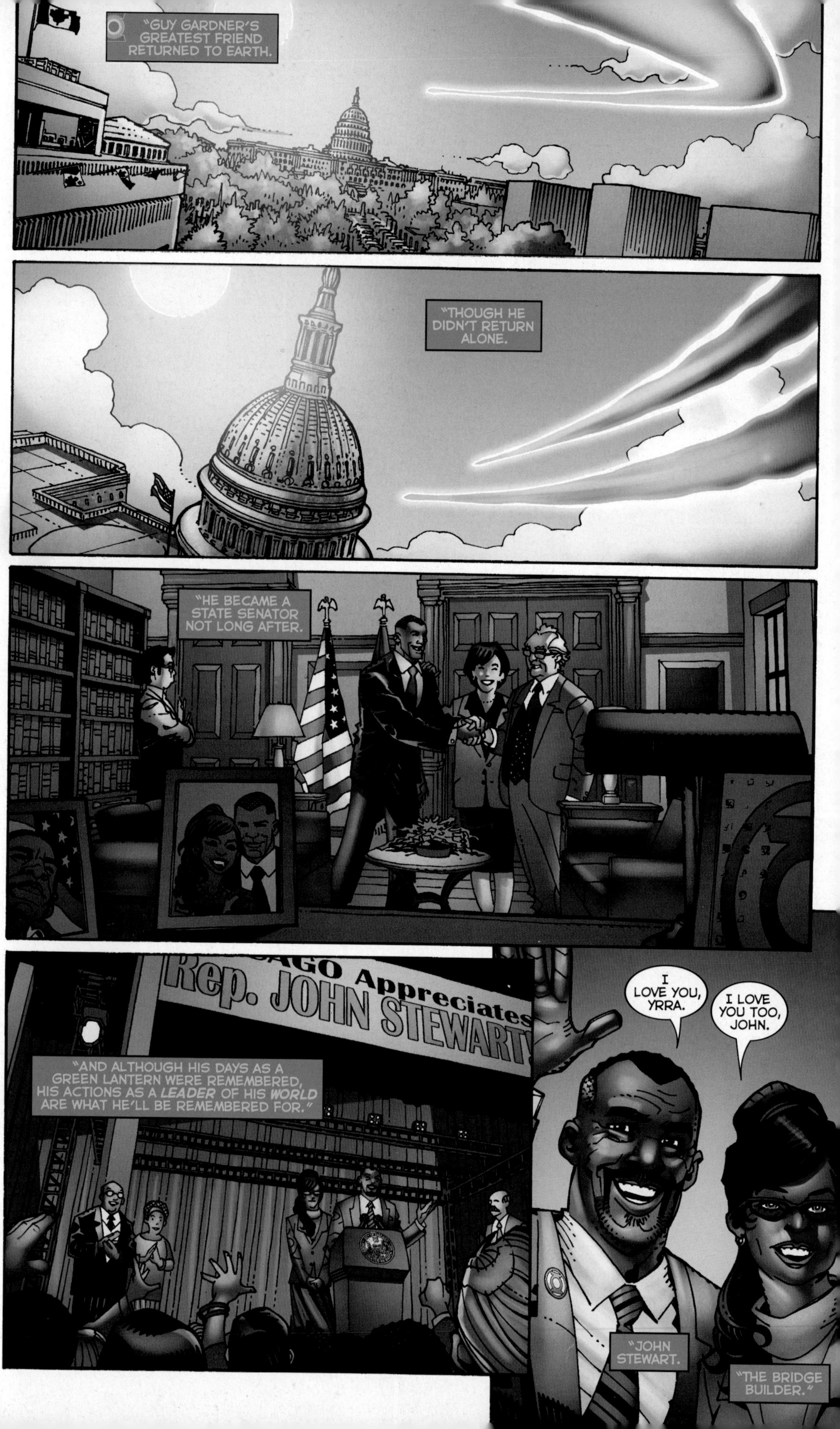
"GUY GARDNER'S GREATEST FRIEND RETURNED TO EARTH.
"THOUGH HE DIDN'T RETURN ALONE.
"HE BECAME A STATE SENATOR NOT LONG AFTER.
Rep. JOHN STEWART
Appreciates
"AND ALTHOUGH HIS DAYS AS A GREEN LANTERN WERE REMEMBERED, HIS ACTIONS AS A *LEADER* OF HIS *WORLD* ARE WHAT HE'LL BE REMEMBERED FOR."
I LOVE YOU, YRRA.
I LOVE YOU TOO, JOHN.
"JOHN STEWART.
"THE BRIDGE BUILDER."

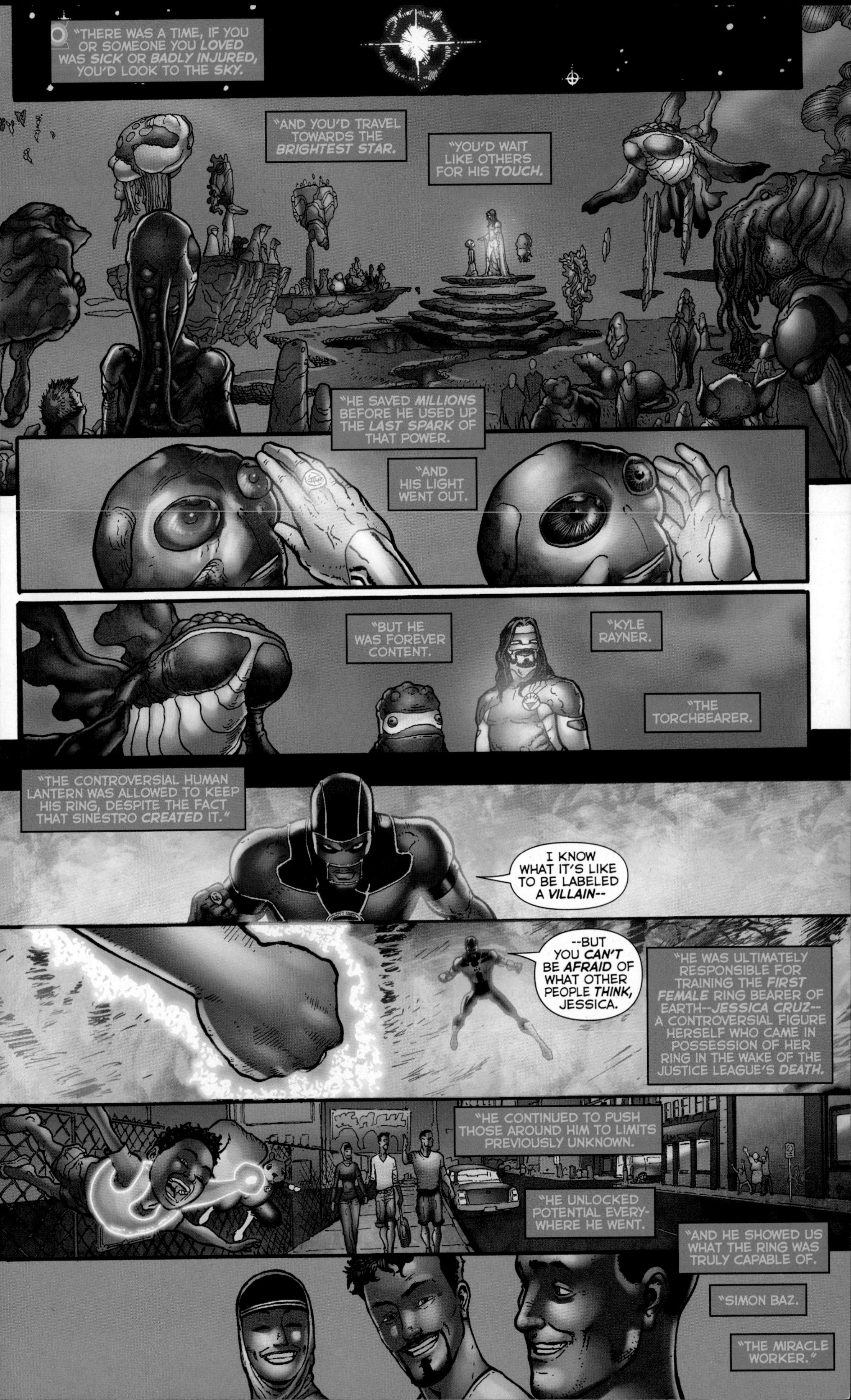

"THERE WAS A TIME, IF YOU OR SOMEONE YOU *LOVED* WAS *SICK* OR *BADLY INJURED*, YOU'D LOOK TO THE *SKY*.
"AND YOU'D TRAVEL TOWARDS THE *BRIGHTEST STAR*.
"YOU'D WAIT LIKE OTHERS FOR HIS *TOUCH*.
"HE SAVED *MILLIONS* BEFORE HE USED UP THE *LAST SPARK* OF THAT POWER.
"AND HIS LIGHT WENT OUT.
"BUT HE WAS FOREVER CONTENT.
"KYLE RAYNER.
"THE TORCHBEARER.
"THE CONTROVERSIAL HUMAN LANTERN WAS ALLOWED TO KEEP HIS RING, DESPITE THE FACT THAT SINESTRO *CREATED* IT."
I KNOW WHAT IT'S LIKE TO BE LABELED A *VILLAIN*--
--BUT YOU *CAN'T* BE *AFRAID* OF WHAT OTHER PEOPLE *THINK*, JESSICA.
"HE WAS ULTIMATELY RESPONSIBLE FOR TRAINING THE *FIRST FEMALE* RING BEARER OF EARTH--*JESSICA CRUZ*--A CONTROVERSIAL FIGURE HERSELF WHO CAME IN POSSESSION OF HER RING IN THE WAKE OF THE JUSTICE LEAGUE'S *DEATH*.
"HE CONTINUED TO PUSH THOSE AROUND HIM TO LIMITS PREVIOUSLY UNKNOWN.
"HE UNLOCKED POTENTIAL EVERY-WHERE HE WENT.
"AND HE SHOWED US WHAT THE RING WAS TRULY CAPABLE OF.
"SIMON BAZ.
"THE *MIRACLE WORKER*."

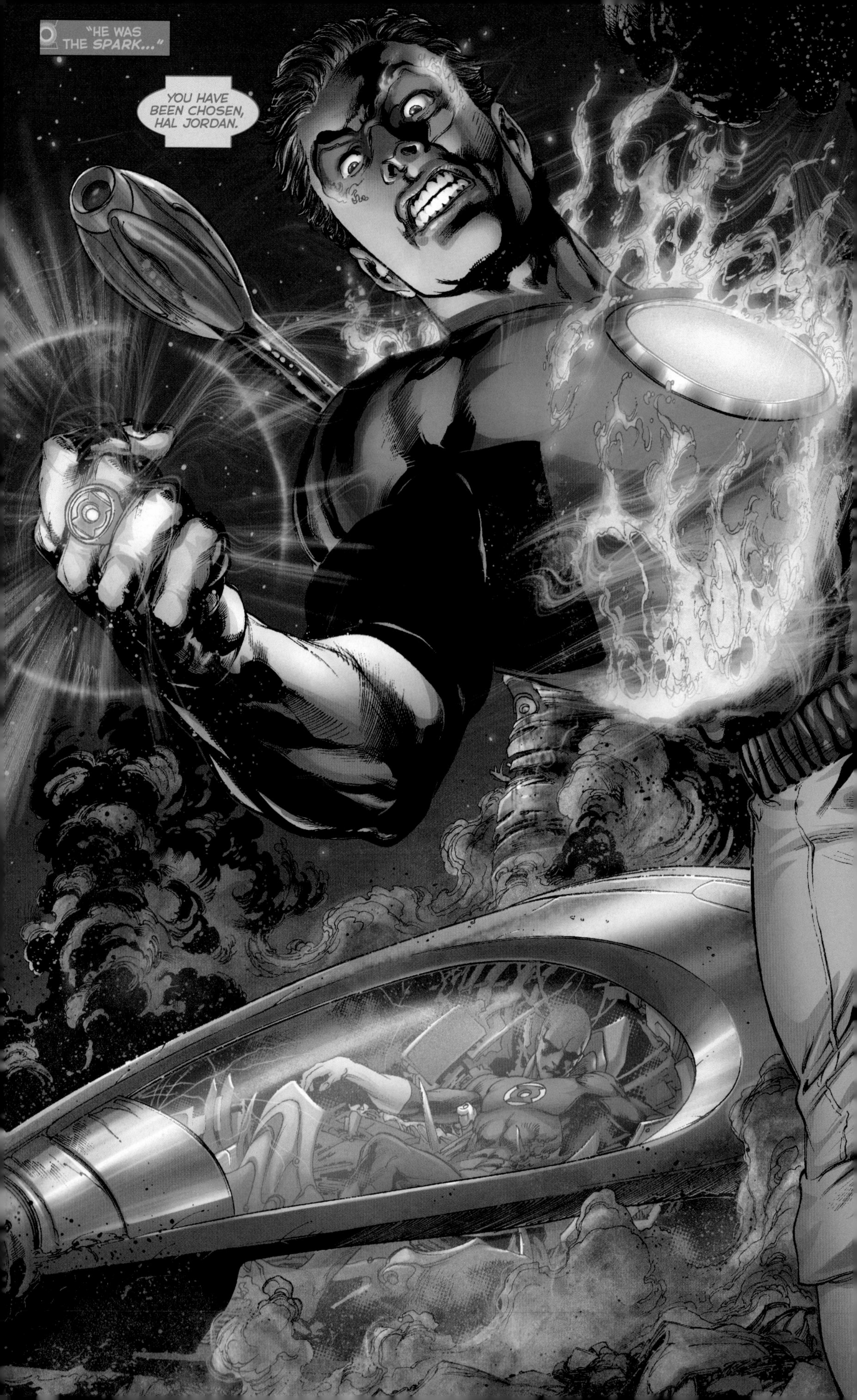
"HE WAS THE SPARK..."
YOU HAVE BEEN CHOSEN, HAL JORDAN.

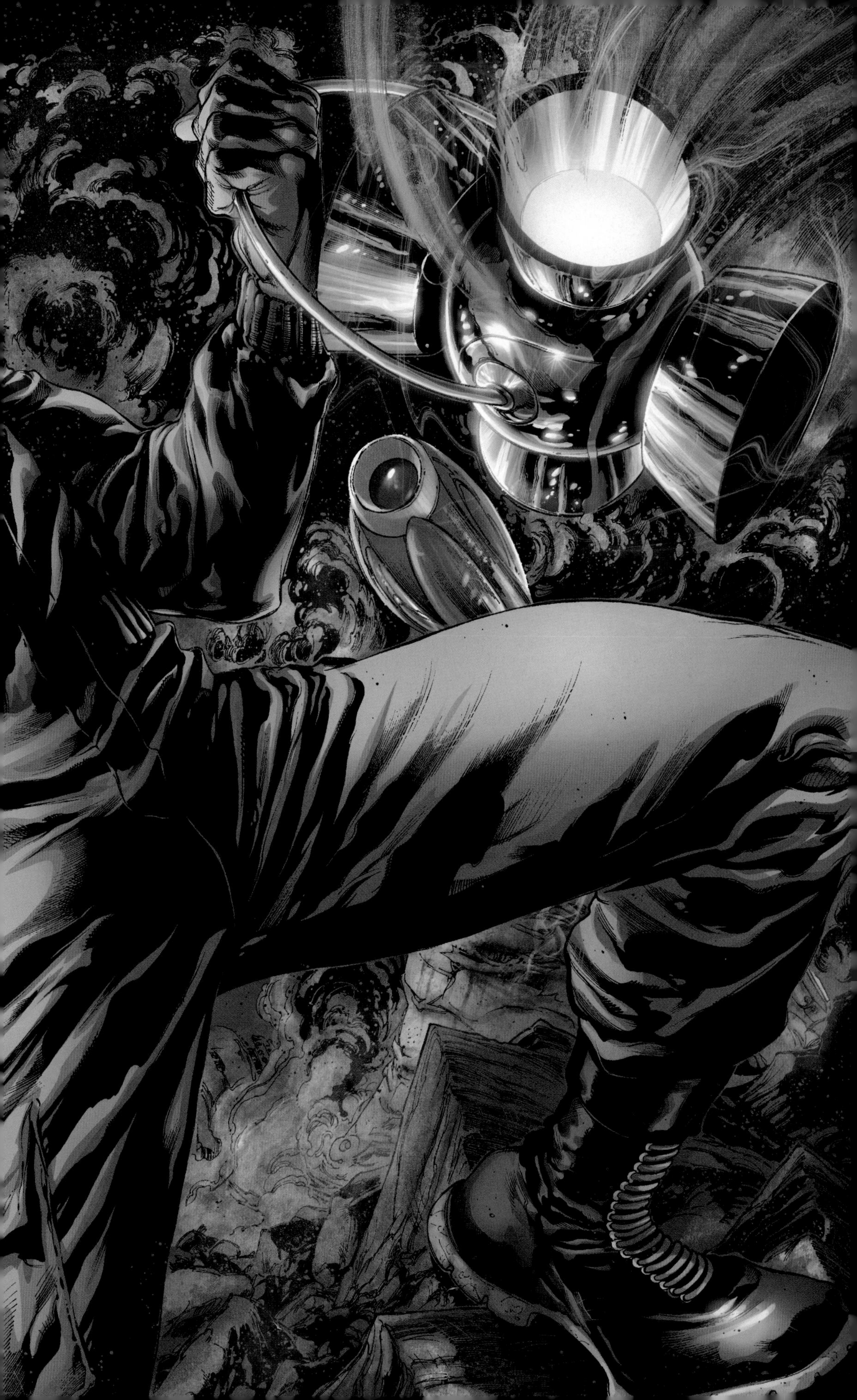

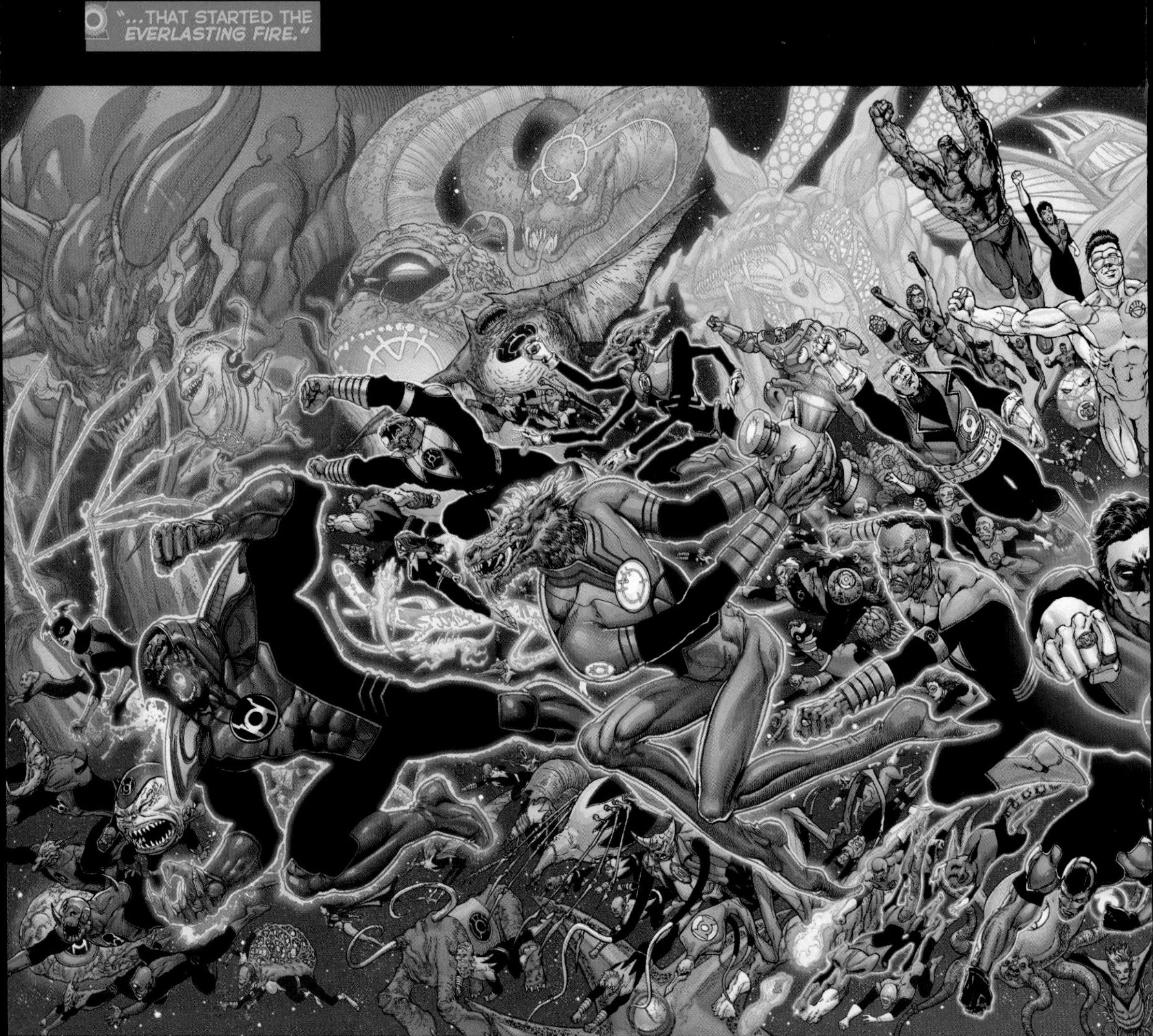
"...THAT STARTED THE EVERLASTING FIRE."

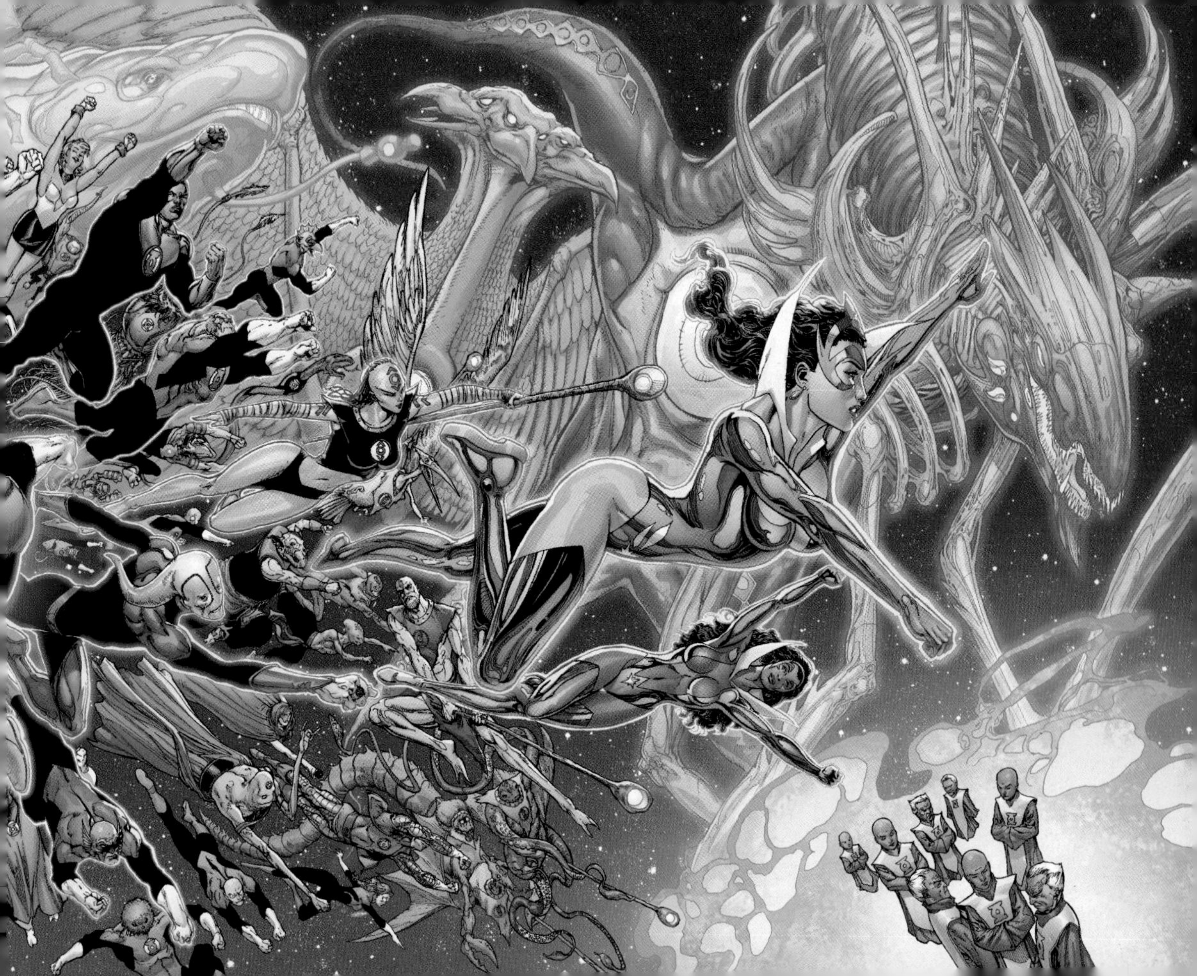

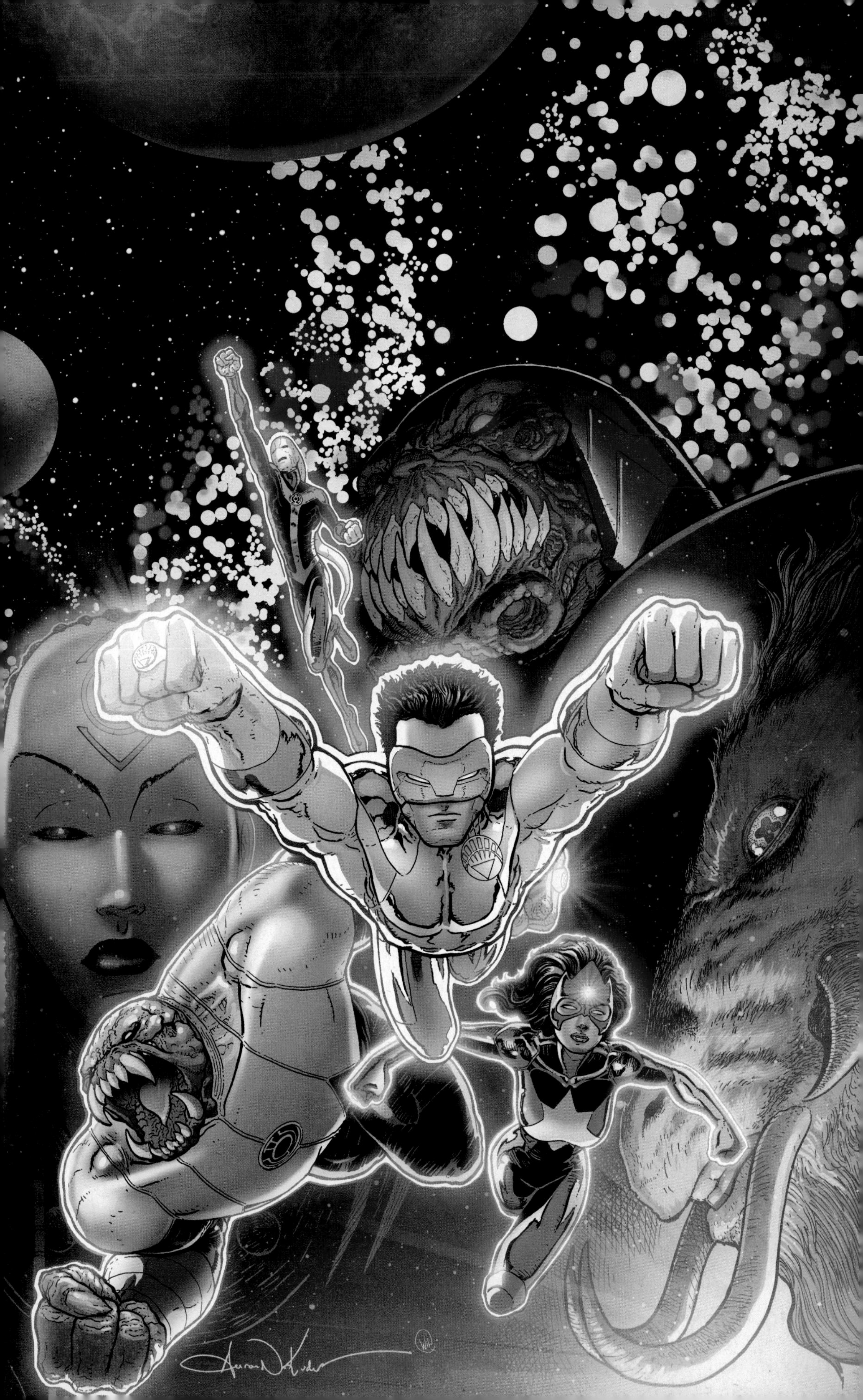

REUNION

TONY BEDARD writer ANDRES GUINALDO penciller RAUL FERNANDEZ inker
AARON KUDER & WIL QUINTANA cover

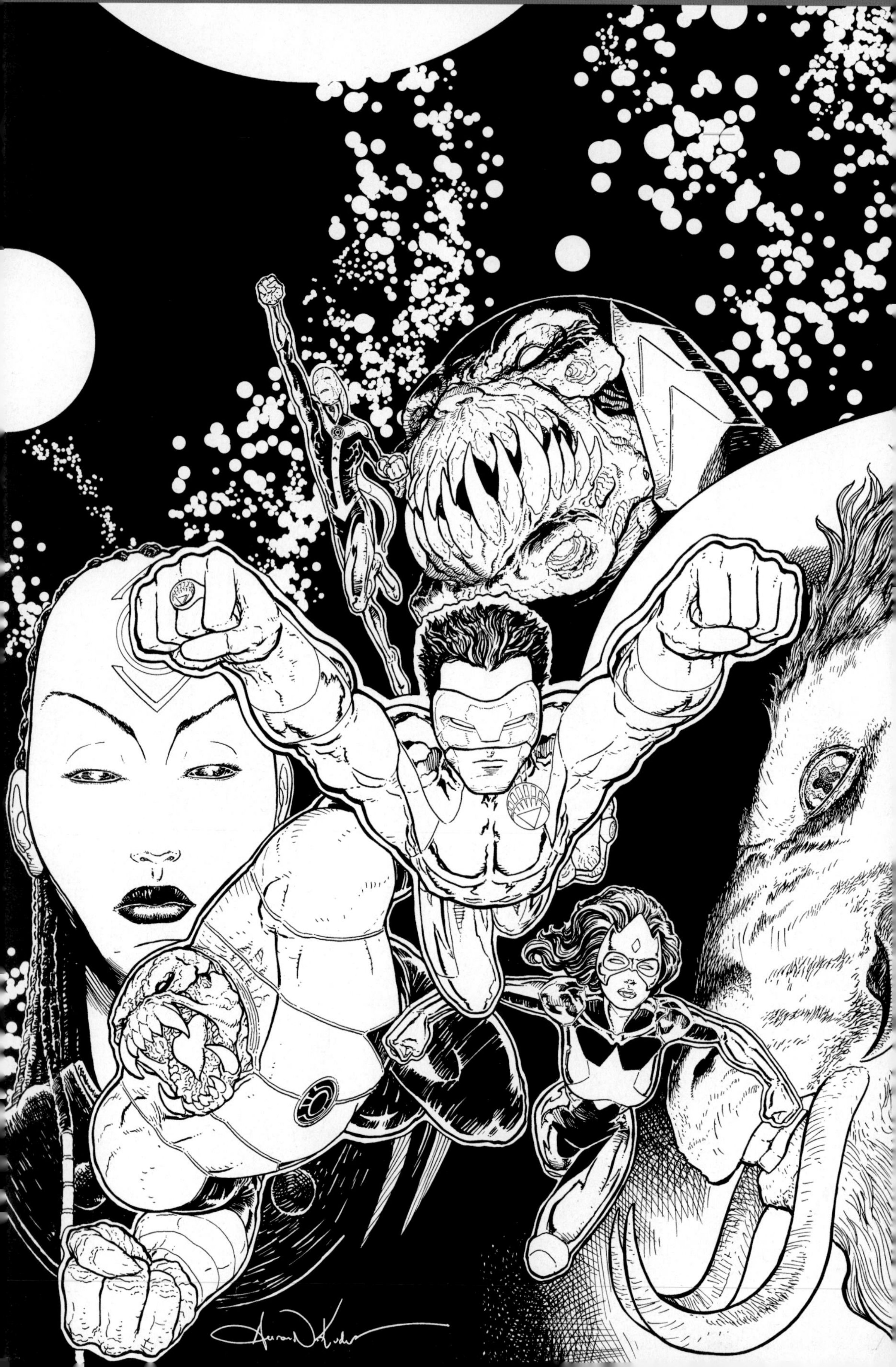

"HE MUST COME TO GRIPS WITH THE ENORMITY OF WHAT HAPPENED ON *OA*.

"SMALL WONDER THAT UPON RETURNING HOME HE SEEKS TO POUR IT ALL OUT THROUGH HIS *BRUSH...*

"...TO EXTERNALIZE HIS FEELINGS FOR HIS *ERSTWHILE COMPANIONS.*

"*SAINT WALKER,* CHAMPION OF HOPE.

"FEARSOME *ARKILLO.*

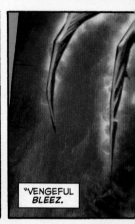

"VENGEFUL *BLEEZ.*

"...AND HIS MISTRESS, *INDIGO-1.*

"RAGING *ATROCITUS.*

"GREEDY *LARFLEEZE,* WHOM WE KNOW ALL TOO WELL...

RING: *TELL ME* SOMETHING.

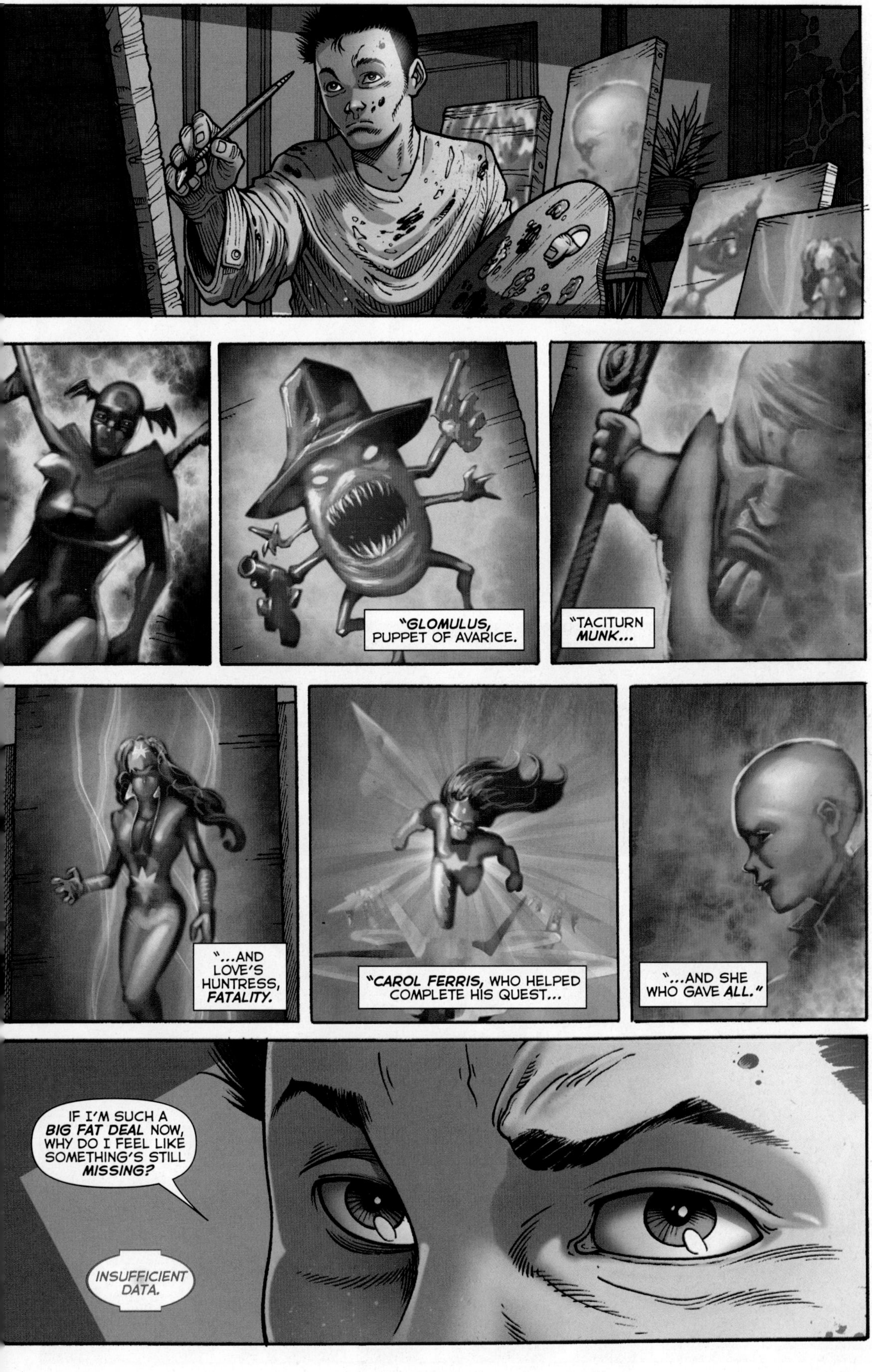
"GLOMULUS, PUPPET OF AVARICE.
"TACITURN MUNK...
"...AND LOVE'S HUNTRESS, FATALITY.
"CAROL FERRIS, WHO HELPED COMPLETE HIS QUEST...
"...AND SHE WHO GAVE ALL."
IF I'M SUCH A BIG FAT DEAL NOW, WHY DO I FEEL LIKE SOMETHING'S STILL MISSING?
INSUFFICIENT DATA.

BE IT EVER SO HUMBLE...

?

NO WAY--

WALKER...?! WHAT'RE YOU DOING ON EARTH?

DIDN'T WE JUST BREAK UP THE BAND?

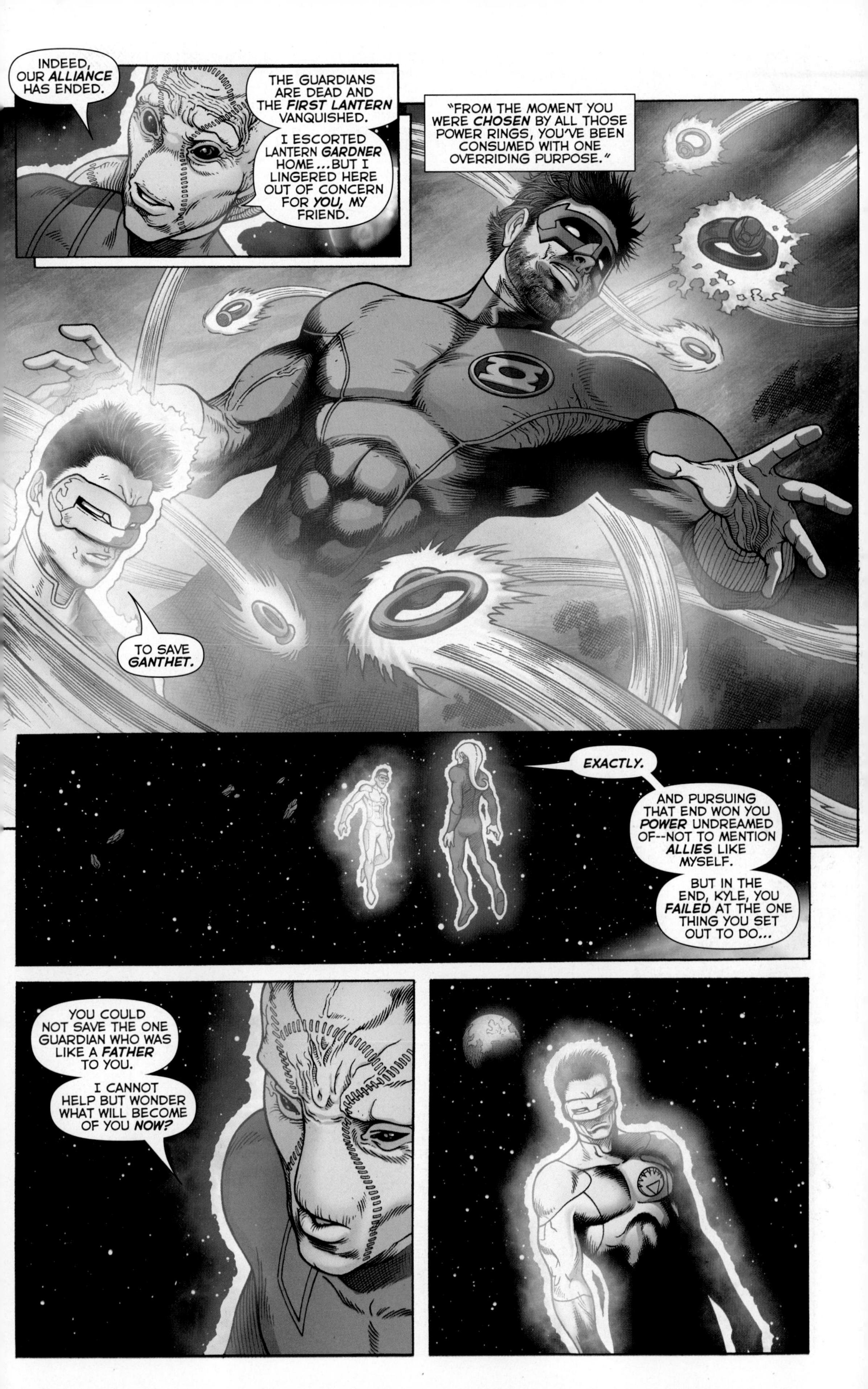
INDEED, OUR ALLIANCE HAS ENDED.
THE GUARDIANS ARE DEAD AND THE FIRST LANTERN VANQUISHED.
I ESCORTED LANTERN GARDNER HOME...BUT I LINGERED HERE OUT OF CONCERN FOR YOU, MY FRIEND.
"FROM THE MOMENT YOU WERE CHOSEN BY ALL THOSE POWER RINGS, YOU'VE BEEN CONSUMED WITH ONE OVERRIDING PURPOSE."
TO SAVE GANTHET.
EXACTLY.
AND PURSUING THAT END WON YOU POWER UNDREAMED OF--NOT TO MENTION ALLIES LIKE MYSELF.
BUT IN THE END, KYLE, YOU FAILED AT THE ONE THING YOU SET OUT TO DO...
YOU COULD NOT SAVE THE ONE GUARDIAN WHO WAS LIKE A FATHER TO YOU.
I CANNOT HELP BUT WONDER WHAT WILL BECOME OF YOU NOW?

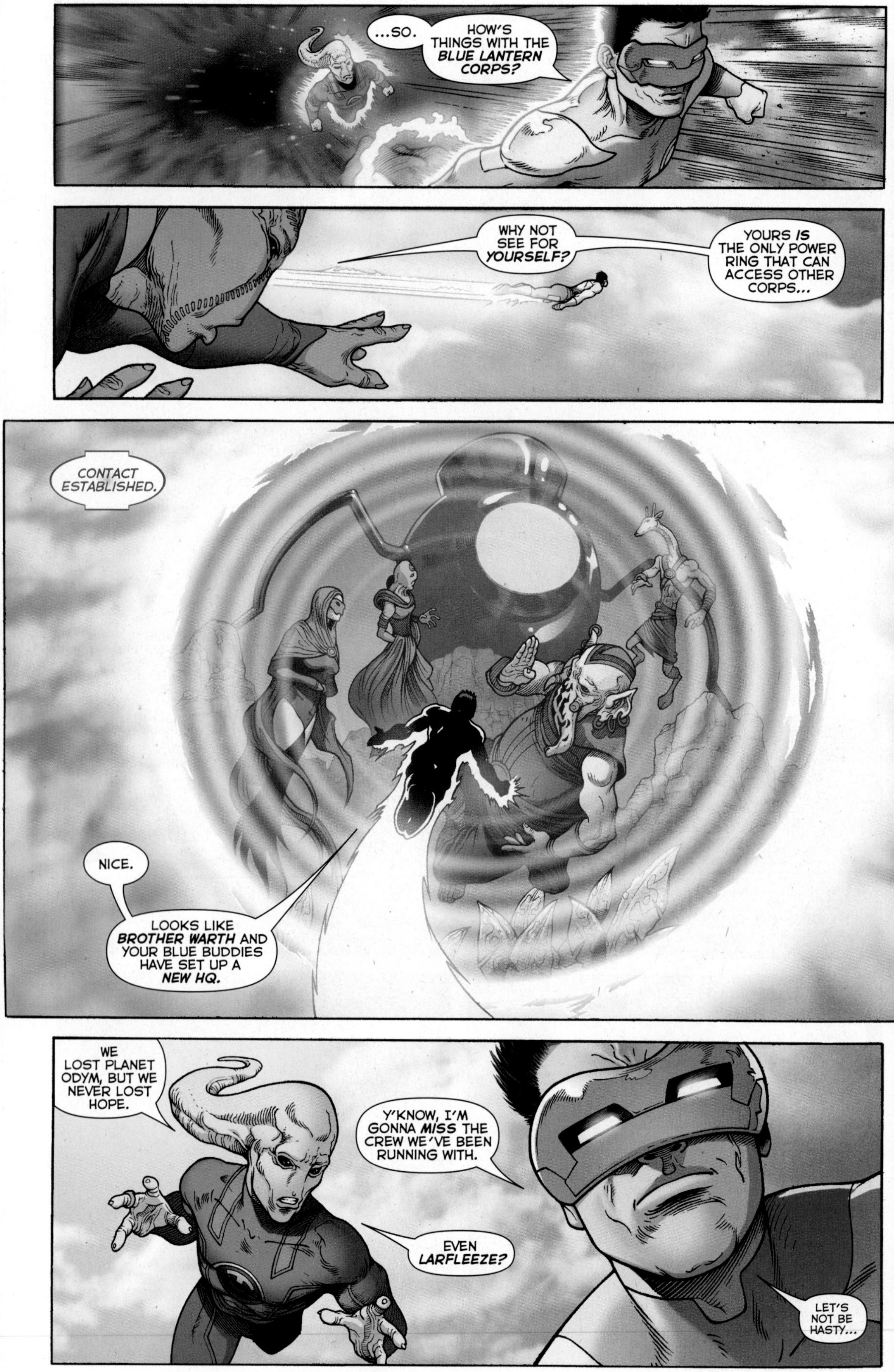
...SO.
HOW'S THINGS WITH THE *BLUE LANTERN CORPS?*
WHY NOT SEE FOR *YOURSELF?*
YOURS *IS* THE ONLY POWER RING THAT CAN ACCESS OTHER CORPS...
CONTACT ESTABLISHED.
NICE.
LOOKS LIKE ***BROTHER WARTH*** AND YOUR BLUE BUDDIES HAVE SET UP A ***NEW HQ.***
WE LOST PLANET ODYM, BUT WE NEVER LOST HOPE.
Y'KNOW, I'M GONNA ***MISS*** THE CREW WE'VE BEEN RUNNING WITH.
EVEN ***LARFLEEZE?***
LET'S NOT BE HASTY...

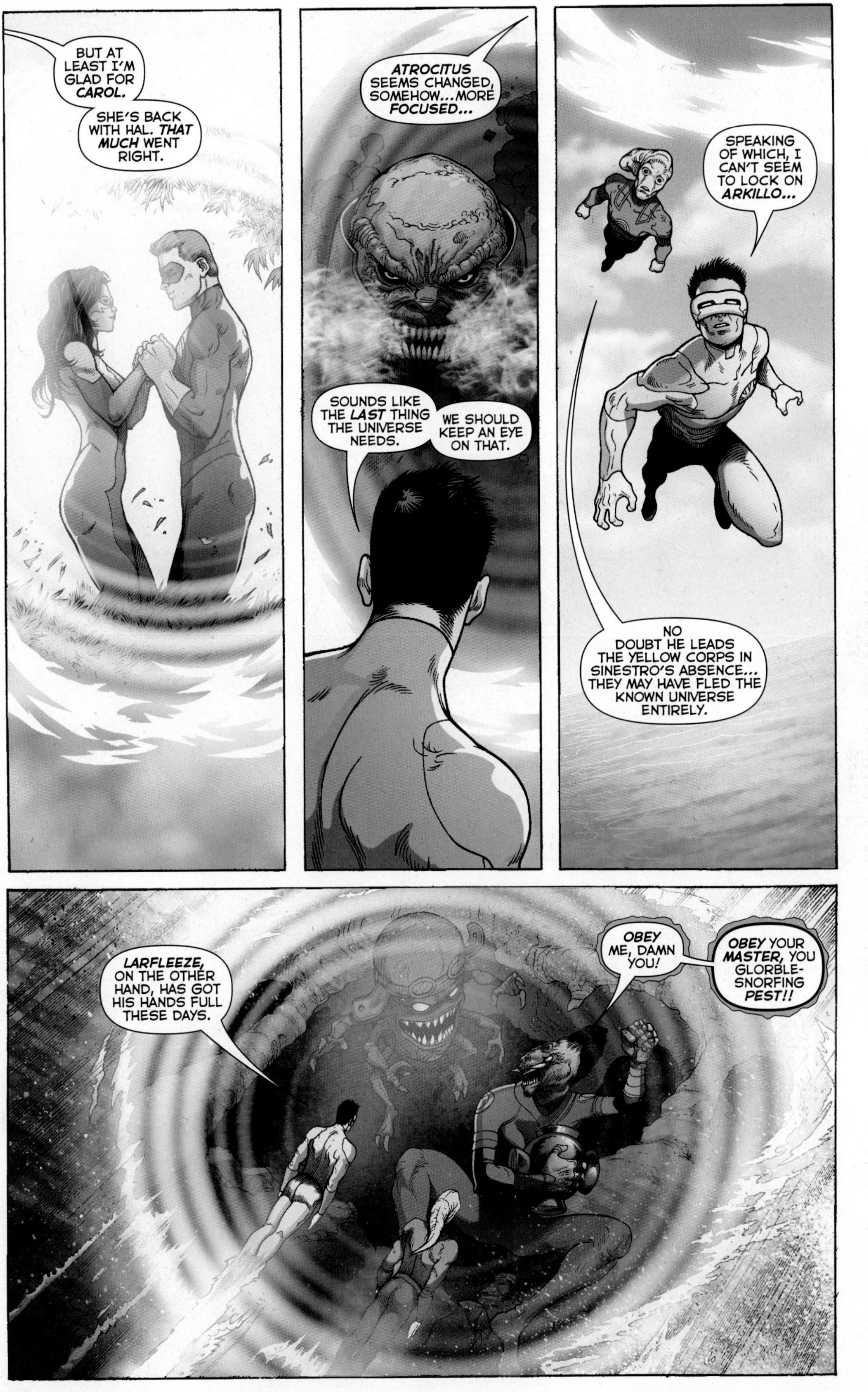

BUT AT LEAST I'M GLAD FOR *CAROL.*
SHE'S BACK WITH HAL. *THAT MUCH* WENT RIGHT.
ATROCITUS SEEMS CHANGED, SOMEHOW...MORE *FOCUSED...*
SOUNDS LIKE THE *LAST* THING THE UNIVERSE NEEDS.
WE SHOULD KEEP AN EYE ON THAT.
SPEAKING OF WHICH, I CAN'T SEEM TO LOCK ON *ARKILLO...*
NO DOUBT HE LEADS THE YELLOW CORPS IN SINESTRO'S ABSENCE... THEY MAY HAVE FLED THE KNOWN UNIVERSE ENTIRELY.
LARFLEEZE, ON THE OTHER HAND, HAS GOT HIS HANDS FULL THESE DAYS.
OBEY ME, DAMN YOU!
OBEY YOUR *MASTER,* YOU GLORBLE-SNORFING *PEST!!*

I MEAN, *THOSE* GUYS DON'T CARE HOW MY RING WORKS, LONG AS IT *DOES*, RIGHT?

ANYHOW, WHAT'S THE BIG DEAL WITH CHANNELING OTHER COLORS? THE *INDIGO TRIBE* DO IT ALL THE TIME...

WHOA. SHE CAN *SEE* ME?

SCOPET KYLE RAYNER--! NOK KLEK?

SORRY FOR *SPYING,* INDIGO-1...

VIP

...WON'T HAPPEN AGAIN.

MOGADISHU, SOMALIA.

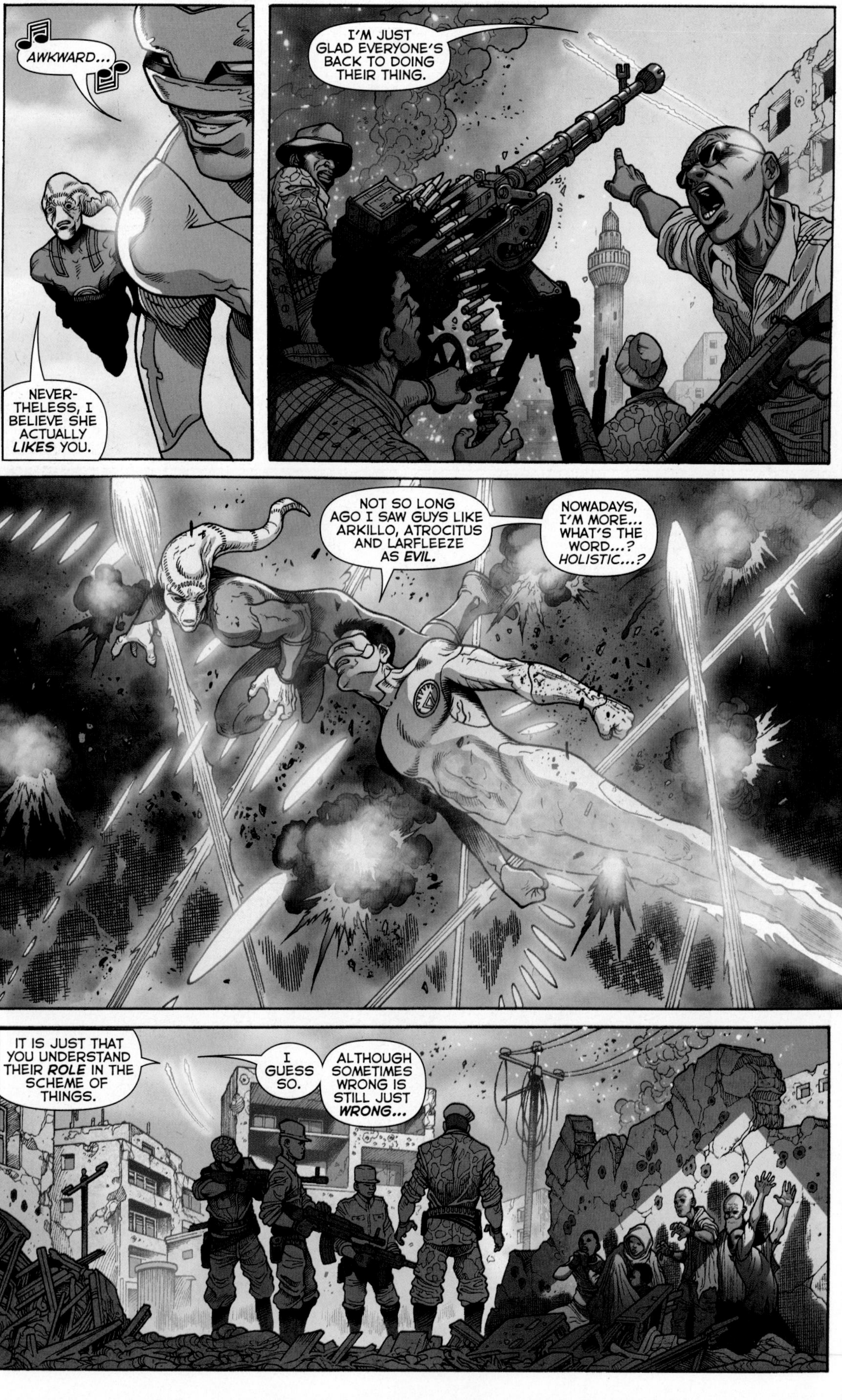
AWKWARD...
NEVER-THELESS, I BELIEVE SHE ACTUALLY LIKES YOU.
I'M JUST GLAD EVERYONE'S BACK TO DOING THEIR THING.
NOT SO LONG AGO I SAW GUYS LIKE ARKILLO, ATROCITUS AND LARFLEEZE AS EVIL.
NOWADAYS, I'M MORE... WHAT'S THE WORD...? HOLISTIC...?
IT IS JUST THAT YOU UNDERSTAND THEIR ROLE IN THE SCHEME OF THINGS.
I GUESS SO.
ALTHOUGH SOMETIMES WRONG IS STILL JUST WRONG...

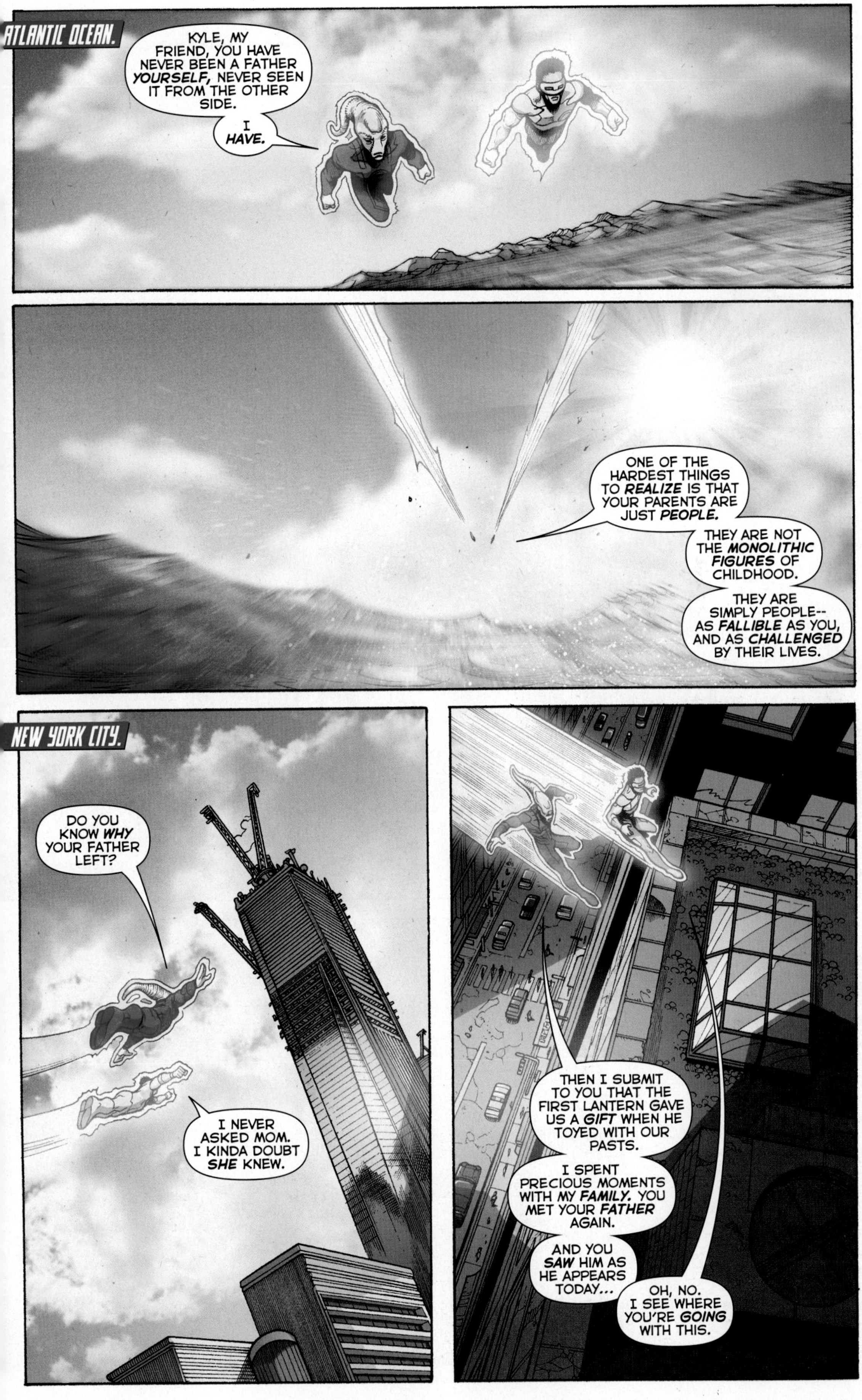
ATLANTIC OCEAN.
KYLE, MY FRIEND, YOU HAVE NEVER BEEN A FATHER YOURSELF, NEVER SEEN IT FROM THE OTHER SIDE.
I HAVE.
ONE OF THE HARDEST THINGS TO REALIZE IS THAT YOUR PARENTS ARE JUST PEOPLE.
THEY ARE NOT THE MONOLITHIC FIGURES OF CHILDHOOD.
THEY ARE SIMPLY PEOPLE-- AS FALLIBLE AS YOU, AND AS CHALLENGED BY THEIR LIVES.
NEW YORK CITY.
DO YOU KNOW WHY YOUR FATHER LEFT?
I NEVER ASKED MOM. I KINDA DOUBT SHE KNEW.
THEN I SUBMIT TO YOU THAT THE FIRST LANTERN GAVE US A GIFT WHEN HE TOYED WITH OUR PASTS.
I SPENT PRECIOUS MOMENTS WITH MY FAMILY. YOU MET YOUR FATHER AGAIN.
AND YOU SAW HIM AS HE APPEARS TODAY...
OH, NO. I SEE WHERE YOU'RE GOING WITH THIS.

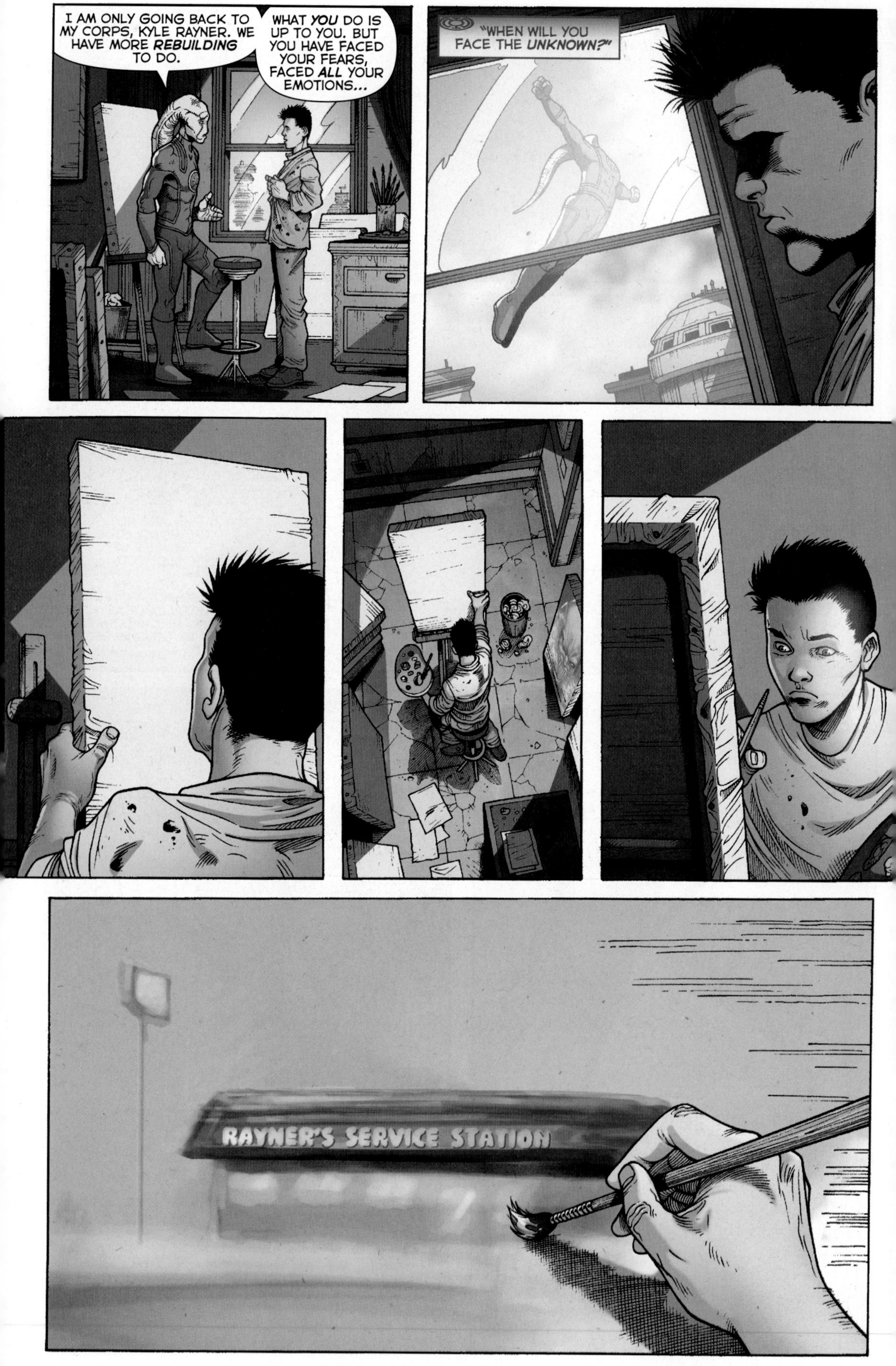
I AM ONLY GOING BACK TO MY CORPS, KYLE RAYNER. WE HAVE MORE *REBUILDING* TO DO.
WHAT *YOU* DO IS UP TO YOU. BUT YOU HAVE FACED YOUR FEARS, FACED *ALL* YOUR EMOTIONS...
"WHEN WILL YOU FACE THE *UNKNOWN?*"
RAYNER'S SERVICE STATION

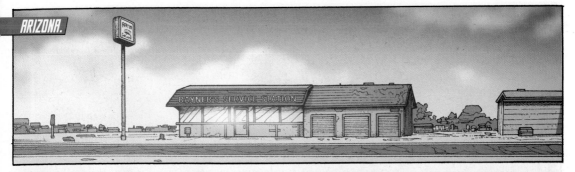

ARIZONA.

RAYNER'S SERVICE STATION

OH--!

Y'*STARTLED* ME, PARTNER.

DIDN'T HEAR A *CAR* PULL UP...

...HOLY....!

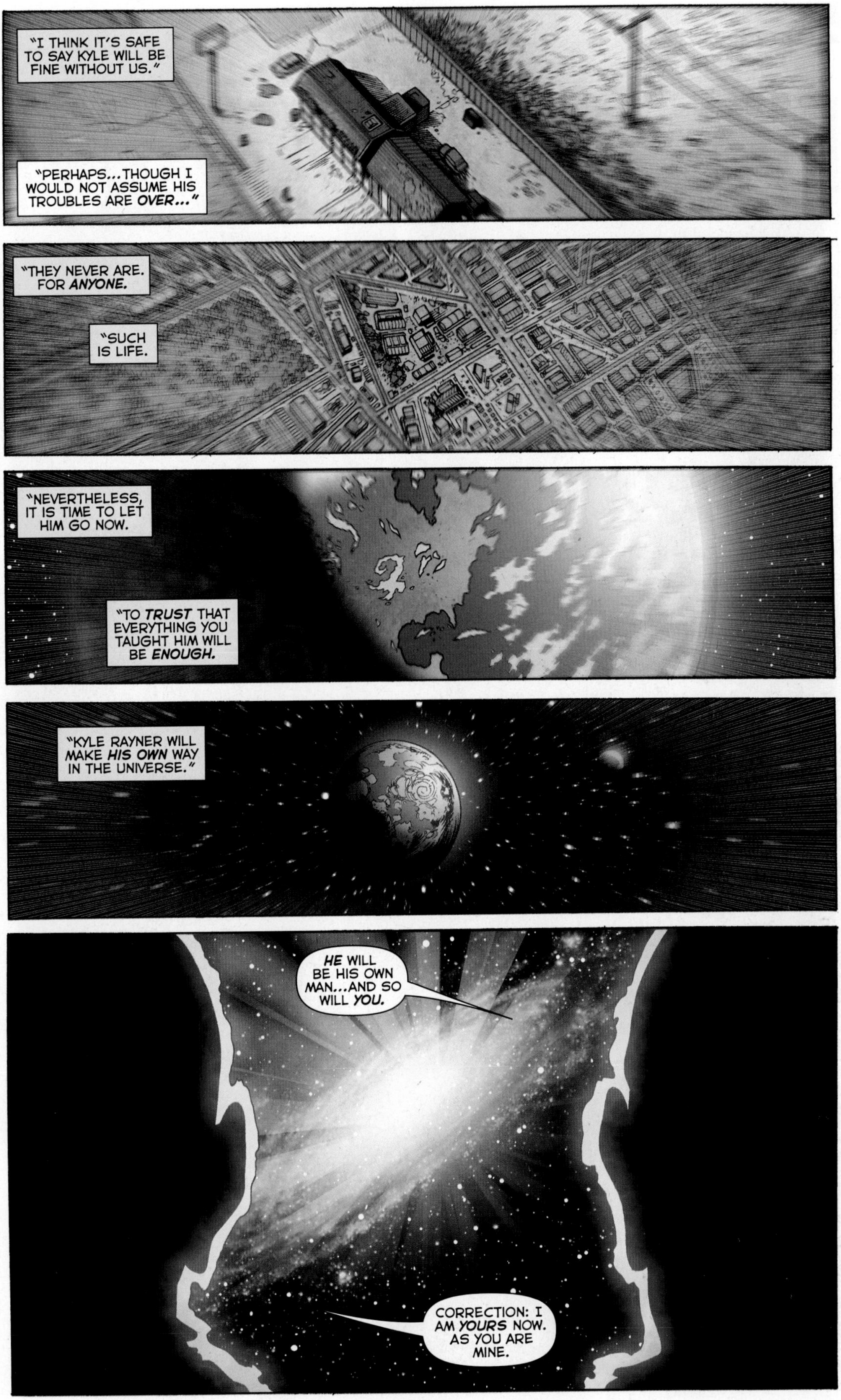
"I THINK IT'S SAFE TO SAY KYLE WILL BE FINE WITHOUT US."
"PERHAPS...THOUGH I WOULD NOT ASSUME HIS TROUBLES ARE OVER..."
"THEY NEVER ARE. FOR ANYONE.
"SUCH IS LIFE.
"NEVERTHELESS, IT IS TIME TO LET HIM GO NOW.
"TO TRUST THAT EVERYTHING YOU TAUGHT HIM WILL BE ENOUGH.
"KYLE RAYNER WILL MAKE HIS OWN WAY IN THE UNIVERSE."
HE WILL BE HIS OWN MAN...AND SO WILL YOU.
CORRECTION: I AM YOURS NOW. AS YOU ARE MINE.

Layout for Issue #15,
Pages 2 and 3

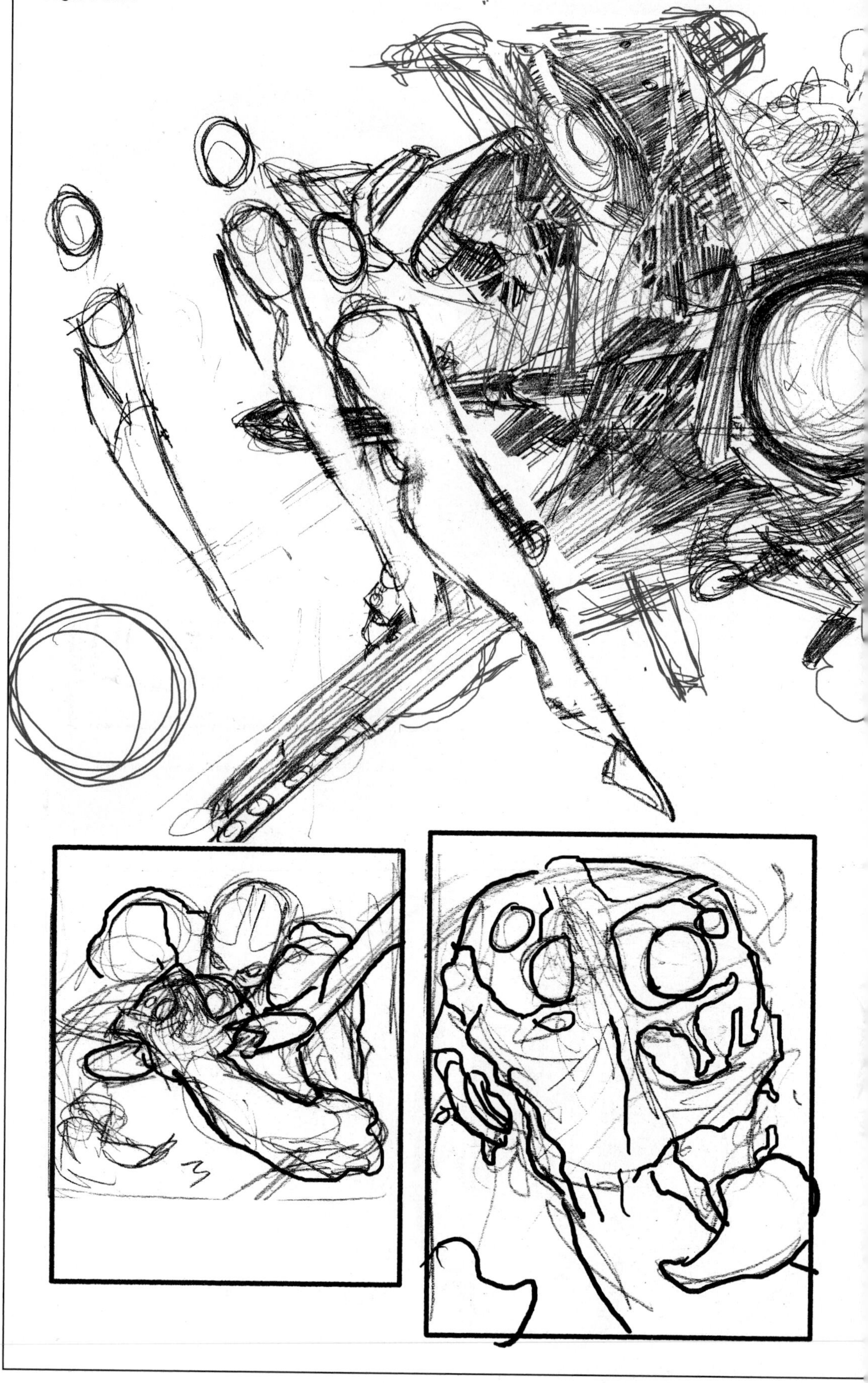

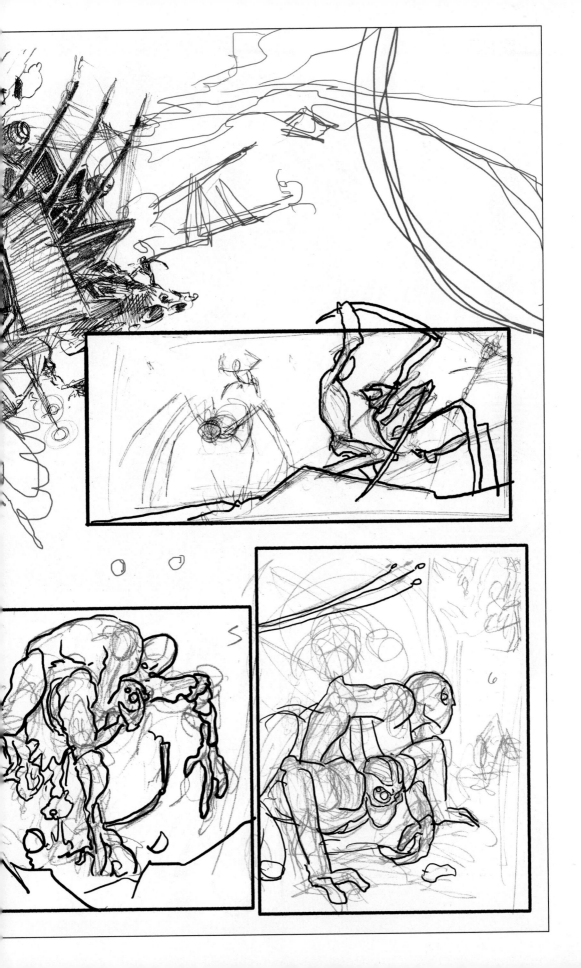

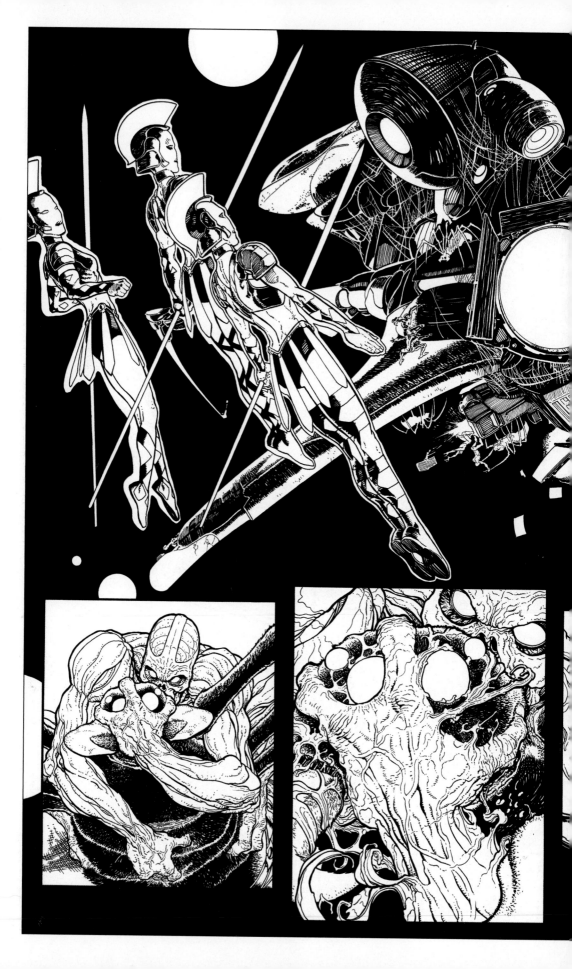

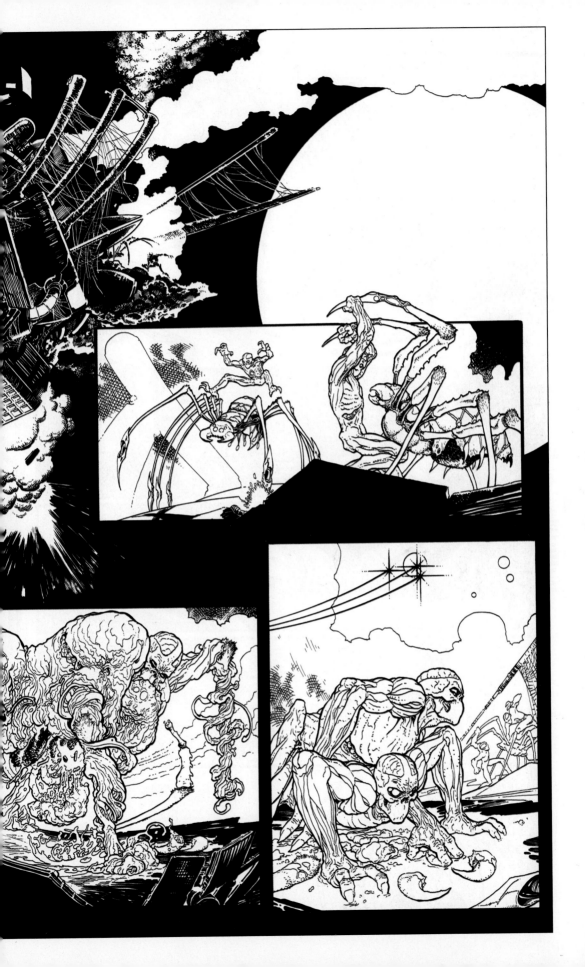

Issue #15, Page 7 inks

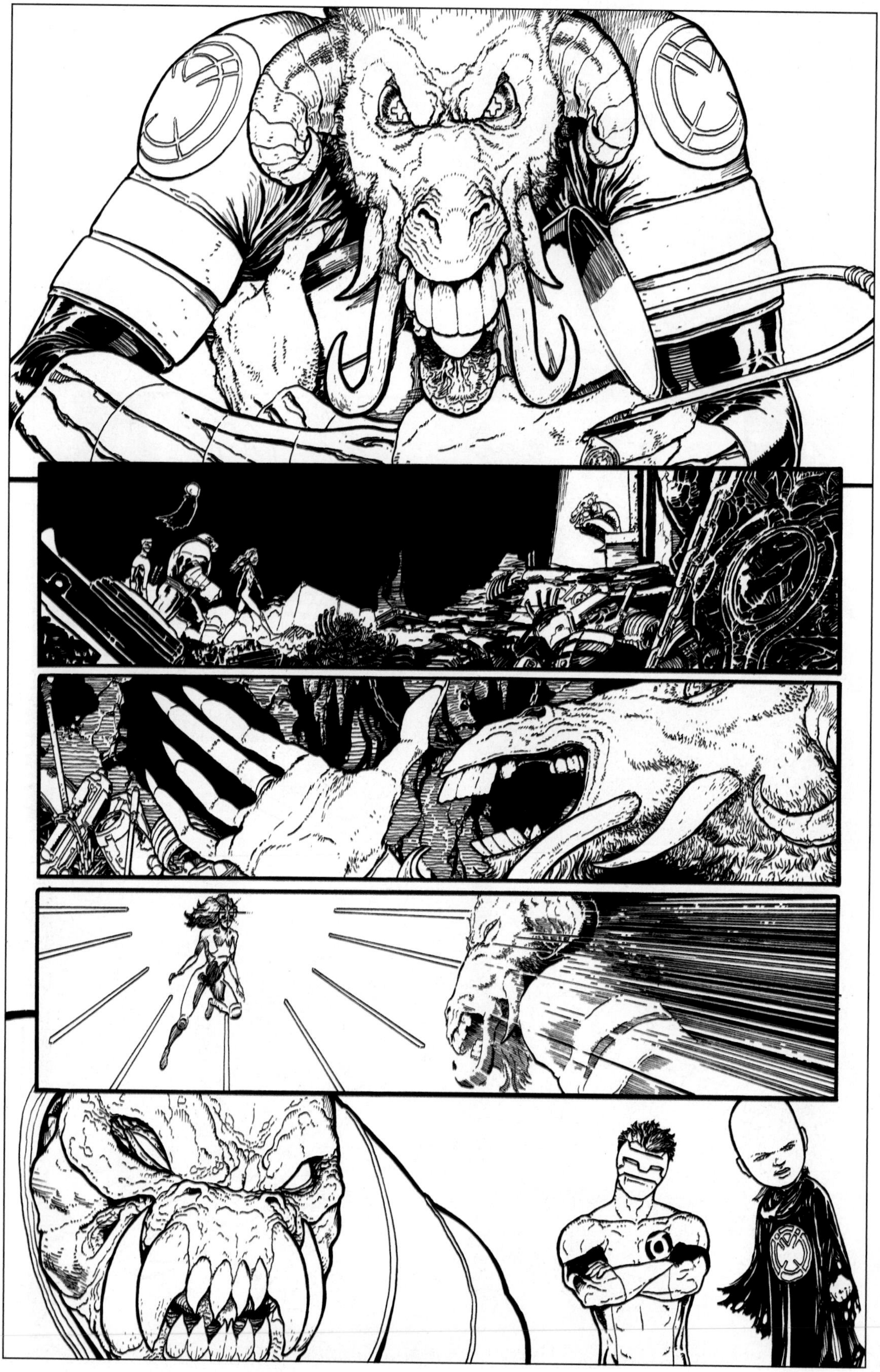

Sketch for unused
Issue #18 cover

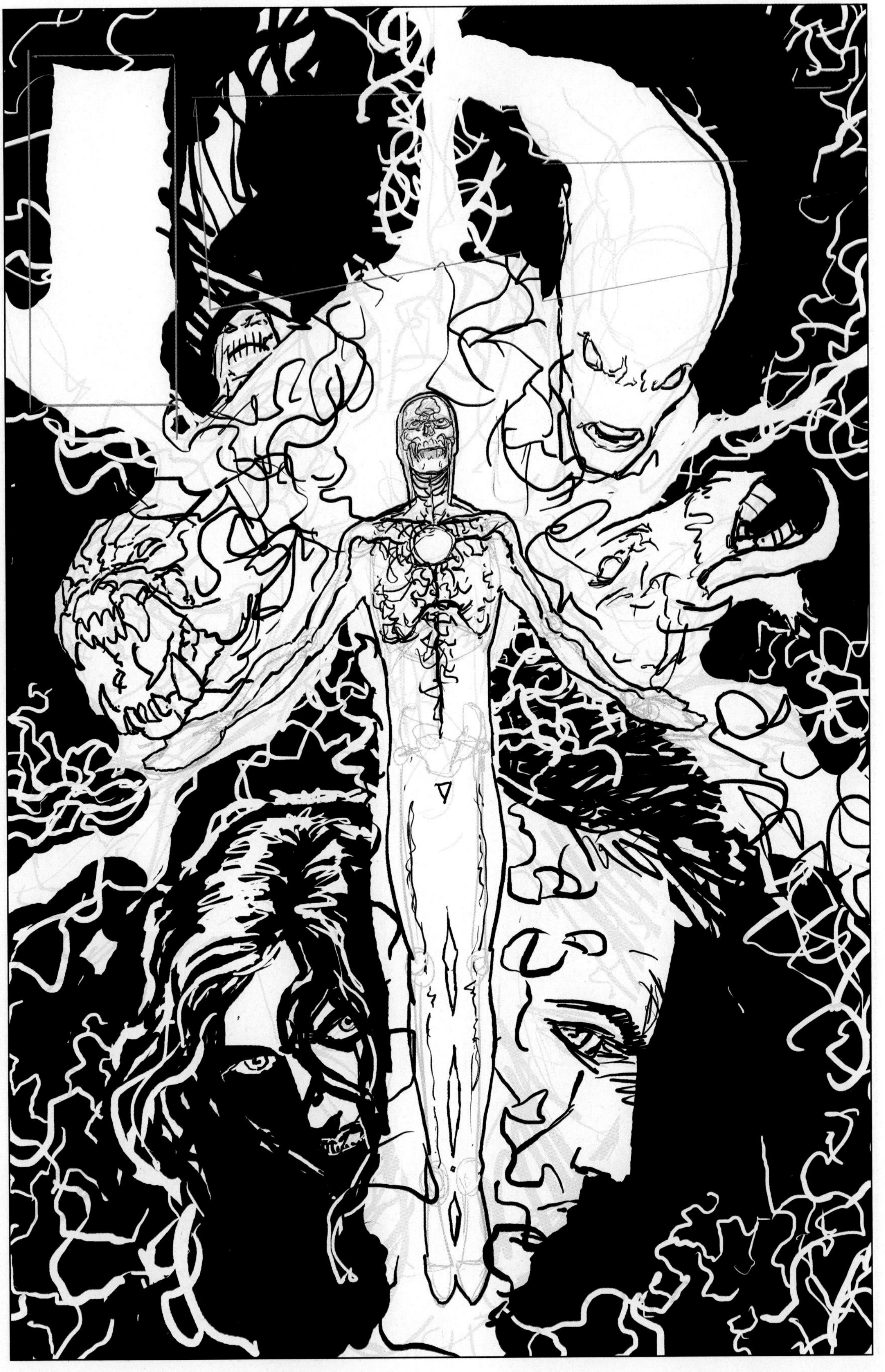

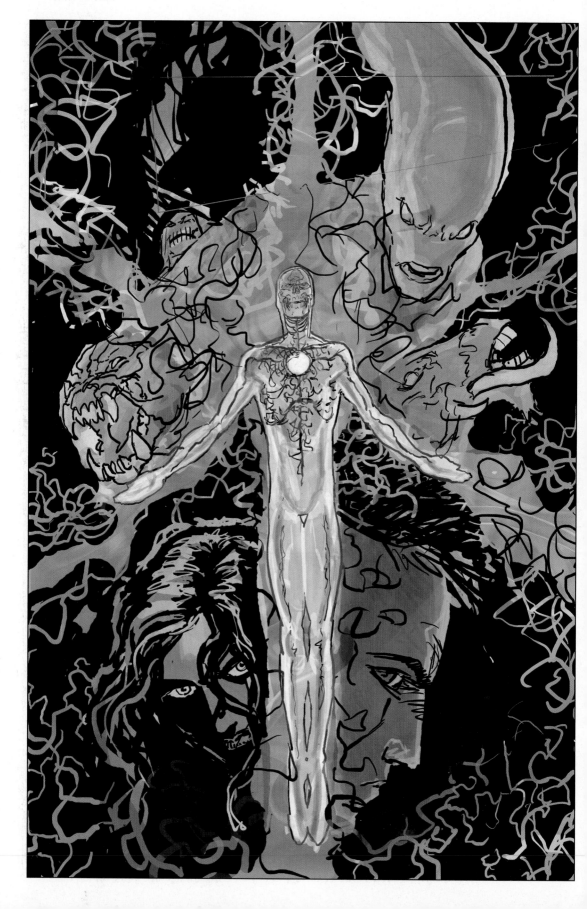

Sketch for Issue #17 cover

DC COMICS™

START AT THE BEGINNING!

GREEN LANTERN
VOLUME 1: SINESTRO

**GREEN LANTERN
CORPS VOLUME 1:
FEARSOME**

**RED LANTERNS
VOLUME 1:
BLOOD AND RAGE**

**GREEN LANTERN:
NEW GUARDIANS
VOLUME 1:
THE RING BEARER**

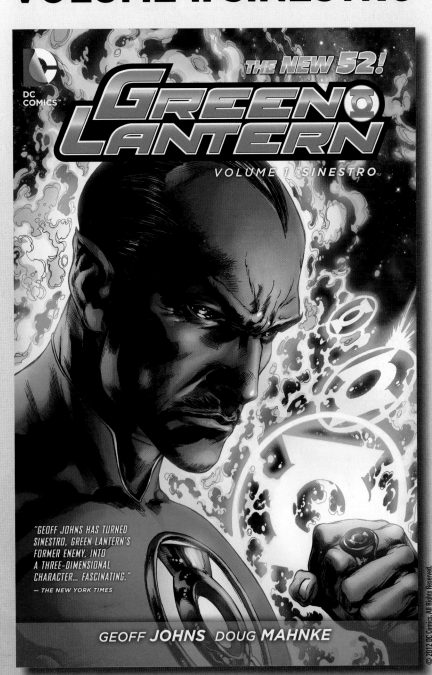

GEOFF JOHNS DOUG MAHNKE

FROM THE WRITER OF *JUSTICE LEAGUE* & *THE FLASH*

GEOFF JOHNS
GREEN LANTERN: REBIRTH

GREEN LANTERN:
BRIGHTEST DAY

GEOFF JOHNS
ETHAN VAN SCIVER

Green Lantern: REBIRTH

Introduction by
BRAD MELTZER